Derivatives

Models on Models

Derivatives

Models on Models

Espen Gaarder Haug

John Wiley & Sons, Ltd

Copyright © 2007 by   John Wiley & Sons Ltd, The Atrium, Southern Gate, Chichester,
West Sussex PO19 8SQ, England

Telephone (+44) 1243 779777

Email (for orders and customer service enquiries): cs-books@wiley.co.uk
Visit our Home Page on www.wileyeurope.com or www.wiley.com

Reprinted July 2007, May 2008, December 2010, May 2012, June 2013, May 2014

Other Wiley Editorial Offices

John Wiley & Sons Inc., 111 River Street, Hoboken, NJ 07030, USA

Jossey-Bass, 989 Market Street, San Francisco, CA 94103-1741, USA

Wiley-VCH Verlag GmbH, Boschstr. 12, D-69469 Weinheim, Germany

John Wiley & Sons Australia Ltd, 42 McDougall Street, Milton, Queensland 4064, Australia

John Wiley & Sons (Asia) Pte Ltd, 2 Clementi Loop #02-01, Jin Xing Distripark, Singapore 129809

John Wiley & Sons Canada Ltd, 6045 Freemont Blvd, Mississauga, Ontario, L5R 4J3, Canada

Wiley also publishes its books in a variety of electronic formats. Some content that appears
in print may not be available in electronic books.

British Library Cataloguing in Publication Data

A catalogue record for this book is available from the British Library

ISBN 978-0-470-01322-9 (H/B)

Typeset in 10/12pt Times by Laserwords Private Limited, Chennai, India
Printed and bound in Great Britain by CPI Group (UK) Ltd, Croydon, CR0 4YY

Contents

Author's "Disclaimer"

This book contains interviews with some of the world's top modelers, researchers, quants, quant-traders, gamblers and philosophers from Wall Street and academia. Their views stand on their own and many of them would probably not agree with each other. This reflects the great depth and width that I tried to get into this book. Also, the views in most of my chapters are my own and the many great modelers interviewed in this book will not necessarily agree with me.

This book should also be read with a sense of humor. By investing in this book you are getting a perpetual American option to read whatever you want and whenever you want, it is not your obligation to read it but your option. If you think the option was overvalued after investing in it you can always try to re-sell it, if you think it was undervalued you can simply buy more copies (options).

Introduction

"Derivatives: Models on Models" is a different book about quantitative finance. In many ways it is two books in one, first of all it contains a series of interviews with some of the world's top modelers, researchers, quants, quant-traders, gamblers and philosophers from Wall Street and academia. On the top of this you get a series of technical chapters covering valuation methods on stocks paying discrete dividend, Asian options, American barrier options, Complex barrier options, reset options, and electricity derivatives. The book doesn't stop there it also takes you into the tails of your imagination and discusses ideas like negative probabilities and space-time finance.

The title "Derivatives: Models on Models" deserves some explanation. It was my former co-worker Dr John Stevenson[1] a great model trader in J.P. Morgan that first came up with the idea of the book title "Models on Models", a title I later changed to "Derivatives: Models on Models". First of all the book is about derivatives models; quantitative finance, option valuation, hedging, and some non-traditional topics in finance like negative probabilities and space-time finance.

"Models on Models" has multiple implications. First of all models are only models and derivatives models are themselves based typically on more fundamental underlying models. For example most derivatives models are based on classic probability theory, that itself is a model that we often take for granted. Many models are based on the assumption of Gaussian distribution (including many of my own formulas). Some of the biggest mistakes in trading and modeling are done because we forget that our models are typically also based on some implicit non-stated assumptions. Typically such models work well (or at least to some degree) most of the time, but then sooner or later the hidden conditions will show up and often cause unexpected problems.

"Models on Models" also points back at the many interesting interviews with many of the world's top modelers and their views on their models: Clive Granger, Emanuel Derman, Edward Thorp, Peter Carr, Aaron Brown, David Bates, Andrei Khrennikov, Elie Ayache, Peter Jäckel, Alan Lewis, Paul Wilmott, Eduardo Schwartz, Knut Aase, Bruno Dupire, Nassim Taleb, and Stephen Ross, all share their great wisdom on quantitative models, trading, gambling and philosophy about modeling. These interesting and fascinating interviews are spread throughout the book. These are modelers with very different backgrounds and personalities; it has been a great pleasure to learn from them through their publications, presentations, and in particular through the interviews for this book. All of these great people stand on their own, and are in no way directly related to my articles if not so stated except in the few cases when some of them are co-authors, Some of them like my work, some of them disagree strongly with me, compared to many of these giants of quantitative finance I am only a footnote, but either you like it or not a footnote that is growing in size!

"Models on Models" also reflects upon early often "forgotten" research and knowledge. The current quantitative finance models are in almost every case extensions that are based on early wisdom and knowledge. Many of the techniques used in finance have their background in physics, engineering, probability theory and ancient wisdom. Many of these theories have developed over thousands of years. It is easy to forget this when working with valuing some advanced derivatives instruments.[2]

For making it easy to remember the importance of understanding models is based on models. This concept is illustrated in an artistic photo in the centre section of the book. After seeing beautiful quantitative finance models painted on beautiful photo models you will hopefully never forget the importance of "Models on Models". Even if the model and the underlying model potential look extremely elegant and beautiful, this does not mean that the surface and the explicitly stated assumption of the model tells the truth about real market behavior. I have myself spent considerable time as a derivatives trader and have seen many of the differences between how the model worked in theory and practice, and I am still learning, it is a life long process. Many of us love beauty and elegance, even if we naturally know beauty and elegance is far from everything. Personally I love the beauty of closed form solutions, but they have their limitations. The beautiful surface of a model says little about how the model actually behaves in practice. Derivatives models are only models and nothing more, often beautiful and elegant on the surface but the real market is much more complex and much more interesting than the model alone, the art of quantitative trading is the understanding of the interaction between the market and the models, and in particular the shortcomings of the model.

The truth about derivatives models as well as photo models is more like this; the first time you see a derivatives model you think it is beautiful and elegant and you fall in love with it. Then when you know the model better, you learn its complexity and that the beautiful and elegant surface is only part of the reality. The more you learn about the model versus reality, the complexities, the weaknesses and strengths the more you tend to like the model despite its weaknesses. Not because it makes the model better, but you know how to get around its shortcomings. Knowing the weaknesses of a model is your best strength in applying the model to the market. Academics and researchers falling blindly in love with the mathematical beauty and elegance of their models without rigorously testing it out on market data, without listening to people with trading experience are like someone falling in love with a photo of a super-model, it has often little to do with the multidimensional reality. A great modeler or trader will test the model against market data, talk with experienced traders and always be open for discussion, and most important will see how the model works over many years in the market. Love based on outer beauty can sometimes be a good start, but only love based on a deep understanding of the weaknesses, strengths and complexities of a model and its interaction with reality can make love last.

Just like fashion models anyone that has followed mathematical finance for some time must also have noticed how fashion here changes over time. In the 1970s to the mid 1980s equity derivatives were in fashion. In the 1980s and early 1990s interest rate modeling was in fashion, every researcher and modeler tried to come up with benchmark yield curve models. In the 1990s exotic options and energy derivatives came into fashion. In late 1990s and until now modeling credit derivatives has been in fashion. It is hard to predict what fashion will be next and when it will end. As the derivatives business has grown dramatically and also the number of people in it, there now tend to be several fashions going on at the same time. The quants and the modelers have a few similarities with fashion designers, sometimes disliking each other's style, design and product. A good modeler should however in my view be open to at least discussing his own work with modelers in the opposite fashion camp. Too often modelers fall in love with their own view of the world (I do it all the time), I guess this is why science has always evolved through paradigm changes, and I don't think that things are any different now, the human brain is more or less unchanged over thousands of years.

Even if this book covers some "serious" ideas and valuation models I see no reason why this cannot be combined with humor and fun. The great sense of humor of the many great researchers and quants interviewed is just one example. To make the book more entertaining I have also added a section filled with comic strips and quant related artistic photos, I hope and think that some of you will like it.

First of all I would like to thank the great modelers, quants, researchers, philosophers, gamblers and traders that shared their knowledge, wisdom and their views through the interviews presented in this book.

I would like to give a special thanks to, Jørgen Haug, Alan Lewis and William Margrabe who I was lucky to have as co-authors in a few of the chapters. Even if this book (besides the interviews) mostly is personal ego trip I have also included a chapter by Professor Knut Aase that is closely related to the subject of one of my chapters.

I am also grateful for interesting discussions, comments and suggestions by Alexander Adamchuk, Gabriel Barton, Christophe Bahadoran, Nicole Branger, Aaron Brown, Peter Carr, Peter Clark, Jin-chuan Duan, Tom Farmen, Stein Erik Fleten, Edwin Fisk, Omar Foda, Gordon Fraser, Stein Frydenberg, Ronald R. Hatch, Steen Koekebakker, John Logie, Xingmin Lu, Hicham Mouline, Svein-Arne Persson, John Ping Shu, Samuel Siren, Gunnar Stensland, Erik Stettler, Svein Stokke, Dan Tudball, James Ward, Sjur Westgaard, Lennart Widlund, Nico van der Wijst and Jiang Xiao Zhong.

I had great fun working with the very talented photographers Amber Gray and Julian Bernstein doing some artistic "Models on Models" shots for this book. For the comic strips I am grateful to the multi-talented Sebastian Conley. The comic strips began by me drafting the story, then Sebastian drew it by hand (black and white) and improved my stories before using computer software to add colors and special effects. Also special thanks are due to my very artistic friend Wenling Wang for her painting "The Path" (oil on canvas shown on page xiv) inspired by the art of ancient wisdom and the vicissitudes of today's financial world that she has witnessed during many years of experience in the some of the top hedge funds of our time.

At John Wiley & Sons I would like to thank Caitlin Cornish, Vivienne Wickham and Emily Pears for helping me put all this material together.

Chapter 1 describes the early and partly forgotten discovery of high-peak/fat-tailed distributions in price data. Chapter 2 describes dynamic delta hedging from theory to practice. Chapter 3 is about how to value options with discrete dividend, a problem that has caused a lot of confusion over the years. Chapters 4 to 8 cover different topics in Exotic option valuation, barrier options, reset options and Asian options. Chapter 9 covers practical valuation of power derivatives. Chapters 10 and 11 look at negative volatility and a interesting symmetry in option valuation. Chapter 12 is a bizarre story about time and frozen time arbitrage. Chapter 13 covers the Relativity Theory's implications for mathematical finance. Chapters 14 and 15 look at probabilities in finance in a non-traditional way.

FOOTNOTES

1. Dr John Stevenson was at that time working on developing quantitative model trading using one of Wall Street's most powerful computers. Basically he was using all the other computers in the bank, and not surprisingly he was often blamed when the network crashed.

2. For a very interesting book on the history of financial economics see Rubinstein, M. (2006) *A History of The Theory of Investments*. New York: John Wiley & Sons, Inc.

The author has received financial support from The Non-Fiction Literature Fund in Norway.

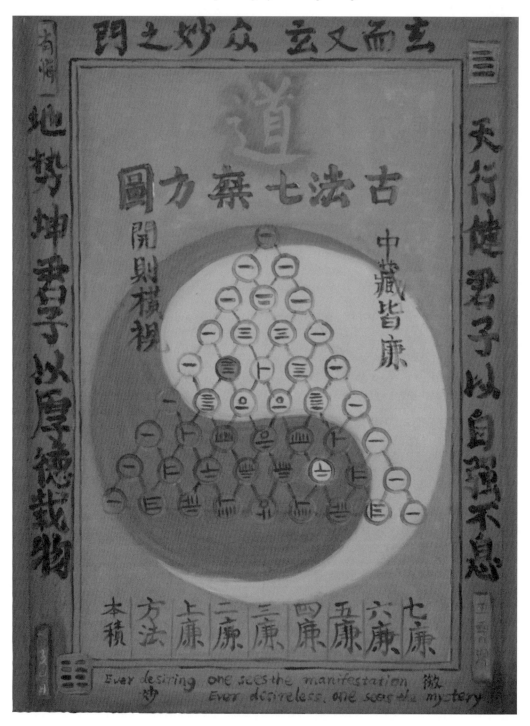

Derivatives
Models on Models

It is easy to forget that many of today's financial models are based on ancient models. For example, an important ingredient in the binomial tree model is Pascal's triangle and the binomial coefficient. The Chinese knew Pascal's triangle long before the Europeans. Figure 0.1 shows a drawing from Chu Shih-chien's book published in (1303). However reading Chinese from right to left we will see that he already in 1303 called this an ancient old method. Chu Shih-chien is actually referring to Yanghui (1261), even today the Chinese mathematical literature refer to this triangle as Yanghui's (or Yang Hui's) triangle. In India there is a book called "Bhagabati Sutra" published 300 years before the birth of Christ that indicates that already back then there was some knowledge of the binomial coefficient. Mahavira (circa 850 A.D.), writing in "Ganita Sara Sangraha" generalized the rule found in the Bhagabati Sutra.

The illustration to your left is an oil painting by Wenling Wang, a hedge fund artist in Greenwich Connecticut. She was inspired by the ancient Yanghui triangle, and the painting is full of ancient wisdom and mystery.

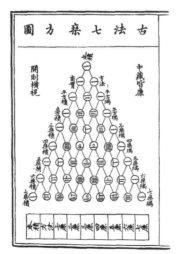

Figure 0.1: Drawing from Chu Shih-chien (1303)

Here together with Nassim Taleb and Benoit Mandelbrot

Nassim Taleb on Black Swans

The first time I heard about Nassim Nicholas Taleb was when, as an option trader, I came across his very interesting book on option trading, "Dynamic Hedging". A few years later I moved to the USA to work for a Hedge Fund in Greenwich, Connecticut. On one of my first days at work I walked over to the coffee room. In order to get up to speed in a new trading job and get rid of my jet lag I needed that caffeine.

There in the coffee room I met someone who looked familiar. It was Nassim Taleb. I recognized him from the photo in his book "Dynamic Hedging". He also recognized me from my book "The Complete Guide to Option Pricing Formulas". I called him Taleb, but he told me to call him Nassim. Nassim was running his own trading firm in the same building, but we shared the coffee room.

Over the next three years or so I met Nassim frequently, he was happy to share his knowledge and loved to get involved in discussions on tail events, advanced option trading and phenomena outside the traditional mainframe of finance. Nassim Taleb was a original thinker, a tail event himself specializing in tail events. He was also not afraid of sharing his knowledge, probably because he knew that human nature and the bonus system in most Wall Street firms would make most traders ignore his ideas anyway. I went skiing a few times with Nassim. Nassim was a great skier and we always did the double black diamonds, something I will come back to in the end of the interview.

Nassim Taleb has more than 20 years of trading experience specializing in option trading and convex payoff structures. In addition to his book on options "Dynamic Hedging" he has also published the best selling book "Fooled by Randomness" and is at the time of writing also coming out with a new book titled "The Black Swan".

Haug : Where did you grow up first of all?

Taleb : This question is appropriate because I'm currently writing the Black Swan, and in it I discuss something I call the narrative-biographical fallacy. The error is as follows: You try to look for the most salient characteristics of someone and impart some link between the person's traits and his background, along causative lines. People look at my background, they see my childhood in the war, in Lebanon, and they think that my idea of the Black Swan comes from that. So I did some empiricism, I looked for every single trader I could find, who had the same background, experienced the same war, and looked at how they trade, they are all short gamma, they are all short the wings, they all bet against the Black

Swan directly or indirectly. So there's no meaningful relevance to the background, I can pretty much say now. This has been studied by a lot of researchers across fields.

Haug : What is your education and trading background?

Taleb : My trading background is more relevant to a description of my personality. I started trading very early on. My education was quite technical but initially I did not have much respect for technical careers. Math was very easy to me and convenient because the books were short and it was not time consuming. I liked its elegance and purity but I feared committing to it career-wise by becoming an engineer – I looked at engineers and saw how they became mostly support staff and I viewed them as a negative role model. I wanted to become a philosopher, understand the world, be a decision-maker; I never wanted to accept that I was bound to have a technical career. After an MBA at Wharton, I became obsessed with convex payoffs and became a option trader very quickly. It was a great compromise between decision-making and technical and mathematical work. And from day one I saw that much of these models was severely grounded in the Gaussian, and that it was nonsense. From day one I thought this application of the Gaussian was nonsense. It was nonsense because the Gaussian was not an approximation to real randomness, but something qualitatively different. Now two decades later, I still believe it is nonsense, nothing has changed.

Haug : But aren't there a lot of other people looking into this through stochastic volatility models?

Taleb : At the time, my biggest mistake was that I started looking at stochastic volatility. I no longer believe in stochastic volatility, because I think it is a fudge but you forget it when you spend too much time with models. A given distribution has four components: first it has a centrality parameter – in other words, for the Gaussian it would be the mean; secondly it has what you call a scale parameter – for a Gaussian, it would be the variance; and it has also a symmetry component – the symmetry attribute is skewness which for a Gaussian is zero; and finally I think the distribution has what I would call the asymptotic tail exponent which for a Gaussian is not relevant because it is infinite. If it does not apply to the Gaussian, it does apply for other classes of distributions, which is where the qualitative difference starts. Building models off the Gaussian do not remedy the lack of tail exponent.

So, given that the Gaussian is not a good representation of the world, the easiest way is to start fudging with it and the mistake I made early on was to use stochastic volatility. Stochastic volatility does the job only up to some degree of out-of-moneyness of the options. If it does a good job sometimes with the body; the problem is that some people believe that stochastic volatility is a real model but it's not. Stochastic volatility is a simple trick to price out-of-the-money options without getting too much into trouble, you see.

Let me summarize my idea. There are two classes of distributions. There is what I call scalable or scale free (they have a tail exponent or no characteristic scale) and there are what I call non-scalable (no tail-exponent). Scalable distribution can have a constant scale parameter, yet they can perfectly mimic stochastic volatility, without your noticing it. Rama Cont and Peter Tankov, in their book[1], made the observation that a student T, with three degrees of freedom (which has a tail exponent alpha of three) will mimic stochastic volatility. You look at it and it resembles what we know. Yet it has infinite stochastic volatility, literally, since it will have an infinite fourth moment. So early on I thought that to fix option models, stochastic volatility was a good patch and luckily realized that it was only a good patch to price some out-of-money options up to fifteen or twenty delta. It did not work really beyond that, in the tails – and the tails are of monstrous importance. Note that the further you go out-of-the money, the higher your model error will be. Also the smaller the probability, the higher the sampling error you're going to have.

So since then I started hunting for models until I found the fractal model. Most people talking mathematics don't fully understand the applications of probability distributions; they don't understand central limit; they don't understand how something becomes Gaussian and they talk about it as a statistical property that hold asymptotically as if it were for real. We don't live in the asymptote. For some parts of the distribution we get to the asymptote very slowly, too slowly for any comfort. The body of the distribution becomes Gaussian, not the tails. We live in the real world so I specialise in out-of-the-money based on that.

Haug : Let's come back to that. One thing is to attack current theories but another thing is to have a good alternative. Do scaling laws and fractal models makes us able to value derivatives?

Taleb : Likewise it is foolish to say "OK I want to have a better theory than the one we have now". That would be similar to saying let's take this medicine because it is the best we have. You do not compare drugs to other drugs; you compare drugs to **nothing!** But it took us a long time to get the FDA to monitor charlatans. Likewise you endorse a model only if it is better than no model. We need to worry about the side effects of models, to see if you are better off having nothing because you should not trade products under unreliable theories.

You should only trade instruments for which you have some degree of comfort – not fall into the trap of back-fitting a theory so you create such unjustified comfort. You should only trade instruments where you are comfortable with the risk because you are sure that you have a good model. It's exactly the opposite of what people seem to do. They take their models and say this is the best model we have and let people trade and labor under the belief that they have the right model.

Here I would like to phrase this in a different framework which is what I call top down versus bottom up. I am a bottom up empiricist. And I would like to live my life as theory free as I can, because I think that theory can be a very dangerous tool, particularly in social science where you don't have good standards of validations. The exact opposite thing to that which is held in the quant world, or in academia, particularly in finance academia: they come with some theory that is very tight, based on some arbitrary assumption. And ludicrously, they are very precise and very coherent in the way they calibrate things to each other, but they never think that their assumption can be bogus. And this is what we see, for example, in Black-Scholes.

So let's discuss Black-Scholes. Black-Scholes makes the assumptions of Gaussianism – that you have a normal distribution, continuous trading. All these assumptions. But then based on that they tell you that you have a **rigorous** way to derive an option formula. That reminds me of Locke's statement that a madman is someone who reasons tightly and rigorously off wrong premises. Well I care not so much about the precision and the "rigor" with which you derive conclusions, I care about how robust your assumptions are and how your model tracks empirical reality. But much of modern finance does not have robust assumptions and tracks nothing.

Much of this is based on another problem: belief in our knowledge about the probability distribution. In real life, you don't observe probability, so even before we talk about fractal or alternative models, we don't observe those probabilities, therefore I want something that does not depend too much on probabilities. The probabilities you observe are uncertain for out-of-the money events. The smaller the probability, the less we know what's going on. So you want to have trading strategies that do not depend too much on these probabilities.

That was the first statement. The second statement is that I want to use the techniques to try to rank portfolios based on their sensitivity to model error. That is **central** to risk management. And they don't allow you to do that. For me a portfolio that is sensitive to model error is not as of high quality as another portfolio that's more insulated from such model error. We do not seem to have a good rigorous method coming from quantitative finance – to the contrary they invent theories and try to turn you into a sucker instead of making you aware of the epistemic opacity of the world.

These people fall into the biggest trap called reification. Reification is when you take completely abstract notions and invest them with concreteness by dint of talking about them. They keep talking about risk as something tangible, they talk about variance, they talk about standard deviations. These things are completely abstract notions that are severely embedded in the Gaussian. If you don't believe in Gaussian you cannot believe in these notions. They don't exist.

Haug : Back to the Black-Scholes and your background in hedging. Black-Scholes and it's risk-neutral valuation is based on continuous dynamic delta hedging, what is your experience with this?

Taleb : First of all we don't use the concepts behind the Black-Scholes derivation and I showed with Derman that we really use a version of the Bachelier-Keynes argument. Black-Scholes is not an equation, the equation existed before them, Black-Scholes is the justification of using that risk neutrality argument, owing to the disappearance of risk for an option operator under continuous time hedging as the risk completely disappears. Now this is grounded in four or five assumptions, and let me read through these assumptions.

- Assumption number 1: Gaussian,
- Assumption number 2: Continuous trading,
- Assumption number 3: No transaction cost,
- Assumption number 4: No price impact.
- Assumption number 5: Knowledge of the parameters of the distribution.

This is not counting sets of other assumptions concerning interest rates and all of that. That the interest rates; etc. also are non-stochastic. No credit risk and so on, I leave these aside.

Now, the fact that all these assumptions are very idealized, I can understand. But at the core, the severe disturbing notion that the Gaussian is not an approximation to other distribution – the risks do not disappear in tails where the payoffs become explosive.

Haug : Merton early on seem to realize this problem by switching to jump diffusion?

Taleb : Jump diffusion still does not enter the class of scalable models and fails in the tails. Jump diffusion is a Poisson jump. Also there is inconsistency in Merton's attitude. Number 1: He said we don't use Bachelier's equation, we use continuous trading, therefore we can take out the risk neutral argument because continuous trading eliminates it, etc. Dynamic hedging eliminates it. Which is, ok, an argument that "if you have no jumps, and believe in Santa Claus". He later said, Well in some cases we have jumps in which case continuous trading doesn't work so we use the Bachelier equation and remove the risk by diversification so we can fudge it by saying jumps are not correlated with the market. If they are not correlated with the market then we can diversify them away. So in other words nobody realized that he went back and said okay, now we are using Bachelier's equation – but in cases the jumps are uncorrelated with the market. Well, if you think about it you would realize that up to 97 % of options trading today are in instruments like fixed income commodities, Forex, and not necessarily correlated to the market. So if I follow his logic we use Bachelier's expectation-based option method (adjusted for Log) 97 % of the time, or perhaps even 100 % of the time since all underlying securities are exposed to jump.

So what I am saying is that all these top down ideas sometimes break down and they patch them with arguments that I've been using all along – that we price options as an expectation under some probability distribution. What we presented, Derman and I, is a very simple statement saying it is rigorous art not defective science. All I need is a distribution that has a finite first moment and some arbitrage constraint and the arbitrage constraint can be put-call parity – and I can produce a number I am comfortable with. If you introduce put-call parity constrains you then end up with something like the Black-Scholes equation under some reasonable assumptions, and that's it. And you don't need to assume continuous trading, all that bogus stuff. And actually that's the way we all traded. I traded for a long time knowing that it was not the continuous trading argument that was behind my pricing. All I knew is put-call parity, which makes time value of the put, equal to the time value of the call. And that you discover yourself, that everything else leads to some arbitrages. I'm looking for something that works, and maybe not 100 % tight, but close enough, rather than something that is perfectly tight off of crazy assumptions and play Locke's madman.

So therefore Black-Scholes is first of all not an equation, it's an argument to be able to remove the risk-free from the Bachelier equation. Bachelier plus some alteration to logs and risk-neutral drift. About 7 or 8 people had it before them. And number 2, Black-Scholes, the argument itself is bogus so we don't use it but people don't notice that they don't use it. There's a universality of the Gaussian distribution that makes people unnecessarily fall into it as a benchmark.

Haug : So the problem is mainly for out-of-money options?

Taleb : Even at-the-money options have problems, but the problem is most severe for out-of-the-money options because they are very nonlinear to model error. Now anyone who has traded options and managed a book knows that you end up with a portfolio loaded with wings because the market moves away from the strikes over time, therefore your model error increases even when you only trade initially at-the-money options. So therefore the dynamic hedging doesn't really work. I know that, I've traded in dynamically hedged portfolio all my life, and I know what it means.

Finance theory has this art of wanting to be married to a top-down paradigm. They also have something nonsensical portfolio theory that they are married to, so they have all these paradigms, they want everything to be consistent with each other and there's no check on them. First of all, when using a non-Gaussian, even if you try to fudge it as Merton did with his jump diffusion, introducing the Poisson, you've got severe misfitness. This is another version of stochastic volatility. It is not scalable in the tails. Furthermore, what type of Poisson jump are you going to use? There are a lot of Poissons you can use, you can use a scalable fractal jump, why did't they choose these fractal jumps? Now empirical evidence shows, that the tails are scalable – up to some limit that is not obvious to us. When tails are scalable, you don't use a nonscalable Poisson that overfits from the past jumps.

Haug : So your alternative is that we hedge options with options?

Taleb : That's exactly how you trade. You traded. Isn't that how you trade?

Haug : Yes

Taleb : Go tell them! We do not rely on delta rebalancing except residually. We trade option against option. I don't know of any operator who dynamically hedges his or her risk. And we told these guys that option dealers have ten billion long, 9 billion and 999 short or vice versa and you'll dynamically hedge a little residual which disappears or increases within a bound. This is not how we trade options.

Finance theory holds that everything is based on dynamic delta hedging. They have not revised it after the failure of Leland O'Brien Rubinstein in the stock market crash of 1987 as they were hedging portfolios by replicating an option synthetically. Somehow finance theory is allergic to empiricism.

Haug : But there are option traders out there relying on dynamic hedging selling options, but they tend to blow up in the long run.

Taleb : In the short run as well they tend to blow up. First of all I don't know of any naked option trader except if the total position size is minimal. Option traders always end up spreading something. Book runners, people who run books – they spread something. Except if you do small amounts. When you sell out-of-the-money options you are very likely to blow up, because as I keep explaining, a 20 sigma events can cost you some 5/6 thousand years of time decay. So I tried to explain the definition of blow up. So if it works for ten years or a thousand years it doesn't even mean anything. Furthermore, out-of-the-money options are more difficult to dynamically hedge than at-the-money options.

Haug : But Black, Scholes and Merton also originally make a connection between their model and CAPM.

Taleb : CAPM is nonsense; empirically, conceptually, mathematically. It is a reverse engineered story where the exact assumptions are found that help produce an "elegant" model. It's top down approach. It relies heavily on Gaussianism. That mean over standard deviation or variance. You think that we know the future return. But on Planet Earth we don't know the mean. We don't know the sigma, and the sigma is not representative of risk. So, this is the kind of stuff that is not compatible with my respect for empirical reality and my awareness of fat-tails. Its grounding in the variance is bothersome.

Mandelbrot and I do not think that variance means anything. The central idea is that if you have what we see the tail exponent equals 3 in the markets[2]. Alpha equals 3 means that the sigma exists but the sampling error is infinite so I don't see the difference between an infinite sigma or a sigma that exists but the sampling error is infinite.

Haug : Is this also related to what you describe as wild randomness and mild randomness?

Taleb : You have type 1 and type 2 randomness. Type 1 is mild in which case you can use a Gaussian. And because of something I call the Ludic fallacy, you cannot use a Gaussian except in very sterilized environments under very strictly narrow conditions. Type 2 is wild randomness, and in wild randomness typically your entire properties are dominated by a very small number of very large moves.

We showed that fifty years of S&P was dominated by the ten most volatile days, so if you have the dominance of the largest moves to the total variance of the portfolio then you have a problem, the problem is that these conventional methods don't apply because these focus on the regular, and the regular is of small consequence for derivation of the moments. So this is why CAPM is nonsense.

Haug : According to Mandelbrot fat-tails were observed as early as 1915 by Mitchell and Mandelbrot who focused strongly on fat-tails in the sixties and then people went back to Gaussian, why did it take so much time before people started to focus on this?

Taleb : I taught in a business school and I'll tell you one thing, a lot of academic finance is intellectually dishonest, because these people are not interested in the truth, they are interested in tools that allow them to keep their jobs and teach students. They're not interested in the truth, or they don't know what it means. If after the stock market crash of 87, they still use sigma as a measure of anything, clearly you can't trust these people. And we've known since Mandelbrot about scalability.

To see the problem, go and buy a book on Investments. Try to evaluate its tools if the sigma does not work, see if any of the conclusions and techniques in it hold once you remove the sigma. See if the book is worth a dollar after that. It will not even be worth a dollar.

Entire finance careers are cancelled if you remove the Gaussian notion of sigma.

Haug : What about risk management? Sharpe and VaR seems to be still very popular measures.

Taleb : Sharpe ratio does not mean anything. Sigma is not a measure of anything so you can't use the Sharpe ratio (which has been known for a long time as the coefficient of variation).

Haug : But people seem to understand it's because they are using stress testing?

Taleb : I remember one person at a conference gave a talk in which she said *Value at Risk is necessary but not sufficient*. This is nihilism. You can stand up and say astrology is necessary but not sufficient.

To me stress testing is dangerous because it can be arbitrary and unrigorous – based on the largest past move which may not be representative of the future. You take a time series, you say what was the worst drop – well it was 10 %. Then you stress test for that – this is the Poisson problem. It means you would have missed the stock market crash in 1987 because it's not part of the sample. You would have stress tested for only 10 %. So the point is, stress testing is a backward looking way not forward looking. With a fractal you can generate far more sophisticated scenarios. The scalables give you a structure of the stress testing – you extrapolate outside your sample set. So there is an intelligent method to stress-test using different tail alphas.

Another problem is institutions use stress testing as an adjunct method not as a central method. You should work backwards. And if you stress test as the central method then you would start writing a portfolio differently. There are non-Poisson ways to do so.

Now let me come back once again to what I said about finance and why I tell you that these guys are dishonest. Any single discipline that is new is starting to use good ideas from statistical physics. Now we know that deaths from terrorist wars are fractal power laws. Power laws are pretty much everywhere. Now why don't they use them in finance? They find obscure reasons not to use them. If you use power laws then you will be able to stress test very well and you can ignore variance because it's totally irrelevant. But if you use power laws then you have to skip portfolio theory. And I show that you have to skip portfolio theory because all your ideas equations are meaningless. And if you use power laws then the Black-Scholes derivation by dynamic replication is not worth even wallpaper. You get the idea.

Haug : You published a book "Fooled by Randomness" and are now coming out with a book entitled "Black Swan", how are these similar and dissimilar?

Taleb : Very dissimilar. "The Black Swan" is a far deeper book; it goes as far as I could into the problem of fat-tails and knowledge. It is about the philosophy of history and epistemology; it's written by the same person, but they are very dissimilar. "Fooled by Randomness" is about randomness, and "The Black Swan" is about extreme wild uncertainty. It's the second level up. It is the one I wanted to write initially but I was mired down by talking about randomness. "The Black Swan" is mostly about the dynamics of history being dominated by these large scale events about which we know nothing and have trouble figuring out their properties. It is also about the social science theories that decrease our understanding of what's going on but are packaged in great pomp.

Haug : Are Black Swans related to fat-tails?

Taleb : The Black Swan is a fat-tail event. Except that it's not a Black Swan as you use a power law, sometimes. If you use a power law of the stock market crash of 87 it is not a Black Swan, or less of a Black Swan. It's perfectly in line with what you can expect. But it was a Black Swan because we don't use power laws.

Haug : Is Extremistan something you are writing about in your new book?

Taleb : Yes. I am discussing the following confusion. We think we live in time with Mediocristan with mild randomness, but we live in Extremistan with wild randomness. We use methods of Mediocristan and applying them to Extremistan is exactly like using tools made for water to describe gas. You can't!

Haug : Many Wall Street traders still seem to be long some types of positive carry trades, believing that they get some signal to get out in time, what's your view on this?

Taleb : I was approached by one guy, a not very intelligent person, who told me well, why don't you sell volatility, all you have to do is buy it back before the event. He was a serious hotshot with authority over large investments. He was also educated. I told him yeah very good, why do we waste our time buying all these lottery tickets? Let's just buy the winning one and save ourselves a lot of money. So you have embedded in the culture this idea that events, before they show up give you a phone call. You get an urgent email telling you what's going to happen. People have that impression, that the next event is going to be preceded by a warning but in the past we have not seen that. The hindsight bias makes us think so.

My problem goes beyond – I'm becoming more and more what I call an academic libertarian. An academic libertarian is this – just like libertarians distrusts Governments, I distrust academia because I think the role of academia is not so much to deliver the truth but self-perpetuation by a guild. And just like civil servants and politicians, they are not there to help you, a politician is out there to find an angle to get power. So this is why I am very suspicious of the academic world in social science, because what we have seen in the last 110 years in economics is quite shocking.

Haug : But how can we test out your own theories, can we back test them against historical data?

Taleb : Of course. You just look at the graph. When I say you don't have to back test the Black Swan, one single example would suffice to tell you that someone is criminal. It's like saying – you don't have to do a lot of empiricism to show someone is criminal. All you have to do is prove one day that you committed a crime. Likewise for a distribution. It's much easier to reject the Gaussian based on these grounds than to accept it. To say a theory is wrong you need one instance. Here we have thousands, right?

Haug : Is the bonus system also affecting how people take risk? People get bonus once a year typically, doesn't this encourage positive carry trading?

Taleb : The bonus system, giving people a yearly bonus based on strategies that take five or ten years to show their properties is foolish. But it's practised everywhere. And banks practise it with their managers. They should wait until the end of the cycle before they pay their managers and the chairmen of their companies. You are paying people in a wild randomness type of environment using tools of mild randomness.

Haug : You also studied the Black Swans in art and literature how is this related to what we have talked about?

Taleb : It is very similar. Actually art and literature are far more interesting for me than finance, because people in finance academia are usually dull, uncultured, lacking in conversation and intellectual curiosity, and these people are more colourful. The problem is that everything in art has fat-tails, everything in literature has fat-tails, everything in ideas has fat-tails. So you have to see how movies, for example, become blockbusters. It does not happen from putting special skills into the movie. Or a good story. All these movies that are competing against each other seem to have pretty much the same calibre of actors and the same quality of plot. What we have is a very arbitrary reason creating a contagious effect, an epidemic that blows things out of proportion. And you have a winner take all. Movies – anything that has the media involved in it are dominated by "the winner take all" effects.

Haug : Going back to finance, is it possible to predict what you call Black Swan risk?

Taleb : I used to think no but now I believe that you can tell simply from the number of positions betting against the Black Swan that these people will be in so much trouble that it's going to make it worse and worse and worse and worse. And the more reliance we're going to have on tools of portfolio theory, the heavier these effects will be. We saw it with LTCM. We will see it again with hedge funds.

Haug : So the construction of the portfolio is maybe more important than looking at all the statistical properties and the standard risk measures?

Taleb : That's the best thing, just seeing how many people are short options – today as we are talking Warren Buffet is short options so visibly you know there's some problem in the offing.

Haug : You spent some time both in academia and on Wall Street, what is the main difference?

Taleb : I spent no time in academia. I ran away in disgust. As I told you academia in finance… I find it intellectually offensive; in mathematics it's beautiful. Wall street – I like trading because traders say things the way they are. And they understand things. I can communicate with traders. It's more fun. Academia bores me to tears – partly because I don't like captive students shooting for grades. I like communicating with researchers, though. Perhaps I might join some research institute–or create one.

Haug : In your new book you are talking about anthropic bias and survivorship bias. How are these related?

Taleb : It's all a wrong reference class problem, in both cases you take the beginning cohort and instead of taking the computing probability for survival based on the beginning cohort you compute them based on the surviving cohort. So you are missing out on some statistical property, in other words you are missing out on a large part of your sample in both cases. It is the confusion of conditional and unconditional probability – or the wrong conditioning.

Haug : Where do you think we are in the evolution of quantitative finance and research?

Taleb : If we start using power laws as risk management tools we'll do very well. If we stay Gaussian-Poisson, I don't think so. But I don't think anyone cares about academic finance. Their idea is to look good, to teach MBAs but they are quite irrelevant. We practitioners do well without them, much like birds do not need onithologists.

Haug : Can you tell us more about your new book?

Taleb : The whole idea is that that out-of-the-money events, regardless of distribution are things we know so little about. And if out-of-the-money events are the ones that dominate in the end then we have a problem, then we know very little about the world. So that's what I'm focusing on currently.

Haug : And GIF what is that?

Taleb : GIF: The Great Intellectual Fraud. It's that Gaussian. The more I think about it the more I realize how people find solutions to the problems of existence, by discovering top down fudges, as Merton did to prove his dynamic hedging argument – he found the assumptions that allow him to produce a proof. What are the problems we face most in real life, what we face is the problem of induction and the fact that going from to the individual to the general is not an easy proposition, it is very painful. It is fraught with errors, It is very hard to derive a confidence level because you do not know how much data you need.

Say I walk into the world and I see a time series, just a series of some points on a page. Say I have a thousand points. How do I know what the distribution is from looking at the data – from these thousand points? How do I know if I have enough points to accept a given distribution? So if you need data to derive the distribution and you then need the distribution to tell if you have enough data then you have what philosophers would call a severe regress argument.

You are asking the data to tell you what distribution it is and the distribution to tell you how many data points you need to ascertain if it is the right distribution. It's like asking someone – are you a liar?

You can't ask the distribution to give its error rate. Likewise you cannot use the same model for risk management as you do for trading. I put it in "Fooled by Randomness". But I went beyond that with a philosopher, Avital Pilpel when we wrote that long paper, calling it "The Problem of Non-Observability of Probability Distribution". Your knowledge has to pre-suppose some probability distribution, otherwise you don't know what's going on. It so happens, very conveniently, that if you have an a priori probability distribution called the Gaussian, then everything becomes easy. So this is why it is was selected, it sort of solves all these problems at one stroke, the Gaussian takes care of everything, and that is what I call the Great Intellectual Fraud, GIF. This is a severe circularity.

Haug : Academics agree and disagree with you, because there are thousands of papers talking about fat-tails?

Taleb : There are thousands of papers on jump or GARCH – the wrong brand of fat-tails. More-over, when you see a fat-tail, you don't know which model to fit. With a fractal – all I know is that we have a fractal distribution, I just don't know how to parameterize it very well. But I personally don't look at one distribution. I look at a family of distributions of fat-tails, and I just make sure that I'm insulated from them. See unlike other people I don't bet against the tail. If I knew the distribution, I would know where to sell out-of-money options. But my knowledge of the properties of the tails is fundamentally incomplete – even with a fractal. I really don't know the upper bound, I know the lower bound. And the lower bound is higher than the Gaussian. And this is what people fail to understand. Yes there have been thousands of papers trying to go into precision, fitting fat-tails, and not realizing the fundamental prob-lem, and this is what the fundamental problem of knowledge is. The Gaussian, guess what? The Gaussian gives you its own error rate. But if you have other distributions, saying I'm going to fatten the tail is not trivial. Because a sampling error of other distribution is very high. So if you select Cauchy you're never going to see anything. Cauchy tells you that you cannot parameterize me. Likewise if you have distribution of infinite variance you have a huge error rate in measuring the variance. So the problem that you have with fat-tails is that these distribution do not deliver their properties easily from data. Assume I have a combina-tion distribution, with a very severe, say jump diffusion with a very severe fat-tail. Nothing moves and *boom* you have a huge event. Now deriving the probability of that very huge event, deriving it from finite set is not possible because by it's very nature it's very rare.

Haug : But do we have good enough statistical tools and mathematical tools to use power laws and scaling laws to price an option?

Taleb : For scaling you can price an option on scale distribution, you can very easily price it. It's done all the time. It is very trivial in fact to do these mathematics of options on that. I wrote this paper saying you don't need variance to price an option; most people don't realise that all you need is finite mean absolute deviation. An option is not sensitive to variance. It's sensitive to MAD.

Haug : Have you published much on this topic?

Taleb : I don't like the process of publishing finance stuff – it is too perishable and I feel I'm wasting time away from more profound issues. There is the time wasted with the referee whose intellectual standards are very low. The best referee is time, not some self-serving academic who thinks he understands the world. I, as a risk-taker have much, much higher standards of rigor, relevance and a no-nonsense need to focus on the bottom line than finance academics. History has treated my work very well. I never submit directly and my dogma is against writing for submission; I usually post on the web and if a journal requests it I still keep it on the web after that. So I wrote a paper called "Who Cares about Infinite Variance" and it is on the web though I may change the title.

Haug : What about variance swaps?

Taleb : Variance swaps are not a real product, try to de-compose a variance swap into real options – you can't. A variance swap is a contract delivering the squares of moves, and an option dose not depend on square of moves, an option is a piecewise linear product you see, the problem we have with variance swaps is that they can deliver an infinite payoff. But delivering infinite payoff means that you don't know how high you can go if you have a company going bankrupt or very large moves.

Haug : Is this why traders or market makers often cap their payout?

Taleb : If you truncate the variance swap then it ends up as finite properties and it is easier to de-compose into regular options, but it has no longer anything to do with variance. The mere fact of capping the tail cuts a lot of it.

Haug : But this seems like market makers are aware of this problem?

Taleb : Market makers are implicitly aware of it. But my point is that we don't need variance to price options, you need variance to price a variance swap. An uncapped variance swap. A capped variance swap becomes very similar to a portfolio of options. But variance is a square. You multiply large moves by large moves. It's dominated in a very small number of observations.

Haug : So incidentally we could maybe change to MAD swaps?

Taleb : MAD is much more stable and is what naturally goes into to the pricing of an option. People don't realise MAD is what an option is priced on. An at-the-money straddle delivers MAD (risk-neutral by put-call parity). It is trivial to show that an option depends on mean absolute deviation, not on variance.

Haug : **You are very well aware of tail events, but some year's back we went skiing and we always went in double black diamond slopes, and you never wore a helmet. How is this consistent with your philosophy and spending most of your time understanding tail events?**

Taleb : If I die it's not the end of the world, you know?! So it's bounded; this tail event is bounded, whereas an integral is not bounded, so my utility is bounded, so you've got to die some day. Also there is domain dependence. Nero, for example, took a lot of physical risks in "Fooled by Randomness", and ended up almost dying as a consequence, while being extremely conservative in his trading: you have a domain dependence of risk aversion, I am very, very risk averse in finance, but I am sometimes thrill-loving in my personal life. So it goes in different ways. Domain dependence is a very striking notion.

Haug : **What about in daily life, like Paul Wilmott told me, you cannot be afraid of walking across the street every day, you can get hit by a car anytime?**

Taleb : This is a pseudo argument. My worst case scenario is not my death, but a catastrophe that kills my relatives, friends, the human race, other mammals, etc. Futhermore such an argument should allow me to cross the street blindfolded. All I am doing is allowing you to see the true risks. The life of society, the economic field is dominated by very small probabilities – but not physical accidents. Let me give you the idea. If I take economic variables, you notice that the world economic variables, dominated by a very small number of companies. Take Google for example. So you have close to a million companies. And probably half that came and went over time, and probably half the capitalization comes from under a hundred companies out of this million companies. Or maybe two hundred companies worldwide. So here we have one event in 100,000 or 10,000 determining the rest of economic variables. You don't have that in real life. We don't have 20 % of the population of a country being killed on any given day crossing the street. So this is where this "crossing the street" argument fails. I take risks crossing the street. The risk is small and computable – and if I die, it is not too consequential for humanity. My death is not the worst case scenario: it is the deaths of members of my family, my friends, the end of humanity in general.

Haug : **What about Black Swan blindness? Is that related?**

Taleb : Black Swan blindness corresponds to the fact that most people don't understand the notion of integral and expectation in economic variables. So that's not compatible with an argument about a single individual crossing the street.

Haug : **You have also mention that extreme events are helpful to understand common events?**

Taleb : Yeah, because common events aren't relevant. It's extreme events which dominate socio economic variables. Whereas in Mediocristan, the uncommon is irrelevant. Let me give you an idea. Moves up to one sigma in the market cumulatively constitute nothing, represent nothing, so you shouldn't worry below one sigma or two sigmas (the equivalent of sigma in a Gaussian world). But the people worry precisely up to that point. You should worry about five or ten sigmas because these are events which eventually in the long run will dominate your P&L. If you stay long enough it's so small that a few rare events are going to dominate everything you do.

Haug : So this is also related to the concentration of wealth and academics getting more citations?

Taleb : Exactly. Academia is dominated by a small number of academics, the arts are dominated by a small number of artists, movies by a small number of movies, books 1 in 800 has about half the readers. I mean these numbers are such that the tail dominates the business. It's not like in real life; in real life, the tail doesn't dominate social life when you cross the street. It dominates social life when you talk about economics. You don't have to worry too much about the rare events when you cross the street. You have to worry about the rare event, if all of economic growth comes from the rare events.

Haug : Why is this?

Taleb : Because of scalability, it becomes non-Gaussian, you see – like Google's success is non-Gaussian. When I talk about the German Mark going from four to a dollar to four trillion to a dollar, you have a problem of fat-tails. You have a problem of fat-tails with Google. Sales going from nothing to several billion is a fat-tail. You don't have a problem of fat-tails for a butcher because for a small shop it's not scalable.

Haug : What about gambling, is that Mediocristan?

Taleb : Gambling is Mediocristan and I call it the Ludic fallacy. The Ludic fallacy is the misapplication of tools imported from the structured world of games. As all these guys Merton and Scholes don't understand randomness, trying to bring in methods from gambling into wild uncertainty. Whereas in fact wild uncertainty is completely different – I tell you, it's qualitatively a different business, it's qualitatively like trying to use water to describe air.

Haug : But this one game that maybe is closer to wild randomness, that's poker?

Taleb : Yes, poker, to some extent.

Haug : And then I win money, but the guy doesn't pay me the money, that's like wild randomness?

Taleb : Casinos – the P&L in a casino is dominated by general risks completely outside the roulette table.

Haug : Can you mention an example?

Taleb : I discuss the casino example in my book "The Black Swan". Their nongambling risks represent a thousand times their gambling swings – gambling P/L obeys the law of large numbers. They are diversifiable. Not the other risks.

Haug : All academics start out with continuous time and continuous prices but in practice we always observe discrete prices and I would also say discrete time, is this just to make the calculations simpler or?

Taleb : That's exactly the reason, it is a tool – but sometimes continuous tools don't work when you have jumps. The infinitesimal matters when you do not have discontinuities. I hold that Ito's Lemma does not work with the scalable, because the errors are dominated by the tails, you cannot set your cutoff at the second moment. A scalable will have some infinite higher moment.

Thank you for this discussion

Some references relevant to the interview are found below:

FOOTNOTES & REFERENCES

1. See Cont and Tankov (2004).
2. The tail exponent α is defined as follows: for some x large enough, the probability of exceeding $x = Kx^{-\alpha}$.

■ Bachelier, L (1990): Theory of speculation in: P. Cootner, ed., 1964, *The random character of stock market prices*. Cambridge, Mass: MIT Press
■ Black, F., and M. Scholes (1973): "The Pricing of Options and Corporate Liabilities," *Journal of Political Economy*, **81**, 637–654.
■ Cont, R., and P. Tankov (2004): *Financial Modelling With Jump Processes*. London: Chapman & Hall.
■ Derman, E., and N. Taleb (2005): "The Illusion of Dynamic Delta Replication," *Quantitative Finance*, **5**(4), 323–326.
■ Keynes, J. M. (1924): *A Tract on Monetary Reform*. Re-printed 2000, Amherst, New York: Prometheus Books.
■ Mandelbrot, B. (1963): "The Variation of Certain Speculative Prices," *Journal of Business*, **36**, 394–419.
■ Mandelbrot, B., and N. Taleb (2006): "A Focus on the Exceptions that Prove the Rule," *Financial Times*, Friday March 24.
■ Merton, R. C. (1973): "Theory of Rational Option Pricing," *Bell Journal of Economics and Management Science*, **4**, 141–183.
■ ——— (1976): "Option Pricing When Underlying Stock Returns are Discontinuous," *Journal of Financial Economics*, **3**, 125–144.
■ Mitchell, Wesley, C. (1915): "The Making and Using of Index Numbers," *Introduction to Index Numbers and Wholesale Prices in the United States and Foreign Countries* (published in 1915 as Bulletin No. 173 of the U.S. Bureau of Labor Statistics, reprinted in 1921 as Bulletin No. 284, and in 1938 as Bulletin No. 656).
■ Taleb, N. (1997): *Dynamic Hedging*. New York: John Wiley & Sons Inc.
■ ——— (2001): *Fooled by Randomness*. New York: Texere.
■ ——— (2006a): *The Black Swan*. New York: Random House.
■ ——— (2006b): "Tales of the Unexpected," *Wilmott Magazine*, March, 30–36.

If you want to survive as an option trader on Wall Street you better take fat-tails into account in your pricing and hedging.

1

The Discovery of Fat-Tails in Price Data

Fat-tails is one of the most important topics in financial economics, in particular for derivatives valuation and hedging, but also for risk management and almost any aspects of the investment process. The early discoveries of fat-tails in price data have in my view received too little attention. Thousands and thousands of papers have been written related to fat-tails; time-varying volatility, stochastic volatility, local volatility, jumps-diffusion, implied distributions, and alternative theoretical fat-tailed distributions are all important tools in derivatives valuation and financial risk management. Few or none of these books and papers refer to the early discoveries on fat-tails in price data,[1] and few traders and quants I have talked with seem to even be aware of that the discovery of fat-tails in price data at the time of writing goes back almost 100 years.[2]

Wesley C. Mitchell (1874–1948) seems to be the very first to empirically detect and describe both time varying "volatility" and high-peaked/fat-tailed distributions in commodity prices. Mitchell was not the first to point to fat-tailed distributions; Vilfredo Pareto had looked at the fat-tailed distributions of income already in the late 1800s and had even developed a theory for such distributions. Mitchell was however the first to empirically show that we had fat-tailed distributions in price data. All this he published in his work titled "The Making and Using of Index Numbers" published in 1915 and updated and re-printed in 1921 and 1938. I am tempted to say that Wesley C. Mitchell in many ways was to empirical finance what Bachelier was to theoretical quantitative finance. They where both far ahead of their time, and some of their most important discoveries was re-discovered long after they were first published. In 1954 Leonard Savage[3] and Paul Samuelson re-discovered in a library a thesis by Bachelier that he defended on March 19, 1900. Since then Bachelier slowly seems to have regained his position in financial economics. One of the reasons for his strong "comeback" is that his thesis was re-printed in the book by Cootner (1964) that was re-printed in 2000. Without access to what the early masters actually wrote how can we give them full credit?

I am the lucky owner of a copy of Cootner's original 1964 version. In Cootner's book there is re-print of several important papers that relatively early on describe fat-tails. One of the papers re-printed in this book is Benoit Mandelbrot's famous 1962/63 paper: "The Variation of Speculative Prices" where he focuses on fat-tailed distributions and also tries to come up with theoretical models that are consistent with fat-tails. Mandelbrot refers to Mitchell (1915) as probably the first to note the existence of high-peaked (fat-tailed) distributions.

Recently I got hold of the 1938 version that is a pure re-print of Mitchell's 1921 version that is described as a update of his 1915 version. The 1938 re-print is 114 pages long with the title "The Making and Using of Index Numbers" and with the text "This is a Reprint of Part I

From Bulletin No. 284 of the Bureau of Labor Statistics". Mitchell's booklet is mainly about how to look statistically at fluctuations in commodity prices, what we today would call volatility. I am not thinking about the statistical measure of variance and standard deviation, but volatility in a broader sense as a measure of price fluctuations. In his introduction "The History of Index Numbers" Mitchell is referring to the earliest work to his knowledge on this subject

> The honor of inventing the device now commonly used to measure changes in the level of prices probably belongs to an Italian. G. R. Carli. In an investigation into the effect of the discovery of America upon the purchasing power of money, he reduced the prices paid for grain, wine, and oil in 1750 to percentage of change from their prices in 1500, added the percentages together, and divided the sum by three, thus making an exceedingly simple index number. Since his book was first published in 1764, index numbers are over 150 years old.

Mitchell also refers to similar work done in England by Sir George Schuckburg-Evelyn 1798, and also to:

> The generation that created the classical political economy was deeply interested in the violent price fluctuations that accompanied the Napoleonic wars and the use of an irredeemable paper currency from 1797 to 1821. Several attempts were made to measure these fluctuations, and in 1883 G. Poulett Scrope suggested the establishment of a 'tabular standard value'.

For Mitchell the main interest in understanding price fluctuations in commodity prices is motivated by political economy. For this reason he and the researcher he refers to were interested mainly in how to come up with a good measure for fluctuations/volatility in the overall commodity market and not so much in individual commodities on their own. Mitchell was clearly aware that fluctuations could be of interest far outside the topic of political economy. For this reason he points out that there are many ways to calculate fluctuations, and what is the best measure will depend on what the measure will be used for.

Mitchell starts out by looking at percentage changes in 252 commodities during the years from 1891 to 1918. He points out that the fluctuations can vary widely from year to year and from commodity to commodity. Next, Mitchell arranges the price changes in the following manner:

> ...from 1891 to 1918, on which the changes from prices in the preceding year were entered in the order of their magnitude, beginning with the greatest percentage fall and running up through no change to the greatest percentage of raise. Then the whole number of recorded for each year was divided in 10 numerically equal groups, again beginning with the greatest fall and counting upward. Finally the nine dividing points between these equal 10 groups were marked off in the percentage scale of fall, 'no change,' or rise.

In this way Mitchell is in what I would consider a quite sophisticated way getting a very good indication for the fluctuations/volatility in the overall commodity market. This method is in many ways more informative than simply calculating the variance (or standard deviation) as we often do today, as this method does not make any theoretical assumptions about the distribution of the commodity prices. The method Mitchell explains here can be seen as a rough way of looking at the whole distribution, and as he does this for every year he is looking at fluctuations/volatility/distributions over time. Mitchell gives a table of this (Table 1 re-print) that he again plots in a very interesting diagram, see Chart 1 that basically shows how the fluctuations vary over time. Mitchell is pointing out

TABLE 1.—CHAIN INDEX NUMBERS OF PRICES AT WHOLESALE IN THE UNITED STATES, BY YEARS, 1891 TO 1918.

[The decils are those points in the percentage scale of rise or fall in price which divide the whole number of price changes recorded each year into 10 equal groups. Based upon the percentages of increase or decrease in price from one year to the next, computed from Table 9 of Bulletin of the United States Bureau of Labor Statistics, No. 269, May, 1920.]

(—indicates a fall; +indicates a rise; ±0 indicates " no change.")

Year.	Greatest fall.	1st decil.	2d decil.	3d decil.	4th decil.	Median.	6th decil.	7th decil.	8th decil.	9th decil.	Greatest rise.
	Per ct.	Per ct.	Per ct.	Per ct.	Per ct.	Per ct.	Per ct.	Per ct.	Per ct.	Per ct.	Per. ct.
1891	−30.5	−13.2	− 8.0	− 4.8	− 1.4	± 0	± 0	+ 1.5	+ 5.0	+15.3	+ 53.0
1892	−41.2	−16.0	−11.2	− 8.5	− 5.4	− 3.1	− 0.5	± 0	+ 1.1	+ 5.5	+ 28.0
1893	−27.5	−11.9	− 8.0	− 5.5	− 2.4	± 0	± 0	+ 1.1	+ 4.8	+11.0	+ 59.1
1894	−44.3	−21.4	−15.8	−13.4	−10.8	− 7.1	− 5.0	− 3.3	− 1.3	± 0	+ 31.1
1895	−38.0	−14.0	− 9.6	− 6.5	− 4.1	− 2.4	± 0	+ .7	+ 4.2	+12.1	+ 61.9
1896	−54.6	−17.8	−11.3	− 7.5	− 3.0	− 1.2	± 0	+ .3	+ 4.3	+10.2	+ 41.5
1897	−50.9	−11.5	− 7.2	− 4.4	− 1.7	± 0	± 0	+ 2.9	+ 6.2	+12.7	+101.6
1898	−21.9	− 7.0	− 3.3	− .4	± 0	+ 1.8	+ 5.0	+ 8.3	+13.3	+19.8	+ 60.4
1899	−20.2	− 3.8	± 0	± 0	+ 2.6	+ 5.5	+ 7.6	+10.6	+16.4	+30.8	+103.3
1900	−29.2	− 3.6	± 0	+ 3.2	+ 5.1	+ 7.5	+ 9.6	+12.7	+17.4	+25.6	+ 72.8
1901	−42.6	−15.0	−10.2	− 6.1	− 3.7	− 1.5	± 0	+ 1.3	+ 4.9	+13.2	+ 53.0
1902	−40.6	− 7.4	− 1.6	± 0	± 0	+ 2.2	+ 4.7	+ 7.1	+12.1	+20.4	+ 58.9
1903	−33.7	−12.6	− 5.3	− 2.1	± 0	+ 1.3	+ 3.7	+ 5.3	+ 8.3	+14.1	+ 37.4
1904	−43.8	−15.0	− 7.6	− 3.5	− .6	± 0	+ 1.3	+ 3.0	+ 5.9	+11.7	+ 39.9
1905	−44.9	− 7.6	− 3.9	− 1.0	± 0	+ .7	+ 3.2	+ 5.9	+ 9.6	+15.9	+ 46.0
1906	−39.1	− 4.8	± 0	± 0	+ 2.8	+ 5.1	+ 6.4	+ 9.7	+14.5	+18.9	+ 40.7
1907	−43.0	− 3.2	± 0	± 0	+ 1.2	+ 3.9	+ 6.6	+ 8.9	+12.3	+17.6	+ 67.8
1908	−39.5	−21.3	−16.0	−10.8	− 5.8	− 3.8	− .9	± 0	+ .8	+ 6.2	+ 44.9
1909	−29.8	− 7.7	− 3.7	− 1.1	± 0	± 0	+ 1.7	+ 5.0	+ 8.1	+16.0	+ 70.1
1910	−37.7	− 6.1	− 2.4	− .4	± 0	+ 1.5	+ 3.6	+ 6.3	+ 9.2	+18.6	+ 49.5
1911	−47.4	−15.1	− 9.8	− 7.0	− 4.2	− .9	± 0	± 0	+ 2.9	+11.0	+ 86.1
1912	−36.1	− 6.8	− 2.9	− .5	± 0	+ 1.0	+ 3.6	+ 6.7	+11.0	+17.7	+ 46.2
1913	−38.5	−10.4	− 3.7	− 1.0	± 0	+ .5	+ 2.4	+ 4.5	+ 7.5	+12.7	+ 58.5
1914	−37.3	−12.0	− 7.4	− 4.1	− 1.3	± 0	± 0	+ 1.5	+ 5.0	+ 9.1	+ 76.4
1915	−60.4	−12.0	− 5.9	− 1.9	− .1	± 0	+ 2.7	+ 6.0	+10.1	+18.7	+172.9
1916	−19.1	+ 2.1	+ 6.7	+10.5	+14.4	+18.6	+24.0	+30.1	+38.7	+53.4	+155.1
1917	−34.1	+ 8.7	+19.4	+25.1	+28.6	+34.8	+42.1	+49.3	+57.5	+69.3	+151.2
1918	−51.0	− 6.0	+ 2.0	+ 8.6	+14.8	+18.5	+22.1	+28.6	+36.1	+46.3	+118.0
Average	−31.9	−10.1	− 5.0	− 2.9	+ .9	+ 3.0	+ 5.1	+ 7.3	+11.5	+19.0	+ 71.0

Time is well spent in studying this chart … The wide range covered by these fluctuations, the erratic occurrence of extremely large changes, and also the fact that the greatest percentages of rise far surpass the greatest percentages of fall are strikingly shown; but so also are the much greater frequency of rather small variations, the dense concentration near the center of the field, the existence of a general drift in the whole complex of changes, and the frequent alternations in the direction and the degree of this drift.

The way he connects the median of each year makes him incorporate the drift over time in the diagram. This is probably the first empirical description of time-varying fluctuation/volatility as well as indication of fat-tails/high-peak and skewed "distribution". Mitchell does not stop here, but also plots the historical distribution based on 5,578 observed percentage price changes as a histogram. He also compares it with the theoretical normal distribution. Mitchell's histogram is re-printed as Chart 2. Among many things Mitchell points out:

The actual distribution is much more pointed then the other, and has much higher mode, or point of greatest density. On the other hand the actual distribution drops away

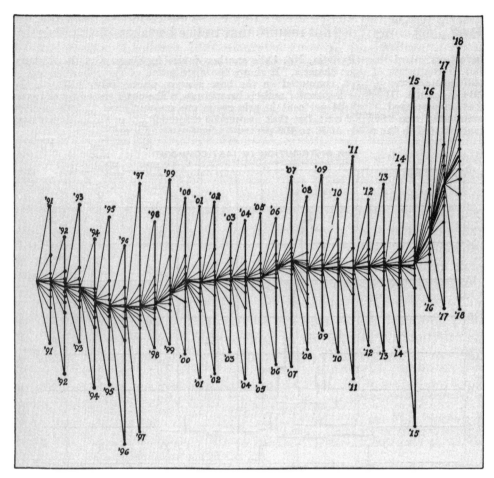

Chart 1.1:   How fluctuations vary over time

rapidly to either side of this mode, so that the curve representing it falls below the curve representing the normal distribution. The actual distribution is skewed instead of being perfectly symmetrical.

Mitchell is focuses mainly on the high-peak, and is not saying that the real histogram also seems to have fat-tails as we can see from studying the "far-out" tails from his histogram. However, he has already pointed this out indirectly with regard to the extreme observations in his time-varying chart and table. The strong positive skewness that he observes both in Chart 1.1 and Chart 1.2 he explains by the fact that the data is from a period when there was a strong positive upward trend in commodity prices. This can naturally be important when the data points are so far apart in time. Another factor that he comments on in a different part of his booklet is that if you simply look at percentage changes then you can not truly expect normal distribution. This is naturally because the maximum drop only can be 100 %, but the maximum increase can be higher. Only if we look at the logarithm of percentage changes we can get a theoretical symmetrical normal distribution. This is pointed out more or less directly by Mitchell.

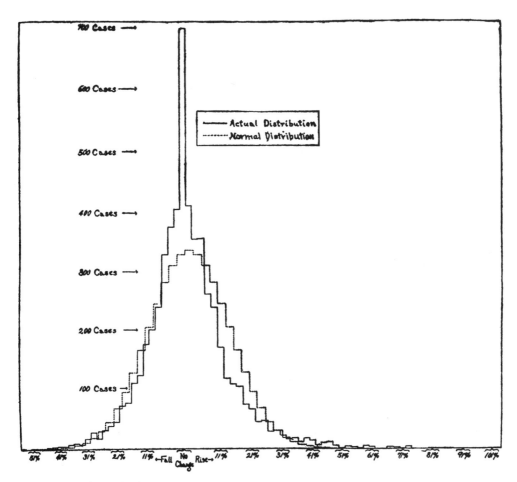

Chart 1.2: Mitchell's histogram

Mitchell also discusses what he calls interrelations (co-movements) between price fluctuations in commodity prices. His conclusion is basically that many commodities have complex forms of interrelations that are too difficult to calculate statistically. However, he is calculating linear correlation between some price indexes and is referring to that which is well known from standard text books on statistics.[4]

To summarize what already is a summary: Wesley C. Mitchell seems clearly to be the first I am aware of that have published empirical statistical findings of time-varying fluctuations/volatility and also the first one to detect and point out that the distributions of real price data have high-peak (and fat-tails) compared to the theoretical normal distribution. His empirical research is quite amazing for his time.

Henry Ludwell Moore was a Professor in political economy at Columbia University. In his book "Forecasting the Yield and the Price of Cotton" published in October 1917 he draws a histogram of spot cotton prices changes relative to the mean. In the same diagram Moore compares the real distribution to the theoretical normal distribution. Even if the histogram from real price changes clearly has high-peak and fat-tails compared to his Gaussian curve, Moore concludes that the real distribution is approximately normally distributed, in other words he ignores the high-peak and fat-tails that he just has detected in his histogram. Moore describes in detail how to measure fluctuations as standard deviation from the mean. Further, he has a lengthy mathematical and empirical discussion on measuring linear correlation in price data.

According to Mandelbrot (1962/63) the first unquestionable proofs for empirical distributions being too "peaked" relative to the Gaussian hypothesis was given by Oliver (1926) and also Mills (1927). At the time of writing I have not been able to get hold of Oliver's work, but I have the book by Mills. His book is 598 pages long and is also mainly about price fluctuations. Mills calculates the skewness and kurtosis from logarithmic returns on a large number of commodities. Based on the skewness and kurtosis numbers in combination with a statistical test that only will reject the normal distribution if the historical distribution is statistically significantly different from it, Mills rejects the Gaussian hypothesis. He concludes that leptokurtic distributions are a characteristic of the distribution of price relatives. Mills not only points out the high peak compared to Gaussian, but also points specifically to the likely reason for fat-tails:

> A distribution may depart widely from the Gaussian type because the influence of one or two extreme price changes.

Then there seems suddenly to be a period with little focus[5] on high-peak/fat-tailed distributions until the late 1950's and the beginning of the 1960's when several papers look into re-discovering fat-tailed distributions. Osborne (1959) detects fat-tails in price data, but basically ignores them and he seems to be a strong believer in normal distributed returns. Larson (1960) looks at the price changes in Chicago corn futures from 1922 to 1931 and from 1949 to 1958 and clearly finds indications of fat-tails:

> The distribution for each 10-year period has mean near zero, and is symmetrical and very nearly normally distributed for the central 80 per cent of the data, but there is an excessive number of extreme values. Also some of these values are quite extreme, being 8 or 9 standard deviations from the mean.

Alexander (1961) looks at observed distributions versus the theory of normal distributed returns and rejects normal distributed returns. He also points out that Osborne (1959) would have needed to dismiss his hypothesis of normality had he done a more rigorous test.

In his doctoral thesis at Yale University 1960:[6] Sprenkle (also re-printed in Cootner (1964)) extends Bachelier's work to log-normal, and is probably also the first to discuss fat-tails in relation to options. Sprenkle rejects log-normal and normal distribution for several stocks based on calculating skewness and kurtosis, but still sticks to log-normal distribution (log-normal price, normal distributed logarithmic returns) in his option formula:

> The ideal distribution would seem to be one which is slightly more peaked than a normal distribution and slightly more skewed than a log-normal distribution. A distribution with these characteristics is not immediately obvious.

Sprenkle rejects normal distributed returns, after skipping the crash of 1929. Sprenkle calculates skewness and kurtosis until just before the crash and then after the crash. Had he included crash he must of course (?) have known that he would have observed even higher kurtosis and probably negative skewness, but it is possible that he thought it was extremely unlikely that such an event would happen again.

In his famous 1962/63 paper Mandelbrot focuses on fat-tails, and tries to come up with a consistent theory based on observed high-peak fat-tailed distribution in price data. Most of the pieces were there before Mandelbrot, but Mandelbrot was one of the first to put together the bits and pieces and to understand the important implications of fat-tails observed in price data. Mandelbrot shows that the second moment of the distribution is highly unstable when one has fat-tails, he suggests replacing the Gaussian distributions with another family of probability distributions: stable-Paretian. Mandelbrot also seems to be one of the few that did his homework by digging out the old texts describing fat-tails before he simply came up with conclusions ignoring the facts that were already known. There is still today a great discussion as to whether or not stable-Paretian is a good solution (Rubinstein, 2006, p. 176: "Unfortunately, it is fair to say that the stable-Paretian assumption has been abandoned by later research, which now seems to favor nonstationarity as the principal source of fat-tails".) However, looking through the recent literature the stable-Paretian hypothesis seems far from dead, see for example Rachev and Mittnik (2000), Mittnik and Schwartz (2002), Rachev, Schwartz, and Tokat (2003).

Ayres (1963) points out that assumptions of normal distributed returns used in option pricing have the great virtue of mathematical simplicity and tractability, but that there is evidence that it is sometimes too simple and are referring to Mandelbrot (1962) in order to point to the problems with fat-tails.

In the 1960's and 1970's there was at the same time a substantial literature on theoretical financial economics that more or less ignored fat-tails and stuck to the Gaussian hypothesis. Many of these models have become very famous, clearly not for their distribution assumptions, but for bringing in other ideas. Probably also on the basis of many researchers being tempted to come up with mathematical simplicity and tractability, unfortunately in many cases at the cost of ignoring well known and observed facts. This has again led to a whole research industry trying to extend Gaussian based models/ideas to apply also to fat-tails. Option valuation and hedging fat-tails in the underlying asset are typically even more important than for investments in the assets themselves, and since the mid 1970's there has been a rapidly expanding literature on jump-diffusion, stochastic volatility, implied distributions, as well as alternative fat-tailed distributions (including the stable-Paretian). Over the last 10 to 30 years there has also been an increase in literature on how to take into account fat-tails in risk-management, asset allocation and capital asset pricing, but this process has in many ways been very slow taking into account that high-peak/fat-tails was an empirically stated fact established in the early 1900s or at least by the late 1920s.

As we have seen, the history of the discovery of high-peak/fat-tailed distributions goes back almost 100 years, but I say that some of the greatest discoveries around our understanding of fat-tailed distributions still lies ahead of us, discoveries that could possibly shake the foundations of financial economics and have consequences far beyond what we can imagine. Are you trying to tell me that the probability for this is extremely low? Yes it is probably low, but when an extreme event first shows up in the form of a stock market crash or a revolutionary idea it often carries with it great power and influence. So look out for the fat-tails, they are here to stay, the question is rather if you and I and our ideas will survive the next tail event.

FOOTNOTES & REFERENCES

1. An exception is Rubinstein (2006) that briefly mentions that Mandelbrot refers to Mitchell (1915) as the first one to discover fat-tails.
2. Or even longer, who knows if I have got hold of the first source? If you are aware of earlier works on discovery of fat-tails in price data I would be more than happy to know.
3. See Poundstone (2005) for more details on the rediscovery of Bachelier's work.
4. Mitchell refers to Yule, Udney G. (1912) "Introduction to the Theory of Statistics", 2nd edition.
5. Or alternatively I am not aware of any work done on fat-tails in this period.
6. According to Cootner this work was submitted to Yale University in 1960, but was probably first published in 1961.

■ Alexander, S. S. (1961): "Price Movements in Speculative Markets: Trends or Random Walks" *Industrial Management Review*, **2**(2), 7–26.
■ Ayres, H. (1963): *Risk Aversion in the Warrant Market*. S.M. thesis M.I.T., summary of it published in Cootner (1964).
■ Bachelier, L. (1900): *Theory of speculation* in: P. Cootner, ed., 1964, *The random character of stock market prices,* MIT Press, Cambridge, Mass.
■ Carli (1764): *Del Valore e della Proporzione de' Metalli Monetati con i generi in Italia prima delle Scoperte dell' Indie col confronto del Valore e della Proporzione de' Tempi nostri.* This Italian title translates to something like "Of the value and the proportion of the Monetary Metals with the kinds in Italy before the Discoveries of the Indians with the comparison of the Value and the Proportion in our times".
■ Cootner, P. H. (1964): *The Random Character of Stock Market Prices.* Cambridge, Mass.: MIT Press. Also re-printed in 2000 by Risk Books.
■ Larson, A. (1960): "Measurement of a Random Process in Future Prices," *Food Research Institute Studies I*, 313–324.
■ Mandelbrot, B. (1962): "The Variation of Certain Speculative Prices," *Thomas J. Watson Research Center Report NC-87: The International Research Center of the International Business Machine Corporation.*
■ —— (1963): "The Variation of Certain Speculative Prices" *Journal of Business*, **36**, 394–419.
■ Mills, F. C. (1927): *The Behaviour of Prices.* New York: National Bureau of Economic Research, Albany: The Messenger Press.
■ Mitchell, Wesley, C. (1915): "The Making and Using of Index Numbers," *Introduction to Index Numbers and Wholesale Prices in the United States and Foreign Countries* (published in 1915 as Bulletin No. 173 of the U.S. Bureau of Labor Statistics, reprinted in 1921 as Bulletin No. 284, and in 1938 as Bulletin No. 656).
■ Mittnik, S. R. S. and E. S. Schwartz (2002): "Value-At-Risk and Asset Allocation with Stable Return Distributions," *Allgemeines Statistisches Archiv*, **86**(1), 53–68.
■ Moore, H. L. (1917): *Forecasting the Yield and Price of Cotton.* New York: The Macmillian Company.
■ Oliver, M. (1926): *Les Nombres Indices de la Variation des Prix.* Paris doctoral dissertation.

■ Osborne, M. F. M. (1959): "Brownian Motion in the Stock Market" *Operations Research*, 145–173.

■ Poundstone, W. (2005): *Fortune's Formula*. New York: Hill and Wang.

■ Rachev, S. and S. Mittnik (2000): *Stable Paretian Models in Finance*. New York: John Wiley & Sons, Inc.

■ Rachev, S., E. S. Schwartz and Y. Tokat (2003): "The Stable non-Gaussian Asset Allocation: A Comparison with the Classical Approach" *Journal of Economic Dynamics and Control*, **27**(6), 937–969.

■ Rubinstein, M. (2006): *A History of The Theory of Investments*. New York: John Wiley & Sons, Inc.

■ Schuckburg-Evelyn, G. (1798): *An Account Of Some Endeavors To Ascertain A Standard Weight And Measure, Part I, Art VIII*. Philosophical Transactions of the Royal Society of London.

■ Scrope, P. G. (1833): *Principles of Political Economy*. London, 405–408.

■ Sprenkle, C. (1961): "Warrant Prices as Indicators of Expectations and Preferences" *Yale Economics Essays*, **1**(2), 178–231.

Ed Thorp is playing cards, using probability theory and taking home some money! This is before he started to concentrate on the Game of all Games – the financial market.

Edward Thorp on Gambling and Trading

Ed Thorp was the first to develop a wearable computer, he made money in Las Vegas using quantitative methods, he was the first to start a market neutral derivatives hedge fund: Princeton Newport and he knew about market neutral delta hedging years before Black, Scholes and Merton published their work. Edward Thorp has published the best selling books "Beat The Dealer" and "Beat The Market" together with Sheen T. Kassouf. He has published numerous articles on gambling, trading and hedge funds. Ed Thorp is a columnist for Wilmott Magazine.

Haug : Where did you grow up?

Thorp : First 10.4 years in Chicago IL then in Southern CA.

Haug : What is your educational background?

Thorp : B.A. and M.A. Physics, Ph.D. Mathematics, all at UCLA. More in "Who's Who in America".

Haug : Why did you decide to give away many if not most of your Black-Jack tricks in the best selling book "Beat the Dealer"?

Thorp : I had no intention of becoming a professional gambler. I was mainly interested in the science of the subject, and figured that I'd collect enough money prepublication to satisfy me. I also wanted to fill a void in the mathematical knowledge of this game and more generally of gambling games in general.

Haug : You worked as a mathematics professor at the University of California at Irvine, why did you decide to leave academia and go into professional trading?

Thorp : "Some are born professional traders, some become professional traders, and some have professional trading thrust upon them." I was in the last category. My increasing success and interest in the markets and the intellectual puzzles that they endlessly present gradually drew me towards full time investing, but my love of academia kept me there until 1983, some 19 years after I became seriously interested in the markets.

Haug : When did you first start trading options?

Thorp : Common stock purchase warrants in 1966 and options in 1967.

Haug : When did you first get in contact with Black and Scholes?

Thorp : The CBOE started trading in, as I recall, March 1973. In anticipation I earlier programmed my options formula into an HP9830A. Then I got a preprint in the mail from someone called Fischer Black with an options formula. It was equivalent to the one I was using and had programmed in preparation for the CBOE opening.

Haug : I heard rumours that you once were betting on horses at Saratoga with Fischer Black, why was this and did you win or lose?

Thorp : I believe this is a story told to Aaron Brown, recounted in his book, without an assertion that it is true or false. It is false. However, I did go to the track (Santa Anita, Hollywood Park) with Bill Ziemba a couple of times to use his system (which worked).

Haug : Do you regret that you were not more involved in publishing more of your ideas in mathematical finance early on rather than trading on them, you could potentially have been close to a Nobel Prize?

Thorp : I wasn't part of the economics/finance tribe so was unaware at the time of the Nobel Prize potential of the discovery. Had I been, I probably would have gone for it, but I have no regrets. Reasoning and history show that there was a tradeoff between fame and money and I prefer having enough money so that I and my family can live comfortably in perpetuity and free ourselves to explore our personal potentials.

Haug : When and how did you first learn about fat tailed distributions?

Thorp : When I devoted the summer of 1964 to reading and learning about the stock market.

Haug : In the late 1970s you also got involved in statistical arbitrage, how is this different from advanced technical analysis?

Thorp : Stat arb, as initially conceived, used price and volume information primarily, so could be called a type of "technical analysis" but wouldn't be grasped by the "chartists". However, as I practiced it, stat arb incorporated other kinds of financial information. The only limits were that it could be reduced to computer algorithms and automatically processed, analyzed and traded.

Haug : When doing statistical arbitrage do you follow it as a "black-box" or do you still use judgment and potential fundamental analysis in addition to the quantitative models?

Thorp : No "extra model" judgments except to decide that a security is, for the time being, to be taken off the trading list because important events (merger, takeover, etc.) have occurred which the model can't evaluate.

Haug : Did your firm ever get involved with the junk bond King Michael Milken?

Thorp : Like most of Wall Street at the time, we did trades with Drexel.

Haug : Your hedge fund Princeton-Newport had great returns also in 1987, how did you manage to do this when most investors lost their shirt?

Thorp : We wore a different kind of shirt.

Haug : At some point you were offered the position to invest as a limited partner in LTCM, why didn't you?

Thorp : Merriweather was a risk-taker and the Nobelists didn't, in my opinion, have trading savvy.

Haug : **Basically all research on derivatives valuation assumes efficient markets, how can this be consistent with your experience of making good returns in trading since the 1960s?**

Thorp : Efficient market theory tells us what the price should be, if it's assumptions are satisfied. In that world, deviations from that price are arbitrageable.

Haug : **What about survivorship bias, if we include the many traders and hedge funds that never made it, blew up or closed down because of low returns and then could not attract enough capital can this be the simple explanation why someone supposedly seems to beat the market?**

Thorp : A weak analogy: think of all the kids who want to be pro basketball players. Most perform below this level and most eventually give up the chase. If we judge performance of the group by that of the survivors, we greatly overestimate. But, does this mean the survivors have little skill? For more thoughts, see my Wilmott articles on market efficiency.

Haug : **Since you started trading do you think the markets have become more efficient over time, or does market efficiency come and go?**

Thorp : Old inefficiencies are (often very slowly) understood and disappear; new ones appear. I'm reminded of the electrical concepts of steady state and transients. New transients are always appearing and disrupting any evolution towards steady state.

Haug : **The number of hedge funds has exploded, in the town where I live Greenwich Connecticut (USA) there are supposedly 330 hedge funds managing more than 150 billion USD, the returns seem to have gone down, is there now an over establishment in the hedge fund business?**

Thorp : Perhaps we'll see some individual funds explode as well? Demand for alpha increases, supply doesn't keep up, amount per buyer decreases. See also my comments in "Time" February 12, 2007, page 54.

Haug : **Back in time you developed systems that gave you a large positive edge in casinos, with Black-Jack and roulette, is this still possible or are the rules now tilted in favor of the casinos?**

Thorp : Looks tight now, but who can say? If I were 20 again I might disagree.

Haug : **Do you still go to casinos gambling?**

Thorp : Not interesting – pales before the greatest game, the markets.

Haug : **Are you still involved in trading?**

Thorp : Not at the moment but this could change.

Haug : **What are your hobbies outside quantitative finance and gambling?**

Thorp : Astronomy, reading (like Charlie Munger's described by his children, some think I'm a book with legs).

Haug : **Where do you think we are in the evolution of quantitative finance?**

Thorp : Too many quants with hammers whacking too few nails too hard.

For an interesting story about quantitative finance applied in practice and a lot of information about Ed Thorp I will recommend the book "Fortune's Formula" by William Poundstone.

REFERENCES

■ Poundstone, W. (2005): *Fortune's Formula*. New York: Hill and Wang.
■ Thorp, E. O. (1966): *Beat the Dealer*. New York: Random House.
■ ——— (1969): "Optimal Gambling Systems for Favorable Games," *Review of the International Statistics Institute*, **37**(3).
■ ——— (1979): "Physical Prediction of Roulette I, II, III, IV," *Gambling Times*, May, July, August, October.

■ ——— (1998): "The Invention of the First Wearable Computer," *Second International Symposium on Wearable Computers in Pittsburg*.

■ ——— (2002): "What I Knew and When I Knew It – Part 1, Part 2, Part 3," *Wilmott Magazine*, Sep-02, Dec-02, Jan-03.

■ ——— (2004a): "Statistical Arbitrage – Part 1 to Part VI," *Wilmott Magazine*, Sep-04, Jan-05, Mar-05, May-05, Jul-05.

■ ——— (2004b): "A Theory of Inefficient Markets – Part 1, Part 2," *Wilmott Magazine*, May-04, Jul-04.

■ ——— (2005): "Inefficient Markets," *Wilmott Magazine*, September, 36–38.

■ Thorp, E. O., and S. T. Kassouf (1967): *Beat the Market*. New York: Random House.

In option trading you need to know your weapon inside out! The author used to be one of the best pistol shooters in Norway.

2

Option Pricing and Hedging from Theory to Practice: Know Your Weapon III*

I sometimes wonder why people still use the Black-Scholes formula, since it is based on such simple assumptions – unrealistic simple assumptions.
Fischer Black 1990

For an option trader an option formula can be seen as a weapon, it is a great tool if you know how to handle it. To really know how to handle it you need to know its ins and outs, its weakness and strengths. Here I will share my current knowledge on some of the most important aspects on option pricing and hedging. I will explain why the very basic option formula is so popular among option traders. I will take you on a journey from the "ancient" past to the present, and from theory to practice. In the end I will take you on a helicopter ride, so hopefully you also can see the forest for the trees. Let's go:

In an idealized fantasy world dynamic delta hedging removes all the risk all the time, but what about the real world? This chapter takes a look at the history as well as the robustness of option pricing and dynamic delta hedging. As we will see the Black-Scholes-Merton idea of dynamic delta hedging is far from robust in practice. Does this mean dynamic delta hedging is dead? Not at all, as I will show dynamic delta hedging is removing a lot of risk compared to not hedging at all. However options are extremely risky instruments, and even after removing a lot of risk there is more than enough risk left. That is in practice dynamic delta hedging alone cannot be used as an argument for risk-neutral valuation.

The great success of option pricing formulas in practice mainly seems to be due to the fact that traders can remove most model risk by hedging options with options. On the top of this delta hedging is helpful, but as we will see it is much more important how you construct your option portfolio than how you delta hedge.

There are many papers on discrete delta hedging and part of what I will tell is repetition of what is already known. The brilliant researchers that have written most of these papers typically

---

* Know Your Weapon Part 1 and 2 can be found as an extra "bonus" on the accompanying CD.

have only one foot on the trading floor. As someone with many years in option trading and market making experience I will try to tell the story from such a perspective. As a trader I am more concerned about approximately understanding how things really work in practice rather than having a model that is 100 % consistent with assumptions that we know will not hold in practice. This will be reflected in my analysis that I hope will shed some new light on option pricing and delta hedging and hopefully also open up further discussion on where we actually are in the evolution of option pricing and hedging.

1   The Partly Ignored and Forgotten History

Let us first start with a quick historical overview of some of the early discoveries in option pricing and hedging. It is worth mentioning that Jules Regnault already in 1863 basically had described the market as random walk where all information was reflected in the prices of the market, see also Girlich (2002). Mathematical description of option valuation goes at least back more than 100 years to the now so famous Bachelier (1900) paper, that was based on his doctoral thesis defended on March 19, 1900. Bachelier assumed a normal distribution for the asset price. This implies a positive probability for observing a negative asset price – a feature that is not popular for stocks and any other asset with limited liability features.

Bachelier viewed the stock market as a gamble, which with perfect competition motivates the zero expected return, see Smith (1976). The call price is given as the expected price at expiration:

$$c = (S - X)N(d_1) + \sigma\sqrt{T}n(d_1), \tag{2.1}$$

where

$$d_1 = \frac{S - X}{\sigma\sqrt{T}},$$

S = stock price.

X = strike price of option.

T = time to expiration in years.

σ = volatility of the underlying asset price.

$N(x)$ = the cumulative normal distribution function.

$n(x)$ = the standard normal density function.

Bachelier did not described dynamic delta hedging, neither market neutral static delta hedging. Yet he describes the purchase of a future contract against a short call and draw the profit and loss (P&L) diagram at maturity that clearly shows that this has same payoff profile as a put, this can be seen as a diffuse description of the put-call parity. We must have in mind that put options were not traded in Paris at that time, which could be the reason Bachelier does not describe this connection in more detail? Bachelier also describes selling two options against long futures and shows P&L of this at maturity. Further, he shows several examples of P&L profile for options against options, like bull spreads and call back spreads (buying one call and selling two calls with a higher strike price against it). So already back then they clearly had at least some intuition about how using combinations of futures and options will alter the risk-reward profile.

The first known published source on the put-call parity for options on forwards seems to go all the way back to Joseph de la Vega (1688), but it is only a "diffuse" description:

> We say of those who buy means of a forward call contract and sell at fixed term or of those who sell by means of a put contract and buy at a fixed term that they shift the course of their speculation.

Knoll (2004) points out the use of put-call parity to avoid usury can potentially be traced back 2000 years. But the "evidence" of the put-call parity at that time is at best diffusely describe as we know it today. Two books ignored and forgotten by the modern option research literature seem to be: "The Put-and-Call" by Leonard R. Higgins (1902) and "The A B C of Options and Arbitrage" by S. A. Nelson published in 1904. Higgins and Nelson fully describe the put-call parity as we know it today. Second, Nelson describes the idea of market neutral delta hedging for at-the-money options. Nelson even gives a rough indication that they had some understanding of the idea behind dynamic delta hedging. Let us start with Nelson's description of market neutral static delta hedging as well as the put-call parity. At page 28 Nelson writes:

> Sellers of options in London as a result of long experience, if they sell a Call, straightway buy half the stock against which the Call is sold; or if a Put is sold; they sell half the stock immediately.

We must see this in the light that standard options in London at that time were always issued at-the-money as is pointed out explicitly by Nelson, further all standard options in London were European style. In London in- or out-of-the-money options were only traded occasionally and were known as "fancy options". It is quite clear from this and the rest of Nelson's book that the option dealers were well aware that the delta from at-the-money options was approximately 50%. As a matter of fact at-the-money options trading in London at that time were always adjusted to be at-the-money forward, Nelson page 73:

> The regular London option is always either a Put or a Call, or both, at the market price of the stock at the time the bargain is made, to which is immediately added the cost of carrying or borrowing the stock until the maturity of the option.

And today we know very well that European options that are-at-the-money forward have a delta of approximately 50% (Naturally −50% for a long put option). Dividends went to the holder of the call and are also discussed by Nelson. There was also an active arbitrage business going on in options and stocks between London and New York at this time. According to Nelson up to 500 messages per hour and typically 2,000 to 3,000 messages per day where sent between the London and the New York markets through the cable companies. Each message flashed over the wire system in less than a minute. Nelson describes many details surrounding this arbitrage business: the cost of shipping shares, the cost of insuring shares, interest expenses, the possibilities to switch shares directly between someone being long securities in New York and short in London and in this way saving shipping and insurance costs, etc. Further:

> The London buyer of options is accustomed to "trade against his options" to a much greater extent than the New Yorker, and trading of this character calls for quite

complicated calculations that would puzzle and confuse the average American stock
speculator who wants a simple, rather than complicated proposition, and who prefer-
ably always demands a quick, rather than a slow decision.

Next it is very clear that they fully understood the put-call parity at this time, Nelson is again
quoting Higgins:

> It may be worthy of remark that "calls" are more often dealt than "puts" the reason
> probably being that the majority of "punters" in stocks and shares are more inclined to
> look at the bright side of things, and therefore more often "see" a rise than a fall in prices.
>   This special inclination to buy "calls" and to leave the "puts" severely alone does
> not, however, tend to make "calls" dear and "puts" cheap, for it can be shown that the
> adroit dealer in options can convert a "put" into a "call," a "call" into a "put", a "call
> o' more" into a "put-and-call," in fact any option into another, by dealing against it
> in the stock. We may therefore assume, with tolerable accuracy, that the "call" of a
> stock at any moment costs the same as the "put" of that stock, and half as much as
> the Put-and-Call.

A "call o' more" was a somewhat "exotic" option trading in London and Paris that gave the
right to buy or sell shares several times. I will not go into detail about that here, such options
are also described by Bachelier. Further, Nelson list six examples of such conversion, once again
quoting Higgins:

1. That a Call of a certain amount of stock can be converted into a Put-and-Call of half as
   much by selling one-half of the original amount.
2. That a Put of a certain amount of stock can be converted into a Put-and-Call of half as
   much by buying one-half of the original amount.
3. That a Call can be turned into a Put by selling all the stock.
4. That a Put can be turned into a Call by buying all the stock.
5. and 6. That a Put-and-Call of a certain amount of a stock can be turned into either a Put
   or twice as much by selling the whole amount, or into a Call of twice as much by buying
   the whole amount.

Numbers 1 and 2 are nothing but initial market neutral delta hedging of at-the-money options.
The Put-and-Call he refers to is nothing but a synthetic straddle, which initially is market neutral
and constructed by buying either a at-the-money call or a put and then doing a 50 % delta hedge
in stocks. Nelson mentions that Put-and-Call was a term used for a put plus a call in London and
that this often was described as a straddle in Wall Street. Numbers 3 and 4 are the pure put-call
parity, as we know it today. Numbers 5 and 6 are simply how a trader can turn a synthetic straddle
(or a real straddle) back into a pure call or a put. We also have to remember that Higgins is only
describing the London market, where options only could be exercised at maturity, while in Wall
Street the options could be exercised at any time. I guess this must have been the origin of the
terms European and American style exercise.

Once again even if Higgins here does not mention how to take into account the funding costs
of the shares in the calculation of the put-call parity we have to remember that this was directly
taken into account by the market practice of adjusting the strike for funding costs immediately
after trading the option. Nelson even mentions the risk in the funding cost changing over the
period of the option. This can be found on page 37 in Nelson's book:

...through buying one-half of the stock to convert the Call into a Put-and-Call – or
loss through an unexpected rise in the money rate.

This sentence is unclear on its own, but by reading the book it is clear that Nelson here is
talking about a dealer that has a short at-the-money call and is creating a market neutral delta
hedge (synthetic short straddle) by buying half of the share underlying the option. The potential
loss he refers to in relation to the money rate is clearly related to the cost of funding the stock
bought. If the money market rate changed and the positions had only locked in the funding short
term, this would naturally create risk.

It is also worth mentioning that the market standard in New York at that time was to first pay
the option premium at option maturity (or at time of exercise of options if American style that
only traded in Wall Street). This could possibly even explain why early option *pricing* formulas
typically did not discount the option premium? Nelson mentions that for this reason someone
selling a option (short) had to take into account the credit risk of the option buyer, as the seller of
the option could not be sure to get paid the option premium at maturity if the counterpart should
default on its obligations. In London this was not the case where the market standard was to pay
the option premium two days after the trade was done.

On page 21 Nelson describes what can possibly be considered the first ever published rough
indication of an early attempt of "dynamic delta hedging":

> Assume that you are a trader and own a Put on 100 Union Pacific at 99. The market
> decline to 98, and against the put you bought 50 shares at 98, and again 50 shares at 97.
> In the event of a rally you could sell out your "long" stock. If there is another decline
> you could rebuy and resell, on a second rally, protected by the Put. Experienced
> traders, however, find that the latter operation works out better in theory than in
> practice.

From this quote it is clear that Nelson knew about the idea of hedging options with shares
in several smaller steps, he starts with buying 50 shares and then another 50 shares as the stock
price falls. The idea of re-selling shares on the way up and buying when it goes down, is not that
far from the main idea behind dynamic delta hedging? It seems likely that Nelson only had a very
rough idea of what the hedge ratio (delta) should be except for at-the-money options. As already
mentioned it seems that option traders knew from experience the delta was approximately 50 %
(naturally −50 % for put options) for at-the-money options.

Nelson is also discussing that it is the expected average price fluctuation that is important
for finding the right option value. He also gives several tables with average percentage price
fluctuations. Nelson points out that the average price fluctuation (volatility) can vary widely over
time and therefore points out that an option dealer needs to do many options over time to have
a chance at getting close to the average expectation based on average fluctuations. Further, he
makes lengthy comparisons with similarities and differences between valuing options and that
of valuing life insurance. In short he concludes that option traders cannot work upon a regular
system or actuarial basis, but must also be guided by what is going on in the market. Nelson also
points out that "...the majority of the great option dealers who have found by experience that it is
the givers, and not the takers, of option money who have gained the advantage in the long run".
In other words most successful option dealers were not "insurance" sellers but buyers, possibly
due to difficulties in creating a perfect delta hedge? As we will soon see for any form of practical
delta hedging the "left over risk" is far from symmetric for long and short option positions.

Recently Hafner and Zimmermann (2007) made an amazing discovery of a Vinzenz Bronzin (1872–1970) ancient and forgotten publication on option pricing. Vinzenz Bronzin a professor of mathematics published in 1908 a book: "Theorie der Prämiengeschäfte" (theory of premium contracts) where he derives the put-call parity and also comes up with a option formula similar to Bachelier. Bronzin looked into option pricing based on several alternative distributions of the asset price, such as rectangular, triangular, parabolic and exponential distribution as well as the normal distribution.

Vinzenz Bronzin used what can be considered risk-neutral valuation taking into account strict arbitrage principles between the spot, the forward and the options, relying to a large degree on the put-call parity. His option formula was basically equivalent to the Black-Scholes-Merton formula, except when deriving it he did not rely on any particulr distribution or on continuous time dynamic delta hedging. I am sure we will hear much more about the interpretation of Bronzin's work in the future. I first became aware of his work while doing the last proof reading of this book. All I can say at the moment is that his work is rather remarkable for his time and I refer to Hafner and Zimmermann (2007) for the details on this discovery.

In 1910 Henry Deutsch (Ph.D.) in the 2nd edition of his book "Arbitrage in Bullion, Coins, Bills, Stocks, Shares and Options" describes the put-call parity in a similar way as Higgins and Nelson, but in less detail. The first edition of the book was published in 1904, but I unfortunately only have the second edition. Deutsch also describes the different option exchanges in Europe; London Stock Exchange, the Continental Bourse, the Berlin Bourse, and the Paris Bourse and how to potential arbitrage options between these exchanges. He states the importance of taking into account different closing times on Paris versus London, etc. Deutsch also mentions that in London the standard is only at-the-money options, while in Paris it was common to quote a lot of different strikes on the same underlying asset. An option issued at-the-money will naturally soon become in or out-of-the-money, but it is unclear if there was much trading in options after they got issued.

Deutsch describes in detail how the forward price between two currencies must be based on arbitrage as we know it today, he shows several detailed calculation examples of this. He even discusses how to take into account different day count basis in different countries. This was probably already known for a very long time and probably published much earlier.

We can so far conclude that hedging options with options as well as initial market neutral static delta hedging were the main principles of option hedging in the early 1900s. The hedge ratio for other than at-the-money options was probably not well understood, or at least not described in the literature I have at hand. For example, I have not got hold of old classic option books like Charles Castelli (1877) "The Theory of Options in Stocks and Shares", that was translated into French in 1882. All I can say is that everybody involved in option trading or research should read Bachelier, Higgins, Nelson, Bronzin and Deutsch in detail, you will be surprised by how much they knew at that time, at least I was.

Kruizenga in his doctoral thesis at MIT (1956) and also in Kruizenga (1964) re-discovered the put-call parity, but in many ways in less detail than was already described by Higgins and Nelson. To offer a few quotes from Kruizenga: "Buying a call plus selling short is equivalent to buying a put", "Writing a put and buying a call is equivalent to buying the stock". Kruizenga also describes a large number of examples of transforming one option strategy into another basically using the put-call parity. Kruizenga is, however, not describing the importance of taking into account the funding cost of going long or short the shares.

The put-call parity was again described in quite some detail by Reinach (1961) who also takes into account interest rate effects in a calculation example and even transaction costs. Traders at

New York stock exchange specializing in using the put-call parity to convert puts into calls or calls into puts was at that time known as Converters. An interesting quote from Reinach book is:

> Although I have no figures to substantiate my claim, I estimate that over 60 per cent of all Calls are made possible by the existence of Converters.

In other words the converters (dealers) that basically operated as market makers were able to operate and hedge most of their risk by "statically" hedging options with options. Actually semi-static hedging is probably a better expression as Reinach clearly also understood that the put-call parity did not hold fully for American options. Reinach describes how converters clearly would try to take advantage of this, by for example preferring to buy a put and convert it into a call that they sold short, if anyone prematurely should exercise the call the converter was left with extra value in the put. Reinach also exploits hedging options with options by taking advantage of options embedded in convertible bonds:

> Writers and traders have figured out other procedures for making profits writing Puts & Calls. Most are too specialized for all but the seasoned professional. One such procedure is the ownership of a convertible bonds and then writing of Calls against the stock into which the bonds are convertible. If the stock is called, the bonds are converted and the stock is delivered.

The put-call parity was later described in mathematical detail by Stoll (1969), but from what I can see there is little or nothing new from what already had been described long before his time.

In 1960[1] Sidney Fried in the booklet "The Speculative Merits of Common Stock Warrants" described empirical relationships between warrants and the common stock price. In several examples the author showed how to try to construct a market neutral static delta hedge both by shorting warrants and going long stocks or by buying warrants and shorting stocks. The hedge ratio Fried described simply seems to be based on a combination of experience, historical relationships between warrants and the stock price and some basic knowledge of factors affecting the value of the warrant. Fried seems in many ways to be less sophisticated than Higgins (1902) and Nelson (1904), but is at the same time adding some new insight, especially when it comes to empirical relationships between the move in the underlying stock and the price of the warrant.

In his doctoral thesis at Yale University (1960) Sprenkle went one step forward in theoretical option pricing and assumed the stock price was log-normal distributed and the returns normal distributed, his thesis was published in 1961 and re-published in the book by Cootner (1964). That is the stock follows a geometric Brownian motion

$$dS = \mu S dt + \sigma S dz,$$

where μ is the expected rate of return on the underlying asset, σ now is the volatility of the rate of return, and dz is a Wiener process, just as in the Black and Scholes (1973) and Merton (1973c) analysis. In this way he ruled out the possibility of negative stock prices, consistent with limited liability. Sprenkle in his option formula allowed for a drift in the asset price:

$$c = Se^{\mu T}N(d_1) - (1-k)XN(d_2) \tag{2.2}$$

$$d_1 = \frac{\ln(S/X) + (\mu + \sigma^2/2)T}{\sigma\sqrt{T}}$$

$$d_2 = d_1 - \sigma\sqrt{T},$$

where k is the adjustment for the degree of market risk aversion.

James Boness (1964) also assumed a lognormal asset price. Boness derives the following formula for the price of a call option:

$$c = SN(d_1) - Xe^{-\mu T}N(d_2) \qquad (2.3)$$

$$d_1 = \frac{\ln(S/X) + (\mu + \sigma^2/2)T}{\sigma\sqrt{T}}$$

$$d_2 = d_1 - \sigma\sqrt{T}.$$

This is actually identical to the Black-Scholes-Merton 1973 formula, but in the way Black, Scholes and Merton derived their formula based on continuous dynamic delta hedging or alternatively based on CAPM they were able to get independent of the expected rate of return. It is in other words not the formula itself that is considered the great discovery done by Black, Scholes and Merton, but how they derived it. This is, among several others, also pointed out by Rubinstein (2006):

> The real significance of the formula to the financial theory of investment lies not in itself, but rather in how it was derived. Ten years earlier the same formula had been derived by Case M. Sprenkle (1962) and A. James Boness (1964).

Paul Samuelson (1965) also assumed the asset price follows a geometric Brownian motion with positive drift, μ:

$$c = Se^{(\mu-w)T}N(d_1) - Xe^{-wT}N(d_2) \qquad (2.4)$$

$$d_1 = \frac{\ln(S/X) + (\mu + \sigma^2/2)T}{\sigma\sqrt{T}}$$

$$d_2 = d_1 - \sigma\sqrt{T},$$

where w is the average rate of growth in the value of the call. This is different from the Boness model in that the Samuelson model can take into account that the expected return from the option is larger than that of the underlying asset $w > \mu$. In Samuelson's paper there is also very interesting appendix by McKean (1965), that comes up with a closed form solution for American perpetual options, but not yet under theoretical risk-neutrality. For that we have to wait for Merton (1973c).

Let us now assume we are trading options in the late 1960s. From the literature we clearly know that log-normal asset price is preferable over normal distribution, further we even know from multiple sources that the market has fat-tails, something we will get back to later on. The best we have at the moment seem to be something like the Boness formula. A good starting point to get a grasp of the change in an option price towards changes in the underlying stock is simply to plot the option value using the Boness formula relative to the underlying stock price. Of course we have to make a guess on the expected rate of return of the stock, or we could alternatively have tried to back it out from empirical data or from the current market.[2] Let us assume the risk free rate is 4 % and that we with a "qualified" guess assume $\mu = 6\%$. Further assume the strike price is 100, time to maturity is 3 months, the current stock price is 96 and the expected volatility of the underlying asset over the lifetime of the option is 20 %.

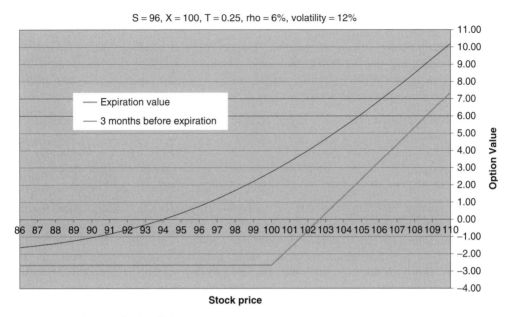

S = 96, X = 100, T = 0.25, rho = 6%, volatility = 12%

Figure 2.1: Boness Option Value

Figure 2.1 shows how the option value will vary with the stock price now 3 months before expiration as well as at expiration.

Simply by inspecting the graph, at least if we had zoom in at the segment close to the current stock price of 96, we would have seen that the option value will increase by about 1/3 point if the stock price goes up by one dollar from 96 to 97. Similar if the stock price drops from 96 to 95 the option value will decrease by about 1/3 point. What if we now are long one stock, how can we remove the risk by selling options against it? As the option locally around the current asset price level moves with approximately 1/3 point for each dollar the stock moves we can remove all risk for a small move in the stock price simply by selling approximately 3 call options against it.

Such market neutral delta hedging is exactly what Thorp and Kassouf are describing in their book "Beat the Dealer" published in 1967. Thorp and Kassouf are describing a very similar example to the one I just described, and let me offer a quote from page 81 of their book:

> If, when the common changed price, the warrant moved along this line, then a 1 point increase in the common would result in a 1/3 point increase in the warrant. If we are short 3 warrants to one common long, then the gain on the common is completely offset by the loss on the warrant.

Thorp and Kassouf (1967) clearly also knew that the hedge ratio was changing both with respect to change in stock price and time, they describe practical approximation rules of when one should adjust the number of options sold with respect to one stock held long. While Higgins and Nelson describe market neutral delta hedging only for options that are at-the-money forward, Thorp and Kassouf can probably be seen as the first to extend and describe how to find a market neutral delta hedge for any level of the strike or asset price. Thorp and Kassouf, however, do not describe how dynamic delta hedging continuous in time can remove all the risk all the time under a set of strict theoretical assumptions.

In 1969 Thorp published a paper describing a option formula similar to that of Sprenkle and Boness, again including the real drift in the stock, see also Thorp (2002) for more details. In his 1969 paper Thorp again describes briefly market neutral static delta hedging, but also points in the direction of dynamic delta hedging:

> We have assumed so far that a hedge position is held unchanged until expiration, then closed out. This static or "desert island" strategy is not optimal. In practice intermediate decisions in the spirit of dynamic programming lead to considerably superior dynamic strategies. The methods, technical details, and probabilistic summary are more complex so we defer the details for possibly subsequent publication.

Another "ignored" and "forgotten" text is a book/booklet published in 1970 by Arnold Bernhard & Co., it is somewhat unclear exactly who the author is, but it says "Written and Edited by the Publisher and Editors of The Value Line Convertible Survey". The authors are clearly aware of market neutral static delta hedging or what they name "balanced hedge" for any level in the strike or asset price. This book has multiple examples of how to buy warrants or convertible bonds and construct a market neutral delta hedge by shorting the right amount of common shares. The book has a focus on going long warrants or convertible bonds with market neutral static delta hedge. To offer a quote from the book:

> Convertible hedges provide a low risk method of investing in securities. Properly established hedges involve only limited possibilities of loss permitting profits to accrue on any sizable move – up or down – in the underlying common stock. Although the potential profits are relatively modest, the technique in its simplest application relieves the investor of the need to correctly gauge the direction of the market in general and in the stock selected in particular.

For example, the author shows an instance when the stock moves with 25 % up or down then the portfolio balanced hedged (market neutral delta hedge) portfolio will be up 5 % no matter the direction of the 25 % move in the stock. The potential 5 % profit no matter direction the stock moves is as the author describes naturally related to the option having convex payoff, while the stock has a linear payoff. The author also points out: "Wide swings in the obtainable security increase the probability of profit in the hedge". This we naturally know must be true for a market-neutral position with long convexity (long options).

Further, the book describes the following formula for calculating the number of shares to short relative to a long (call) warrant: $\frac{(A+C)\times 2}{S}$ when assuming a 25 % rise or fall in the price of the common stock, where A is the change in the warrant or convertible bond price for a raise of 25 % in the common, and C is the change in the warrant or convertible bond price for a 25 % fall in the common. For a 50 % move the author gives the formula of number of shares to short as: $\frac{B+D}{S}$, where B and D now is the change in the warrant or convertible bond price for respectively a 50 % rise and fall in the common. These simple formulas are for the chosen size of moves in the stock price ΔS consistent with the more generalized and well known finite-difference approximation typically used in delta calculations today for finite difference methods and often also for closed form option formulas:

$$\Delta \approx \frac{f(S + \Delta S, \ldots) - f(S - \Delta S, \ldots)}{2\Delta S}$$

where f stands for the price of the derivatives instrument and ΔS the move in the asset. Except that Arnold Bernhard & Co. are looking at change in option value for a percentage change in asset price rather than absolute change. When $\Delta S = 25\%$ and $A = [f(S(1 + \Delta S), \ldots) - f(S, \ldots)]$ and $C = [f(S, \ldots) - f(S(1 - \Delta S), \ldots)]$ then the delta of the option is given by

$$
\Delta \approx \frac{[f(S(1 + \Delta S), \ldots) - f(S, \ldots)] + [f(S, \ldots) - f(S(1 - \Delta S), \ldots)]}{S \times 2\Delta S}
$$

$$
= \frac{A + C}{S \times 2\Delta S} = \frac{(A + C) \times 2}{S}
$$

And for $\Delta S = 50\%$ we naturally get $\frac{B+D}{S}$, so Arnold Bernhard & Co. clearly seemed to be aware of how to calculate the delta numerically. For frequent dynamic hedging it naturally make sense to make ΔS much smaller than Arnold Bernhard & Co. are describing. We should have in mind that the authors are not discussing continuous-time dynamic delta hedging, but only market neutral static delta hedging over a long holding period. Convertible bonds and warrants typically have much longer time to maturity than exchange traded standard stock options. For a more "optimal" static delta over a long holding period it makes sense to make ΔS reasonably large. The book also contains re-prints of a convertible bond and warrant sheets published and I assume sent out to customers (investors). These sheets contain hedge ratios for a large number of warrants and convertible bonds, all based on 25% moves up or down in the common share price. It is somewhat unclear how Arnold Bernhard & Co. calculate how much a warrant or a convertible bond should move for given move in the underlying share. The book describes no option formulas, but it seems to be a combination of empirical relationships potential in combination with a model?

By 1970 we can conclude that hedging options with options through the knowledge of the put-call parity had been well established for a long time and probably was the most central arbitrage and hedging principle for many experienced option traders. Market neutral static delta hedging was, as we have seen, well known from the literature and used by multiple investors and traders. The idea of dynamic delta hedging had been pointed at and loosely discussed. However the idea of continuous time dynamic delta hedging as a method to remove all the risk all the time was from what I have seen clearly not yet published.

Black and Scholes (1973) in their famous paper, among other things, extending on the idea of market neutral delta hedging:

> One of the concepts that we use in developing our model is expressed by Thorp and Kassouf (1967). They obtain an empirical valuation formula for warrants by fitting a curve to actual warrant prices. Then they use this formula to calculate the ratio of shares of stock options needed to create a hedge position by going long in one security and short in the other. What they fail to pursue is the fact that in equilibrium, the expected return on such a hedge position must be equal to the return on a riskless asset. What we show below is that this equilibrium condition can be used to derive a theoretical valuation formula.

What in modern times often is considered as the greatest break through in delta hedging and derivatives valuation was to see that by continuously dynamically delta hedging under some strict theoretical assumptions one could remove all risk all the time, or as stated by Black and Scholes (1973):

If the hedge is maintained continuously, then the approximations mentioned above become exact, and the return on the hedged position is completely independent of the change in the value of the stock. In fact, the return on the hedged position becomes certain. This was pointed out to us by Robert Merton.

This is the brilliant mathematical idea of continuous dynamic delta hedging. The mathematical proof is quite simple (at least when someone has first pointed it out) and can today be found in standard option books like Wilmott (2006) or Haug (2006). As we can see Black and Scholes are giving the credit of this idea to Robert Merton, see also Merton (1973c) and Merton (1998). There is no doubt that this is a brilliant mathematical discovery, but finance is unfortunately not pure math. Robert Merton himself did naturally not fully believe in continuous-time dynamic delta hedging. When moving to practice the idea of continuous-time dynamic delta hedging was naturally only meant as a good approximation. A model is only a model and never the full reality. The original Black-Scholes-Merton model was naturally based on a lot of unrealistic assumptions that the trio was well aware of, see, for example, Black (1989) and Black (1990). We should not criticise a model because there in practice are a few breaks on it assumptions. What is important is if the main idea and concept of the model is robust. Here we will concentrate on the robustness of dynamic delta hedging. This question is an important one that Merton (1998) himself has pointed out:

> A broader, and still open, research issue is the robustness of the pricing formula in the absence of a dynamic portfolio strategy that exactly replicates the payoffs to the option security. Obviously, the conclusion on that issue depends on why perfect replication is not feasible as well as on the magnitude of the imperfection. Continuous trading, is, of course, only an idealized prospect, not literally obtainable; therefore with discrete trading intervals, replication is at best only approximate. Subsequent simulation work has shown that within the actual trading intervals available and the volatility levels of speculative prices, the error in replication is manageable, provided, however that the other assumptions about the underlying process obtain... Without a continuous sample path, replication is not possible and that rules out a strict no-arbitrage derivation. Instead, the derivation is completed by using equilibrium asset pricing models such as the Intertemporal CAPM Merton 1973a and the Arbitrage Pricing Theory Ross 1976.

2 Discrete Dynamic Delta Hedging under Geometric Brownian Motion

Even if geometric Brownian motion is very different from real asset price behavior let us start with such an idealized world before we get closer to the real market behavior. If assets really were following a geometric Brownian motion and we could hedge continuous in time then we could hedge out all the risk all the time, as first pointed out by Merton.

There exists a special case under discrete hedging assuming geometric Brownian motion (GBM) where we basically can remove "all" risk "all" the time. That is in the binomial tree model of Cox, Ross and Rubinstein (1979) and Rendleman and Bartter (1979). The reason dynamic delta hedging here works so well is that the price jumps in the tree are of known size and at known time points, and that there only are two states of the "world". The binomial method naturally only converges fully to the Black-Scholes-Merton formula when the number of time steps goes towards infinite, but even at relatively few time steps it is a very good approximation.

This is not the case of discrete dynamic delta hedging under real geometric Brownian motion, the convergence is here much slower.

Assuming discrete hedging under GBM; Boyle and Emanuel (1980) and Leland (1985) show how to analytically calculate the hedging error over one hedging period. Derman and Kamal (1999) gives a analytical approximations for the hedging error over the whole lifetime of the option. Here we will basically repeat what is already known from the literature by simply using Monte Carlo simulation.

In almost any option valuation problem when using Monte Carlo simulation we would prefer quasi-random (also known as low-discrepancy) numbers for fast convergence. Here we actually want to simulate something extremely close to a real GBM and we want our random numbers to be as close to random as possible. A reasonably good random number generator is therefore important in such simulations. For example, the random number generator that comes with Excel will fail, it will actually over estimate the hedging errors.[3]

We will be running 100 thousand simulated stock price paths for each number presented in the table. Before we start to look at how effective discrete dynamic delta hedging is at removing risk, it is a good idea to have something to compare with. To do this we start out with no delta hedging (naked options) and alternatively market neutral static delta hedging. Static delta hedging also known as initial market neutral delta hedging simply consists of delta hedging the option once (in this case according to the Black-Scholes-Merton delta) in the beginning of the period under consideration. The delta hedge is kept unchanged until option expiration, therefore the name static delta hedging.

For simplicity we will assume zero drift and zero interest rate. This so we can concentrate on hedging errors alone.

Table 2.1 shows the standard deviation in the P&L in percent of initial option premium for a one month put option for different volatilities and strikes. The asset price is 100 and the table looks at at-the-money put options that roughly have -50% delta no matter volatility level, further we look at -25% and -10% delta put options.

TABLE 2.1:   MONTE CARLO SIMULATION PUT OPTION NO HEDGE AND STATIC DELTA HEDGE, 100,000 SIMULATIONS
($S = 100$, $T = 30/365$, $\mu = 0$, $r = 0$.)

Vol	Strike	Delta	Value	Stdev %	"Max"	Stdev %	"Max"
				No Hedge		Static Delta Hedge	
10%	100.0000	−49.4%	1.14369	144.2%	856.2%	75.7%	457.9%
10%	98.1252	−25.0%	0.43383	231.9%	2204.3%	166.3%	1520.6%
10%	96.4322	−10.0%	0.13736	395.9%	5740.3%	339.5%	4897.5%
30%	100.0000	−48.3%	3.43014	139.1%	855.5%	75.6%	548.0%
30%	94.7136	−25.0%	1.34026	221.0%	1817.0%	159.9%	1239.6%
30%	89.8953	−10.0%	0.42222	374.2%	5390.1%	321.4%	4600.8%
60%	100.0000	−46.6%	6.85394	132.8%	680.4%	75.5%	619.1%
60%	90.3727	−25.0%	2.80468	202.2%	1380.2%	148.6%	981.0%
60%	81.4117	−10.0%	0.87655	335.6%	3620.1%	291.3%	3036.7%

As we can see the risks in naked options are huge. For example the standard deviation in P&L as a percentage of the option premium for a -10% delta put with 10% volatility is 395.9% of the option premium. I have also calculated the maximum error "Max", this is simply the maximum error from the single path giving the highest P&L error out of the 100 thousand paths simulated. If you try to repeat this study the standard deviation in P&L should be close to the numbers I have in my table, the maximum error could naturally vary somewhat more from study to study, but it gives a rough indication of how bad things can go. The maximum hedging error could always be larger than given in the table. It would naturally be even better to look at the whole distribution of P&L (and hedging errors), but I was running out of time and I leave this work up to others.

From the last two columns we can see that static market neutral delta hedging reduces the standard deviation in P&L by about half for at-the-money options. For far out-of-the-money options the hedge has much less impact. It is naturally important to be aware that the hedging error not is symmetric for long and short option positions. For example, the standard deviation of 339.5% for a -10% delta put, assuming 10% known continuous-time volatility tells you that you easily can lose approximately 3 times the option premium if you are short a put option with initial delta hedge. If you are long the same option then you can naturally also lose money, but your losses will naturally be limited to the option premium paid, that is 100%. Still you could naturally end up making 300% return or even better close to 5000% return for the "maximum" error (4897.5% for this particular 100 thousand run). This does not mean you have a positive edge; you could still bleed to death (time decay). But this is why experienced option traders in general never sell naked options and only to a very limited degree also options with a static delta hedge.

Now assume that you knew that a -10% put very likely was 20% over priced, would you sell it naked or even with initial delta hedge in large quantities? With limited capital the answer is probably no, even if the edge is on your side the risk is unbearable at least for large quantities of options. Of course if you could remove most risk towards moves in the underlying asset by dynamic delta hedging or another hedging approach it would be a very good idea to sell such options, as we soon will see dynamic delta hedging is not a good solution, but there is another solution.

Next let us move to dynamic delta hedging. Table 2.2 gives the standard deviation for the dynamic delta replication hedging error for a one month put option for different volatilities and strikes. We look at re-hedging the option once a day, that is 30 times over the option lifetime ($n = 30$), two times a day ($n = 60$), and ten times a day ($n = 300$). The column marked "Value" is simply the theoretically Black-Scholes-Merton value for the option.

There are several interesting observations we can make from this table. Let's start to look at at-the-money options. We see that when re-hedging 30 times and the volatility is 10% the standard deviation in the replication error as a percentage of option premium is about 15.6%, further the standard error hardly changes as we change the volatility. For an option trader the standard hedging error is not really the most important, possibly more important is worst-case hedging error. The maximum hedging error we cannot really know, but we can at least look at the maximum hedging error from the 100 thousand simulated paths and use this as a rough indication, at least to get an idea of how large the maximum error can be compared to the standard error. The maximum hedging error from 100 thousand simulations is 100.7% for this option (at-the-money option with 10% volatility).

Even in the idealized world of GBM we naturally do not know if the "maximum" error would show up on the first option traded or the last or a trade in between. If it was the first option you did after getting hired as an option trader you would possibly get fired. On Wall Street in

TABLE 2.2:   MONTE CARLO SIMULATION OF DYNAMIC DELTA REPLICATION PUT OPTION, 100,000 SIMULATIONS
$(S = 100, T = 30/365, \mu = 0, r = 0.)$

Vol	Strike	Delta	Value	Stdev %	"Max"	Stdev %	"Max"	Stdev %	"Max"
				$n = 30$		$n = 60$		$n = 300$	
10%	100.0000	−49.4%	1.14369	15.6%	100.7%	11.2%	70.2%	5.1%	35.0%
10%	98.1252	−25.0%	0.43383	34.9%	304.6%	25.3%	246.7%	11.4%	88.9%
10%	96.4322	−10.0%	0.13736	76.9%	854.8%	55.1%	663.0%	24.8%	275.6%
30%	100.0000	−48.3%	3.43014	15.6%	123.1%	11.2%	80.4%	5.1%	37.9%
30%	94.7136	−25.0%	1.34026	34.2%	304.2%	24.4%	216.4%	11.0%	77.6%
30%	89.8953	−10.0%	0.42222	73.4%	763.6%	52.0%	518.6%	23.7%	269.4%
60%	100.0000	−46.6%	6.85394	15.7%	127.6%	11.1%	93.8%	5.1%	35.4%
60%	90.3727	−25.0%	2.80468	31.9%	436.7%	22.7%	352.2%	10.3%	83.7%
60%	81.4117	−10.0%	0.87655	67.0%	661.5%	48.0%	534.9%	21.9%	262.9%

general it does not help to explain to your boss that this simply was an hedging error caused by randomness, and that your standard hedging error only will be about 15% when you have finished doing lot's of trades. Capital is limited and time is limited. When I worked many years ago as a market maker in Norwegian bond options there were probably only about 30 option trades going on over a whole year, so it would not help to tell my boss that the standard deviation in my hedging error would be reduced to 15% over the next 3,000 years.[4] In other words I could naturally not rely on dynamic delta hedging. I had to rely on something else, something we will get back to later on, and remember we are still talking about the idealized world of geometric Brownian motion. Defenders of the dynamic delta hedging argument would naturally like to turn this argument around; claiming that the probability of getting hit by the "maximum" error early on is incredibly small or negligible, yes I partly agree, but we are still in the Gaussian world (GBM), soon we will get closer to real market behavior and you will hopefully see the importance of this argument before you learn the hard way, from the market itself.

As we move out-of-the money we see the replication error increases dramatically. Going from at-the-money to a −25% delta option the standard hedging error is going from 15.6% to more than 30%. Also here the hedging error is roughly unaffected by the volatility levels. The "maximum" hedging error observed for the 100 thousand simulations is now more than 300% of the option premium. For −10% delta options the standard hedging error is around 70%, and the "maximum" hedging error varies from approximately 854% to 661% dependent on the volatility level. An option trader can naturally not accept living with such large replication errors.

The Merton argument is based on continuous hedging so what if we hedge more frequently? As we increase the hedging frequency the hedging error naturally reduces. When re-hedging 10 times a day that is 300 times for a 1 month option the standard error for at-the-money options goes down to about 5.1% of the option premium, not without risk, but not bad. Still the "maximum" hedging error is more than 35%. When we move further out-of-the-money the hedging error again increases. For −25% delta options the standard hedging error is more than 10%, and the "maximum" error varies from 77% to 88%, for a −10% delta put option the standard error is more than 20 %, and the "maximum" error more than 260 %. So even when re-hedging 10 times a day the hedging errors in particular for out-of-the-money options are simply too high to live with, and far too high to argue for risk-neutral valuation.

We could increase the hedge frequency further, but are then running into the problem of transaction costs. Potentially we could hedge even more frequently in some of the most liquid currency markets where the transaction costs in some of the major currencies can be very small, but in many markets hedging more than 10 times a day would mean the transaction costs in form of bid-offer spreads etc. would turn the hedging strategy into a sure way of losing money. In many markets hedging more than a couple of times a day is unrealistic due to high transaction costs, and at 10 or more times a day we have a problem.

Looking at table 2.2 it is obvious that dynamic delta hedging leaves us with a lot of risk. Still we should not forget the bright side. Comparing table 2.2 with table 2.1 we see that dynamic delta hedging is removing a lot of risk compared to no hedging or static delta hedging.

Our little Monte Carlo simulation has mainly confirmed what is already known from the literature, see for example Mello and Neuhaus (1998) and Bertsimas, Kogan and Lo (2001). We have presented the replication errors as a percentage of the option premium, also known as relative replication error. As we have seen, the relative hedging error is largest for out-of-the-money options. Another way to express the replication error is simply as the absolute dollar value. In this case the hedging error would be highest for approximately at-the-money options, in general the options with highest gamma. From the tables presented you can easily find the absolute dollar error simply by multiplying the percentage replication error with the option premium. If we should use relative or absolute values as expression for hedging errors is naturally a important question. In general everyone has a limited amount of capital that can be invested so in that case relative hedging error seems the most relevant, but it is much more complex than this. Actually both relative and absolute hedging error are relevant. In practice we typically also have a volatility smile; deep out-of-the-money options typically trade at a higher Black-Scholes-Merton implied volatilities relative to options around at-the-money. This will reduce the relative hedging error for out-of-the money options considerably and slightly increase it for at-the-money options relative to the tables presented here.

During our analysis we have been unrealistic in several ways. Option traders and market makers do not simply spread their delta hedging "bullets" uniformly over time as done in the naive Monte Carlo simulation. Sometimes the market does not move much and why would you then hedge and cause transaction costs? Further, the Black-Scholes-Merton delta is the optimal delta for continuous-time hedging, for discrete-time hedging it is not the optimal delta, and several authors have shown how to improve the delta for discrete hedging, see for example Schachter and Robins (1994), Hoggard, Whalley, and Wilmott (1994), Bertsimas, Kogan and Lo (2001) and Wilmott (2006). Knowledgeable option traders typically delta hedge as a function of the size of the move in the underlying asset, the size of their net delta and the gamma risk, transaction costs, etc. For example, when the market is moving a lot and their gamma is high they tend to hedge more frequently. Some option traders use quantitative models to optimize their delta hedging, others use experience and intuition or some type of combination of experience and quantitative methods. In other words the hedging errors and in particular the "maximum" hedging error's presented in table 2.2 are over estimated (under assumption of GBM). It is obvious that we can do better than table 2.2 for discrete hedging under GBM, but markets are not following GBM. So even if we can reduce the hedging error under GBM there are important factors like jumps and stochastic volatility that will strongly increase the hedging errors.

TABLE 2.3: DERMAN-KAMAL THEORETICAL DYNAMIC DELTA HEDGING REPLICATION ERROR PUT OPTION
($S = 100, T = 30/365, \mu = 0, r = 0.$)

Vol	Strike	Delta	Value	Stdev % $n = 30$	Stdev % $n = 60$	Stdev % $n = 300$
10%	100.0000	−49.4%	1.14369	16.2%	11.4%	5.1%
10%	98.1252	−25.0%	0.43383	34.0%	24.0%	10.7%
10%	96.4322	−10.0%	0.13736	59.3%	41.9%	18.7%
30%	100.0000	−48.3%	3.43014	16.2%	11.4%	5.1%
30%	94.7136	−25.0%	1.34026	33.0%	23.3%	10.4%
30%	89.8953	−10.0%	0.42222	57.8%	40.9%	18.3%
60%	100.0000	−46.6%	6.85394	16.1%	11.4%	5.1%
60%	90.3727	−25.0%	2.80468	31.5%	22.3%	10.0%
60%	81.4117	−10.0%	0.87655	55.7%	39.4%	17.6%

For comparison as well as a simple control check of my Monte Carlo Simulation I am repeating the calculations from table 2.2, but now using the analytical approximation given by Derman and Kamal (1999).[5] As mentioned by Derman and Kamal their theoretical approximation works best for at-the-money options, this we can confirm by comparing tables 2.2 and 2.3. The Derman and Kamal approximation for standard replication error seems to under estimate the real error somewhat for deep out-of-the-money options. For at-the-money options the two methods gives almost the same values as they should, which is a good indication that my Monte Carlo Simulation is not messed up.

Further, the Derman and Kamal closed form approximation only gives standard error and gives us no indication about potential "maximum" replication error, however in their paper they also show a few figures of the distribution in hedging errors based on Monte Carlo simulation.

Before we move on, let us analyse briefly why dynamic delta hedging does not work as well as "expected" even in the idealized world of GBM. We have so far assumed constant volatility and that option traders know the volatility of the underlying asset. But it is only in continuous-time the volatility is known and constant. When going from continuous-time to discrete-time the volatility is no longer constant, this is well known from the statistical literature. You can call it sampling error or whatever you want, it is a real effect that is very important for discrete-time delta hedging. The relevant volatility for the delta hedger is the discrete monitored volatility. So instead of a known volatility in the Monte Carlo simulation we actually have different volatility for each path, even if we are using the same input volatility for each simulation, see for example Haug (2006) for how to calculate the confidence interval for volatility when measured discretely, assuming normal-distributed returns.

Another factor that is worth mentioning is DdeltaDvol, that is the sensitivity to delta for a change in volatility, see Know Your Weapon part 1 (on the accompanying CD) as well as Taleb (1997). At-the-money options have very low DdeltaDvol, while deep-out-of-the-money options have high DdeltaDvol. As the volatility is uncertain under discrete hedging this means the delta for deep-out-of-the-money options often will be far off. This is probably another reason why dynamic delta hedging works relatively well for at-the-money options, but is less reliable for out-of-the-money options. Of course an option that initially is at-the-money can end up out-of-the-money etc.. A detailed analysis of the hedging error for a given path is naturally more complex than this, as we know from the literature it is path dependent, see for example Wilmott (2006). The high DdeltaDvol for deep-out-of-the-money options you will also find in local volatility, stochastic volatility and jump-diffusion models. So even in periods without jumps such models will have similar problems for discrete hedging in particular for deep-out-of-the-money options. In addition dynamic delta hedging will naturally work even worse by introducing stochastic-volatility. Now let us jump straight to the most important market-factor affecting delta hedging, that is jumps!

3   Dynamic Delta Hedging Under Jump-Diffusion

We have so far stayed in the unrealistic world of GBM. Asset prices are not normal distributed, but have fat-tails. Detection of fat-tails in price data goes at least all the way back to Mitchell (1915), see Chapter 1: "The Discovery of Fat-Tails in Price Data". In relation to option valuation Sprenkle (1961) (if not Bronzin, 1908) is probably the first to show some concern about high peaked/fat-tailed distributions. Later there were literally thousands of papers looking at fat-tail distribution in relation to derivatives valuation and risk management.

We will start out simply by assuming traders are using the Black-Scholes-Merton formula to calculate their delta. Naively we are assuming they know the continuous-time constant volatility in a normal market environment, the diffusion part, and are using this to calculate their delta. Further we assume the market from time to time makes an un-expected jump to the downside. The timing and the size of the jump we assume for simplicity is completely unexpected by the delta hedger. So for simplicity we have not reflected the fear of jumps in out-of-the-money option volatilities. Even if we assume such jumps happen infrequently we are interested in how well the dynamic delta hedging works for options that actually are affected by the jump, we have already looked at the case of no jumps. Our naive model assumes GBM as the diffusion part then with a single jump at a random time during the option lifetime. For each number in table 2.4 we have 100 thousand simulations. We are here only looking at the case of 30 % diffusion volatility (excluding the jump).

The table reports standard deviation and "maximum" errors for delta replication for jump-size of 3 %, 5 % and 10 %. First of all we now see that the hedging errors are much larger than without jumps (tables 2.2 and 2.3). Second, we can see that the benefit of hedging more frequently is not of much help anymore, in particular for a jump of 5 % or higher. Here the hedging error is completely dominated by the unexpected jump and it hardly matters how frequent we hedge.

We can argue that it is extremely seldom we get jumps of this magnitude and that we typically will be able to hedge several times as the asset often jumps down in several smaller intraday steps. Even if I have not presented empirical evidence that stocks and other assets can easily make jumps of 3 %, 5 %, 10 %, or even larger jumps without any good hedging opportunity, I have been in the market long enough to observe this actually happening, and more frequently than most of us probably would like to think.

When studying intraday data it is not enough to see at what levels the assets have traded to calculate the jump-size. What is the real jump-size will actually often vary from trader seat to trader seat. For example if a stock trading at 100 intraday goes down to 97 and then down to 95, how big is the largest intraday jump? Some would probably say 3 %. But if the liquidity at the 97 level was limited to 100 shares traded and I needed to sell 100 thousand shares then the realistic jump for me is at least 5%. For someone that needs to sell up to 100 shares and that also got filled at 97 could argue that the maximum jump-size that day only was 3%, from his perspective this is a correct observation. Only traders know how much they need to buy or sell and can know the real jump-size from their trading seat. This information is hidden from researchers and even other traders, but is a very important effect in real trading. And you don't need to be a big player for this to have effects, even the most liquid markets can dry up very quickly, and market makers then often only show their minimum bid-offer, or as I have observed even refuse to pick up their phone, pretending that they are in the bathroom. Diffusion for some can be jumps for others; a series of small intraday jumps for one trader can be a mega jump for another trader. It all depends on your trading seat, and every seat has a different view of the world! This is what I like to call; "The Many-World's Interpretation of Jump-Diffusion".[6] Historical intraday data even including volumes can "only" detect the minimum jump-size, such data can say little about maximum jump-size, except of course in super liquid market situation where everyone can get filled at almost any price and for any volume, but in such market periods there are not many large jumps anyway.

Again our Monte Carlo simulation is far too naive, knowledgeable option traders knows that assets make jumps, it is more or less priced into the option prices. They can optimize their delta hedge based on knowledge or using more sophisticated jump-diffusion models, etc. For example Bertsimas, Kogan and Lo (2001) optimize their delta hedge ratio based on jump-diffusion. However, they are limiting their analysis to very small jump-size, thus only if the jumps are very small can we argue that the market is close to complete, and of course only then will delta hedging have any hope of working at all.

Further, in practice the higher price for out-of-the-money options due to the volatility smile will reduce the hedging error relative to table 2.4. Then again there are so many factors that would increase the hedging error, one of them is jumps in realized and implied volatility that in a complex way often are correlated to jumps in the asset. Option traders naturally also do not know

TABLE 2.4: MONTE CARLO SIMULATION OF DISCRETE DYNAMIC DELTA REPLICATION WITH JUMPS IN THE UNDERLYING ASSET, 100,000 SIMULATIONS, PUT OPTION

$(S = 100, T = 30/365, \mu = 0, r = 0, \sigma = 0.3)$

Jump-size	Strike	Delta	Value	Stdev %	"Max"	Stdev %	"Max"	Stdev %	"Max"
				$n = 30$		$n = 60$		$n = 300$	
3%	100.0000	−48.3%	3.43014	17.7%	141.6%	13.7%	104.2%	9.1%	73.7%
3%	94.7136	−25.0%	1.34026	41.6%	349.7%	32.0%	252.0%	20.9%	191.0%
3%	89.8953	−10.0%	0.42222	97.4%	1014.9%	74.7%	731.8%	47.4%	619.0%
5%	100.0000	−48.3%	3.43014	25.6%	173.1%	23.1%	160.0%	20.8%	127.1%
5%	94.7136	−25.0%	1.34026	62.3%	394.6%	55.1%	403.1%	48.9%	312.8%
5%	89.8953	−10.0%	0.42222	149.1%	1504.2%	131.3%	1040.0%	114.1%	950.4%
10%	100.0000	−48.3%	3.43014	73.7%	287.9%	73.6%	275.2%	73.6%	268.8%
10%	94.7136	−25.0%	1.34026	189.1%	773.7%	188.5%	658.1%	188.1%	680.9%
10%	89.8953	−10.0%	0.42222	478.8%	2314.6%	473.3%	2026.8%	468.9%	2089.0%

the diffusion volatility as we have assumed here, that is the volatility is partly deterministic and partly stochastic. We can argue back and forth if the hedging errors should be cut by 5%, 10%, in half, or even by two thirds, or alternatively be doubled relative to table 2.4. The point is not to find the exact theoretical hedging error, if there even is such a thing, the point is that dynamic delta hedging clearly cannot be used as argument alone for risk-neutral valuation.

Merton (1976) in his jump-diffusion model no longer assumes we can hedge away all the risk by dynamic delta hedging. Instead he returns to some type of equilibrium model. Merton assumes that all jumps are unsystematic, that is the jump risk can be hedged away by simply holding a well diversified portfolio of assets. Merton's (1976) model is a good model to understand about how jump risk can affect option values, for example it is clear from his model that out-of-the-money options with short time to maturity should have a higher value than at-the-money options compared to the Black-Scholes-Merton formula.

Personally I like the main idea behind equilibrium models that unsystematic risk can be hedged away by holding a well-diversified portfolio, and that unsystematic risk for this reason should not be priced. Most famous ideas in financial economics are in my view unfortunately too black and white; the real world is almost always full of shades and even colours. Black and white[7] models are easier to come up with and are often the simplest way to isolate various effects and ideas into a simple theoretical model framework, but such models typically give too rough a picture of the reality. If you want to survive as a trader it is of great importance to also see the shades and even the colours of the real world. That we do not have a fully consistent theoretical model for colours yet does not mean that we cannot observe and partly understand shades and colours in the market place.

Academics have recently started to see more and more evidence of shades and colours, for example how unsystematic risk to some degree actually seems to matter, see Goyal and Santa-Clara (2003). Several papers have given support for the claim that both individual and many mutual funds are surprisingly un-diversified; see for example Barber and Odean (2000), Benartzi and Thaler (2001) and Falkenstein (1996). However, these papers seem to fail to see that unsystematic risk and particularly unsystematic jumps also count for trading decisions in large well-diversified banks and institutions that on an aggregate basis are not affected much by such jumps. This seem contradictory, but is easy to see for anyone who knows how market making and trading is set up in most big banks.

Most individuals working as market makers in options are typically only managing a book of options on a few underlying assets. For example, one individual can be a market maker in options on gold and possibly also other precious metals, another market maker on crude oil options, another a market maker in options on Scandinavian currencies and so on. In few if any big banks will you find an individual that is a market maker in a well-diversified portfolio of all types of underlying assets. Further, the currency desk is typically separated from the equity desk, the fixed income desk from the energy desk, etc. A bank as a whole is typically very well diversified and is well aware of the benefits of diversification. If someone loses 50 million on gold options and another trader makes 50 million the same day on some equity option trading, the CEO of the big bank would possibly not even be informed, or at least not worried, he she is mainly interested in aggregated trading results. CEO's are typically not daily decision makers at the trading floor, except for possibly being involved in setting some major risk limits. Inside their risk limits (that can be considerable) traders and market makers rule the trading floors. Sometimes top traders even get paid more than their CEO.

Proprietary traders and market makers in most big Wall Street banks are mainly rewarded in terms of bonus based on the performance in their own portfolio (trading book), and typically only based slightly on overall performance of the whole investment bank. The market maker is an individual and not a computer trying to optimize risk reward for the whole portfolio of the bank. Even on the same small trading desk one trader making lots of money trading in a few underlying assets can get paid several million dollars in bonus while someone sitting next to him/her trading some other assets, but with moderate losses can get zero bonus or even get fired. Individual traders in general simply do not get paid based on returns from the banks well diversified portfolio, and often not even much on the desk's performance, but from their own specific trading portfolios. May be they should get paid more based on the whole of the bank's performance? This is a completely different discussion, as a trader you have to trade based on how markets are, not on how some equilibrium model tells you that the market (and bonus system) should be based on a series of strict theoretical assumptions.

Let us for a moment assume a gold option market maker that has sold a lot of short-term out-of-the-money puts that he is delta hedging. Then suddenly the market is gapping down and down, as we know his delta hedging will not work that well, his losses are increased further by the implied volatility exploding to the upside. He is losing millions and millions and millions and soon blowing through his risk limits. Soon enough he is called into the head of precious metals and commodity trading:

- **The Boss**: What on earth is going on? You have been blowing through your risk limits, why did you not cover your tails by buying back some of these puts on the way down!
- **Market maker**: Don't worry Sir, what I have lost someone else in our bank must for sure have made. When I got hired you specifically told me that the bank is extremely well diversified in all types of markets and businesses. You should thank me for not wasting money on protecting us for unsystematic risk by paying up for those puts. The other banks have been driving up the prices on these put options to unrealistic levels and are clearly not acting rational. Actually my diversification model told me to sell more puts on the way down, and I did. I expect a raise in salary and a good bonus, on aggregate the bank is probably making loads of money, thanks to their well-diversified portfolio and traders like me!
- **The Boss**: Guards get this nut out of our building now!

I think this would be close to reality on many trading floors in such a case. We can argue whether financial economists are incorrectly assuming that unsystematic never should be priced as we always can hedge it(?) by holding a well-diversified portfolio, or alternatively we can argue that most Wall Street banks are irrational when it comes to decisions making on the trading floor. Personally I think the truth is something in between, the bonus and reward system is probably not optimal, but unsystematic risk is probably also more important than traditional financial theories claims?

We can also ask why there is so much trading in options on individual stocks, individual currencies, and individual commodities, if most investors are assumed to be rational and that rational investors supposedly should be holding a very well diversified portfolio of assets? I would think that we in that case would see mainly interest only for index option products? For me it seems quite clear that in today's financial markets unsystematic risk counts more than financial economists with there idealized models would like us to think.

Market makers are supposed to take care of their own risk in general without relying on the rest of the institution. Options are particularly vulnerable to jumps, and as we have seen dynamic delta hedging is almost useless under jumps. Market makers and option traders are well aware of this. The way they survive is by how they construct their option portfolio, and as we know the risk is not symmetrical for long and short option positions. Knowledgeable market makers and option traders will in general at least try to truncate their wing exposure. Net they can be short vega and or gamma, but only for a given interval in the underlying asset where they feel comfortable with their exposure. Some market makers and traders however seems to think they will get a phone call[8] telling them when the jump will happen. Such option traders seem to be happy to sell far out-of-the-money options even at low premiums (or other types of tail event risk). Experienced traders can potentially make a good living from such an attitude? But again this is another discussion somewhat outside the topic here.

Back to the Merton jump-diffusion model, it is also quite clear that jump risk is not only unsystematic. In large market moves like crashes, most assets tend to jump in the same direction, and the jump risk is then more or less systematic. Bates (1991) has developed a more generalized jump-diffusion model going in this direction. Bates assumes all markets can jump in the same direction. Bates is also basing his option formula on a equilibrium model, but he is justifying his risk-neutral jump-diffusion valuation to some degree by using options to hedge options. Hedging jump risk with options is very close to what traders actually do. The most important way to hedge for jump risk is how you construct your option portfolio, not how you delta hedge.

In the idealized world of GBM with continuous-time delta hedging then demand and supply for options should not affect the price of options. If someone wants to buy more options market makers can simply manufacture them by dynamic delta hedging that will be a perfect substitute for the option itself. In a world where dynamic delta hedging is not robust the story is naturally a very different one. Now suddenly supply and demand for options will affect option values themselves, and this is also what the academics recently have started to recognize, see Gârleanu, Pedersen, and Poteshman (2006).

4   Equilibrium Models

When strict arbitrage arguments like dynamic delta hedging obviously do not hold academics tend to fall back on equilibrium models. According to an interview with Robert Merton[9] Fischer Black preferred the capital asset pricing model version of deriving the Black-Scholes formula. The reason was because he thought anything close to continuous trading was not really possible in practice.

Black and Scholes originally derived their formula consistent with the Sharpe-Linter-Mossin CAPM. CAPM and many of its extensions have obvious weaknesses. A clear indication of the limitations of most capital asset pricing models can be found in the financial economic literature itself, namely the well known equity premium puzzle, see Rubinstein (1976) and Mehera and Prescott (1985).

The equity premium puzzle is not really a market puzzle, but in many ways a clear indication that most equilibrium models measure risk incorrectly. The original CAPM assume that returns are normally distributed and that volatility is constant, it is rooted in the Gaussian world. In practice we have fat-tails that we know was pointed out already by Mitchell (1915). Interestingly, using a jump-diffusion consumption-based capital asset pricing model Aase (1993) seems to be able to explain at least part of the equity premium puzzle, see also Aase (2005).

Second, I have already commented that unsystematic risk probably seems to count more than most of us would like to think.

Third, even if today we have more realistic equilibrium models including time varying volatility and even jumps, when relying on equilibrium models we typically have to make assumptions about a series of non-observable factors like consumption, attitudes to risk, utility functions, etc. Even if such models clearly have their purpose and we can learn a lot from them, few option traders will feel comfortable basing their trading and hedging on a specific equilibrium model. This is why the continuous-time dynamic delta hedging argument was so wonderful, the only problem is that it unfortunately only holds under very strict theoretical assumptions.

5   Portfolio Construction and Options Against Options

We know that dynamic delta hedging is not even close to giving us risk-neutral valuation. Further, option traders do not like to rely on the CAPM that again is based on the Gaussian. So why then do option traders rely so much on option pricing formulas? The most popular option pricing formula for standard options is still by far what is known as the Black-Scholes-Merton formula.[10]

The main reason is option traders **can** remove most of the risk simply by trading options against options, a method developed in multiple steps over a period of at least 100 years, starting with the put-call parity. In more recent times the benefits and robustness of hedging options with options have created a whole new area of quantitative research often known as static hedging, semi-static hedging as well as dynamic static hedging. For example Mello and Neuhaus (1998) illustrates that discrete delta hedging can cause substantial risk, further they suggest that a large part of this risk can be hedged away by using options against options. They assume a quite practical situation were a market maker often not can hedge a option with another option with exactly the same strike and maturity. As a market maker you will typically not be able to buy back exactly the same option you just sold at a profit or even at flat, at least not immediately, but typically you will be able to hedge an option with some other options with a slightly different strike and or maturity. When we have jumps in the asset price Carr and Wu (2002) shows how hedging options with options is superior to delta hedging. According to Carr and Wu simulations indicate that the inferior performance of the delta hedge in the presence of jumps cannot be improved upon by increasing the rebalancing frequency, see also Hyungsok and Wilmott (2007). Bates (1991) is basing his risk-neutral valuation for a jump-diffusion model partly on the idea that traders can hedge jump risk with other options. Hua and Wilmott (1995) describes a great example of the asymmetry in delta hedging replication error for long and short options. If you are delta hedging a long option position the worst case scenario for you is that there is no crash. This is actually because the delta hedging works poorly for any jumps, but if you are long options you will benefit from this hedging error when the market crash. Among the many papers looking into hedging options with options are for example Choie and Novomestky (1989), Carr and Madan (2001), Andreasen and Carr (2002) and Haug (1993). Ross (1976), Breeden and Litzenberger (1978), Green and Jarrow (1987) and Nachman (1988) can probably be seen as early publications pointing in this direction. Hua and Wilmott (1996) describe the importance of using options to hedge against tail events. When it comes to exotic options there is a fast growing literature on static and semi-static hedging, to mention a few of the papers here: Carr and Bowie (1994),

Derman, Ergener, and Kani (1995), Carr and Chou (1998), Carr, Ellis, and Gupta (1998) and Haug (1998).

Hedging options with options is typically superior to simply relay on dynamic delta hedging. It can be shown that dynamic delta hedging works reasonably well to replicate certain path dependent options like Asian options, but for standard European or American option it fails to give us anything close to risk-neutral valuation in practice. Here I will look at some aspects of hedging options with options in the framework of the basic option formula most traders use. Many of the principles already described in the litterature can potentially be seen as methods adding quantitative insight to the analysis below.

If you hedge an option with an identical option all risk is basically gone. One of the most central principles in hedging options with options is the put-call parity. This gives a strict arbitrage link between the forward price and the call and the put options. The forward price is again linked by strict arbitrage to the spot price. Bronzin (1908) based his risk-neutral option valuation to a large degree on such robust arbitrage principles. In this way he did not need to rely on a particular distribution of the underlying asset. Derman and Taleb (2005) also derive a option pricing formula similar to the Black-Scholes-Merton formula based on the put-call parity and forward price arbitrage principles. If their method is theoretically tight it is still an ongoing discussion.

Hedging options with an identical option or a synthetically identical option by using the put-call parity removes all the risk all the time – it not only hedges your delta, but also your gamma, vega and theta, etc. The method of hedging options with options is therefore extremely robust and is fully consistent with discrete as well as continuous-time trading (in practice we naturally only have discrete trading). This approach is also not very sensitive to transaction costs in the underlying asset as little or no dynamic delta hedging is necessary. It is a robust hedge against jumps in the asset price and what is known as stochastic volatility. Still to get an option formula consistent with the market behavior is not a simple task, but as we will soon see such an approach is actually hanging just in front of our nose.

That option traders can rely on hedging away most unwanted risk in options with other options have some very important implications. That is the price of an option **should** be expected to be affected by supply and demand for options. This is in strong contrast to the Black-Scholes-Merton arguments, where supply and demand for options should have no impact on the market price or valuation of options. Every knowledgeable market maker or option trader knows very well that they cannot remove all risk or even most of the risk by dynamic delta replication. In many option markets it is considered bad "market practice" for a trader to lift many market makers for their maximum bid-offer size on a specific option at the same time. Why? simply because the market makers cannot hedge away most of their risk with delta hedging, and in such cases they will not even be able to buy back part of the options they just sold short from other market makers, that also just got lifted on the same option, at least not on a price close to the price they just traded.

I remember a well-known option trader that lifted several market makers for their maximum offer size in some currency options; more precisely straddles with short time to maturity. The market makers that got short the options in large quantity was not even in need to initially delta hedge as the straddles initially were delta neutral. The underlying spot price was hardly moving that day, there was basically no news entering the market place, and still the price on short-dated options in this currency spiked. The reason was obvious, the market makers now suddenly short a lot of options knew it would be risky to be short so much gamma. They knew delta hedging naturally was far from robust. They tried to lift other market makers, but many of these were already short the option. The result was that the market makers were running after each other to reduce their risk. The price of these options spiked for no other reason than sudden large and unexpected demand for these options.

Option traders are in particular relying on the strict arbitrage principles, that is the put-call parity, this ensures that options with the same strike and maturity basically have the same implied volatility. Further they rely on relative-value option arbitrage. That is trading options against options with different strikes and time to maturity. For a minute assume you are a market maker using the Black-Scholes-Merton formula with the same volatility for every strike, not based on dynamic delta hedging, but based on the hedging options with options argument. Now you will try to hedge every option with an option with the same strike and maturity. But some traders are smarter than you, they know there are fat-tails and high-peaked distributions caused by jumps in the asset price and they will arbitrage you. While not strictly risk-free arbitrage, but relative-value option arbitrage. They just keep buying a lot of out-of-the-money options from you and are selling at-the-money options to you at the same Black-Scholes-Merton implied volatility. As you cannot construct these options synthetically by dynamic delta hedging without taking on a lot of risk, you will soon be forced to increase your price for out-of-the-money options and decrease your prices for at-the-money options, if not you will sooner or later go out of business. You just have to wait for the next big jump as you now are short the tail risk, and you have not even got paid a fair price for it. If you are a rational market maker the market will quickly be forced into "equilibrium" by relative-value option arbitrage trading.

The traders arbitraging you are basically simply trading options against options and on top of this using delta hedging. Based on knowledge about jumps, stochastic volatility and fat-tailed/high-peaked distribution they are getting an edge over you. Initially they don't even need a more sophisticated formula, simply by looking at various option greeks from their basic option formula they will also have a good idea of what strikes to sell and what strikes to buy, see "Know Your Weapon" parts 1 and 2 (on CD).[11] Of course after some type of volatility smile starts to evolve things will get a bit more complicated. You think this is a unrealistic example? This is exactly what was going on in the Nordic electricity market around years 1999 and 2000. The volatility smile from the standard option formula in that market was basically flat. Looking at historical return distributions in the underlying forwards there was clearly some fat-tails (see Chapter 9) and an option trader did not need a sophisticated model to get an edge by doing simple relative-value option arbitrage.

Further what came first the chicken or the egg? As a market maker or option trader you will to a large degree rely on implied volatilities from the market; the current market volatility-surface, quotes from other market makers, brokers, your last trades, and the positions already on your book as guidance to quote prices and implied volatilities. You will try to optimize risk/reward and avoid being arbitraged and try to arbitrage others. Supply and demand based option pricing is something that you would expect from this approach, while the continuous dynamic delta hedging and even the Merton (1976) jump-diffusion equilibrium model is not consistent with supply-demand based option pricing. Everyone[12] that has ever worked as an option market maker for some time naturally knows option pricing is supply and demand based, something recently academics have started to grasp, see Gârleanu, Pedersen, and Poteshman (2006).

The way option traders use the Black-Scholes-Merton formula with a different volatility for every strike and maturity evolving dynamically over time is evidently inconsistent with geometric Brownian motion, CAPM, the Gaussian and most principles underlying the Black-Scholes-Merton model. Many researchers have for this reason concluded that the Black-Scholes-Merton model and formula has to be replaced, or rather extended by something more sophisticated, like local volatility models, stochastic volatility, jump-diffusion or combinations of such models. They are partly right–that the market is not consistent with the Black-Scholes-Merton model. What they missed out is that option traders are actually not using the Black-Scholes-Merton formula or model even if most of us think we are.

Option trading is not about coming up with strict theoretical assumptions that only hold in a strict theoretical world (and potentially also inside a university campus) to get every theoretical model consistent with each other. Trading is about having robust tools and methods that can help you hedge and arbitrage and find prices consistent with other tradable instruments. Traders are still relying on the very fundament of quantitative finance; strict arbitrage, relative-value arbitrage, market liquidity and risk versus reward, as well as such things as gamblers ruin; we all have limited capital. But in practice the risk cannot simply be measured by standard deviation, and all the risk in options cannot simply be removed with continuous time delta hedging.

In supply-demand based option pricing what is known as the implied volatility will not simply be: "the markets best estimate of the expected future realized standard deviation". In real option trading there is not the strict and absolute link between options and the Black-Scholes-Merton dynamic delta hedging way of capturing the stochastic behavior of the asset price. In the traders way of using the formula the future realized volatility is just one of the many factors that goes into what I would like to call the "supply-demand parameter" or "basket-parameter". Yes we can call it implied volatility as this is the term used by traders (and academics), but we should know what implied volatility actually imply before we imply too much about implied volatility, see also Ayache (2006) who seems to be one of the few that have been thinking or at least writing about this topic.[13] As implied volatility from the option formula is not what many researchers think it is, let us for a moment not call implied volatility simply σ but let us call it $\sigma_{X,T}$. That is the "implied volatility" or rather the "basket parameter" has to be the same for every strike X and time to maturity T (based on the put-call parity). Excepting that the restrictions are relatively loose and dynamic. Relative-value option arbitrage will play an important role here, and on the top of this comes delta hedging. There are several empirical findings supporting that implied volatility is not simply the markets best estimate of future realized standard deviation. For example Canina and Figlewski (1998) studying S&P 100 index options, one of the most active equity option markets found virtually no correlation between implied and realized volatility. On the other hand for example Jorion (1995) doing similar research on the FX option market found that implied volatility had good prediction power. Is this a market puzzle? No under supply-demand based option pricing both of these empirical findings are consistent with the market formula.

In a supply-demand based option pricing we would also expect the supply and demand of options to change with news entering the market. I am talking about news in a broader sense. The relevant news are not longer limited to news that would affect the future fluctuations and the distribution of the underlying asset, but also news about flows in the option market itself. Professional option market makers and traders are often very focused also on flows in the option market. News about strong supply or demand for a certain maturity or strike can affect the prices on such options. If a trader suddenly observes massive buying of certain options, he/she would possibly buy this option or at least try to quickly get out of a short position in such a option, and in this way potentially generate additional demand for this option. Under the Black-Scholes-Merton model of deriving the formula this should never happen. The trader observing the massive bid for the option without any other news should instead short this option and dynamically delta hedge it. This idea is as we all know based on the idea of a strict and absolute link between the option and the continuous dynamic delta hedging argument.

The traders way of using the market option formula is also fully consistent with what is known as calibration and re-calibration of the volatility-surface, even if a better word for the volatility-surface probably would be supply-demand parameter surface. Under this approach calibration and re-calibration is actually something built into the traders way of hedging and pricing. When researchers test out their local-volatility, stochastic volatility models or jump-diffusion models they typically test it out against the naive Black-Scholes-Merton model and formula. However traders do not rely on the Black-Scholes-Merton model or formula.

The option formula most option traders actually use looks like this (the market option formula):

$$c = SN(d_1) - Xe^{-rT}N(d_2)$$
$$p = Xe^{-rT}N(-d_2) - SN(-d_1)$$

where

$$d_1 = \frac{\ln(S/X) + (r + \sigma_{X,T}^2/2)T}{\sigma_{X,T}\sqrt{T}}$$
$$d_2 = d_1 - \sigma_{X,T}\sqrt{T}$$

where S is the asset price, T time to maturity, r the risk-free rate, X the strike price, and $N(d_{X,T})$ is typically the cumulative normal distribution function for strike X and time to maturity T. As we will see this is not simply a fudge of the Black-Scholes-Merton formula. If a fudge it is a fudge of the models and principles developed precursor to Black-Scholes-Merton. In the traders formula $\sigma_{X,T}$ is a "basket parameter" better known as "implied volatility", that takes into account supply and demand of options for each strike and maturity. The supply and demand is again based on pure arbitrage and relative-value option arbitrage and on top of this delta hedging as well as other factors such as option liquidity etc. The parameter $\sigma_{X,T}$ can be different for every strike and maturity, and thereby we will also have a different $N(d_{X,T})$ for every strike and maturity. The traders formula is thereby not restricted to a given distribution or stochastic process of the underlying asset. The traders formula is not a model directly telling us how the "volatility" or "volatility-surface" should evolve over time, but it is probably the simplest model/formula/tool that fits and generates what is known as "volatility-surface" in a close to arbitrage free way. Used in the right way this formula is a flexible and robust traders tool, it is a weapon. If used under the assumptions of getting the formula consistent with the CAPM or based on continuous time dynamic delta hedging to remove all the risk all the time it is a trap. A trap that many inexperienced traders have fallen into, and as a result lost their shirt.

So how did I derive this formula, now suddenly with a partly stochastic partly deterministic "basket/supply-demand parameter"? How can this formula be consistent if not based on the CAPM and continuous time dynamic delta hedging to get risk-neutral valuation? Where are my mathematical proofs? Sorry I do not have the mathematical proofs, and it was not me coming up with this formula. This is actually the option formula most knowledgeable option traders use and have used for a very long time. Do formulas and tools used by the market actually have to be derived from scratch in an academic consistent fashion to make them consistent with a series of theoretical unrealistic assumptions? What are the alternatives? Except from concluding that this is a crank formula used by some option traders that do not understand stochastic calculus?

There is an alternative, a formula used by the market can evolve over time, not necessarily consistent with all the theoretical ideas at the university campus, but consistent with what is going on in the market, that is in particular tradeable arbitrage principles, and not pure theoretical arbitrage principles. The trader version of the option formula did not evolve in one step; it evolved over many steps with inputs from academics like: Bachelier, Bronzin, Sprenkle, Boness and quantitative-traders like Higgins, Nelson, and Thorp. Traders rely in particular on the put-call parity (strict arbitrage principle), relative-value arbitrage; using options with different strikes against each other–generating and at the same time getting consistent with what is known as the volatility-surface–and on the top of this using delta hedging, static and dynamic. Again the market formula is not consistent with continuous-time delta hedging or the CAPM to get risk-neutral valuation, these principles are as we know from empirical data, intuition and trading experience not even close to robust in practice.

It is somewhat ironic that it is the last step or idea of continuous time delta replication and to make the formula fully consistent with the Gaussian and the CAPM that the market option formula is best known for. As an option trader these are the only principles I cannot rely on. I think that many researchers fall in love with the continuous time delta hedging replication argument, the CAPM, the Sharpe ratio and the Gaussian world simply because under that paradigm every model could be made **theoretically consistent** with other models (Models on Models). Or as once told by Fisher Black

> "In the end, a theory is accepted not because it is confirmed by conventional empirical tests, but because researchers persuade one another that the theory is correct and relevant."

The cost of this was to ignore the empirical facts, the robust ideas and how traders actually used option formulas/models/tools, see also Taleb (2007) for more on this topic. I have even myself spent some time (not much in trading, but some of my research) under this theoretical paradigm, as should be evident from some of my chapters in this book. The Black, Scholes and Merton derivation of the formula made it 100% tight with other theoretical models. At the same time the option formula based on their assumptions lost most of its practical flexibility and robustness. This again created several model puzzles that hundreds if not thousands of researchers have tried to solve. How could option traders be so naive and stick to an option model assuming constant volatility? How could they rely on a model rooted in the Gaussian when we clearly had fat-tails and high-peak asset distribution in every market? How could a simple fudge of the Black-Scholes-Merton model work so well? The reason is options traders never relied on the Black-Scholes-Merton model or formula, we used a much more robust version of the option formula. Option traders kept relying on the hedging and pricing principles developed precursor to the Black-Scholes-Merton model. Still over time these principles got known as fudging of the Black-Scholes-Merton formula, this even if they had little or nothing to do with the Black-Scholes-Merton way of deriving the formula.

The academics were in ecstasy, they finally had a derivation of the option formula that was theoretically consistent with their other theoretical models, like the CAPM, the Sharpe ratio and the Gaussian. This simply had to be the correct method and solution. Over time even these researchers agreed it was an approximation, but they claimed it was a robust approximation. And any improvement of the model had to be extensions of this model framework, rather than a replacement consistent with how the market actually operates. Any new model had to be consistent across other models. The empirical data and hedging principles that was not consistent with such an approach was soon ignored ad partly forgotten in the academic literature. It is more than 100 years since Mitchell pointed at fat-tails in price data. Still most well accepted models in academia were rooted in the Gaussian. Merton soon extended the Black-Scholes-Merton model to include jumps, but again new unrealistic assumptions were invented to get models consistent across models.

What about risk-neutrality, how can we get full risk-neutrality if not all risk can be removed with continuous-time delta hedging? In most situations in liquid option markets most unwanted risk can robustly be hedged away with other options. Still this is also only a model, but a reasonably robust one. In practice at least during some periods and or markets it can be difficult to get hold of the options necessary to remove the unwanted risk. But who told you that option traders assumed full risk-neutrality even if we use a risk-free rate as input in our option formula? I already told you that what is known as the implied volatility is rather a "basket-parameter" where traders input a series of elements to try to arbitrage, avoid getting arbitraged and to maximize returns relative to risk. From time to time option traders are even throwing in some "risk premium" directly into this parameter known as implied volatility, rather than in the risk-free rate parameter (r). I know this sounds absurd but this is how it is actually done in the option market.

In periods when option liquidity dries up, volatility spreads tend to widen, even if the liquidity in the underlying still should be very good. Further market makers in illiquid option markets are quick at coloring the prices they are quoting based on what positions they already have on their books. How can this be? According to Black-Scholes-Merton this should not happen. In the Black-Scholes-Merton world only low liquidity in the underlying asset could potentially have an effect on option prices. I have not seen empirical research published on this, but during my trading career I have seen several examples of how option spreads tend to be wider in illiquid option markets than in liquid option markets, this even on underlying assets with good liquidity relative to the option market.

I remember being the very first and only market maker in Norwegian bond options. As the bond market maker was letting me hedge at close to mid-market for basically any size (I needed) the delta hedging was not the problem. The problem was I could not find other options to hedge with. As a result I had to quote wide bid offer spreads and quickly color my quotations based on what positions I already had on my book. Risk-neutrality is only a robust approximation when option traders have the opportunity to hedge with other options. I had to remove risk with delta hedging without relying on delta hedging for larger moves. I was quickly coloring my quotes so I at least was not caught with too much short tail risk (trying to truncate my tail exposure). The risk-premium or whatever you call it in this way simply got baked into my implied volatility. From someone standing on the outside not paying close attention and only looking at my option formula would possibly think I based my trading even now on risk-neutral valuation. If customers kept selling options and I already was short I was obviously quoting too low prices (and/or potentially too narrow bid-offer spread). Based on supply and demand for options in the market I "quickly" got approximately the "right" market risk premium baked into my option pricing. This is the markets invisible arbitrage-hand way of taking into account the risk premium. I can tell you that this "risk-premium" is not constant, it is dynamic dependent on the supply-and demand in the options and in the underlying asset. On the other hand to simply ignore that you actually have risk in situations like this thinking you can rely on delta hedging to get risk-neutrality, when this obviously is not the case will make you vulnerable to getting arbitraged. To adjust for "risk-premium" in the volatility by widening bid-offer spreads and coloring the prices you quote can certainly be seen as a ad hoc method. Thanks to the markets invisible arbitrage-hand such a method probably works better than many would think. The risk premium is anyway incredibly difficult to estimate, academics have still not got a reliable method to do this, but I think the market has a method to do this. However to extract the risk-premium and interpret it in terms of theoretical equilibrium model is something I leave up to the academics.

Several great researchers on volatility modeling that I talked with over the years, and that I have the highest respect for, have told me they are somewhat surprised how few professional option traders have actually switched to stochastic volatility models, models that obviously are much more realistic than the Black-Scholes-Merton model. Don't get me wrong: stochastic volatility models, jump-diffusion models etc. have their purpose and have given us some great insight, and is even part of the toolbox for many option traders. Still option traders are not in a desperate need to get away from the basic market option formula, simply because they do not rely on the Black-Scholes-Merton way of deriving it. The way the option formula is used by experienced traders makes it much more robust than most researchers think. The way option traders hedge options with options make their portfolio highly robust towards both stochastic volatility and jumps. You can call it fudge if you want, but it is a robust fudge and actually a consistent fudge. Built in to this fudge is at least a hundred years of accumulated experience by a living and evolving organism called the option market. The option market has over time been putting together the most robust ideas from academics and traders to get a formula consistent with a series of tradeable arbitrage principles, but not to get a model or formula consistent with other popular models at the university campus.

After 1973 we know there initially were many people relying too much on the Black-Scholes-Merton way of deriving the formula. For example Leland O'Brien Rubinstein Associates and their way of constructing synthetic options (portfolio insurance) based on dynamic delta hedging basically failed in the crash of 1987. Many investors that actually followed the arguments behind the Black-Scholes-Merton model without taking into account how experienced option traders were hedging unwanted option risk with other options, or at least truncating their tails simply went out of business, and keep going out of business to this day. I am thanking the business schools for every Gaussian delta hedger they send into the market, they are feeding my bread and butter trading machine.

Does this mean delta hedging is dead and that all market makers and option traders simply hedge options with options. No, I never told you so, market makers often hedge residual risk with delta hedging, but they tend to try truncating their tail risk. Not because this reduces the hedging error, but as we already have discussed delta hedging errors are non-symmetric for long and short option positions. Going long or truncating your wing risk do not necessarily mean you get an edge with expected profit, it is just a way to make you less vulnerable for how poorly dynamic delta hedging really works in many situations, and it will insure you from blowing up.

Option trading is a dynamic process, and the option formula the market uses is consistent with this. For example if you hedge a 12 month option with a 9 month option with the same strike the hedge will typically work reasonably well for the first few months as the options basically will have similar risk characteristics. However as time evolves and the 9-month option only has one week left and the 12-month option has 3 months and one week left this will definitely not be a good hedge. Long before this the market maker would probably have changed his option portfolio and re-hedged with one or more options.

6   Conclusions

- Hedging and pricing of options developed in many small steps rather than one or two big steps as we often feel when reading most modern text books on options and derivatives (including some of my own work). Even the development in option pricing and hedging has clearly been in discrete time-steps, not continuous ;-) Robust option pricing and hedging principles evolved over many steps with inputs from academics like Bachelier, Bronzin, Sprenkle, Boness and quantitative-traders like Higgins, Nelson, and Thorp–and I am sure some people I have forgotten as well as researchers we still have to re-discover, as well as many traders that never wrote down their ideas, but still had a influence on how the market option formula and hedging principles evolved over time.

- Dynamic delta hedging removes a lot of risk compared to not hedging or to static delta hedging, but there is plenty of risk left, and far too much to argue for risk-neutral valuation in practice. The idea of continuous dynamic delta hedging to get risk-neutrality is simply not a robust idea.

- Dynamic delta hedging works extremely poorly when we have jumps. And we have jumps. We have unsystematic jumps that seem to matter for some players, and we also have systematic jumps.

- Option traders do not like to rely on option models built on equilibrium models alone, and in particular not on the CAPM and the Gaussian. How do we know the utility function, the consumption, etc.? How can we be so sure unsystematic risk never counts? Further, jump risk is often systematic; in particular the largest jumps that basically can only be hedged with other options.

- Option traders rely mainly on hedging away unwanted risk by hedging options with options, a concept that was more or less understood at least 100 years ago.

- Option traders also use delta hedging, but they construct their portfolios in such a way that they are not vulnerable to how poorly delta hedging works in many situations, that means using options against options at least to protect yourself for large jumps. The risk in delta hedging is not symmetric for long and short option positions. Nelson's (1904) argument that most experienced option traders/dealers had a tendency to be long options rather than short seems to be consistent with what experienced option traders are saying today. The reason is simply that this makes a trader less vulnerable for the risk he/she is left with when doing static or dynamic delta hedging. It will not necessarily give you an edge, but at least it insures you against blowing up.

- How you construct your option portfolio is far more important than how you delta hedge.

- This means supply and demand of options will affect option prices, which has become evident from the academic literature. In supply and demand based option pricing what is known as calibration and re-calibration is what you would expect, it is part of the framework. I expect to see much more research on this topic in the future.

- What is known as implied volatility is simply not only the markets best estimate of future realized standard deviation. Implied volatility is a "basket parameter" taking into account the supply and demand of options that again is related to strict option arbitrage (put-call parity), relative-value option arbitrage and on top of this delta hedging, as well as liquidity in the option market and the underlying asset etc. All this together creates what is known as the "volatility-surface" and at the same time makes the option formula the market use consistent with the "volatility-surface".

- In a illiquid option market where we only can remove risk by delta hedging we cannot rely on risk-neutral valuation. Experienced option market makers then typically take such risk into account by widening their bid-offer spreads as well as coloring theirs price quotations based on what positions they already have on their books. The markets invisible arbitrage-hand is baking the risk-premium into what is known as implied-volatility that actually is a basket-parameter.

Herbert Filer was an option trader who was involved in option trading from 1919 to the 1960s. In his book first published in 1959 Filer describes what must be considered a reasonably active option markets in New York and Europe in the 1920s and early 1930s. Filer mentions however that due to World War II there was no trading on the European Exchanges, for they were closed. Further he mentions that in London option trading did not return before 1958. In the early 1900s option traders in Europe were known to be more sophisticated than in New York, according to Nelson, he himself was a New York option trader. Could it be that World War II and the close down of option trading for many years to come was part of the reason known robust arbitrage principles and option formulas got partly forgotten and almost lost? Could this also explain the current myth: that option trading became popular basically because the Black-Scholes-Merton formula got published in 1973, and that option traders before this time only had some simple rule of thumb principles? As we know from studying part of the ignored and forgotten literature this was clearly not the case, basically every option pricing and hedging principle used by traders were developed and in use already before 1973. Hedging options with options, delta hedging was all there. Ed Thorp had the option formula programmed into his calculator before 1973. I think the invention of electronic computers had much more to do with an explosive growth in option trading than the invention of non-robust hedging principles such as continuous time delta hedging and making the formula consistent with CAPM and the Gaussian. I am sure more discoveries will be done on the history of the development of option pricing and hedging. The discussion of how to interpret the "ancient" rediscovered literature and what traders do versus how academics describe what traders do I am sure will be an ongoing discussion.

FOOTNOTES & REFERENCES

1. The first version of this booklet was published in 1949, but I have only been able to get hold of the 1960 version at time of writing.
2. See for example Thorp (1969).
3. Naturally assuming we not take advantage of the known lack of randomness in the random number generator, in that case we could actually reduce the hedging error compared to hedging under real geometric Brownian motion.
4. Here we would naturally need to look at how fast the convergence is.
5. This paper was first distributed as a Goldman Sachs working paper in 1998.
6. See my Blog June 3, 2006 for more detailed explanation on this, you can find a web link to my blog at www.espenhaug.com.
7. I am not talking about some joint model by Fischer Black and Alan White.
8. See interview with Nassim Taleb.

9. The interview can be found at http://www.afajof.org/association/historyfinance.asp.

10. And its many variations, Merton (1973c), Black (1976), Asay (1982),Garman and Kohlhagen (1983), etc. See Haug (2006) for a detailed overview of its many variations.

11. When writing part 1 and 2 I was still under the illusion I was using the Black-Scholes-Merton formula, most of what is written there still holds. But not because the Black-Scholes-Merton argument of continuous time delta hedging or the argument of making the model consistent with the CAPM.

12. Except the few that believed fully in dynamic delta hedging and went out of business.

13. Pablo Triana is another fellow that has considered this topic and has some insight here. Triana (2006) shows that the market is strongly breaking with all the assumptions of the Black-Scholes-Merton model basically concluding that the Black-Scholes-Merton formula is very robust (basically what I also did in my "Know Your Weapon 1" and 2). Triana points out "The model is mathematically wrong, but it can be righted through its built-in self-correction mechanism". His idea is that traders are fudging the Black-Scholes-Merton formula, and that the formula still works remarkably well, if not how could so many traders use the formula? He is right in much of his analysis, but he got the wrong conclusion. Most traders including me have been living under the illusion that we actually have been fudging the Black-Scholes-Merton formula, while in fact we are basically relying on hedging principles and an option formula developed over multiple steps before Black-Scholes-Merton. We were all told we used the Black-Scholes-Merton formula and we partly thought so.

■ Aase, K. K. (1993) "A Jump/Diffusion Consumption-based Capital Asset Pricing Model and the Equity Premium Puzzle" *Mathematical Finance*, **3**(2), 65–84.

■ ——— (2005) "Using Option Pricing Theory to Infer About Equity Premiums," *Working paper UCLA and Norwegian School of Economics and Business Administration*.

■ Asay, M. R. (1982) "A Note on the Design of Commodity Option Contracts" *Journal of Futures Markets*, **52**, 1–7.

■ Andreasen, J., and P. Carr (2002): "Put Call Reversal," *Working paper, Corant Institute, New York*.

■ Ayache, E. (2006): "What is Implied Volatility?" *Wilmott Magazine*, January, 28–35.

■ Bachelier, L. (1900) *Theory of speculation* in: P. Cootner, ed., 1964, *The random character of stock market prices*. Cambridge, Mass.: MIT Press.

■ Barber, B. M. and T. Odean (2000) "Trading is Hazardous to Your Wealth: The Common Stock Investment Performance of Individual Investors" *Journal of Finance*, **55**, 773–806.

■ Bates, D. S. (1991) "The Crash of '87: Was It Expected? The Evidence from Options Markets" *Journal of Finance*, **46**(3), 1009–1044.

■ Benartzi, S. and R. H. Thaler (2001) "Naive Diversification Strategies in Defined Contribution Saving Plan" *American Economic Review*, **91**(1), 79–98.

■ Bernhard, A. (1970) *More Profit and Less Risk: Convertible Securities and Warrants*. Written and Edited by the Publisher and Editors of The Value Line Convertible Survey, Arnold Bernhard & Co., Inc.

■ Bertsimas, D., L. Kogan and A. W. Lo (2001) "Hedging Derivative Securities and Incomplete Markets: An ϵ-Arbitrage Approach" *Operations Research*, **49**(3), 372–397.

■ Black, F. (1976) "The Pricing of Commodity Contracts" *Journal of Financial Economics*, **3**, 167–179.

■ ——— (1989) "How to Use the Holes in Black-Scholes" *Journal of Applied Corporate Finance*, **1**(4), 67–73.

■ Black, F. (1990) "Living Up to The Model" *Risk Magazine*, **3**(3), 11–13.

■ Black, F. and M. Scholes (1973) "The Pricing of Options and Corporate Liabilities," *Journal of Political Economy*, 81, 637–654.

■ Blau, G. (1944-1945) "Some Aspects of The Theory of Futures Trading," *The Review of Economic Studies*, 12(1), 1–30.

■ Boness, A. (1964) "Elements of a Theory of Stock-Option Value" *Journal of Political Economy*, **72**, 163–175.

■ Boyle, P., and D. Emanuel (1980) "Discretely Adjusted Option Hedges" *Journal of Financial Economics*, **8**, 259–282.

■ Breeden, D. T., and R. H. Litzenberger (1978): "Price of State-Contigent Claimes Implicit in Option Prices," *Journal of Business*, 51, 621–651.

■ Bronzin, V. (1908): *Theorie der Prämiengeschäfte*. Leipzig und Wien: Verlag Franz Deticke.

■ Canina, L. and S. Figlewski (1998): "The Information Content of Implied Volatility" *The Review of Financial Studies*, **6**(3), 659–681.

■ Castelli, C. (1877) *The Theory of Options in Stocks and Shares*. London: F.C. Mathieson.

■ Carr, P., and J. Bowie (1994): "Static Simplicity," *Risk Magazine*, 7(8).

■ Carr, P., and A. Chou (1998): "Static Hedging of Complex Barrier Options," *Banc of America Securities Working paper*.

■ Carr, P., K. Ellis, and V. Gupta (1998): "Static Hedging of Exotic Options," *Journal of Finance*, 53.

■ Carr, P., and D. Madan (2001): "Optimal Positioning in Derivative Securities," *Quantitative Finance*, 1, 19–37.

■ Carr, P., and L. Wu (2002): "Static Hedging of Standard Options," *Working paper, Courant Institute, New York University*.

■ Choie, K. S., and F. Novomestky (1989): "Replication of Long-Term with Short-Term Options," *Journal of Portfolio Management*, Winter, 17–19.

■ Cootner, P. H. (1964) *The Random Character of Stock Market Prices*. Cambridge, Mass.: MIT Press. Also re-printed in 2000 by Risk Books.

■ Cox, J. C., S. A. Ross and M. Rubinstein (1979): "Option Pricing: A Simplified Approach," *Journal of Financial Economics*, **7**, 229–263.

■ de la Vega, J. (1688): *Confusión de Confusiones*. Re-printed in the book: 'Extraordinary Popular Delusions and the Madness of Crowds & Confusión de Confusiones' edited by Martin S. Fridson, 1996, New York: John Wiley & Sons, Inc.

■ Derman, E., D. Ergener, and I. Kani (1995): "Static Options Replication," *Journal of Derivatives*, 2, 78–95.

■ Derman, E. and M. Kamal (1999) "When You Cannot Hedge Continuously, The Corrections of Black-Scholes" *Risk Magazine*, **12**, 82–85.

■ Derman, E. and N. Taleb (2005) "The Illusion of Dynamic Delta Replication" *Quantitative Finance*, **5**(4), 323–326.

■ Deutsch, H. (1910) *Arbitrage in Bullion, Coins, Bills, Stocks, Shares and Options*, 2nd Edition (first version 1904). London: Effingham Wilson.

■ Falkenstein, E. G. (1996) "Preferences for Stock Characterstics as Revealed by Mutual Fund Portfolio Holdings" *Journal of Finance*, **51**, 111–135.

■ Filer, H. (1959): *Understanding Put and Call Option's*. New York: Popular Library.

■ Fried, S. (1960) *The Speculative Merits of Common Stock Warrants*. New York: RHM Associates. There were at least 4 different versions of this book, 1949, 1951, 1956, and 1960.

■ Gârleanu, N., L. H. Pedersen and Poteshman (2006): *Demand-Based Option Pricing*. Working Paper: New York University – Leonard N. Stern School of Business.

■ Garman, M. and S. W. Kohlhagen (1983): "Foreign Currency Option Values" *Journal of International Money and Finance*, **2**, 231–237.

■ Girlich, H.-J. (2002) "Bachelier's Predecessors," Working Paper: University of Leipzig.

■ Goyal, A. and P. Santa-Clara (2003) "Idiosyncratic Risk Matters!" *Journal of Finance*, **58**(3), 975–1008.

■ Green, R., and R. A. Jarrow (1987): "Spanning and Completeness in markets with Contingent Claims," *Journal of Economic Theory*, 41, 202–210.

■ Hafner, W. and H. Zimmermann (2007): "Amazing Discovery: Vincenz Bronzin's Option Pricing Models" *Journal of Banking and Finance*, **31**, 531–546.

■ Haug, E. G. (2006) *The Complete Guide To Option Pricing Formulas*, 2nd Edition. New York: McGraw-Hill.

■ Haug, E. G. (1993): "Opportunities and Perils of Using Option Sensitivities," *Journal of Financial Engineering*, 2(3), 253–269.

■ Higgins, L. R. (1902): *The Put-and-Call*. London: E. Wilson.

■ Hoggard, T., A. E. Whalley and P. Wilmott (1994): "Hedging Option Portfolios in the Presence of Transaction Costs" *Advances in Futures and Options Research*, **7**, 21–35.

■ Hua, P., and P. Wilmott (1995): "Modelling Market Crashes: the Worst-case Scenario," *Working Paper*.

■ ——— (1996): "Crash Modelling, Value at Risk and Optimal Hedging," *Working Paper*.

■ Hyungsok, A., and P. Wilmott (2007): "Jump Diffusion, Mean and Variance: How to Dynamically Hedge, Statically Hedge and to Price," *Working Paper Forthcoming Wilmott Magazine*.

■ Jorion, P. (1995): "Predicting Volatility in the Foreign Exchange Market" *Journal of Finance*, **50**(2), 507–528.

■ Keynes, J. M. (1924) *A Tract on Monetary Reform*. Re-printed 2000, Amherst, New York: Prometheus Books.

■ Knoll, M. (2004) "Ancient Roots of Modern Financial Innovation: The Early History of Regulatory Arbitrage", Working paper 49, University of Pennsylvania Law School.

■ Kruizenga, R. J. (1956) "Put and Call Options: A Theoretical and Market Analysis," Unpublished Ph.D. thesis, Massachusetts Institute of Technology.

■ ——— (1964) *Introduction to the Option Contract*, Dr. thesis 1956 at MIT, published in P. Cootner, ed., 1964, *The Random Character of Stock Market Prices*, MIT Press, Cambridge, Mass.

■ Leland, H. (1985) ""Option Pricing and Replication with Transactions Costs"" *Journal of Finance*, **XL**(5), 1283–1301.

■ McKean, H. P. (1965) "A Free Boundary Problem For The Heat Equation Arising From A Problem In Mathematical Economics" *Industrial Management Review*, **6**(2), 32–39.

■ Mehera, R. and E. C. Prescott (1985) "The Equity Premium: a Puzzle" *Journal of Monetary Economics*, **15**, 145–161.

■ Mello, A. S. and H. J. Neuhaus (1998) "A Portfolio Approach to Risk Reduction in Discretely Rebalanced Option Hedges" *Management Science*, **44**(7), 921–934.

■ Merton, R. C. (1973a) "An Intertemporal Capital Asset Pricing Model" *Econometrica*, **41**, 867–887.

■ ———— (1973b): "The Relationship Between Put and Call Prices: Comment" *Journal of Finance*, **28**(1), 183–184.

■ ———— (1973c) "Theory of Rational Option Pricing" *Bell Journal of Economics and Management Science*, **4**, 141–183.

■ ———— (1976) "Option Pricing When Underlying Stock Returns are Discontinuous" *Journal of Financial Economics*, **3**, 125–144.

■ ———— (1998): "Application of Option-Pricing Theory: Twenty-Five Years Later" *American Economic Review*, **3**, 323–349.

■ Mitchell, Wesley, C. (1915) "The Making and Using of Index Numbers," *Introduction to Index Numbers and Wholesale Prices in the United States and Foreign Countries* (published in 1915 as Bulletin No. 173 of the U.S. Bureau of Labor Statistics, reprinted in 1921 as Bulletin No. 284, and in 1938 as Bulletin No. 656).

■ Nachman, D. (1988): "Spanning and Completeness with Options," *Review of Financial Studies*, 31(3), 311–328.

■ Nelson, S. A. (1904) *The A B C of Options and Arbitrage*. New York: The Wall Street Library.

■ Regnault, J. (1863) *Calcul des Chances et Philosophie de la Bourse*. Paris: Mallet-Bachelier. Re-print here http://driout.club.fr/Calcul_de_Regnault.html.

■ Reinach, A. M. (1961) *The Nature of Puts & Calls*. New York: The Bookmailer.

■ Rendleman, R. J. and B. J. Bartter (1979) "Two-State Option Pricing" *Journal of Finance*, **34**, 1093–1110.

■ Ross, S. A. (1976) "The Arbitrage Theory of Capital Asset Pricing. Journal of Economic Theory" **13**, 341–360.

■ Ross, S. A. (1976): "Options and Efficiency," *Quarterly Journal of Economics*, 90, 75–89.

■ Rubinstein, M. (1976) "The Valuation of Uncertain Income Streams and the Pricing of Options" *Bell Journal of Economics and Management Science*, **7**(2), 407–425.

■ ———— (2006): *A History of The Theory of Investments*. New York: John Wiley & Sons, Inc.

■ Samuelson, P. (1965): "Rational Theory of Warrant Pricing" *Industrial Management Review*, **6**, 13–31.

■ Schachter, B., and R. Robins (1994) "An Analysis of the Risk in Discretely Rebalanced Option Hedges and Delta-Based Techniques" *Management Science*, **40**(6), 798–808.

■ Smith, Jr., C. W. (1976) "Option Pricing: A Review" *Journal of Financial Economics*, **3**, 3–51.

■ Sprenkle, C. (1961) "Warrant Prices as Indicators of Expectations and Preferences" *Yale Economics Essays*, **1**(2), 178–231.

■ Stoll, H. (1969) "The Relationship Between Put And Call Prices" *Journal of Finance*, **24**(5), 801–824.

■ Taleb, N. (1997) *Dynamic Hedging*. New York: John Wiley & Sons, Inc.

■ Taleb, N. (2007): *The Black Swan*. New York: Random House.

■ Thorp, E. O. (1969) "Optimal Gambling Systems for Favorable Games" *Review of the International Statistics Institute*, **37**(3).

■ ———— (2002): "What I Knew and When I Knew It – Part 1, Part 2, Part 3," *Wilmott Magazine*, Sep-02, Dec-02, Jan-03.

■ Thorp, E. O., and S. T. Kassouf (1967) *Beat the Market*. New York: Random House.

■ Triana, P. (2006): "Smiling at Black-Scholes" *GARP Risk Review*, **33**, 27–31.

■ Wilmott, P. (2006) *Paul Wilmott on Quantiative Finance, Second Edition*. New York: John Wiley & Sons, Inc.

Alan Lewis

Alan Lewis on Stochastic Volatility and Jumps

Alan Lewis has worked with option valuation and related financial research for over twenty years. He served as Director of Research, Chief Investment Officer, and President of the mutual fund family at Analytic Investment Management, a money management firm specializing in derivative securities. He has published articles in many of the leading financial journals, including The Journal of Business, The Journal of Finance, The Financial Analysts Journal, and Mathematical Finance and Wilmott Magazine. He is probably best known for his book "Option Valuation under Stochastic Volatility", one of the very first books covering this topic in detail.

I was lucky to write a paper together with Alan Lewis and my brother on valuation of options when the underlying asset pays discrete dividend. To write a paper together with Alan Lewis and my brother was a great pleasure. As an option trader and option formula collector I was quite familiar with the problem within current models trying to value options with discrete dividend. However, to solve and understand the problem in depth I needed to team up with someone with great mathematical quant skills, and here Alan Lewis together with my brother came in. While I worked on implementation and testing out as many models as we could find in the literature, Alan Lewis and my brother figured out how to come up with a model that did not inherit the problems affecting current models and formulae. I felt we emerged with an interesting model and essay covering options on an asset paying discrete cash dividend, the essay is included as Chapter 3 in this book.

I only met Alan Lewis once during the Global Derivatives conference in Madrid 2004. The first thing I noticed was that Alan Lewis had a great tan, not surprisingly for someone working in Newport Beach, California.

Haug : Where did you grow up?

Lewis: A lot of places because my father was in the Air Force. But we finally settled in Tucson, Arizona for most of my youth.

Haug : What is your educational background?

Lewis: I have two physics degrees: a bachelor of science from Caltech and a PhD from the University of California at Berkeley.

Haug : Why and when did you decide to move from physics to finance?

Lewis: During a post-doctoral position at the University of California at Santa Cruz, (this was in the late 70s), I discovered some of the early options literature. Perhaps the first book I ran across was Kassouf and Thorp's "Beat the Market" about the OTC warrant market. Then I learned Sheen Kassouf and his brother Ned had a firm down in Irvine, Calif. which specialized in derivatives. I interviewed with them, they offered me a position, and it seemed to me a great opportunity. Also, I wasn't sure I wanted to continue in my area (critical phenomena) which had been recently "solved" by the brilliant Ken Wilson. So I joined their firm (Analytic Investment Management) and made it my career for 19 years.

Haug : What are the main differences between physics and finance?

Lewis: Well, of course, in physics one tries to discover the invariant laws of nature – in finance, nothing is invariant!

Haug : How did you first get interested in stochastic volatility and jumps?

Lewis: A lot of my time at Analytic was devoted to improving our option analysis system. Extending the modeling to include stochastic volatility was a big project for me in the early 90s. I left the firm to work on a book on that topic, which I completed toward the end of that decade. After completing that, I began to pay more attention to extending the models to include jumps.

Haug : What are the fundamental factors that create stochastic volatility and jumps?

Lewis: In equities, which is my main interest, there are a lot of things going on to create stochastic volatility. Of course, one could just say that "constant volatility" is an idealization that Black and Scholes knew from the beginning was flawed. Volatility expresses uncertainty and the "rate" of that is always changing due to all the macro and micro events that impact the markets. There are business cycles, technology cycles, political cycles, etc. where I am using cycles in a very loose way. Jumps are due to the same...only more so.

Haug : What is the simplest form of stochastic volatility model described in the option literature, is this the CEV (constant elasticity of variance) model?

Lewis: There is a CEV model for stock prices, which would be called a "local volatility" model. It's a limited type of stochastic volatility model, stochastic in the sense that the Black-Scholes implied volatility is not a constant. The simplest "true" stochastic volatility model (with a new source of randomness) is probably Steve Heston's 1993 model. There is also a CEV volatility model.

Haug : What is the difference between stochastic volatility and GARCH models?

Lewis: It's that same distinction I was just talking about – usually by true stochastic volatility, we mean a new source of randomness. GARCH models don't have that, but generate a changing volatility from changing stock prices.

Haug : The Heston model seems to be often mentioned in the stochastic volatility literature, what are the strength and weakness with this model?

Lewis: Some strengths: all the parameters have good intuitive meanings, the option model is analytically tractable, and there is a lot of good evidence that it significantly improves upon the Black-Scholes-Merton constant volatility case. Some weaknesses: calibrated parameters from options often suggest the volatility hits the origin; this may be a serious weakness. At a minimum, such a calibration result must be reconciled with the real-world process. Like all stochastic volatility models, it excludes jumps, and the specific functional form is somewhat arbitrary.

Haug : In your book I think you mention that the Heston model is somewhat related to a GARCH model?

Lewis: You may be thinking of a stochastic volatility model I termed the "GARCH diffusion", which is a continuous time limit of a GARCH model. Then, one can place both the GARCH diffusion model and the Heston model together in a larger class of models, sometimes called the CEV volatility models.

Haug : Don't the principles of risk-neutral valuation break down if the volatility is stochastic? The argument of dynamic delta hedging cannot remove my risk towards volatility of volatility?

Lewis: There are two principles: the principle that traded security prices (relative to some bond, say) are martingales (essentially, a fair game) under some risk-neutral probability measure still holds. But the principle that option values are uniquely determined by a delta hedging arbitrage with the stock and bond fails.

Haug : Am I right when I say that most stochastic volatility models assume a continuous process for the volatility while we in practice often also observe jumps in the realized as well as the implied volatility any views on this?

Lewis: In general, I agree with this, but there are difficult problems of interpretation in my opinion. With major stock price jumps – you see it all the time in the exploratory drug stocks – there is no question. On the other hand, the VIX index jumps a lot at the opening, but it is mostly just catching up with the overnight market or the opening market. You have to infer a lot with volatility jumps; it's tricky econometrics.

Haug : In your book "Option Valuation under Stochastic Volatility" you talk about Volatility Explosions and how derivatives valued under some stochastic volatility models are not true martingales. Can you explain a bit about this, and also what are local martingales, and are explosions in volatility in any way related to jumps in volatility?

Lewis: Many common stochastic models allow the volatility to range from zero to infinity. The trouble with diffusion processes is that they sometimes run off to one boundary or another. When they run off to infinity that is called an explosion. In the models where this happens, this can cause the local martingale vs. martingale distinction. Jumps are a separate modeling issue, although I suspect you are thinking that if we have a real jump, it will look like an infinite volatility, which is true.

Haug : Can you shortly also comment on Explosion probabilities, what is this and how are such probabilities useful in option valuation?

Lewis: My current thinking is that models with volatility explosions are probably ones to be avoided. They can always be avoided by putting an upper bound on volatility. The problematic ones lead to difficulties with multiple pde solutions and put/call parity ambiguities.

Haug : As an option trader I often distinguish between stochastic realized volatility and stochastic implied volatility. Do current stochastic volatility models take this into account?

Lewis: In principle, yes. Short term implieds can change because of price moves in the underlying, or mean reversion of volatility, or changing risk aversion. Stochastic volatility models incorporate these things through leverage effects, mean reversion, and risk-aversion parameters. But if the implieds are changing because the market is getting more worried about a jump, then the effect may be much stronger than a stochastic volatility model can handle.

Haug : For what type of options are jumps in the underlying asset most important to take into account and what are the problems one faces when trying to include jumps in the model?

Lewis: Certainly individual stocks frequently jump up or and down, due to all sorts of things, earnings releases, analyst opinions sometimes, regulators, corporate actions, etc., etc. But there are many modeling difficulties, due to the overall rarity of these events compared to the daily grind, so to speak.

Haug : In practice is there any realistic way we can hedge against jumps in the underlying asset and what about jumps in the volatility?

Lewis: In practice, your first hedging defense for individual names is, of course, diversification, since most jumps are idiosyncratic to the name. I don't deal with credit derivatives but perhaps those offer some possibilities. Market wide jumps in the underlying asset can be hedged with deep out of the money puts – imperfectly, of course. Jumps in market volatility might be helped by the new VIX options if they develop some liquidity or perhaps some volatility swaps. But, in general, I agree with the implication of your question: namely, that it is very difficult to hedge against rare events that are hard to model.

Haug : As a option trader that is paid to take good bets I sometimes think the volatility surface from liquid options potentially simply is wrong, can I then feed a stochastic volatility model with my own subjective parameters and use this as a tool to try to find which options on the volatility surface are most over or under priced?

Lewis: Of course, with the usual caveats that the liquid options may reflect a jump risk (or other factor) that simply is missing from your model. And, even if you are correct in your judgments, your bets may only pay off in a statistical sense. As an experienced option trader, these caveats are well-known to you, but perhaps not to a novice.

Haug : When calibrating volatility models to historic data isn't there always a danger that we have too little data. We could easily miss out on extreme jumps in the asset and

volatility or other tail events that happen extremely infrequently, how can we adjust or compensate for this?

Lewis: One partial compensation is to always give important weight to the current market (implieds). The market will always reflect a forward looking view. For example, the SPX historical option skew is often fairly flat on the upside, but there was a good positive skew there just prior to the most recent Iraq war. But, your point about the data is well-founded, too, as intraday jumps are completely missed by end of day series. That may partly explain why tail events seem to be much more important when inferred from option prices than when simply looked for in the historical record.

Haug : When it comes to correlation between volatility and the asset I would think the correlation often change dramatically in disaster/crises situations, do current stochastic volatility models capture this?

Lewis: You could: the correlation parameter can be made a function of the current volatility or promoted to its own stochastic process, say with a switching model (normal/crisis). I know Robert Engle has done some work on dynamic correlations. Peter Carr and Liuren Wu have modeled stochastic skews in currency options by combining a Levy process with time changes–this is their very clever mechanism for generating stochastic parameters. And, in some very nice recent work, Christoffersen, Heston, and Jacobs generate stochastic equity correlations with two stochastic volatility factors.

Haug : In the jungle of stochastic volatility models how can a trader decide what model best suits his needs?

Lewis: One rule might be to have at least three models: the Heston model, a more general stochastic volatility model, and at least one model with jumps. Then, at least you can gain a sense of the model risk.

Haug : Where is the trade off between having a model that captures the most important aspects of the asset price behavior and a model that has too many parameters to estimate?

Lewis: That's difficult; at a minimum, one should have a good intuitive understanding of all the parameters, so that you can sense when they're wrong and what might be missing.

Haug : In the case of constant or time dependent deterministic volatility the Black-Scholes-Merton formula is the market standard and the benchmark model, do you think the market will develop a similar standard model for stochastic volatility?

Lewis: Yes, I believe the Heston 1993 model will become a standard in the sense that you will always look at what it has to say.

Haug : If the first ever published reasonable option model had stochastic volatility to start with did you think the Black-Scholes-Merton model with constant volatility would be as popular as it still is with practitioners?

Lewis: Maybe. Once somebody discovered there was a model where the option prices were independent of hard-to-estimate drifts, it could become very popular.

Haug : Living and working in Newport Beach California do you spend much time on the beach?

Lewis: Yes, I love the beaches here, and try to get my work done in the mornings in the summer to take advantage of them.

Haug : How important is it to also know some programming when working with developing quantitative finance models?

Lewis: In my opinion, it's critically important. If your theories don't lead to numbers, they will never be influential. To check the numbers, everything should be done at least two ways. This requires some programming skills. Also, sometimes you simply need some numerical support for a conjecture about something.

Haug : Any views on patenting in quantitative finance? Could this be a way to distribute some of the big bonuses from traders using the quantitative finance models over to the researchers and quants that did the hard work coming up with the models?

Lewis: It's probably a waste of time. My sense is that it's both too easy and too costly to get a patent, and then, what are you going to do with it? Has anybody ever licensed a quantitative finance related patent and made enough royalties to cover the legal costs?

Haug : Do you ever get fed up with quantitative finance?

Lewis: Not really.

Haug : Do you have any hobbies outside quantitative finance?

Lewis: I enjoy the southern California music scene, especially many of the big festivals. Some of my favorites are the annual Bob Marley day (a reggae festival every February), Coachella (a new music/alternative rock festival in the desert every spring), Hootenanny (a rockabilly fest every July 4th weekend in Irvine) and Street Scene (an end-of-summer festival in San Diego). As you can see, something for every season!

Haug : In physics researchers are searching for the theory of everything, do you think there could be such a thing as the theory of everything when it comes to asset price behavior?

Lewis: I doubt it; I think that models will simply get bigger as smaller things become more important and computer power increases.

Haug : If I remember right you once told me you worked on a second volume of your stochastic volatility book, how is this project going, and what will it be about?

Lewis: It's going well – thanks for asking. The working title is simply "Option Valuation under Stochastic Volatility: Volume II". I hope to have a 2007 release. Some expected topics are: the Heston model in more depth, some exotics (barriers, asians, cliquets), jumps, and the geometrical approach to smile asymptotics. The last topic treats the fascinating resolution of some questions involving the short-dated smile that I could only conjecture about in my first volume. Recent work by a number of researchers shows how geodesics, Riemannian geometry, and large deviation principles combine to answer these questions. In my view, this work marks a major theoretical success that will spawn a lot of new research in the next few years.

Haug : In your view where are we in the evolution of quantitative finance?

Lewis: In physics terms, I think we have made it through early quantum mechanics: we understand a lot of simple systems and have some powerful tools like stochastic calculus. I wonder what people will be working on in 100 years – figuring out how to hedge those Martian weather derivative contracts?

REFERENCES

■ Black, F., and M. Scholes (1973): "The Pricing of Options and Corporate Liabilities" *Journal of Political Economy*, **81**, 637–654.
■ Cox, J. (1975): "Notes on Option Pricing I: Constant Elasticity of Variance Diffusions" *Working paper, Stanford University*.
■ Haug, E. G., J. Haug and A. Lewis (2003): "Back to Basics A New Approach to the Discrete Dividend Problem" *Wilmott Magazine, September*.
■ Heston, S. L. (1993): "A Closed-Form Solution for Options with Stochastic Volatility, with Applications to Bond and Currency Options" *Review of Financial Studies*, **6**, 327–343.
■ Lewis, A. (1988): "A Simple Algorithm for the Portfolio Selection Problem" *Journal of Finance*, **43**(1), 7–81.
■ —— (2000): *Option Valuation under Stochastic Volatility*. Newport Beach, CA: Finance Press.
■ Merton, R. C. (1973): "Theory of Rational Option Pricing" *Bell Journal of Economics and Management Science*, **4**, 141–183.
■ Thorp, E. O., and S. T. Kassouf (1967): *Beat the Market*. New York: Random House.

3

Back to Basics: A New Approach to the Discrete Dividend Problem*

Together with Jørgen Haug[†] and Alan Lewis[‡]

1 Introduction

Stocks frequently pay dividends, which has implications for the value of options on these stocks. For options on a large portfolio of stocks, one can approximate discrete dividend payouts with a dividend yield and use the generalized Black-Scholes-Merton (BSM) model. For options on one stock, this is not a viable approximation, and the discreteness of the dividend has to be modeled explicitly.[1] We discuss how to properly make the necessary adjustments.

It might come as a surprise to many readers that we write an entire chapter about a supposedly mundane issue – which is treated thoroughly in any decent derivatives text books (including, but not limited to Cox and Rubinstein, 1985; Chriss, 1997; Haug, 1997; Hull, 2000; McDonald, 2003; Stoll and Whaley, 1993; Wilmott, 2000). It turns out, however, that some of the adjustments suggested in the extant literature admit arbitrage – which is fine if all your competitors use these models, but you know how to do the arbitrage-free adjustment.

1.1 Existing methods

Escrowed dividend model: The simplest escrowed dividend approach makes a simple adjustment to the BSM formula. The adjustment consists of replacing the stock price S_0 by the stock price minus the present value of the dividend $S_0 - e^{-rt_D}D$, where D is the size of the cash dividend to be paid at time t_D. Because the stock price is lowered, the approach will typically lead to too little absolute price volatility ($\sigma_t S_t$) in the period before the dividend is paid. Moreover, it is just an approximation used to fit the ex-dividend price process into the geometric Brownian

---

*We would like to thank Samuel Siren, Paul Wilmott, and participants in the Wilmott forum (www.wilmott.com) for useful comments and suggestions. All the usual disclaimers apply. Copyright Espen Gaarder Haug, Jørgen Haug and Alan Lewis.

[†]Norwegian School of Economics and Business Administration.

[‡]OptionCity.net.

motion (GBM) assumption of the BSM formula. The approach will in general undervalue call options, and the mispricing is larger the later in the option's lifetime the dividend is paid. The approximation suggested by Black (1975) for American options suffers from the same problem, as does the Roll-Geske-Whaley (RGW) model (Roll, 1977; Geske, 1979, 1981; Whaley, 1981). The RGW model uses this approximation of the stock price process, and applies a compound option approach to take into account the possibility of early exercise. Not only does this yield a poor approximation in certain circumstances, but it can open up arbitrage opportunities!

Several papers discuss the weakness of the escrowed dividend approach. In the case of European options, suggested fixes are often based on adjustments of the volatility, in combination with the escrowed dividend adjustment. We shortly discuss three such approaches, all of which assume that the stock price can be described by a GBM:

1. An adjustment popular among practitioners is to replace the volatility σ with $\sigma_2 = \frac{\sigma S}{S - De^{-rt_D}}$, (see for instance Chriss, 1997). This approach increases the volatility relative to the basic escrowed divided process. However, the adjustment yields too high volatility if the dividend is paid out early in the option's lifetime. The approach typically overprices call options in this situation.

2. A more sophisticated volatility adjustment also takes into account the timing of the dividend (Haug and Haug, 1998; Beneder and Vorst, 2001). It replaces σ with σ_2 as before, but not for the entire lifetime of the option. The idea behind the approximation is to leave volatility unchanged in the time before the dividend payment, and to apply the volatility σ_2 after the dividend payment. Since the BSM model requires one volatility as input, some sort of weight must be assigned to each of σ and σ_2. This is accomplished by looking at the period after the dividend payment as a forward volatility period (Haug and Haug, 1996). The single input volatility is then computed as

    $$\hat{\sigma} = \sqrt{\frac{\sigma^2 t_D + \sigma_2^2 (T - t_D)}{T}},$$

    where T is the time of expiration for the option. The adjustment in the presence of multiple dividends is described in Appendix A. This is still simply an adjustment to *parameters* of the GBM price process, that ensures the adjusted price process remains a GBM – at odds with the true ex-dividend price process. The adjustment therefore remains an approximation. One can easily show numerically that this method performs particularly poorly in the presence of multiple dividends.

3. Bos et al. (2003) suggest a more sophisticated volatility adjustment, described in Appendix B. Still, this is just another "quick fix" to try to get around the problems with the escrowed dividend price process. Numerical calculations show that this approach offers quite accurate values provided the dividend is small to moderate. For very high dividends the method performs poorly. The poor performance seemingly also occurs for long term options with multiple dividends.

4. A slightly different way to implement the escrowed dividend process is to adjust the stock price and strike (Bos and Vandermark, 2002). Even if this approach seems to work better than the approximations mentioned above, it suffers from approximation errors for large dividends just like approximation 3.

Lattice models: An alternative to the escrowed dividend approximation is to use non-recombining lattice methods (see for instance Hull, 2000). If implemented as a binomial tree one builds a new tree from each node on each dividend payment date. A problem with all non-recombining lattices is that they are time consuming to evaluate. This problem is amplified with multiple dividends. Schroder (1988) describes how to implement discrete dividends in a recombining tree. The approach is based on the escrowed dividend process idea, however, and the method will therefore significantly misprice options. Wilmott et al. (1993, p. 402) indicate what seems to be a sounder approach to ensure a recombining tree for the spot price process with a discrete dividend.

1.2   Problems and weaknesses of current approaches

In fact, the admission of arbitrage is merely the most egregious example among problems or weaknesses in current approaches. Of course, we cannot claim to have seen every paper written on this subject, but of those we have seen, we note one or more of the following weaknesses:

(i) *Logical flaws.* Many approaches use the idea of an escrowed dividend process, as discussed above. The idea is to break up the stock price process into two pieces, a risky part and an escrowed dividend part. The admirable goal is to "guarantee" that the declared dividend will be received. The logical flaw is that the resulting stock price process changes with the option expiration. Whatever the stock price process is, it cannot depend upon which option you happen to be considering. The fact that this is a logical fallacy is, to our thinking, under-appreciated.

(ii) *Ill-defined stock price processes.* Some treatments just don't "get it" that a constant dividend D can't be paid at arbitrarily low stock prices. This tends to be a problem with discussions of "non-recombining trees". The problem is (a) the discussion "never" mention that something must be said about this issue.[2] A related issue, which we have seen in some recent models is that (b) negative stock prices are explicitly allowed. The reason that authors can get away with (a) is that, in many computations, the problematic region is a very low probability event. But, this is no excuse for failing to completely define your model. The reader should be able to say similar bad things about (b).

(iii) *Only geometric Brownian motion* is discussed. This is understandable in the early literature, but not now a days. The weaknesses of GBM are well-known. Some fixes include stochastic volatility, jumps, and other ideas. A dividend treatment needs to accommodate these models.

(iv) *Arbitrage issues.* This has been mentioned above and an example is given below. All we will add here is that the source of this problem is (i) or (ii) above. Finally, to paraphrase the physicist Sidney Coleman, who was speaking in another context, just because a theory is dead wrong, doesn't mean it can't be highly accurate. In other words, the reader will observe below many instances of highly accurate numerical agreement between our current approach and some existing approximations that suffer from (ii) for example. Nevertheless, we would argue that a theory that predicts negative stock prices must be "dead wrong" in Coleman's sense.[3]

Arbitrage example: In the case of European options, the above techniques are *ad hoc*, but get the job done (in most cases) when the corrections are properly carried out. To give you an idea of when it really goes wrong, consider the model of choice for American call options on stocks whose cum dividend price is a GBM. The Roll-Geske-Whaley (RGW) model has for decades been considered a brilliant closed form solution to price American calls on dividend paying stocks. Consider the case of an initial stock price of 100, strike 130, risk free rate 6%, volatility 30%, one year to maturity, and an expected dividend payment of 7 in 0.9999 years. Using this input the RGW model posits a value of 4.3007. Consider now another option, expiring just before the dividend payment, say in 0.9998 years. Since this in effect is an American call on a non-dividend paying stock it is not optimal to exercise it before maturity. In the absence of arbitrage the value must therefore equal the BSM price of 4.9183. This is, however, an arbitrage opportunity! The arbitrage occurs because the RGW model is mis-specified, in that the dynamics of the stock price process depends on the timing of the dividend. Similar examples have been discussed by Beneder and Vorst (2001) and Frishling (2002). This is not just an esoteric example, as several well known software systems use the RGW model and other similar mis-specified models. In more complex situations than described in this example the arbitrage will not necessarily be quite so obvious, and one would need an accurate model to confidently take advantage of it. It is precisely such a model we present in the present chapter.

2 General Solution

2.1 A single dividend

You wish to value a Euro-style or American-style equity option on a stock that pays a discrete (point-in-time) dividend at time $t = t_D$. The simpler problem is to first specify a price process whereby any dividends are reinvested immediately back into the security – this is the so-called cum-dividend process $S_t = S(t)$. In general, S_t is not the market price of the security, but instead is the market price of a hypothetical mutual fund that only invests in the security. To distinguish the concepts, we will write the market price of the security at time t as Y_t, which we will sometimes call the ex-dividend process. Of course, if there are no dividends, then $Y_t = S_t$ for all t. Even if the company pays a dividend, we can always arrange things so that $Y_0 = S_0$, which guarantees (by the law of one price) that $Y_t = S_t$ for all $t < t_D$.

In our treatment, we allow S_t to follow a very general continuous-time stochastic process. For example, your process might be one of the following (to keep things simple, we suppose a world with a constant interest rate r):

Example (cum-dividend) processes

(P1). GBM: $dS_t = r S_t \, dt + \sigma S_t \, dB_t$, where σ is a constant volatility and B is a standard Brownian motion.

(P2). Jump-diffusion: $dS_t = (r - \lambda k) S_t \, dt + \sigma S_t \, dB_t + S_t \, dJ_t$, where dJ_t is a Poisson driven jump process with mean jump arrival rate λ, and mean jump size k.

(P3). Jump-diffusion with stochastic volatility: $dS_t = (r - \lambda k) S_t \, dt + \sigma_t S_t \, dB_t + S_t \, dJ_t$, where σ_t follows its own separate, possibly correlated, diffusion or jump-diffusion.

Consider an option at time t, expiring at time T, and assume for a moment that there are no dividends so that $Y_t = S_t$ for all $t \leq T$. In that case, clearly, models (P1) and (P2) are one-factor models: the option value $V(S_t, t)$ depends only upon the current state of one random variable. Model (P3) is a two-factor model, $V(S_t, \sigma_t, t)$. Obviously, "n-factor" models are possible in principle, for arbitrary n, and our treatment will apply to those too. Note that we leave the dependence on many parameters implicit.

What the examples have in common is that the stock price, with zero or more additional factors, jointly form a Markov process,[4] in which the discounted stock price is a martingale. Also, for simplicity, we will consider only time-homogenous processes; this means that transition densities for the state variables depend only on the length of the time period in question, and not on the beginning and end dates of the time period.

Choosing a dividend policy   Now we want to create an option formula for the case where the company declares a single discrete dividend of size D, where the "ex-dividend date" is at time t_D during the option holding period. We consider an unprotected Euro-style option, so that the option holder will not receive the dividend. Since option prices depend upon the market price of the security, for one factor models, we must now write $V(Y_t, t)$.

Note that we are being very careful with our choice of words; we have said that the company "declares" a dividend D. What we mean by that is that it is the company's stated intention to pay the amount D *if that is possible*. When will it be impossible? We assume that the company cannot pay out more equity than exists. For simplicity, we imagine a world where there are no distortions from taxes or other frictions, so that a dollar of dividends is valued the same as a dollar of equity. In addition, we always assume that there are no arbitrage opportunities. In such a world, if the company pays a dividend D, the stock price at the ex-dividend date must drop by the same amount: $Y(t_D) = Y(t_D^-) - D = S(t_D^-) - D$. Our notation is that t_D^- is the time instantaneously before the ex-dividend date t_D (in a world of continuous trading). Since stock prices represent the price of a limited liability security, we must have $Y(t_D) \geq 0$, so we have a contradiction between these last two concepts if $S(t_D^-) < D$.

This is the fundamental contradiction that every discrete dividend model must resolve. We resolve it here by the following minimal modification to the dividend policy. We assume that the company will indeed pay out its declared amount D if $S^- > D$, abbreviating $S^- = S(t_D^-)$. However, in the case where $S^- < D$, we assume that the company pays some *lesser* amount $\Delta(S^-)$ whereby $0 \leq \Delta(S^-) \leq S^-$. That is our general model, a "minimally modified dividend policy." In later sections, we show numerical results for two natural policy choices, namely $\Delta(S^-) = S^-$ (liquidator), and $\Delta(S^-) = 0$ (survivor). The first case allows liquidation because the ex-dividend stock price (at least in all of the sample models P1–P3 above) would be absorbed at zero. We will assume that a zero stock price is always an absorbing state. The second case (and, indeed any model where $\Delta(S) < S$) allows survival because the stock price process can then attain strictly positive values after the dividend payment.

These choices, liquidation versus survival, sound dramatically different. In cases of financial distress, where indeed the stock price is very low, they would be. But such cases are relatively rare. As a practical matter, we want to stress that for most applications, the choice of $\Delta(S)$ for $S < D$ has a negligible financial effect; the main point is that *some* choice must be made to fully specify the model. There is little financial effect in most applications because the probability that an initial stock price S_0 becomes as small as a declared dividend D is typically negligible; if this is not obvious, then a short computation with the log-normal distribution should convince you. In any event, we will demonstrate various cases in numerical examples.

To re-state what we have said in terms of an SDE for the security price process, our general model is that the actual dividend paid becomes the random variable $\mathcal{D}(S)$, where

$$\mathcal{D}(S) = \begin{cases} D, & \text{if } S > D \\ \Delta(S) \leq S, & \text{if } S \leq D \end{cases}.$$ (3.1)

In (3.1) D is the declared (or projected) dividend – a constant, independent of S. The functional form for $\mathcal{D}(S)$ is any function that preserves limited liability. Then, the market price of the security evolves, using GBM as the prototype, as the SDE:

$$dY_t = \left[rY_t - \delta(t - t_D)\mathcal{D}(Y_{t_D^-}) \right] dt + \sigma Y_t \, dB_t, \tag{3.2}$$

where $\delta(t - t_D)$ is Dirac's delta function centered at t_D. The same SDE drift modification occurs for (P2), (P3), or any other security price process you wish to model.

It's worth stressing that the Brownian motion B_t that appears in (P1) and (P1a) have *identical realizations*. You might want to picture a realization of B_t for $0 \le t \le T$. Your mental picture will ensure that $Y_t = S_t$ for all $t < t_D$ and $Y_{t_D} = S_{t_D} - \mathcal{D}(S_{t_D})$. Note that Y_t is completely determined by knowledge of S_t alone for all $t \le t_D$ (the fact that $Y_{t_D} = f(S_{t_D})$, where f is a deterministic function, will be crucial later). What about $t > t_D$? For those (post ex-dividend date) times, little can be said about Y_t given only knowledge of S_t (all you can say is that $Y_t < S_t$ if $D > 0$).

For our results to be useful, you need to be able to solve your model in the absence of dividends. By that, we mean that you know how to find the option values and the transition density for the stock price (and any other state variables) to evolve. Note that you need not have these functions in so-called "closed-form", but merely that you have some method of obtaining them. This method may be an analytic formula, a lattice method, a Monte Carlo procedure, a series solution, or whatever.

It's awkward to keep placeholders for arbitrary state variables, so we will simply write $\phi(S_0, S_t, t)$ (the cum-dividend transition density), with the understanding that additional state variable arguments should be inserted if your model needs them. To be explicit, the transition density is the probability density for an initial state (stock price plus other state variables) S_0 to evolve to the final state S_t in a time t. This evolution occurs under the risk-adjusted, cum-dividend process (or measure) such as the ones given under "Example (cum-dividend) processes" above. For GBM, $\phi(S_0, S_t, t)$ is the familiar log-normal density. Option formulas are similarly displayed only for the one-factor model, with additional state variables to be inserted by the reader if necessary.

With this discussion, let's collect all of our stated assumptions in one place:

(A1) Markets are perfect (frictionless, arbitrage-free), and trading is in continuous-time.

(A2) After risk adjustment, every cum-dividend stock price S_t, jointly with $n \ge 0$ additional factors (which are suppressed), evolve under a time-homogenous, (Markov) stochastic process. S_t is non-negative; if $S_t = 0$ is reached, it's a trap state (absorbing). All these statements also apply to the market price (ex-dividend process) Y_t.

(A3) If a company declares (or you project) a discrete dividend D, this is promoted to a random dividend policy $\mathcal{D}(S)$ in the minimal manner of (3.1). This causes the market price of the stock to drop instantaneously on an ex-dividend date, as prototyped by (P1a).

Our Main Result We write $V_E(S_t, t; D, t_D)$ for the time-t fair value of a European-style option that expires at time T, in the presence of a discrete dividend D paid at time t_D. The last two arguments are the main parameters in the fully specified dividend policy $\{t_D, \mathcal{D}(S)\}$ where $t < t_D < T$. If there is no dividend between time t and the option expiration T, we simply drop the last two arguments and write $V_E(S_t, t)$. So, to be clear about notation, when you see an option value $V(\cdot)$ that has *only two arguments*, this will be a formula that you know in the absence of dividends, like the BSM formula. Again, the strike price X, option expiration T, and other parameters and state variables have been suppressed for simplicity. Then, here is our main result:

Proposition 1 Under assumptions **(A1)–(A3)**, the adoption by the company of a single discrete dividend policy $\{t_D, \mathcal{D}(S)\}$, causes the fair value of a Euro-style option to change from $V_E(S_0, 0)$ to $V_E(S_0, 0; D, t_D)$, where

$$V_E(S_0, 0; D, t_D) = \mathrm{e}^{-rt_D} \int_0^\infty V_E(S - \mathcal{D}(S), t_D)\phi(S_0, S, t_D)\,\mathrm{d}S. \tag{3.3}$$

A very elaborate argument is:

(i) Let S be the cum-dividend process, and Y the ex-dividend process as before. Assume dividend policy $\mathcal{D}(S)$, paid on date t_D. Then $Y_t = S_t$ for all $t < t_D$, $Y_{t_D} = S_{t_D} - \mathcal{D}(S_{t_D})$, and typically $Y_t \neq S_t$ for $t > t_D$. Assume the distribution function F_S for S and that the option pays off $g(Y_T)$ at time T.

(ii) Relative to time $t < T$ the payoff from the option is *a random variable*/uncertain cash flow. The absence of arbitrage then implies that the price at time t for this cash flow is

$$\mathrm{e}^{-r(T-t)}\mathrm{E}_t\{g(Y_T)\}.$$

Let's call this value $V(Y_t, t)$, which again is *a random variable* relative to any time $t' < t$. For any $t \geq t_D$ this random variable is the price of an option on a non-dividend paying stock, and therefore assumed known for any value of Y_t.

(iii) We're interested in the value of the option on Y at time 0. Since $V(Y_t, t)$ is simply a random variable relative to today (time 0), we can use the exact same argument as in (ii) above. Its value at time 0 must therefore, in the absence of arbitrage, be

$$\mathrm{e}^{-rt}\mathrm{E}_0\{V(Y_t, t)\}. \tag{3.4}$$

So far, the only result we've used is the (almost) equivalence of no arbitrage and the martingale property of prices (Harrison & Kreps, 1979; Harrison & Pliska, 1981; Delbaen & Schachermayer, 1995, among others), and we haven't said anything about what specific date $t \geq t_D$ is (the argument would hold for $t < t_D$ too, but we want $V(Y_t, t)$ to be "known").

(iv) Assuming sufficient regularity, we can write (3.4) in integral form wrt. a distribution function

$$\mathrm{E}_0\{V(Y_t, t)\} = \int_0^\infty V(y, t)\,dF_Y(y; Y_0, 0, t).$$

The trouble with this integral is that we typically do not know the distribution function F_Y unless $t < t_D$ – but in that case V is unknown (orthogonal knowledge ;-).

(v) The main insight is now that by considering $t = t_D$ we *know* that $Y_{t_D} = S_{t_D} - \mathcal{D}(S_{t_D})$. This means that we do not need to know F_Y, since by the "Law of the Unconscious Statistician"

$$E_0 \left\{ V(Y_{t_D}, t_D) \right\} = \int_0^\infty V(y, t_D) \, dF_Y(y; Y_0, 0, t_D)$$

$$= \int_0^\infty V(s - \mathcal{D}(s), t_D) \, dF_S(s; S_0, 0, t_D).$$

In other words, at time $t = t_D$ we know both how to compute V and how to compute its expectation $E_0 \left\{ V(Y_{t_D}, t_D) \right\}$, and this is the only date for which this holds. With a time-homogeneous transition density $dF_S(s; S_0, 0, t_D) = \phi(S_0, s, t_D) \, ds$, and we arrive at (3.3).

An Example: Take GBM, where the dividend policy is $\Delta(S) = S$ (liquidator) for $S \leq D$. Then (3.3) for a call option becomes

$$C_E(S_0, 0; D, t_D) = e^{-rt_D} \int_D^\infty C_E(S - D, t_D) \phi(S_0, S, t_D) \, dS. \tag{3.5}$$

Note that the call price in the integrand of (3.3) is zero for $S - \mathcal{D}(S) = 0$ ($S \leq D$). In (3.5), $\phi(S_0, S, t)$ is simply the (no-dividend) log-normal density and $C_E(S - D, t_D)$ is simply the no-dividend BSM formula with time-to-go $T - t_D$. For example, suppose $S_0 = X = 100$, $T = 1$ (year), $r = 0.06$, $\sigma = 0.30$, and $D = 7$. Then, consider two cases; (i) $t_D = 0.01$, and (ii) $t_D = 0.99$. We find from (3.5) the high precision results: (i) $C_E(100, 0; 7, 0.01) = 10.59143873835989$ and (ii) $C_E(100, 0; 7, 0.99) = 11.57961536099359$.

American-style options It is well-known, and easily proved that, for an American-style call option with a discrete dividend, early exercise is only optimal instantaneously prior to the ex-dividend date (Merton, 1973). This result of course applies to the present model. Hence, to value an American-style call option with a single discrete dividend, you merely replace (3.3) with

$$C_A(S_0, 0; D, t_D) = e^{-rt_D} \int_0^\infty \max\{(S - X)^+, C_E(S - \mathcal{D}(S), t_D)\} \phi(S_0, S, t_D) \, dS, \tag{3.6}$$

Early exercise is never optimal unless there is a finite solution S^* to $S^* - X = C_E(S^* - D, t_D)$, where we are assuming that $X > D$ (a virtual certainty in practice). In this case, the reader may want to break up the integral into two pieces, but we shall just leave it at (3.6).

For American-style put options, as is also well-known, it can be optimal to exercise at any time prior to expiration, even in the absence of dividends. So, in this case, you are generally forced to a numerical solution, evolving the stock price according to your model. This is the well-known backward iteration. What may differ from what you are used to is that you must allow for an instantaneous drop of $\mathcal{D}(S)$ on the ex-date.

2.2 One down, *n–1* to go

With the sequence of dividends $\{(D_i, t_i)\}_{i=1}^n$, $t_1 < t_2 < \ldots < t_n$, the argument leading to formula (3.3) still holds. Simply repeat it iteratively, starting at time t_{n-1} by applying (3.3) to the last dividend (D_n, t_n). While straight forward, this procedure involves evaluating an n-fold integral. We therefore show a simpler way to compute it in Section 4.

3   Dividend Models

It is now time to compare specific dividend models, $\Delta(S)$. We consider the two extreme cases for $\Delta(S)$, use these to develop an inequality for an arbitrary dividend model, and then illustrate the impact on option prices.

Liquidator: We consider first the situation where the dividend is reduced to S_{t_D} when $S_{t_D} < D$, i.e., $\Delta(S) = \Delta^l(S) = S$ for $S < D$. This is tantamount to the firm being liquidated if the cum dividend stock price falls below the declared dividend. Although this might seem an extreme assumption, keep in mind that for most reasonable parameter values, this will be close to a zero-probability event. It is a simple approximation that succeeds in ensuring a non-negative ex-dividend stock price. In this case (3.3) reduces to

$$V_E^l(S_0, 0; D, t_D) = e^{-rt_D} \int_D^\infty V_E(S - D, t_D)\phi(S_0, S, t_D)\, dS$$

$$+ e^{-rt_D} \int_0^D V_E(S - \Delta^l(S), t_D)\phi(S_0, S, t_D)\, dS,$$

$$= e^{-rt_D} \left\{ \int_D^\infty V_E(S - D, t_D)\phi(S_0, S, t_D)\, dS + V_E(0, t_D) \int_0^D \phi(S_0, S, t_D)\, dS \right\}.$$

In this decomposition the "tail value" $e^{-rt_D} V_E(0, t_D) \int_0^D \phi(S_0, S, t_D)\, dS$ will vanish for a call option, but not for a put option.

Survivor: Consider next the situation where the dividend is canceled when $S_{t_D} < D$, i.e., $\Delta(S) = \Delta^s(S) = 0$ for $S \le D$. This approximation also succeeds in ensuring a non-negative ex-dividend stock price, and also allows the firm to live on with probability one after the dividend payout. The option price is now similar to the one for the liquidator dividend, with a slight modification to the tail value of the option contract:

$$V_E^s(S_0, 0; D, t_D) = e^{-rt_D} \left\{ \int_D^\infty V_E(S - D, t_D)\phi(S_0, S, t_D)\, dS \right.$$

$$\left. + \int_0^D V_E(S, t_D)\phi(S_0, S, t_D)\, dS \right\}. \tag{3.7}$$

From (3.3) and (3.7) we can now establish a result that should enable you to sleep better at night if you are concerned with your choice of dividend policy $\Delta(\cdot)$.

Corollary 1   Let $C_E(S_0, 0; D, t_D)$ be given by (3.3) for a generic dividend policy $\Delta(S)$ such that $0 \le \Delta(S) \le S$. For European call options

$$C_E^l(S_0, 0; D, t_D) \le C_E(S_0, 0; D, t_D) \le C_E^s(S_0, 0; D, t_D).$$

If $S_{t_D} < D$ with positive probability then additionally $C^l_E(S_0, 0; D, t_D) < C^s_E(S_0, 0; D, t_D)$.

The $\int_D^\infty$-integral is identical for all three options. Since $0 \leq \Delta(S) \leq S$ it follows that

$$\int_0^D C_E(S - \Delta^l(S), t_D)\phi(S_0, S, t_D)\, dS$$

$$\leq \int_0^D C_E(S - \Delta(S), t_D)\phi(S_0, S, t_D)\, dS$$

$$\leq \int_0^D C_E(S - \Delta^s(S), t_D)\phi(S_0, S, t_D)\, dS.$$

The strict inequality follows from a similar argument.

We could easily have established the same inequality for American call options, by simply using more cumbersome notation that takes early exercise into account. The interesting part of the result is the weak inequality. It tells us that if there's a negligible difference in prices between the liquidator and survivor dividend policies, then it doesn't matter what assumption you make about $\Delta(S)$ as long as it satisfies limited liability.

We end this section with an illustration of the relevance of the dividend model $\Delta(S)$. We do so by illustrating the pricing implications of the two extreme dividend policies, liquidator and survivor, in a specific case.

A financial fairy "tail": A long-lived financial service firm, let's call them Ye Olde Reliable Insurance, paid a hefty dividend once a year, which they liked to declare well in advance. Once declared, they had never missed a payment, not once in their 103-year history.

As their usual practice, they went ex-dividend every June 30 and declared their next dividend in November. One November, with their stock approaching the $100 mark, the Ye Olde board decided that 6% seemed fair and easily do-able, so they declared a $6 dividend for the next June 30.

Unfortunately, during the very next month (December), the outbreak of a mysterious new virus coupled with an 8.2 temblor centered in Newport Beach devastated both their property/casualty and health insurance subs and their stock plummeted to the $10 range.

The CBOE dutifully opened a new option series striking at $10 with a leaps version expiring one year later. To keep things simple, we will imagine this series expires exactly in one year with an ex-dividend date at exactly the 1/2 year mark. Of course, there was much speculation and uncertainty about the declared $6 dividend. The company's only comment was a terse press release saying "the board has spoken."

So, the potential option buyer was faced with a contract with $S = 10$, $X = 10$, $T = 1$ year and $t_D = 0.5$. If they paid in full, then $D = 6$. Interest rates were at 6%.

Our "liquidator" option model postulates that the company would pay in full unless the stock price S_{t_D} at mid-year was below $D = 6$, in which case they would pay out all the remaining equity, namely S_{t_D}. The skeptics said "no way" and proposed a new "survivor" option model in which the board would completely drop the dividend if $S_{t_D} \leq D$. The call price in this new model was larger by a "tail value". The big debate in the Wilmott forums became what volatility should one use to compute these values and, in the end, of course, no one knew. But everyone could agree that the stock price sure was volatile. So one way to proceed was to compute the option

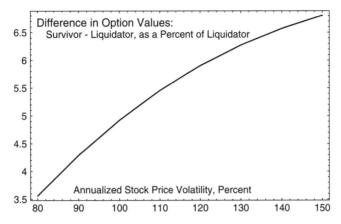

Figure 3.1: Relative tail value for a European call option

price in both models for volatilities ranging from 80 % to 150 % and the results are shown in the figure. Interestingly, the results only differed by 3.5 to 7 % even in this extreme scenario with a doubtful yield, if paid, in the 60 % range.

4 Applications

To illustrate the application of the pricing formula we now specialize the option contracts as well as the stock price process.

European call and put options: It is straightforward to derive the following put-call parity:

Proposition 2 For a general cum-dividend price process S_t and dividend policy $\mathcal{D}(S)$ as in (3.1),

$$C_E(S_0, 0; D, t_D) + e^{-rT}X + e^{-rt_D}\overline{D} = P_E(S_0, 0; D, t_D) + S_0, \tag{3.8}$$

where

$$\overline{D} = D - \int_0^D \phi(S_0, S, t_D)(D - \Delta(S))\, dS$$

is the expected received dividend.

The idea of the argument is standard (Merton, 1973): Since $C_E(Y, T; D, t_D) + X = (Y - X)^+ + X = P_E(Y, T, D, t_D) + Y$, these two portfolios must have the same value today. Consider first the LHS. Its value is $e^{-rT}E_0\left\{(Y - X)^+ + X\right\} = C_E(S_0, 0; D, t_D) + e^{-rT}X$. Consider next the RHS. Its value is similarly given by $e^{-rT}E_0\left\{(X - Y)^+ + Y\right\} = P_E(S_0, 0; D, t_D) + e^{-rT}E_0\left\{(Y + \overline{D}_T) - \overline{D}_T\right\} = P_E(S_0, 0; D, t_D) + S_0 + e^{-rT}E_0\left\{\overline{D}_T\right\}$, where $\overline{D}_T$ is the future value (at time T) of the dividend received (a random variable). Since

$$E_0\left\{\overline{D}_T\right\} = e^{r(T-t_D)}\int_0^D \Delta(S)\phi(S_0, S, t_D)\, dS + e^{r(T-t_D)}D\int_D^\infty \phi(S_0, S, t_D)\, dS$$

the result follows.

For the case of GBM stock price and liquidator dividend, $\Delta(S) = S$ for $S < D$, the value of a European call option can be written explicitly as

$$C_E(S_0, 0; D, t_D) = e^{-rt_D} \int_d^{\infty} C_E\left(S_0 e^{\left[r-\sigma^2/2\right]t_D + \sigma\sqrt{t_D}x} - D, t_D\right) \frac{1}{\sqrt{2\pi}} e^{-\frac{1}{2}x^2} \, dx,$$

$$d = \frac{\ln(D/S_0) - \left(r - \sigma^2/2\right) t_D}{\sigma\sqrt{t_D}}.$$

A similar expression can be written down for the put option, but this is really not necessary in light of (3.8). Tables 3.1 and 3.2 report option prices for European call options for small and large dividends. The tables use the symbols:

BSM is the plain vanilla Black-Scholes-Merton model.
M73 is the BSM model with $S - e^{-rt_D}D$ substituted for S – the escrowed dividend adjustment (Merton, 1973).
Vol1 is identical to M73, but with an adjusted volatility. The volatility of the asset is replaced with $\sigma_2 = \sigma \frac{S}{S - e^{-rt_D}D}$ (see for instance Chriss, 1997).
Vol2 is a slightly more sophisticated volatility adjustment than Vol1 (see Appendix A for a short description of this technique).
Vol3 is the volatility adjustment suggested by Bos et al. (2003) (see Appendix B for a short description of this adjustment).
BV adjusts the strike and stock price, to take into account the effects of the discrete dividend payment (Bos and Vandermark, 2002).
Num is a non-recombining binomial tree with 500 time steps, and no adjustment to prevent the event that $S - D < 0$ (see for instance Hull, 2000, for the idea behind this method).
HHL(3.5) is the *exact* solution in (3.5).

Table 3.1 illustrates that the M73 adjustment is inaccurate, especially in the case when the dividend is paid close to the option's expiration. Moreover the Vol1 adjustment, often used by practitioners, gives significantly inaccurate values when the dividend is close to the beginning of the option's lifetime. Both Vol2 and BV do much better at accurately pricing the options. Vol3 yields values very close to the BV model. The non-recombining tree (Num) and our exact solution (HHL(3.5)) give very similar values in all cases. However, the non-recombining tree is not ensured to converge to the true solution (HHL(3.5)) in all situations, unless the non-recombining tree is set up to prevent negative stock prices in the nodes where $S - D < 0$. This problem will typically be relevant only with a very high dividend, as we discussed in Section 3. For low to moderate cash dividends one can assume that even the "naive" non-recombining tree and our exact solution agree to economically significant accuracy.

Table 3.2 shows that the BV and the non-recombining tree have significant differences when there's a significant dividend in the middle of the option's lifetime. The latter is closer to the true value. The Vol3 model strongly underprices the option when the dividend is this high.

American call and put options: Most traded stock options are American. We now do a numerical comparison of stock options with a single cash dividend payment. Tables 3.3–3.5 use the following models that differ from the European options considered above:

B75 is the approximation to the value of an American call on a dividend paying stock suggested by Black (1975). This is basically the escrowed dividend method, where the stock price in

TABLE 3.1:   EUROPEAN CALLS WITH DIVIDEND OF 7
$(s = 100, t = 1, r = 6\%, \sigma = 30\%)$

	BSM	Mer73	Vol1	Vol2	Vol3	BV	Num	HHL(3.5)
t				$X = 100$				
0.0001	14.7171	10.5805	11.4128	10.5806	10.5806	10.5806	10.5829	10.5806
0.5000	14.7171	10.6932	11.5001	11.1039	11.0781	11.0979	11.1079	11.1062
0.9999	14.7171	10.8031	11.5855	11.5854	11.5383	11.5887	11.5704	11.5887
				$X = 130$				
0.0001	4.9196	3.0976	3.7403	3.0977	3.0977	3.0977	3.0987	3.0977
0.5000	4.9196	3.1437	3.7701	3.4583	3.4203	3.4159	3.4368	3.4383
0.9999	4.9196	3.1889	3.7993	3.7993	3.6949	3.7263	3.7140	3.7263
				$X = 70$				
0.0001	34.9844	28.5332	28.9113	28.5332	28.5332	28.5332	28.5343	28.5332
0.5000	34.9844	28.7200	29.0832	28.9009	28.9047	28.9350	28.9218	28.9215
0.9999	34.9844	28.9016	29.2504	29.2504	29.2920	29.3257	29.3140	29.3257

TABLE 3.2:   EUROPEAN CALLS WITH DIVIDEND OF 50
$(s = 100, t = 1, r = 6\%, \sigma = 30\%)$

	BSM	Mer73	Vol1	Vol2	Vol3	BV	Num	HHL(3.5)
t				$X = 100$				
0.0001	14.7171	0.1282	2.9961	0.1283	0.1282	0.1283	0.1273	0.1283
0.5000	14.7171	0.1696	3.0678	1.4323	0.5755	0.8444	1.0687	1.0704
0.9999	14.7171	0.2192	3.1472	3.1469	1.1566	2.1907	2.1825	2.1908
				$X = 130$				
0.0001	4.9196	0.0094	1.3547	0.0094	0.0094	0.0094	0.0092	0.0094
0.5000	4.9196	0.0133	1.3556	0.4313	0.0947	0.1516	0.2264	0.2279
0.9999	4.9196	0.0184	1.3609	1.3607	0.2510	0.6120	0.6072	0.6120
				$X = 70$				
0.0001	34.9844	1.6510	7.0798	1.6517	1.6513	1.6514	1.6515	1.6517
0.5000	34.9844	1.9982	7.3874	4.9953	3.3697	4.2808	4.7304	4.7299
0.9999	34.9844	2.3780	7.7100	7.7096	4.9966	7.2247	7.2122	7.2248

the BSM formula is replaced with the stock price minus the present value of the dividend. To take into account the possibility of early exercise one also computes an option value just before the dividend payment, without subtracting the dividend. The value of the option is considered to be the maximum of these values.

RGW is the model of Roll (1977); Geske (1979); Whaley (1981). It is considered a closed form solution for American call options on dividend paying stocks. As we already know, the model is seriously flawed.

HHL(3.6) it the exact solution in (3.6), again using the liquidator policy.

TABLE 3.3: AMERICAN CALLS WITH DIVIDEND OF 7
$(D = 7, S = 100, T = 1, r = 6\%, \sigma = 30\%)$

	B75	RGW	Num	HHL(3.6)
t		$X = 100$		
0.0001	10.5805	10.5805	10.5829	10.5806
0.5000	10.6932	11.1971	11.6601	11.6564
0.9999	14.7162	13.9468	14.7053	14.7162
		$X = 130$		
0.0001	3.0976	3.0976	3.0987	3.0977
0.5000	3.1437	3.1586	3.4578	3.4595
0.9999	4.9189	4.3007	4.9071	4.9189
		$X = 70$		
0.0001	30.0004	30.0004	30.0000	30.0004
0.5000	32.3034	32.3365	32.4604	32.4608
0.9999	34.9839	34.7065	34.9737	34.9839

Table 3.3 shows that the RGW model works reasonably well when the dividend is in the very beginning of the option lifetime. The RGW model exhibits the same problems as the simpler M73 or escrowed dividend method used for European options. The pricing error is particularly large when the dividend occurs at the end of the option's lifetime. The B75 approximation also significantly misprices options.

For very high dividend, as in Table 3.5, the mispricing in the RGW formula is even more clear; the values are significantly off compared with both non-recombining tree (Num) and our exact solution (HHL(3.6)). The simple B75 approximation is remarkably accurate. The intuition behind this is naturally that a very high dividend makes it very likely to be optimal to exercise just before the dividend date – a situation where the B75 approximation for good reasons should be accurate.

TABLE 3.4: AMERICAN CALLS WITH DIVIDEND OF 30
   $(D = 30, S = 100, T = 1, r = 6\%, \sigma = 30\%)$

	B75	RGW	Num	HHL(3.5)
t		$X = 100$		
0.0001	2.0579	2.0579	2.0574	2.0583
0.5000	9.8827	7.5202	9.9296	9.9283
0.9999	14.7162	11.4406	14.7053	14.7162
		$X = 130$		
0.0001	0.3345	0.3345	0.3322	0.3346
0.5000	1.6439	0.6742	1.7851	1.7855
0.9999	4.9189	2.4289	4.9071	4.9189
		$X = 70$		
0.0001	30.0004	30.0004	30.0000	30.0004
0.5000	32.3034	32.0762	32.3033	32.3037
0.9999	34.9839	34.1637	34.9737	34.9839

TABLE 3.5: AMERICAN CALLS WITH DIVIDEND OF 50
   $(D = 50, S = 100, T = 1, r = 6\%, \sigma = 30\%)$

	B75	RGW	Num	HHL(3.5)
t		$X = 100$		
0.0001	0.1282	0.1437	0.1273	0.1922
0.5000	9.8827	5.8639	9.8745	9.8828
0.9999	14.7162	9.3137	14.7053	14.7162
		$X = 130$		
0.0001	0.0094	0.0094	0.0092	0.0094
0.5000	1.6439	0.1375	0.5112	1.6492
0.9999	4.9189	1.1029	4.9071	4.9189
		$X = 70$		
0.0001	30.0004	30.0004	30.0000	30.0004
0.5000	32.3034	32.0762	32.6600	32.3034
0.9999	34.9839	34.1637	34.9737	34.9839

4.1 Multiple dividend approximation

We showed in Section 2 that it is necessary to evaluate an n-fold integral when there are multiple dividends. It is therefore useful to have a fast, accurate approximation. We now show how to approximate the option value in the case of a call option on a stock whose cum-dividend price follows a GBM, using the liquidator dividend policy.

First, let's write the exact answer on date t with a sequence of n dividends prior to T as $C_n(S, X, t, T)$, where X is the strike and T is the expiration date. Then, the first iteration of (3.5) in an exact treatment becomes

$$C_1(S, X, t_{n-1}, T) = e^{-r(t_n - t_{n-1})} \int_{D_n}^{\infty} C_{\text{BSM}}(S_1 - D_n, X, t_n, T)\phi(S, S_1, t_n - t_{n-1})S_1, \quad (3.9)$$

where $C_{\text{BSM}}(\cdot)$ is the BSM model. This integral is quick to evaluate, just as in the single dividend cases tabulated above. The second iteration becomes

$$C_2(S, X, t_{n-2}, T) = e^{-r(t_{n-1} - t_{n-2})} \int_{D_{n-1}}^{\infty} C_1(S_1 - D_{n-1}, X, t_{n-1}, T)\phi(S, S_1, t_{n-1} - t_{n-2})S_1.$$

$$(3.10)$$

Notice that we now integrate not over the BSM model, but rather the option price derived in the first iteration (3.9). Evaluation of (3.10) therefore involves a double integral. We know, however, that $C_1(\cdot)$ will look like an option solution and hence will have many of the characteristics of the BSM formula. If we can effectively parametrize $C_1(\cdot)$ with a BSM formula then it will be quick to evaluate (3.10).

Some key characteristics of $C_1(S, X, t_{n-1}, T)$ are as follows. First, it vanishes as $S \to 0$. Second, because (standard) put-call parity becomes asymptotically exact for large S,

$$C_1(S, X, t_{n-1}, T) \approx S - e^{-r(T - t_{n-1})}X - e^{-r(t_n - t_{n-1})}D_n.$$

This suggests the BSM parametrization

$$C_1(S, X, t_{n-1}, T) \approx C_{\text{BSM}}(S, X_{\text{adj}}, t_{n-1}, T), \quad (3.11)$$

where $X_{\text{adj}} = X + D_n e^{-r(t_n - T)}$. The strike adjustment ensures correct large-S behavior.

A little experimentation will show that the approximating BSM formula just suggested is inaccurate for S near the money. Still, we have another degree of freedom in our ability to adjust the volatility in the right-hand-side of (3.11). By choosing σ_{adj} so that $C_1(S_0, X, t_{n-1}, T) \equiv C_{\text{BSM}}(S_0, X_{\text{adj}}, \sigma_{\text{adj}}, t_{n-1}, T)$, where S_0 is the original stock price of the problem, we obtain an accurate approximation

$$C_1(S, X, t_{n-1}, T) \approx C_{\text{BSM}}(S, X_{\text{adj}}, \sigma_{\text{adj}}, t_{n-1}, T)$$

that often differs by less than a penny over the full range of S on $(0, \infty)$.

This same scheme is used at successive iterations of the exact integration. That is, the "previous" iteration will always be fast because it uses the BSM formula. Then, after you get the answer, you approximate that answer by a BSM formula parameterization. In that parameterization, you

TABLE 3.6:   EUROPEAN CALLS WITH MULTIPLE DIVIDENDS OF 4
($S = 100$, $X = 100$, $r = 6\%$, $\sigma = 25\%$, $D = 4$)

T	Num	Vol2	Vol3	BV	HHL	Appr	Adjusted strike	Adjusted volatility
1	10.6615	10.6585	10.6530	10.6596	10.6606	10.6606	104.122	0.2467
2	15.2024	15.1780	15.1673	15.1992	15.1989	15.1996	108.499	0.2421
3	18.5798	18.5348	18.5241	18.5981	18.5984	18.5998	113.146	0.2375
4	–	21.2297	21.2304	21.3592	–	21.3644	118.081	0.2328
5	–	23.4666	23.4941	23.6868	–	23.6978	123.320	0.2282
6	–	23.3556	25.4279	25.6907	–	25.7100	128.884	0.2237
7	–	26.9661	27.1023	27.4395	–	27.4695	–	–

choose an adjusted strike price and an adjusted volatility to fit the large-S behavior and the S_0 value. This enables you to move on to the next iteration.

Table 3.6 reports call option values when there is a dividend payment of 4 in the middle of each year. The first column shows the years to expiration for the contracts we consider. The models Vol2, Vol3, BV, and Num are identical to the ones described earlier. HHL is our closed form solution from Section 2 evaluated by numerical quadrature. As we have already mentioned, this approach is computer intensive. We have therefore limited ourselves to value options with this method with up to three dividend payments. An efficient implementation in for instance C++ will naturally make this approach viable for any practical number of dividend payments. Non-recombining trees are even more computer intensive, especially for multiple dividends. They also entail problems with propagation of errors when the number of time steps is increased, so we limited ourselves to compute option values for three dividends (3 years to maturity), with 500 time steps for $T = 1, 2$, and 1000 time steps for $T = 3$. The column Appr is the approximation just described above. The two rightmost columns report the adjusted strike and volatility used in this approximation method.

The approximation we suggest above (Appr) is clearly very accurate, when compared to our exact integration (HHL). Also the non-recombining binomial implementation (Num) of the spot process yields results very close to our exact integration. Vol2 and Vol3 seems to give rise to significant mispricing with multiple dividends. The BV approximation seems somewhat more accurate. However, as we already know, it significantly misprices options when the dividend is very high. From a trader's perspective, our approach seems to be a clear choice – at least if you care about having a robust and accurate model that will work in "any" situation. Remember also that our method is valid for any price process, including stochastic volatility, jumps, and other factors that can have a significant impact on pricing and hedging.

Exotic and real options: Several exotic options trade in the OTC equity market, and many are embedded in warrants and other complex equity derivatives. The exact model treatment of options on dividend paying stocks presented in this chapter holds also in these cases. Many exotic options, in particular barrier options, are known to be very sensitive to stochastic volatility. Luckily the model described above also holds for stochastic volatility, jumps, volatility term structure, as well as other factors that can be of vital importance when pricing exotic options. The model we have suggested should also be relevant to real options pricing, when the underlying asset offers known discrete payouts (of generic nature) during the lifetime of the real option.

Appendix A

The following is a volatility adjustment that has been suggested used in combination with the escrowed dividend model. The adjustment seems to have been discovered independently by Haug and Haug (1998) (unpublished working paper), as well as by Beneder and Vorst (2001). σ in the BSM formula is replaced with σ_{adj}, and the stock price minus the present value of the dividends until expiration is substituted for the stock price.

$$
\sigma_{\mathrm{adj}}^2 = \left(\frac{S\sigma}{S - \sum_{i=1}^{n} D_i e^{rt_i}}\right)^2 (t_1 - t_0) + \left(\frac{S\sigma}{S - \sum_{i=2}^{n} D_i e^{rt_i}}\right)^2 (t_2 - t_1) + \cdots + \sigma^2(T - t_n)
$$

$$
= \sum_{j=1}^{n} \left(\frac{S\sigma}{S - \sum_{i=j}^{n} D_i e^{rt_i}}\right)^2 (t_j - t_{j-1}) + \sigma^2(T - t_n)
$$

This method seems to work better than for instance the volatility adjustment discussed by Chriss (1997), among others. However, this is still simply a rough approximation, without much of a theory behind it. For this reason, there is no guarantee for it to be accurate in all circumstances. Any such model could be dangerous for a trader to use.

Appendix B

Bos et al. (2003) suggest the following volatility adjustment to be used in combination with the escrowed dividend adjustment:

$$
\sigma(S, X, T)^2 = \sigma^2 + \sigma\sqrt{\frac{\pi}{2T}}\left\{4e^{\frac{z_1^2}{2}-s}\sum_{i=1}^{n} D_i e^{-rt_i}\left[N(z_1) - N\left(z_1 - \sigma\frac{t_i}{\sqrt{T}}\right)\right]\right.
$$

$$
\left. + e^{\frac{z_2^2}{2}-2s}\sum_{i}^{n}\sum_{j}^{n} D_i D_j e^{-r(t_i+t_j)}\left[N(z_2) - N\left(z_2 - \frac{2\sigma\min(t_i, t_j)}{\sqrt{T}}\right)\right]\right\},
$$

where n is the number of dividends in the option's lifetime, $s = \ln(S)$, $x = \ln[(X + D_T)e^{-rT}]$, where $D_T = \sum_{i}^{n} D_i e^{-rt_i}$, and

$$
z_1 = \frac{s - x}{\sigma\sqrt{T}} + \frac{\sigma\sqrt{T}}{2}, \qquad z_2 = z_1 + \frac{\sigma\sqrt{T}}{2}.
$$

FOOTNOTES & REFERENCES

1. An alternative to discrete cash dividend is discrete dividend yield. Implementation of discrete dividend yield is well known and straight forward using recombining lattice models (see for instance Haug, 1997; Hull, 2000). Typically, however, at least the first dividend is known in advance with some confidence. Discrete cash dividend models consequently seem to have been the models of choice among practitioners, despite having to deal with a more complex modeling problem. For very long term options the predictability of future dividends is less pronounced, and dividends should be somewhat correlated with the stock price level. Moreover, cash dividends tend to be reduced following a significant stock price decrease. If the stock price rallies, on the other hand, it indicates that the company is doing better than expected, which again can result in higher cash dividends. For very long term options then, it is likely that the discrete dividend yield model can be a competing model to the discrete cash dividend model.

2. Except, to our knowledge (which, unlike the universe, is limited) Wilmott et al. (1993, p. 399), who mention this problem and suggest to let the company go bankrupt if the dividend is larger than the asset price. This approach avoids negative stock prices. Moreover, McDonald (2003, p. 352) points out this problem, and suggests using the approach of Schroder (1988). As we have already pointed out, this method has other flaws.

3. Coleman (1985), speaking of Fermi's theory of the 'Weak force': *Phrased another way, the Fermi theory is obviously dead wrong because it predicts infinite higher-order corrections, but it is experimentally near perfect, because there are few experiments for which lowest-order Fermi theory is inadequate.*

4. The Markov assumption is for simplicity. Perhaps it can be relaxed. We leave this issue open.

■ **Beneder, R. and T. Vorst** (2001) "Options on Dividends Paying Stocks," in "Proceedings of the International Conference on Mathematical Finance". Shanghai.

■ **Black, F.** (1975) "Fact and Fantasy In the Use of Options," *Financial Analysts Journal*, July–August, 36–72.

■ ———— **and M. Scholes** (1973) "The Pricing of Options and Corporate Liabilities," *Journal of Political Economy*, May–June, **81**, 637–654.

■ **Bos, R., A. Gairat and A. Shepeleva** (2003) "Dealing with Discrete Dividends," *Risk*, **16**(1), 109–112.

■ ———— **and S. Vandermark** (2002) "Finesssing Fixed Dividends," *Risk*, **15**(9), 157–158.

■ **Chriss, N. A.** (1997) *Black-Scholes and Beyond: Option Pricing Models*. New York: McGraw-Hill.

■ **Coleman, S.** (1985) *Aspects of Symmetry: Selected Erice Lectures*. Cambridge: Cambridge University Press.

■ **Cox, J. C. and M. Rubinstein** (1985) *Options Markets*. Englewood Cliffs, New Jersey: Prentice-Hall.

■ **Delbaen, F. and W. Schachermayer** (1995) "The Existence of Absolutely Continuous Local Martingale Measures," *Annals of Applied Probability*, **5**(4), 926–945.

■ **Frishling, V.** (2002) "A Discrete Question," *Risk*, **15**(1).

■ **Geske, R.** (1979) "A Note on an Analytic Valuation Formula for Unprotected American Call Options on Stocks with Known Dividends," *Journal of Financial Economics*, **7**, 375–380.

■ ———— (1981) "Comments on Whaley's Note," *Journal of Financial Economics*, **9**, 213–215.

■ **Harrison, M. J. and D. M. Kreps** (1979) "Martingales and Arbitrage in Multiperiod Securities Markets," *Journal of Economic Theory*, **20**, 381–408.

■ **Harrison, J.M. and S. Pliska** (1981) "Martingales and Stochastic Integrals in the Theory of Continuous Trading," *Stochastic Processes and Their Applications*, **11**, 215–260.

■ **Haug, E. G.** (1997) *The Complete Guide to Option Pricing Formulas*. New York: McGraw-Hill, 1997.

■ ——— **and J. Haug** (1996) "Implied Forward Volatility" Presented at the Third Nordic Symposium on Contingent Claims Analysis in Finance.

■ ——— **and J. Haug** (1998) "A New Look at Pricing Options with Time Varying Volatility" Unpublished working paper.

■ **Hull, J.** (2000) *Options, Futures, and Other Derivatives*, 4th ed. Englewood Cliffs, New Jersey: Prentice-Hall.

■ **McDonald, R. L.** (2003) *Derivatives Markets*. Upper Saddle River, New Jersey: Pearson Education.

■ **Merton, R. C.** (1973) "Theory of Rational Option Pricing," *Bell Journal of Economics and Management Science*, **4**, 141–183.

■ **Roll, R.** (1977) "An Analytical Formula for Unprotected American Call Options on Stocks with Known Dividends," *Journal of Financial Economics*, **5**, 251–258.

■ **Schroder, M.** (1988) "Adapting the Binomial Model to Value Options on Assets with Fixed-cash Payouts," *Financial Analysts Journal*, **44**(6), 54–62.

■ **Stoll, H. R. and R. E. Whaley** (1993) *Futures and Options: Theory and Applications The Current Issues in Finance*. Cincinnati, Ohio: South-Western.

■ **Whaley, R. E.** (1981) "On the Valuation of American Call Options on Stocks with Known Dividends," *Journal of Financial Economics*, **9**, 207–211.

■ **Wilmott, P.,** (2000) *Paul Wilmott on Quantitative Finance*, Chichester: John Wiley & Sons, Ltd.

■ ——— **, J. Dewynne and S. Howison** (1993) *Option Pricing: Mathematical Models and Computation*, Oxford: Oxford Financial Press.

Professor Emanuel Derman in his office at Columbia University (Photo: Amber Gray)

Emanuel Derman
the Wall Street Quant

Emanuel Derman was one of the first on Wall Street to leave theoretical physics and become a successful quant. He started out with a PhD in theoretical particle physics from Columbia University. He worked for several years as a post doctorate doing research in theoretical physics. He then worked for several years for Bell Laboratories before he moved to Wall Street and Goldman Sachs. Here he came into contact with Fischer Black and together with Bill Toy they came up with the Black-Derman-Toy one factor interest rate model. After spending a short period in Salomon Brothers he again returned to Goldman Sachs where Fischer Black had just moved to a different position, so Derman took over running the Quantitative Strategies group. This group did some very interesting research on convertible bonds, exotic options, implied tree models, variance swaps and much more. Some years ago Emanuel Derman returned to academia and is now a Professor at Columbia University, but still with a foot in Wall Street, being involved in a hedge fund.

Between 1991 and 1996 I was working with trading and market making of fixed income options for Den norske Bank and Chemical Bank (now J.P. Morgan Chase). The Black-Derman-Toy model had been one of the option models I was most interested in, the entire bond option market was talking about the BDT model at that time. While writing my book "Option Pricing Formulas" I was looking into implementation of implied tree models. Here also Derman together with Iraj Kani (also at Goldman) had been among those who pioneered the idea of extracting implied stochastic risk neutral process of the underlying asset from the volatility surface of liquid options.

In 1998 I was visiting my brother at Wharton in Philadelphia where he had just finished part of his PhD studies in mathematical finance. I was planning to visit New York City one day. I contacted Emanuel Derman by email for the first time and asked if he had time to meet for a cup of coffee. A few days later I was walking around down town Manhattan. I made sure I was there early, deciding that it was better to walk around the Goldman building at 85 Broad Street a few times instead of being late. I took the elevator up to the twenty-ninth floor, where Emanuel Derman himself met me. He was extremely friendly and the complete opposite of an arrogant Wall Street hot shot. My experience has been that most good quants on Wall Streets seem in general much nicer than most traders or political managers. Quants are typically in the business not only for the money, but also just as much if not more so for the joy of being able to apply their math and imagination to the fast growing field of quantitative finance. Derman first took me to his office where we had a nice chat. Next he showed me around the Quantitative Strategy group and introduced me to a couple of the people he worked with on some research ideas. Derman seemed happy to share his knowledge and he gave me copies of a large stack of Quantitive Strategy research working papers. The entire Quantitative Strategy group had in my view made Goldman Sachs famous among quant traders. This was one of the reasons one wanted to do business with Goldman, in order to get hold of their state of the art derivatives research.

Derman later on the same day asked if I was looking for a job. Well actually I had been thinking about it, and who would not dream of working for Goldman Sachs and for a guru like Derman? However, I felt Derman and his team were light years ahead of me when it came to quant skills. I felt I had little to offer, not that he had offered me a job. My edge was a combination of quant skills with considerable trading experience, something I still consider to be my edge. I told Derman so, and the same day he set me up with an interview with the head of a trading department. The chemistry between myself and the head of trading was not good, he had a very different personality than Derman. I felt like the head of trading was talking down to me, but anyway it was a great experience, and in particular the meeting with Derman and his Quantitative Strategy group was very inspiring.

A year later I moved to the US, trading for a hedge fund in Greenwich Connecticut. I have maintained contact with Emanuel Derman, since then meeting up at some quant related dinner or conference.

Haug : You started out with theoretical physics and switched to quantitative finance, why?

Derman : Destiny of some kind, I suppose, plus an affection for a little personal risk. I was a product of the Sixties, when everything – personal, social and scientific – seemed possible. Wonderful breakthroughs were being made in particle physics and I had a strong desire to do something wonderful myself.

I switched to quantitative finance much later, more or less by accident. If you'd told me even five years before I switched that I would end up working on Wall Street, I wouldn't even have bothered to laugh. But life takes its own course. I left physics mainly because getting a job in a suitable location became exceedingly difficult. So, I took a job at Bell Labs in 1980, when Bell was the haven for career-switching physicists that Wall Street is now. I didn't like it there, and so, five years later, I took another chance and accepted a position at Goldman.

Haug : What are the main differences between physics and finance?

Derman : There's one gigantic difference: in physics, divination (i.e. theorizing, modeling, plucking ideas out of your head) works well. God knows why (at least I hope he does). In finance, it works poorly.

The problem is the (ostensible) difference between mind and matter. Physics is concerned with matter. A true theory can predict the future to an astonishing degree of accuracy.

To make a theory you have to look long and hard at the world, detect the hint of a pattern, and then somehow miraculously come up with a structure that incorporates and extends that pattern. Once in a while it turns out to be pretty close to true. You can't read a theory in the book of nature; you have to divine it. And divination works amazingly well.

Finance is entirely different. It's concerned with things of the mind: money and value. You can write down all the partial or stochastic differential equations you are capable of, and the way people behave will still confound your theory. Theorizing isn't useless in finance and other social sciences, it's just much less effective. One of the hard parts is figuring out how to make good use of theories that are only very very approximately correct.

Haug : In physics many researchers are searching for the Theory of Everything, do you believe there are such thing in physics and what about finance?

Derman : I don't believe there is a Theory of Everything for finance at all. Ask rather: **Is There a Theory of Anything?**

I suppose it's unlikely there's a Theory of Everything for physics either.

There are many *Models of Anything*. But are they real theories? There have been great conceptual advances in the last fifty years, but to a large extent they are magnificent engineering advances rather than scientific ones. Mechanical engineering is built on Newton's laws, which are pretty accurate, almost true. Financial engineering is built largely on geometric Brownian motion, which is less accurate. Mean-variance theory is elegant but it assumes you know the expected means and variances, and you don't. It assumes normality of returns, and they aren't normal (fat-tails etc.). CAPM builds on that. Dynamic replication is the greatest triumph, but has its limits too: you need to know the stochastic process beneath the replication, and you need to be able to hedge more or less continuously without friction.

One of the things I've noticed recently during conversations with academic economists or students of the subject is that they often don't clearly understand the difference between "right" and "true." "Right" means self-consistent, logically correct. "True" means describing the real world accurately. Some economists conflate the two; they think if something is right then it's equivalent to being true. Physicists, who've seen theories that are correct to ten significant figures, can't help but know the difference between right and true.

Because of the mismatch between true and right, I'm very negative about optimization in finance. Optimization is great when you have a GPS navigation system and you want to find the shortest route, because you know the lengths of each segment of parkway or road. But optimization makes little sense when the future scenarios you're optimizing over are right but not true.

I don't mean to be a spoilsport or a sour graper; I'd be ecstatic if I'd invented any of the theories I mentioned above, but they have their limits, and there will never be a theory of everything in this discipline.

I think that models are metaphors. A theory of everything means a single metaphor for everything. Is there one? I'm tempted to say Ommmmmm. Somehow this reminds me of a deep metaphor I read by Schopenhauer: "Sleep is the interest we have to pay on the capital which is called in at death; and the higher the rate of interest and the more regularly it is paid, the further the date of redemption is postponed." Now there's a metaphor worth many right but not true models.

Haug : During what period did you work with Fischer Black?

Derman : The first time was for about 18 months from mid-1986 to the end of 1987 when we worked on BDT. And the second time was in the early 90s when Fischer, Iraj Kani and I collaborated on a two-factor version of BDT which we never completed. Aside from that that we had occasional regular interactions.

Haug : **How long did it take Fischer Black, Bill Toy and yourself from starting to develop a new bond option model to your publishing the model in 1990?**

Derman : We finished a version of the model in early 1987, and had traders using it shortly thereafter. But Fischer was a perfectionist, and didn't want to publish it until he was happy with the model and the write-up. Next we tried to generalize BDT to two factors, the level of rates and their slope. Then we started to incorporate mean reversion, which later blossomed into Black-Karasinski. Though BDT had been completed and in production for several years, we submitted a paper to FAJ much later, most likely in 1989.

Haug : **Was it Fischer Black who inspired you to write papers about complex ideas in a way that also is understandable for traders who are often less interested in pages filled with mathematical proofs?**

Derman : Definitely so. Fischer was obsessive to the point of mania about writing simply. His style was his own, but he did motivate me to write as qualitatively and clearly as possible. I grew to enjoy exposition and writing at least as much as I liked finance.

Haug : **Back in 1994 you and a couple of people in the Quantitative Strategy group did some work on convertible bonds. The model despite its simplicity became to my knowledge very popular among convertible bond traders, can you describe briefly the main idea behind the model?**

Derman : It was a very simple model that took account of the equity-linked options in a convertible bond: the right to convert, the right to put and the possibility of being called. It treated all of these as hedgeable options in a Cox-Ross-Rubinstein binomial framework. Our model became popular because both the idea and the exposition were clear and it was therefore easy to put into production. Few trading desks had the resources to treat convertibles that way before. One other nice feature of the model was that it incorporated credit risk (in a naive and flawed but nevertheless useful way) by making the discount rate in the option valuation model interpolate between the riskless rate and the corporate risky rate systematically.

In those days convertibles were cheap relative to the model, but I think many hedge funds started to use our model and later prices tracked those of the model more closely, or so I'm told.

Haug : **In 1994 you published a paper together with Iraj Kani, "The Volatility Smile and Its Implied Tree", how was this related to Dupire's and Mark Rubinstein's work on the same topic published about the same year?**

Derman : That's kind of ancient history, described at length in my book. Black-Scholes assumes a constant stock volatility in the future, no matter what the stock price does. Rubinstein, Dupire and I all had the idea that you could explain the volatility smile by assuming that volatility depends on market level. For the S&P you find that volatility often does seem to rise when the market falls, and vice versa. Iraj and I showed that, given the implied volatilities at some instant of time of options of all strikes and expirations, i.e the volatility smile, you could extract a unique volatility (the local volatility) as function of future stock price and time, and we demonstrated how to do that in a binomial context. Dupire did the same thing in a continuous time framework. And Rubinstein did something similar too, but he had to make more restrictive assumptions about how local volatilities vary with time.

The key point is that the future volatility of the stock or index in the model is calibrated so as to make all the dynamically replicated option prices with this variable volatility exactly match current options market prices.

Haug : For people having a hard time grasping implied tree models; can we say that this in one way is a very sophisticated form of interpolation?

Derman : If you work as a practitioner, and you pay attention to the world around you, you soon realize that all options models are rational sophisticated forms of interpolation to take you from the prices of liquid fungible securities to the values of illiquid exotic ones. Black-Scholes interpolates from the known prices of a stock and a riskless bond to the value of an option. A convertible bond is a centaur, half risky bond, half stock. Convertible bond models take you from the liquid stock price and the liquid risky bond price to the value of the centaur, the hybrid itself.

Similarly, implied trees interpolate or extrapolate from the known prices of standard options of all strikes and expirations (the smile) to the value of an exotic option via a rational model based on dynamic replication.

Haug : One of the main weaknesses with the standard implied tree models seems to be that they do not take into account that the volatility surface actually is changing over time. In 1998 you and Iraj Kani tried to extend the implied tree method to take this into account, can you give us a quick briefing on this topic?

Derman : Implied tree models assume fixed future local volatilities after the calibration, and you know of course that that can't be true. Volatilities change. As a result, the process underlying implied tree models doesn't match the true stock process (assuming you can ever know what that is), and so implied tree models have to be recalibrated regularly. But, show me an options model (or indeed any financial model) that doesn't need regular recalibration and I'll show you something that isn't of much use.

Re the weaknesses of implied tree models: A few years after we developed the implied tree model, I actually looked at the behavior of implied volatilities in a paper called Regimes of Volatility, and found that index equity markets tend to drift up slowly or crash down fast. Stéphane Crépey recently wrote a very nice paper in Quantitative Finance showing that, given this characteristic of index equity markets, regularly recalibrated implied tree models should provide better hedging than Black-Scholes. He then examined the empirical behavior of past index options prices and found that this seems to be true. Implied trees led to less P&L variance than Black-Scholes.

Kani and I extended the implied tree model by allowing the evolution of the local volatilities to be stochastic, a la HJM. (The HJM interest rate model makes forward rates stochastic. We made local volatilities, which are the analogs of forward rates in fixed income, to be stochastic.) The advantage of this approach is that there are fewer constraints on forward volatilities than on implied volatilities, so satisfying the no-arbitrage condition is relatively easy. But the model turned out to be very complicated and calculation-intensive.

Haug : How are the implied tree models different from stochastic volatility models?

Derman : In implied tree models, the future (local) volatility of the stock varies with stock price; volatility is a deterministic function of a stochastic stock price. Implied tree models are one-factor models. In stochastic volatility models the volatility of the stock is genuinely random in its own right, with a volatility of volatility. So, a stochastic volatility model has two (possibly correlated) random variables, the stock price and its volatility.

Haug : In the Jungle of models trying to describe the volatility smile how should a trader or risk manager decide on what model to use?

Derman : The sad truth is the impossibility of an absolutely right model. A model in finance is merely a useful approximation to the real world. What you should do is use perturbation theory. Decide, if you can, what's the dominant contributor to the volatility smile in the particular market you trade. Start with that kind of model. Then add corrections for other contributing factors.

For example, in the world of currency options the most important deviation from the Black-Scholes assumptions is probably stochastic volatility, so start with that type of model. Then, add local volatility corrections to the stochastic volatility model. In contrast, for interest rates, where volatility seems to vary systematically with the level of rates, the dominant contribution to the smile is local volatility, so begin with that and then add stochastic volatility effects. For equity options, jumps may be most important for short expirations; begin with that and then add bits of the other models.

In each case you should assess your market, use the dominant model to get the zeroth order effects, and then add the next most critical mechanism to achieve the final calibration. None of this is going to be perfect, and at various times market forces will confound even well-constructed and realistic models, so a trader has to overlay the model with a great deal of common sense and experience about how regimes change.

Haug : In the long run how does the market choose between what models to use, is it the survival of the fittest or do you think marketing of the model also plays an important role?

Derman : I think you've put your finger on it. It isn't one thing because no single model is correct. In finance, models are more of an aid to insight than an algorithm for getting the right value. I think there are three qualities that count: (1) whether the model does do a reasonable job of describing the dynamics of the underlyer and its volatility; (2) how well the model allows you to gain insight by giving you a few clear conceptual variables you can use to stress your view of the world; and (3) how well it's marketed.

I always think of OAS in this connection; it's useful but by no means perfect, and it isn't necessarily a good measure of value. But Salomon Bros. marketed it to all their clients in the Eighties, and it became a standard.

Why do people need models so badly? Because they want a metric, a one-dimensional scale on which to rank value. But value isn't one-dimensional; nevertheless, people yearn for a model that lines up a wide range of instruments on a one-dimensional value scale. Look at OAS, yield-to-maturity, implied volatility, etc. And, if you want an even better example, look at IQ. It's clear that intelligence is a multi-dimensional, soft quality, and yet they've marketed the model of IQ as a hard quantity very successfully.

Haug : Do you think the price on derivatives is mainly driven by stochastic process of the underlying asset, or can it be that a model and our understanding of a model at any given time influence the derivatives prices? In other words do the most popular quant models impact the prices?

Derman : I think models do impact the prices. Once a model gives the market a way to think about things, people use it to set prices too.

I know one very clear example of this. When I worked at Salomon Bros on adjustable rate mortgages, the traders used the OAS model to back out OAS's from mortgage prices. One day we decided to take the desk's historical mortgage prices (marked by the traders in an OTC market) and then try to build a factor model. The first thing we did was convert the mortgage prices the traders gave us to OAS, only to discover that the OAS remained constant for long periods of time and then suddenly changed to a new value, then remaining there for a long period, and so on. What was happening was that the traders were generating the mortgage prices from their estimates of OAS's, and their OAS estimates stayed constant for a long period and then suddenly changed. Maybe they were too lazy to change them every day; equally likely it was hard to figure out how to change them in small increments.

I've seen the same thing with volatilities ten years ago. I tried to back out the volatility spread between at-the-money and 25-delta CAC options from our traders marks on options prices. It turned out that, though the implied volatilities of at-the-money and out-of-the-money options varied widely over time, the spread between stayed constant for long periods. The traders were generating the marks for out-of-the-money options from at-the-money volatility and their estimate of the spread, which they changed rarely.

Haug : In your book you say, "complexity without calibration is pointless". Can you comment on this principle?

Derman : The most effective use of models is as tools to determine relative value. Relative to what? Relative to the liquid securities you calibrate to. Simple is better, because models take parameters you have a feel for as inputs. A complex model – I've seen naive people build models that simultaneously allow for stochastic volatility, local volatility, jump diffusion and God knows what else – can lead to any result you like. Simplicity and then calibration are critical to priming the model.

If you don't calibrate you are trying to calculate absolute value relative to nothing, and that doesn't work well in finance. It works miserably.

Haug : You also published some work in 1999 on discontinuous hedging in relation to the Black-Scholes formula, what were the main results from this work?

Derman : This was a paper (*When You Cannot Hedge Continuously*) written together with Mike Kamal, now a bio-informatics guy at M.I.T. (He started as a physicist, worked on Wall Street, and now does something totally different. One of the great things about the U.S.A. is how you can change careers with no prejudice.)

The main result, and it wasn't really a new one, as I later found out, was that when you of necessity hedge discretely rather than continuously, you get large errors in the cost of replicating the option, even if you pretend to know the future volatility. The error in an at-the-money option price corresponds to an error in the volatility of order $1/\sqrt{N}$, where N

is the number of times you hedge over the life of the option. That's a large error for typical values of N, and makes you wonder how market-makers use Black-Scholes to make money reliably. I think the answer is that they don't hedge single options – if they're sensible they try to run an approximately vega- and gamma-neutral book of as many options as possible, and just hedge the residual gamma sensitivity. *Minimize your dependence on the model* is the rule of the game.

Haug : How important is timing in quant finance, to be at the right place at the right time as opposed to hard work and excellent quant skills, or do you need it all?

Derman : The more gifts you can get from the universe, the better. But timing is very important: you want to get into a field early when zeroth order insights will have a large impact; it's much more difficult to have an impact on an already sophisticated field. It also helps to have smart and interesting colleagues on both the trading and quant sides who can bring challenging phenomena to your attention.

Hard work and excellent skills are prerequisites, but you also need good fortune, in all fields. But then again, fortune favors the well-prepared.

Haug : In 1999 you and some co-workers also came out with some interesting research on variance/volatility swaps and how to hedge such products, can you tell us briefly about this work?

Derman : After our work on local volatility models and exotic options, we began to think of volatility as an asset class. Furthermore, in 1996 some of our traders were beginning to try to trade volatility more in a more organized fashion by means of positions in straddles. We (Kresimir Demeterfi, Mike Kamal, Iraj Kani, Joe Zou, and myself) began to look at the problem more systematically.

The trouble with trading stock volatility by means of hedged stock options positions is that, though you do indeed get volatility exposure, that exposure varies with the stock price level. You don't get a clean exposure to volatility. It's a bit like trying to trade credit by trading corporate bonds, which are sensitive to both riskless interest rates and credit, and are also relatively illiquid. The solution to that challenge was to create credit default swaps, which give you pure credit exposure. One wants to do the same for volatility, i.e. get pure volatility exposure independent of stock price.

Sometime in 1996 we came across Neuberger's very clever paper on the log contract. We then wrote a Quantitative Strategies Research Note called *Investing in Volatility*. We pointed out that if you buy a single option, and hedge it, your exposure to variance (the variance-vega) varies with stock price. If you want to trade variance alone, then you want a variance-vega that is independent of stock price. We showed that a portfolio of options, suitably weighted by the inverse of the strike squared, has a variance-vega that's independent of the stock price. We also showed that the sum of those options has the payoff of the log contract that Neuberger discussed. So, you can replicate a log contract with a bunch of options.

In the 1999 paper, we expanded on this by analyzing how well the replication worked when you couldn't trade continuous or far out-of-the-money strikes. We also estimated the fair value of these contracts in the presence of the ubiquitous volatility smile. Finally, we showed that volatility should be thought of as a derivative contract on variance, since volatility is the square root of variance, and therefore a volatility contract's value depends on the volatility of variance.

Eventually the CBOE used our replication formula to redefine the VIX volatility index.

Variance swaps became a big business. Zhenyu Duanmu of Merrill Lynch once pointed out in a talk at Columbia that what allowed variance swaps to become a high volume business was the fact that there existed in advance a model to replicate it. He thought that the best sequence was for a simple usable model to drive product development rather than a product to demand (often complex) model development.

Haug : You have been full time both in academia and on Wall Street, what is the main difference between working as a quant in academia as opposed to Wall Street?

Derman : On Wall Steet you're putting your money where your mouth is, and you have to walk a delicate line between theory and practicality. Simple is beautiful.

In academia you're freer to think about whatever you like, but that freedom isn't always productive. The convex combination of academia and Wall Street would be very nice.

Haug : Any views on patenting in quantitative finance? Could this be a way to distribute some of the big bonuses from traders using the quantitative finance models over to the researchers and quants that did the hard work coming up with the models?

Derman : In my gut I'm against patenting formulas and models and algorithms. It may be irrational, but I find it weird to patent mental things. I suppose you could argue that a new computer chip is also a mental thing in origin, so perhaps I'm inconsistent. But nevertheless.

I don't think patenting will help quantitative people to get paid more, except in rare cases. It's perception of quants that counts, and, as the Beatles said, it's getting better all the time.

Haug : From your interesting book "My Life as a Quant", I see that you have been involved in long distance running, do you think physical exercise has also been an important part of your winning formula in quantitative finance?

Derman : My winning formula? You must be kidding. Actually, I came up with it by running a gigantic Monte Carlo simulation over all scenarios weighted by my utility function.

I just like running. It's exhilarating to run far, be tired, and yet still feel you can accelerate when you have to. When I was a kid long distance runners were our heroes. And it's one of the few things you can do in NYC without great start-up costs in time and money and travel. But it is true that sometimes, if you've been working on something very hard for a long time without success, the solution comes to you while you're taking a run or showering.

Haug : Some years back when submitting a paper I once used the word Quant, the referee told me I had to remove the word Quant as it was not part of the English vocabulary. Is the word Quant still a slang word or is becoming a well-established word in the English finance vocabulary?

Derman : Years ago I disliked the word, and then one day I read in Gary Gastineau's and Mark Kritzman's Dictionary of Financial Risk Management that the word was "often pejorative".

I liked that because I thought it was true then, though it's less true today. I chose the title of my book, "My Life as a Quant" because it reminded me of Lasse Hallstrom's movie "My Life as a Dog"; it's a dog's life, it's a quant's life. You can call yourself a quant, but it used to be insulting when other people called you that. It reminds me of the way black or gay people have developed a similar way of referring to themselves by formerly disparaging adjectives. It takes the sting out of it.

Haug : When did you come up with most of your ideas, in the office, when talking to others or when out doing long distance running? In other words what do you think is the best environment for coming up with good quant finance ideas?

Derman : I think investment banks or hedge funds are great places to come up with ideas. Work with markets and people who live by them, talk to people around you, learn how they use models, experience what works and what doesn't, and then go to a quiet place and struggle for a long time. Then take a break. If you're lucky you'll think of a good solution.

Haug : In trading my experience is that traders are often more than happy to "steal" good trading ideas or strategies from competitors (and also from co-workers), it is more or less accepted and part of the game. I have heard some academics claiming that similar things are going on in quantitative research. Is it important to hold the cards close to your chest until you get published?

Derman : Finance is largely an ideas business. Assets are more mental than material. And there's always a little theft in all creative work. It's not a bad idea to keep research ideas in narrow circulation until you publish them. But it is important to get them published.

Haug : Goldman Sachs and other investment banks seemed to be more willing to share their quantitative research in form of publications during the 1980s and 1990s than they are today. Today many investment banks seem to be holding on to their research, any views on this?

Derman : It's not a trend I like, though I can understand it. I liked the attitude of the 1980s and 1990s. I thought of finance as a science in which you contributed to the whole field of knowledge, and I ran the Quantitative Strategies group at Goldman that way as much as I could, as long as it didn't conflict with our business. And the truth is it helped our business; more clients wanted to talk to us and read our publications, and it made it easier to attract outstanding employees when we had a research team that was highly visible in the outside world.

Nowadays everyone is forced to be unnecessarily secretive. I've sometimes invited people from industry to give talks to my class at Columbia – merely introductory talks that are not intended to reveal any sorcerer's secrets about making money or committing arbitrage. Nevertheless, the people I invite are often reluctant to give a talk because they feel their managers will disapprove; they're reluctant to even ask their managers for permission for fear they'll seem too disloyal or too academic. To me that's a misguided notion of loyalty and paranoia. You obviously need some secrecy in a business, but minimize it rather than keep everything secret.

Haug : When working on some of my more "crazy" ideas (some of them in this book) I sometimes feel that I am in the zone between being a crank and a scientist. Have you ever felt the same and also how does one know one has not stepped over the line?

Derman : Finance is a strange field, one part science and three parts opinion. As a result it's very hard to tell what's cranky and what's right. Nutrition is similar. What they both have in common is that their clients desperately want the practitioner to have an opinion, right or wrong. So practitioners of both fields tell their clients anything that sounds right and is more or less defensible.

You know you've begun to step on the line when you take your models and formulas too seriously and think the world has to obey them. But it's very tempting to think you can find a formula that explains everything. Science is a miraculous kind of magic; cranks and scientists aren't that different – same aims, not totally dissimilar methods.

You know how people – cranks? – in the "spiritual" business talk about "energy?" Nowadays energy has a precise quantitative meaning in physics; it's not vague at all. But I once read somewhere that Newton took the word energy from a much vaguer use of it that was closer to the way people in the spiritual business use it today.

Haug : **Is there any advice that you would give to someone fresh from school that is seeking a Wall Street career. Should they get a Masters degree in Financial Engineering or a PhD?**

Derman : Try and work for a year in a finance business and see what it's like before spending a long time getting a degree in it. Do what you like doing, not what people think is good for you. Give it a shot and then compromise if you can't make a go of it.

Haug : **Do you have any hobbies outside quantitative finance and long distance running?**

Derman : Reading, movies, theatre, and most of all writing, which I enjoy the most. I'm working on a textbook and maybe a novel.

Haug : **In your view where are we in the evolution of quantitative finance?**

Derman : I would guess that dramatic advances in the theory of derivatives are reaching an end. You can go only so far with replication, no matter how many theorems you prove. The next big step, if there is one, is to develop much better theories of underlyers.

Look how underdeveloped our theory of underlyers is.

Mean-variance theory, though it sparked much of the quantitative approach to financial modeling, is not that useful in practice, because it deals with optimizing over estimated future means and estimated variances, and those estimations are wildly inaccurate.

The Capital Asset Pricing Model in the end doesn't do practitioners that much good either. Both CapM and mean-variance theory are theories of underlyers, and their trouble is that they are tightly linked to geometric Brownian motion. Options pricing theory is much more useful and robust, because it can transcend geometric Brownian motion more easily, and because it's a theory of relative value, of interpolation.

The place where you can get the most bang for your buck is dealing with underlyers. One needs better empirical data (the econophysicists are providing this) and better models to explain it – fat-tails, jumps, volatility spikes and their persistence, scaling, the works.

Behavioral finance is obviously an evolving area, but I'm a little skeptical about its potential as a positive field. From the outside it seems to have more of a negative tone: this is wrong, that doesn't work, people are bad at estimation. But what should you do about it?

I've always been a little fascinated by theories that involve changes of time scale, and in particular theories that involve changes in the perception of time. Clark introduced the idea of trading time many years ago, and it's plausible to me that people perceive short term risk in trading time rather than calendar time. Various researchers have claimed that returns appear more normal in trading time. These studies seem to close the gap between behavioral and neoclassical finance in a quantitative rather than merely qualitative fashion

Haug : Do you think the derivatives markets and the most popular models used can affect the underlying asset price behavior itself?

Derman : Yes. Lasse Pedersen wrote a paper on this subject recently. When there is a large volume of derivatives held by market makers who hedge them, then the hedging itself can move the underlying market, much the way portfolio insurance did in the late 1980s. Marco Avellaneda and Mike Lipkin demonstrated that pinning, the tendency for underlying prices to move towards the strike as options approach expiration, can be caused by hedging.

Haug : Why did financial researchers start out with continuous time and then use numerical methods like binomial trees to approximate the continuous process? I thought that price movement and possibly even time are discrete so why not the other way round? All price moves that I have seen in practice are discrete, and my *clock says tick tick tick*. As a physicist and quant any views on this?

Derman : Very interesting question. Once you have the analytic powers provided by the calculus and its descendants it's easier to analyze models in continuous time. You avoid all the combinatorics of discreteness. A pendulum is also a bunch of atoms, but to a good approximation it's effective to treat it as a continuum. But then, if you want to really study the details of a pendulum to great accuracy, you have to go back and add in the consequences of discreteness, and that isn't easy.

Continuous methods provide great power. On the other hand, from a pedagogic point of view, discrete time and price models are much easier to understand and teach. In finance all the change-of-measure theorems become relatively trivial. I think that's the right way to teach quantitative finance: start with discrete time and prices, then later generalize to the continuous case, which, as you point out, doesn't strictly describe the price-tick-clock-tick world either. I notice an increasing number of authors that take the discrete approach – Kerry Back more recently, as well as LeRoy and Werner.

Personally I love the binomial model; it provided my first exposure to quantitative finance and it provides such a clear mental model of evolution that I can't think without it.

Some references related to this interview can be found below, more references to Emanuel Derman's many publications can be found at his homepage www.ederman.com.

REFERENCES

■ Avellaneda, M. and M. Lipkin (2003) "A Market-induced Mechanism for Stock Pinning" *Quantitiative Finance*, **3**, 417–425.
■ Back, K. (2005) *A Course in Derivatives Securities*. New York: Springer Verlag.
■ Bardhan, I., A. Bergier, E. Derman, C. Dosembet and I. Kan (1994) "Valuing Convertible Bonds as Derivatives" *Goldman Sachs, Quantitative Strategies Research Notes*.
■ Black, F., E. Derman, and W. Toy (1990) "A One-Factor Model of Interest Rates and Its Application to Treasury Bond Options" *Financial Analysts Journal*, 33–39.
■ Black, F. and P. Karasinski (1991) "Bond and Option Pricing when Short Rates are Lognormal" *Financial Analysts Journal*, 52–59.
■ Black, F. and M. Scholes (1973) "The Pricing of Options and Corporate Liabilities" *Journal of Political Economy*, **81**, 637–654.
■ Clark, P. K. (1973) "A Subordinated Stochastic Process Model with Finite Variance for Speculative Prices" *Econometrica*, **41**(1), 135–155.
■ Cox, J. C., S. A. Ross and M. Rubinstein (1979) "Option Pricing: A Simplified Approach," *Journal of Financial Economics*, **7**, 229–263.
■ Crépey, S. (2004) "Delta-hedging Vega-Risk?" *Quantitative Finance*, **4** (October), 559–579.
■ Demeterifi, K., E. Derman, M. Kamal and J. Zou (1999) "More Than You Ever Wanted to Know About Volatility Swaps" Working paper, Goldman Sachs.
■ Derman, E. (1999) "Regimes of Volatility," *Risk Magazine*, April.

■ ——— (2004) *My Life as a Quant*. New York: John Wiley & Sons, Inc.
■ Derman, E. and M. Kamal (1999) "When You Cannot Hedge Continuously, The Corrections of Black-Scholes" *Risk Magazine*, **12**, 82–85.
■ Derman, E., M. Kamal, I. Kani, J. McClure, C. Pirasteh and J. Z. Zou (1998) "Investing in Volatility" *Working paper, Goldman Sachs*.
■ Derman, E. and I. Kani (1994) "Riding on a Smile," *Risk Magazine*, **7**(2).
■ ——— (1997) "Stochastic Implied Trees: Arbitrage Pricing With Stochastic Term and Strike Structure of Volatility" *Working paper, Goldman Sachs*.
■ Dupire, B. (1994) "Pricing with a Smile," *Risk Magazine*, **7**(1).
■ Gârleanu, N., L. H. Pedersen and Poteshman (2006) *Demand-Based Option Pricing*. Working Paper: New York University–Leonard N. Stern School of Business.
■ Gastineau, G. and M. Kritzman (1999) *Dictionary of Financial Risk Management, Third Edition*. New York: John Wiley & Sons, Inc.
■ Heath, D., J. R. and A. Merton (1992) "Bond Pricing and the Term Structure of Interest Rates: A New Methodology" *Econometrica*, **60**(1), 77–105.
■ LeRoy, S. and J. Werner (2001) *Principles of Financial Economics*. Cambridge University Press.
■ Merton, R. C. (1973) "Theory of Rational Option Pricing" *Bell Journal of Economics and Management Science*, **4**, 141–183.
■ Neuberger, A. (1994) "The Log Contract: A New Instrument to Hedge Volatility," *Journal of Portfolio Management*, Winter, 74–80.
■ ——— (1996): "The Log Contract and Other Power Contracts" in *The Handbook of Exotic Options*, edited by I. Nelken, Winter, 200–212.
■ Rubinstein, M. (1994): "Implied Binomial Trees" *Journal of Finance*, **49**(3), 771–818.

4

Closed Form Valuation of American Barrier Options*

C losed form formulae for European barrier options are well known in the literature. This is not the case for American barrier options, for which no closed form formulae have been published. One has therefore had to resort to numerical methods. Lattice models like a binomial or a trinomial tree, for valuation of barrier options are known to converge extremely slowly, compared to plain vanilla options. Methods for improving the algorithms have been described by several authors. However, these are still numerical methods that are quite computer intensive. In this chapter we show how some American barrier options can be valued analytically in a very simple way. This speeds up the valuation dramatically as well as giving new insight into barrier option valuation.

1 Analytical Valuation of American Barrier Options

Closed form solutions and valuation techniques for standard European barrier options are well known from the literature, see for instance Merton (1973); Reiner and Rubinstein (1991); Rich (1994); Haug (1997). No closed form solution for American barrier options exist in the current literature. The technique used to value American barrier options has therefore been numerical methods. Lattice models have been especially popular. Without doing any adjustments lattice models have been shown to converge extremely slowly. Although several methods that improve on the technique have been published, they are still quite computer intensive: Boyle and Lau (1994); Ritchken (1994); Derman, Bardhan, Ergener and Kani (1995). In this present chapter we suggest an analytical solution. This offers both speeding up the valuation process and giving new insight into the valuation of barrier options. We limit ourselves by assuming that the underlying asset price follows a geometric Brownian motion in the risk adjusted economy (i.e., we consider the process after an appropriate change of probability measure).

$$dS_t = \mu S_t dt + \sigma S_t dz_t$$

*First printed as Haug, E. G. (2001): "Closed-Form Valuation of American Barrier Options," *International Journal of Theoretical and Applied Finance*, XIX, 175–192. I would like to thank Edwin Fisk, Jørgen Haug, John Logie, Gunnar Stensland and Jiang Xiao Zhong for helpful comments on this chapter. Needless to say, I remain solely responsible for any remaining errors.

where S is the asset price, μ is the expected instantaneous rate of return, σ is the instantaneous standard deviation of the rate of return, and dz is a standard Wiener process.

The idea is to use the reflection principle Harrison (1985). In a barrier context (e.g. a down-and-in call) the reflection principle basically states that the number of paths leading from S_t to a point higher than X, that touch a barrier level $H(H < S_t)$ before maturity, is equal to the number of paths from an asset that starts from $H^2 = S_t$ and that reach a point higher than X. Using the reflection principle we can then simply value both European and American barrier options on the basis of formulas from plain vanilla options. Using the reflection principle the value of a European or American down-and-in call is equal to (assuming $H \leq S_t$)[1]:

$$C_{di}(S_t, X, H, T, r, b, \sigma) = \left(\frac{S}{H}\right)^{1-\frac{2b}{\sigma^2}} C\left(\frac{H^2}{S_t}, X, T, r, b, \sigma\right), \tag{4.1}$$

where $C_{di}(S_t, X, H, T, r, b, \sigma)$ is a call down-and-in (the subscript indicating the type of barrier option $di = $ down-and-in) with asset price S_t, strike X, barrier H, time to maturity in years T, risk free rate r, cost of carry b, and volatility σ. $C(\frac{H^2}{S_t}, X, T, r, b, \sigma)$ is a plain vanilla American call with asset price equal to $\frac{H^2}{S_t}$ and strike price equal to X. For European barrier options we could naturally just replace the American plain vanilla call with a European c. This implies that all we need to value an American down-and-in call analytically is a closed form solution for a plain vanilla American call option. This involves using a closed form approximation, such as the popular closed form model of Barone-Adesi and Whaley (1987), or the closed form method of Bjerksund and Stensland (1993). Similarly, using the reflection principle, the value of a European or American up-and-in put when $H \geq X$ can be shown to be equal to

$$P_{ui}(S_t, X, H, T, r, b, \sigma) = \left(\frac{S_t}{H}\right)^{1-\frac{2b}{\sigma^2}} P\left(\frac{H^2}{S_t}, X, T, r, b, \sigma\right). \tag{4.2}$$

2   Numerical Comparison

In this section we will compare some well known methods for barrier option valuation with our closed form solution method.

Table 4.1 compares European barrier option values. Column one is calculated using the closed form barrier formulas derived by Reiner and Rubinstein (1991). Column two is calculated using the formula of Black and Scholes (1973) and Merton (1973) in combination with the reflection principle. As expected, these two columns contain identical values. Columns three and four contain values calculated using a binomial tree without any adjustments. It is evident that using a tree without any corrections is more or less useless. Columns five and six are calculated using the trinomial tree of Boyle (1986), in combination with the barrier technique developed by Derman, Bardhan, Ergener and Kani (1995). Using 300 time steps this method gives quite accurate values, except when the barrier is very close to the asset price. The last column is based on the binomial tree of Cox, Ross and Rubinstein (1979) in combination with the barrier technique described by Boyle and Lau (1994). The Boyle-Lau method does not allow direct control of the number of time steps. The method instead offers choices of the optimal number of time steps. The numbers in brackets are

TABLE 4.1: COMPARISON OF EUROPEAN DOWN-AND-IN CALL BARRIER OPTION VALUES

$(S_t = 94.5, X = 105, T = 1, r = 0.10, b = -0.05, \sigma = 0.20)$

H	Barrier formula	BSM reflection	Plain tree 50 steps	Plain tree 300 steps	Derman 50 steps	Derman 300 steps	Boyle-Lau binomial
94	4.3230	4.3230	3.2464	4.0079	3.7469	4.2184	4.3240 (1421)
93	3.7876	3.7876	3.2464	3.4578	3.6169	3.8093	3.7933 (156)
90	2.4105	2.4105	2.1429	2.1042	2.4240	2.4308	2.4118 (151)
80	0.2501	0.2501	0.2302	0.2128	0.2754	0.2640	0.2456 (116)

the number of time steps used. We have chosen to have the number of time steps equal to the first number higher than 100 of the time steps given by the Boyle-Lau formula. As can be seen from the table the Boyle-Lau method gives accurate values in all cases. However, the number of time steps has to be extremely large (1,421) when the barrier is very close to the asset price ($H = 94$).

American barrier option values are compared in Table 4.2. The first column is calculated using the closed form approximation method suggested by Bjerksund and Stensland in combination with the reflection principle.

TABLE 4.2: COMPARISON OF AMERICAN DOWN-AND-IN CALL BARRIER OPTION VALUES

$(S_t = 94.5, X = 105, T = 1, r = 0.10, b = -0.05, \sigma = 0.20)$

H	BS reflection	Binomial reflection	Plain tree 50 steps	Plain tree 300 steps	Derman 50 steps	Derman 300 steps	Boyle-Lau binomial
94	4.8535	4.9236	3.6279	4.5401	4.2120	4.7902	4.9213 (1421)
93	4.2120	4.2807	3.6279	3.8844	4.0579	4.3008	4.2816 (156)
90	2.6134	2.6690	2.3576	2.3160	2.6698	2.6878	2.6659 (151)
80	0.2572	0.2645	0.2428	0.2245	0.2906	0.2791	0.2595 (116)

The second column is computed using a plain Cox-Ross-Rubinstein binomial tree in combination with the reflection principle. Using 300 time steps these values should be very accurate and can be seen as a benchmark against the other models. The unadjusted binomial tree is also more or less useless in this case, as it is extremely slow to converge. Both the method of Boyle and Lau, and the method of Derman et al. work well as long as the barrier is not too close to the asset price. The reflection principle is an analytical solution. It is therefore naturally much faster than the lattice models. The closed form reflection principle should thus be of great interest in valuing American barrier options, when assuming geometric Brownian motion. The accuracy of the model will naturally depend on the accuracy of the plain vanilla American option formula used. We have only been able to develop our method for knock-in options (down-and-in call and up-and-in put). For European barrier options knock-out options can be found from knock-in options by using the well known in-out barrier parity:

$$\text{Out-option} = \text{long plain vanilla option} + \text{short in-barrier option}$$

Unfortunately the in-out barrier parity will, in general, not hold for American options. However, for knock-in options traditional numerical lattice models are particularly computer intensive. To find the value of an down-and-in (up-and-in) option one has to calculate the value of an American option for every node just below (above) the barrier. So, for example, using a 128 step Boyle-Lau binomial tree one has to calculate more than a hundred American option values to get the value of a single down-and-in call or up-and-in put. For out options this is not necessary, and they are for this reason much better suited to lattice models.

It is also worth noting that our approach will not work in general, when one moves away from the assumption of geometric Brownian motion, or when working with complex barrier options. For instance, when working with an implied tree model calibrated to the volatility smile found in the market, the only available methodology is still numerical methods, see Dupire (1994); Derman and Kani (1994); Rubinstein (1994). The method of Boyle and Lau will, in general, only work on a standard Cox-Ross-Rubinstein (CRR) tree. On the other hand, the method of Derman et al. is very flexible and independent of the underlying tree model (binomial, trinomial, multinomial, implied trees). This makes theirs the method of choice when valuing complex barrier options. The method of Boyle and Lau is basically built for barrier valuation in a CRR binomial tree. This implies an additional weakness in their method. In situations when the risk-free rate is very high and the volatility is very low the CRR tree can give negative probabilities Chriss (1996); Haug (2004). In most practical situations this is not a problem, but it could certainly happen in special market situations.

3 Conclusion

We have shown how to price American barrier options using a plain vanilla American option formula, utilizing the reflection principle. This enables fast and accurate valuation of American barrier options. For valuation of more complex barrier options numerical solutions are still the only game in town. Further research in this field is needed if we are to extend our results for valuation of more complex forms of barrier options.

FOOTNOTE & REFERENCES

1. I had not pointed this out in a earlier version of this work Haug (2001) and the result has later been generalized by an excellent paper by Dai and Kwok (2004).

■ Barone-Adesi, G. and R. E. Whaley (1987) "Efficient Analytic Approximation of American Option Values" *Journal of Finance*, **42**(2), 301–320.
■ Bjerksund, P. and G. Stensland (1993) "Closed-Form Approximation of American Options" *Scandinavian Journal of Management*, **9**, 87–99.
■ Black, F. and M. Scholes (1973) "The Pricing of Options and Corporate Liabilities" *Journal of Political Economy*, **81**, 637–654.
■ Boyle, P. P. (1986) "Option Valuation Using a Three Jump Process" *International Options Journal*, **3**, 7–12.
■ Boyle, P. P., and S. H. Lau (1994) "Bumping Up Against the Barrier with the Binomial Method" *Journal of Derivatives*, **1**, 6–14.
■ Chriss, N. A. (1996): *Black-Scholes and Beyond*. Chicago: Irwin Professional Publishing.

■ Cox, J. C., S. A. Ross and M. Rubinstein (1979) "Option Pricing: A Simplified Approach" *Journal of Financial Economics*, **7**, 229–263.

■ Dai, M. and Y. K. Kwok (2004) "Knock-in American Option" *The Journal of Futures Markets*, **24**(2), 179–192.

■ Derman, E., I. Bardhan, D. Ergener and I. Kani (1995) "Enhanced Numerical Methods for Options with Barriers" *Financial Analysts Journal*, November–December, 65–74.

■ Derman, E., and I. Kani (1994) "Riding on a Smile," *Risk Magazine*, **7**(2).

■ Dupire, B. (1994) "Pricing with a Smile," *Risk Magazine*, **7**(1).

■ Harrison, M. J. (1985) *Brownian Motion and Stochastic Flow Systems*. New York: John Wiley & Sons, Inc.

■ Haug, E. G. (1997) *The Complete Guide To Option Pricing Formulas*. McGraw-Hill, New York.

■ ——— (2001) "Closed form Valuation of American Barrier Options" *International Journal of Theoretical and Applied Finance*, **XIX**, 175–192.

■ ——— (2004) "Why so Negative to Negative Probabilities?," *Wilmott Magazine Sep/Oct*.

■ Merton, R. C. (1973) "Theory of Rational Option Pricing" *Bell Journal of Economics and Management Science*, **4**, 141–183.

■ Reiner, E. and M. Rubinstein (1991) "Breaking Down the Barriers" *Risk Magazine*, **4**(8).

■ Rich, D. R. (1994) "The Mathematical Foundation of Barrier Option-Pricing Theory" *Advances in Futures and Options Research*, **7**, 267–311.

■ Ritchken, P. (1994) "On Pricing Barrier Options" *Journal of Derivatives*, **3**, 19–28.

■ Rubinstein, M. (1994) "Implied Binomial Trees" *Journal of Finance*, **49**, 771–818.

Peter Carr doing quant finance on napkins in a coffee shop in Manhattan (Photo: Amber Gray)

Peter Carr, The Wall Street Wizard of Option Symmetry and Volatility

Peter Carr is head of the Bloomberg quantitative financial research team in New York. Aside from Peter Carr, the team consists of quant stars like Bruno Dupire (one of the founders of local volatility surface models) and Bjørn Flesaker (best known for his work in fixed income research). In addition, they have several other PhDs in physics, computer science and math. There is no quant finance problem that this team cannot solve, and the number of innovative as well as practical implementations emerging from this team is just astonishing. What else would one expect from such a quant dream team? Peter Carr is the Director of the Masters in Math Finance program at the world famous Courant Institute at New York University. He has been involved for many years in the industry, through working or consulting, for firms like Bank of Tokyo, Mitsubishi, Susquehanna, Morgan Stanley, Bank of America, etc. Peter Carr has received many awards, among them "quant of the year" from Risk Magazine and the Wilmott award for Cutting Edge Research.

I first met Peter Carr at a derivatives conference many years ago. He was presenting some of his work on static hedging of barrier options. I was at that time involved in trading barrier options and was shortly thereafter applying successfully several of Peter Carr's ideas to the market.

Since that first meeting, we have met every now and then for lunch or dinner. Some quants in this business try to avoid talking about quantitative finance as they only became involved to make a good living. Peter Carr seems to be the opposite, during every meeting we end up not just talking about quantitative models, he also ends up drawing 3-dimensional illustrations cluttered with equations and stochastic analysis on the back of napkins or even on the restaurant table. Every time I walk out from a lunch with Peter, my brain is boiling with equations and 3-dimensional charts, and my pockets are filled with napkins with even more equations. Complex models and equations that were hard to grasp suddenly seem clear and intuitive.

Haug : Where did you grow up?

Carr : I grew up playing road hockey in a suburb of Toronto. I had dreams that I would make my living playing hockey professionally. Funnily enough, I now play with hockey sticks everyday.

Haug : When did you first get interested in math and finance?

Carr : I remember being impressed as a kid that money earned interest and that interest earned interest as well. In high school, my main interest in math was part of a lame attempt to impress girls. You can imagine how successful that was.

Haug : Were you particularly talented in math as a kid?

Carr : I scored well on aptitude tests but I was much more interested in scoring well in hockey.

Haug : What is your educational background?

Carr : I have an accounting undergrad degree from University of Toronto and a PhD in Finance from UCLA. I'm self-taught in math. I learned much from Dan Thornton and Laurence Booth at University of Toronto and from Eduardo Schwartz and Michael Brennan from UCLA.

Haug : You came up early on with the idea of static hedging of barrier options. What is the main idea behind static hedging and what is the advantage of static hedging techniques versus dynamic delta hedging?

Carr : The main idea stems from the observation that barrier options are fundamentally more closely linked to the corresponding vanilla option than they are to the underlying currency. The so-called static hedging strategy is actually dynamic since a self-financing option trade is required at the barrier crossing time. Thus the fundamental distinction is not static versus dynamic, but rather that vanilla options are used as hedge instruments rather than the underlying currency. Due to the close link between barrier options and vanillas, at most one option trade is needed to replicate the barrier options payoff. The reflection principle is used to ensure that any such trade is self-financing.

A surprising aspect of the so-called static hedge is that it works perfectly under independent stochastic volatility, even when the volatility process is unknown. In contrast, delta hedging fails under stochastic volatility. Static hedging doesn't always work, but neither does dynamic delta hedging. Whenever anyone runs a hedging horse race, static hedging always finishes in the money.

Haug : Can static hedging also be used for products like variance, volatility and correlation swaps?

Carr : The standard hedge for a variance swap has a static option hedge as well as dynamic trading in the underlying. Roger Lee and I have shown that volatility swaps can be robustly replicated only by dynamic option trading. To my knowledge, no one knows how to robustly hedge correlation swaps. Model based hedges don't interest me.

Haug : In 2000 you wrote a paper on "Deriving Derivatives of Derivatives Securities" where you claim that the partial derivatives of path-independent derivatives can be represented in terms of spatial derivatives. What are spatial derivatives and how does this approach work?

Carr : That paper focused on single security path independent claims in the Black Scholes model. Merton observed that in this setting, normalized option values depend only on moneyness and term volatility and I extrapolated the implications of his observation to greeks. The first spatial derivative is just delta and the second spatial derivative is just gamma. It turns out that every possible greek can be expressed in terms of delta, gamma, and higher order spatial derivatives.

Haug : You have also worked a great deal with stochastic volatility models. There are many stochastic volatility and jump models out there, and new ones are coming out all the time. Is this a never ending topic, or are certain models now taking the lead and becoming the benchmark, in the way that the Black-Scholes-Merton model has become the benchmark for constant volatility?

Carr : At Bloomberg, we are trying to establish certain models as benchmarks, but the jury is still out. Any model is an attempt to establish the invariants of a dynamical system. Determining these invariants is very difficult, especially when humans are an intrinsic part of the system.

Haug : Why is it that stochastic volatility models seem to work best for mid to long term options, while jump-diffusion seems to work better for short term options, and does this mean that a great model should combine stochastic volatility with jumps?

Carr : I'm a firm believer that options prices reflect both jumps in the price of the underlying asset and one or more additional sources of uncertainty, which you can call either stochastic volatility, feedback effects, or supply and demand. The failure of stochastic volatility models at short maturities is due to jumps and the failure of jump diffusions at longer terms is due to the independent increments assumption and the neglect of other factors. A great model must accommodate both jumps and additional factors to price the cross section of option prices correctly over calendar time.

Haug : In the different areas of derivatives models there are many competing models, and in every paper we can read about why one particular model is so important. How does the market choose between which models to use, is it the survival of the fittest or do you think marketing of the model can also play a central role?

Carr : Models are used for many purposes and by diverse users. In deciding what features a model should have, you must first decide on the user and the use. For example, consider the often trumpeted property that a model has an exact fit to all data. For a market maker making his money off buying at the bid and selling at the ask, this is a good property as off market quotes lead to either no trades or bad trades.

For a proprietary trader who uses a model to identify mispriced assets, an exact fit to data is a bad property as no trade is suggested. Regarding the relative importance of marketing vs markets, I think marketing plays only a minor role; I have found that there is often a hidden wisdom in standard market practice.

Haug : Do you think that prices of derivatives are driven mainly by the underlying stochastic process, or can it be that a model and our understanding of a model at any given time influences the prices of derivatives? In other words do the most popular derivatives models impact the prices of derivatives?

Carr : It is a tautology that the risk-neutral process determines (a range for) derivatives prices and a big mistake to think that the real world stochastic process is the sole determinant of value.

The measure change is a very general thing that can incorporate effects like supply and demand, risk aversion, inventories, feedback effects, and even irrationality, which includes our limited understanding of a model.

However, models which forbid both discrete trading and price jumps restrict the measure change so that only a shift in the mean can be accommodated. In general, the shape of the whole distribution can change and does.

Haug : Do you think that trading in derivatives can also influence the stochastic process of the underlying asset?

Carr : There is a lot of empirical evidence in support of this. For example Allan Poteshman has recent work strongly suggesting that stock option holdings forecast subsequent stock price changes.

Haug : You have done a lot of work on volatility derivatives, like volatility swaps, volatility options, correlation swaps, etc. How do you see the future for these products, and how should a trader choose between the many ways of valuing them described in the literature?

Carr : The future of volatility derivatives looks bright. Options on the VIX have now launched and I know that several other exchanges are contemplating similar products. As with any other derivative, the choice of model depends heavily on the use to which it is to be put.

Haug : What is the difference between a standard variance swap and a corridor variance swap and how do you value a corridor variance swap?

Carr : A standard variance swap is actually a forward contract written on the average of squared daily returns. A corridor variance swap only includes a squared daily return in the averaging if the underlying price started or ended a day inside a given corridor. As I mentioned above, the standard hedge for a variance swap combines a static position in options of literally all strikes with daily trading in the underlying. In contrast, a corridor variance swap only requires holding options struck within the corridor and only requires daily trading in the underlying when its price is within the corridor.

Haug : What makes valuing volatility swaps more complicated than variance swaps?

Carr : Under some conditions, the volatility swap rate can be easier to value than the variance swap rate. More specifically, when the underlying price is continuous and implied volatility is a symmetric function of log moneyness, then Roger Lee and I have shown that the initial volatility swap rate is well-approximated by ATM implied vol. However, this does not apply for seasoned vol swaps. For seasoned contracts, the Pythagorean theorem makes variance swaps easy to value, while Jensen's inequality makes vol swaps hard to value.

Haug : Most models for valuing volatility derivatives such as variance, volatility swaps and options assume that the underlying returns process is continuous, while in practice we can often observe that the asset price makes jumps. You have done some work on this, can you give us a brief overview?

Carr : My work on this has been with Dilip Madan who I regard as a somewhat unheralded genius. Consider any nonlinear function of the average of squared daily returns, e.g. vol swaps or options. If daily returns are assumed to be independent, then the law of large numbers tells us that the underlying average becomes less volatile as we average more and more returns together. Hence, the volatility value of volatility derivatives will die away with increasing maturity. So, the important modeling issue is how to realistically relax the artificial independence assumption.

Haug : **Should one value the futures contracts on the VIX index trading at CBOE (Chicago Board Option Exchange) as a variance or volatility swap, and can you tell us something about your recent work on this?**

Carr : Futures on VIX are neither a variance swap nor a volatility swap. Bloomberg has created an interesting model for valuing VIX futures and Bruno Dupire and Arun Verma deserve the lion's share of the credit for the research behind it.

Haug : **In one of your recent papers you describe an interesting result, namely how volatility swaps should initially be priced close to the implied volatility from a straddle with maturity equal to the volatility swap, can you comment on this?**

Carr : The reason that the initial vol swap rate is close to the at-the-money (ATM) implied under some conditions is that ATM options prices increase with maturity in a square root fashion. For continuous processes, random variance and fixed maturity is equivalent to fixed variance and random maturity. Thus an ATM option price is just an expectation of the square root of a random variable and so is the vol swap rate.

Haug : **During the lunches and meetings we've had over the years you always end up drawing 3-dimensional, if not 4-dimensional figures on napkins cluttered with equations. When you work on a new idea in quant finance do you always visualize the problem first, or do you do the equations first and then the visualize it?**

Carr : I visualize everything first. This explains why I rarely work with more than one underlying asset. The big advantage of visualizing everything is that it becomes easy to determine the effect of discrete operations such as reflection or inversion. In my job, it doesn't hurt that you can do math on the subway as well.

Haug : **In the spring of 2004 I listened to a talk you gave at Columbia University about a stochastic volatility model driven by stochastic clocks, something you called time-changed Levy processes. I know you looked at time reversal in option pricing in another paper. For an outsider this must seem absurd, how can stochastic clocks and time reversal make any sense in practical finance?**

Carr : The Pythagoreans stoned someone for proving that the square root of two is irrational. As you know, purely mathematical explorations in non-Euclidean geometry were later used by Einstein to conclude that space is curved. He also showed that time is relative, not absolute. I was taught early on that the same word e.g. time is often used to describe distinct objects. When time is regarded as the index of a stochastic process rather than what your watch measures, it becomes natural to randomize it, flip it, or invert it.

Haug : In all your papers and ideas is there any one of your ideas that you are particularly proud of?

Carr : A common theme in my work is that option prices convey information and the challenge is to not bring prejudices when listening to what they are trying to say.

Haug : After publishing a paper have you ever found out that you made an error or that there were typos that you not were happy with?

Carr : A paper in Risk on covariance swaps has an error that arose from not considering the units of measurement. Since then I have insisted that every step in a derivation carry a financial meaning. I learned a lot from that mistake.

Haug : I have seen that many people in the industry are very secretive about their quantitative models while you seem to be happy to share most of your ideas through papers and conference talks. Why do you think so many quants and institutions are afraid to share their knowledge?

Carr : People working for Draconian Hacks are afraid of being fired. Fortunately, Bloomberg is much more enlightened. We are hiring by the way.

Haug : You have worked both in academia and on Wall Street, what is the main difference between working as a quant in academia as opposed to Wall Street?

Carr : As Emanuel Derman has observed, academics work in silos, while industry quants are much more collegial.

Haug : Is it more political in academic publishing or on Wall Street?

Carr : Academia. Henry Kissinger wrote that the politics in academia are so vicious because the stakes are so low. Larry Summers has just resigned as president of Harvard, the pinnacle of academic success. His academic salary is $563,000.

Haug : Do you have any advice to give to new financial engineers or PhDs when going from academia to work on Wall Street?

Carr : Yes, it is to not scoff at industry practice, as it is often wiser than you think.

Haug : Many investment banks are still controlled by old time non-quantitative traders, while in other firms I see that quant and quant traders are in charge. Do you think quantitative oriented traders and researchers will take over Wall Street and investment banking, or will it always be the place for the old fashioned "rule of thumb trader"?

Carr : Yes, I think that as quants continue to embrace computers, they will rise further to the top. Extrapolating forward, we may all be working for a silicon chip one day.

Haug : Do you have any views on patenting in quantitative finance? Could this be a way to distribute some of the big bonuses from traders using the quantitative finance models to the researchers and quants that did the hard work in coming up with the models?

Carr : That's an interesting idea. I once tried to patent an idea and gave up due to the difficulty in explaining the idea to lawyers. If that bridge can be overcome, your suggestion sounds reasonable.

Haug : From my own experience it seems that politics plays an important role if you want to get to the top in many of the larger financial institutions. Quants often seem too busy with coming up with new ideas in quantitative finance to get ahead in the game of corporate politics. Have you ever been distracted by corporate politics that lost you valuable research time, or is it possible to combine the two?

Carr : Unfortunately, politics and publishing don't mix. Pick your poison and live with it.

Haug : Do you also apply quantitative models to option-like decisions (real options) in your daily life?

Carr : I used to think getting married was like exercising an American call early but that idea was trumped by the hidden wisdom of markets (including marriage markets). I think that if I tried to be rational about my personal life, I would have to change it dramatically.

Haug : Where do you find the energy to come up with so many ideas and write so many papers in record time, do you have a secret diet or is it simply the hunger for knowledge that drives you?

Carr : Well, co-authors deserve an awful lot of credit especially Dilip Madan, Liuren Wu, and Roger Lee. The main thing that drives me to write papers is to get the ideas down before I lose them.

Haug : Do you and your wife exchange napkins with 3-dimensional figures and equations during dinner, or is that something you only do when meeting up with geeks/nerds like me?

Carr : My wife refuses to listen to any technical discussions whatsoever. It's too bad because she's the smartest person I know.

Haug : You have written a great number of papers, many quite heavy with mathematics, have you thought about writing down some of your main results in a more intuitive book?

Carr : I've always thought I would write a book when I figured it all out. I now realize that's not going to happen. If I did write a book, I would want it to have a lot of pictures. So I may wait until the technology for doing that improves.

Haug : Do you have any hobbies outside quantitative finance, when I click on the hobbies link on your homepage nothing comes up. I assume that this means that you have no hobbies?

Carr : I run religiously and know more about the Beatles than I do about options. When I was younger I realized that my life revolves around the four F's: Food, Fun, Finance, and Females, but not necessarily in that order.

Haug : In your view where are we in the evolution of quantitative finance?

Carr : I think we are presently in a chapter that will be regarded as extremely curious a hundred years from now. Just over a hundred years ago, a mathematician named Perrin proved that it was possible to construct a function that is continuous everywhere and differentiable nowhere. At present, the predominant world view is that only such outcomes are possible. On top of that, if all such sample paths occupy our universe, then the constant volatility view is that the only possibility is that we live on the surface of a sphere. While we do in fact live on the surface of a sphere (or oblate spheroid actually), I'm still hopeful that we'll raise our horizons, both physically and metaphorically.

Some references are given below for more information about Peter Carr's research and for a long list of his papers visit his website at: http://www.math.nyu.edu/fellows/carrp/.

REFERENCES

■ Andreasen, J. and P. Carr (2002) "Put Call Reversal," Working paper, Corant Institute New York.

■ Carr, P. (2000) "Deriving Derivatives of Derivative Securities" *Journal of Computational Finance*, **4**(2), 5–29.

■ Carr, P. and J. Bowie (1994) "Static Simplicity," *Risk Magazine*, **7**(8), 44–50.

■ Carr, P. and M. Chesney (1998) "American Put Call Symmetry" *Journal of Financial Engineering*.

■ Carr, P. and A. Chou (1998) "Static Hedging of Complex Barrier Options" Bank of America Securities Working paper.

■ Carr, P. and A. Corso (2001) "Commodity Covariance Contracting" *Energy and Power Risk Management*, April.

■ Carr, P. and K. Ellis (1995) "Static Hedging of Exotic Options" Working paper, Cornell University.

■ Carr, P., H. Geman, D. B. Madan and M. Yor (2003) "Stochastic Volatility for Lévy Processes" *Mathematical Finance*, **13**(3), 345–382.

■ Carr, P. and R. Lee (2003) "Robust Replication of Volatility Derivatives" Risk Congress USA, Boston, June 10.

■ Carr, P. and K. Lewis (2004) "Corridor Variance Swaps," *Risk Magazine*, February.

■ Carr, P. and D. Madan (1998) "Towards a Theory of Volatility Trading." In *Volatility*. London: Risk Book Publications.

5

Valuation of Complex Barrier Options Using Barrier Symmetry*

T his chapter shows how a mathematical symmetry between standard barrier call and put options can be used to construct a static hedge and valuation formulae for more complex barrier options. The relationship can, for example, be used to value double barrier options in a intuitive way. Double barrier options and other complex barrier options trade quite actively in the financial markets, in particular in the foreign exchange market, and a good understanding of valuation and hedging of such options is of great importance to investment banks, hedge funds and corporations involved in such options.

1 Plain Vanilla Put–Call Symmetry

Assume that the underlying asset follows a geometric Brownian motion $dS_t = \mu S_t dt + \sigma S_t dz_t$, where as usual μ is the expected instantaneous rate of return on the underlying asset, σ is the instantaneous standard deviation of the rate of return, and dz is a standard Wiener process. The put–call symmetry for European options where first described by Bates (1991)

$$c_t(S_t, X, T, r, b, \sigma) = \frac{X}{S_t} p_t\left(S_t, \frac{S_t^2}{X}, T, r - b, -b, \sigma\right),\qquad(5.1)$$

Where S is the asset price, X the strike price, T time to maturity, r the risk free rate, and b the cost of carry,[1] further c and p stands for European call and put price using the well known Black–Scholes–Merton formula, see Black and Scholes (1973) and Merton (1973). Carr and Bowie (1994) describes how the put–call symmetry can be used for static hedging of barrier options using plain vanilla options. This not only simplifies valuation, but also makes it possible to find a much more robust hedge than one would have by using traditional dynamic delta hedging.

---

*This chapter is extended work based on my Presentation at the Danske Bank Symposium on Securities with Embedded Options (1998).

Put–call symmetry also holds for American options as described by Bjerksund and Stensland (1993) and Carr and Chesney (1998). Bjerksund and Stensland (1993) describe what they call a put–call transformation

$$C_t(S_t, X, T, r, b, \sigma) = P_t(X, S_t, T, r - b, -b, \sigma),$$ (5.2)

The power of this symmetry is that if we already have a formula for an American call option we no longer need a separate formula for a put option, and visa versa. However, the usefulness of this transformation for static hedging and valuation of a large class of exotic options we first have when rewriting it on the form of put–call symmetry. We can easily rewrite the payoff function from a call (or similarly for a put) option, $\max(S - X, 0)$, into $\frac{X}{S} \max\left(\frac{S^2}{X} - S, 0\right)$. Then by combining this with the put–call transformation we simply get the American put–call symmetry, Carr and Chesney (1998):

$$C_t(S_t, X, T, r, b, \sigma) = \frac{X}{S_t} P_t\left(S_t, \frac{S_t^2}{X}, T, r - b, -b, \sigma\right),$$ (5.3)

For more on static hedging of Exotic options using plain vanilla put–call symmetry see also Carr, Ellis and Gupta (1998).

2   Barrier Put–Call Symmetry

Barrier options have become extremely popular and constitute one of the most popular classes of exotic options in the financial markets. Closed form solutions for valuation of single barrier options have been published by Merton (1973), Reiner and Rubinstein (1991) and Rich (1994), and for double barrier options by Ikeda and Kunitomo (1992) and Geman and Yor (1996). Further, the relationship between in and out options is well known, as the in-out barrier parity. A long out option is equal to a long plain vanilla option plus short an in option. However, it is worth mentioning that in-out barrier parity only holds, in general, for European barrier options and not for American style, as mentioned by Haug (2001a).

In this chapter we go one step further and state the put–call symmetry for European and American single and double barrier options. This was first described by Haug (1998). In a different context the symmetry between standard single barrier options is also described by Gao, Huang and Subrahmanyam (2000), see also Haug (2001b). Given that the plain vanilla put–call symmetry holds the intuition behind the put–call barrier symmetry is quite intuitive. The only difference between a plain vanilla put–call symmetry and a put–call barrier symmetry is the probability of barrier hits. Given the same volatility and drift towards the barrier the probability of barrier hits only depend on the distance between the asset price and the barrier. In the put–call symmetry the drifts are different on the call and the put, b versus $-b$. However, given that the asset price of the call is above (below) the barrier and the asset price of the put is below (above) the barrier this will naturally ensure the same drift towards the barrier. In the case of a put–call symmetry between a down-call with asset price S_t and an up-put with asset price X it must be that

$$\ln\left(\frac{S_t}{H_c}\right) = \ln\left(\frac{H_p}{X}\right)$$ (5.4)

where the call barrier $H_c < S_t$ and the put barrier $H_p > X$. In the case of a put-call symmetry between an up-call and a down-put the barriers and strike must satisfy;

$$\ln\left(\frac{H_c}{S_t}\right) = \ln\left(\frac{X}{H_p}\right) \tag{5.5}$$

where $H_c > S_t$ and $H_p < X$. In both cases we can rewrite the put barrier as $\frac{S_t X}{H_c}$. For standard barrier options the put–call symmetry between in-options must from this be given by

$$C_t^{di}(S_t, X, H, r, b, \sigma) = P_t^{ui}\left(X, S_t, \frac{SX}{H}, r - b, -b, \sigma\right) \tag{5.6}$$

$$= \frac{X}{S_t} P_t^{ui}\left(S_t, \frac{S_t^2}{X}, \frac{S_t^2}{H}, r - b, -b, \sigma\right)$$

$$C_t^{ui}(S_t, X, H, r, b, \sigma) = P_t^{di}\left(X, S_t, \frac{SX}{H}, r - b, -b, \sigma\right) \tag{5.7}$$

$$= \frac{X}{S_t} P_t^{di}\left(S_t, \frac{S_t^2}{X}, \frac{S_t^2}{H}, r - b, -b, \sigma\right)$$

where C_t^{di} stands for a down-and-in call at time t, and C_t^{ui} stands for a up-and-in call (similarly for puts). The put-call symmetry between out barrier options is given by:

$$C_t^{do}(S_t, X, H, r, b, \sigma) = P_t^{uo}\left(X, S_t, \frac{SX}{H}, r - b, -b, \sigma\right) \tag{5.8}$$

$$= \frac{X}{S_t} P_t^{uo}\left(S_t, \frac{S_t^2}{X}, \frac{S_t^2}{H}, r - b, -b, \sigma\right)$$

$$C_t^{uo}(S_t, X, H, r, b, \sigma) = P_t^{do}\left(X, S_t, \frac{SX}{H}, r - b, -b, \sigma\right) \tag{5.9}$$

$$= \frac{X}{S_t} P_t^{do}\left(S_t, \frac{S_t^2}{X}, \frac{S_t^2}{H}, r - b, -b, \sigma\right)$$

and for double barrier options we have:

$$C_t^o(S_t, X, L, U, r, b, \sigma) = P_t^o\left(X, S_t, \frac{SX}{U}, \frac{SX}{L}, r - b, -b, \sigma\right) \tag{5.10}$$

$$= \frac{X}{S_t} P_t^o\left(S_t, \frac{S_t^2}{X}, \frac{S_t^2}{U}, \frac{S_t^2}{L}, r - b, -b, \sigma\right)$$

$$C_t^i(S_t, X, L, U, r, b, \sigma) = P_t^i\left(X, S_t, \frac{SX}{U}, \frac{SX}{L}, r - b, -b, \sigma\right) \tag{5.11}$$

$$= \frac{X}{S_t} P_t^i\left(S_t, \frac{S_t^2}{X}, \frac{S_t^2}{U}, \frac{S_t^2}{L}, r - b, -b, \sigma\right)$$

where L is the lower barrier and U is the upper barrier level. These symmetry relationships also hold for partial-time single and double barrier options, described by Heynen and Kat (1994) and Hui (1997).

These new symmetry relationships give new insight and should be useful when calculating barrier option values. If one has a formula for a barrier call, the relationship will give the value for the barrier put and vice versa. The relationship also gives new opportunities for static hedging and valuation of "second-generation" exotic options. An example of this would be a first-down-then-up-and-in call. In a first-down-then-up-and-in call $C_t^{dui}(S_t, X, L, U)$ the option holder gets a standard up-and-in call with barrier $U(U > S_t)$ and strike X if the asset first hit a lower barrier $L(L < S_t < U)$. Using the up-and-in call down-and-in put barrier symmetry described above we can simply construct a static hedge and thereby a valuation formula for this new type of barrier option;

$$C_t^{dui}(S_t, X, L, U, r, 0, \sigma) = \frac{X}{L} P_t^{di}\left(S_t, \frac{L^2}{X}, \frac{L^2}{U}, r, b, \sigma\right) \qquad (5.12)$$

In other words to hedge a first-down-then-up-and-in barrier call option all we need to do is buy $\frac{X}{L}$ number of standard down-and-in puts with strike $\frac{L^2}{X}$ and barrier $\frac{L^2}{U}$. If the asset price never touches L both the first-down-then-up-and-in call and the standard down-and-in put will expire worthless. On the other hand, if the asset price hits the lower barrier L the value of the $\frac{X}{L}$ down-and-in puts will be exactly equal to the value of the up-and-in call. So in that case all we need to do is sell the down-and-in put and simultaneously buy the up-and-in call. As we can see we have created a perfect static hedge for this new barrier option using only standard barrier options and the barrier symmetry principle.

In a similar fashion one can easily construct static hedges and valuation formulas for a large class of new barrier options.

3 Simple, Intuitive and Accurate Valuation of Double Barrier Options

Ikeda and Kunitomo (1992) and Geman and Yor (1996) have developed closed form formulae for double barrier options using quite complex mathematics.

An alternative is to value double barrier options using the single barrier put-call symmetry in combination with some simple intuition. The idea can best be illustrated by first trying to construct a static hedge for a double barrier option by using only single barrier options. Let's assume we want to try to statically hedge a double barrier knock-in-call option with lower barrier L, upper barrier U, and strike price X.

A natural first step could be to buy an up-and-in-call and a down-and-in-call. As long as the asset does not touch any of the two barriers, or only touches one of the barriers this hedge works fine. The problem with this strategy is naturally that if the asset touches both barriers we end up with two call options instead of one. In other words we are over hedged. This makes our static hedge unnecessarily expensive.

To avoid this we could simply add a short position in a first-up-then-down-and-in-call and a first-down-then-up-and-in-call. In this case when the asset for the first time hits a barrier we get a call. Then if the asset should hit the other barrier we get two new options at the same time; a long call plus a short call which cancel each other out. We are only left with the call we got at the first barrier hit, as we should.

The problem with this strategy occurs if the asset first hits the upper barrier, then hits the lower barrier, and then hits the upper barrier. Or alternatively, if the asset first hits the lower barrier, then hits the upper barrier, and then hits the lower barrier. In any of these cases we will end up with zero call options. To avoid this we could simply add a long position in a first-down-then-up-then-down-and-in call plus a first-up-then-down-then-up-and-in call.

Now we will get into trouble if the asset first hits the upper barrier, then the lower barrier, then the upper barrier and then the lower barrier. Or alternatively if the asset first hits the lower barrier, then hits the upper barrier, then hits the lower barrier, and then hits the upper barrier. To avoid this we could simply add a short position in a first-up-then-down-then-up-then-down-and-in and a first-down-then-up-then-down-then-up-and-in call.

Continuing this way one will soon find that a double barrier option is nothing more than an infinite series of the new type of barrier options introduced in section 2. Since these new types of barrier options (e.g. a first-down-then-up-then-down ... and-in) can be constructed simply by using the single barrier put–call symmetry, a double barrier option is nothing more than an infinite series of single barrier options:

$$\text{Double barrier option} = \sum_{i=1}^{\infty} \text{Single barrier options} \tag{5.13}$$

To value an infinite series is naturally not practical if not impossible. However, the probability of the asset first touching the upper barrier then touching the lower barrier, then touching the upper barrier, then touching the lower barrier... then touching the upper barrier is in most cases fast becoming extremely small. Numerical investigation shows that our method converges very fast in most cases only using the first three or four correction terms. Using four terms, the value of a double barrier in-call option can be approximated by

$$C_i(S, X, L, U, T, r, \sigma) \approx C_{ui}(S, X, U, T, r, \sigma) + C_{di}(S, X, L, T, r, \sigma) \tag{5.14}$$

$$- \frac{X}{U} P_{ui}\left(S, \frac{U^2}{X}, \frac{U^2}{L}, T, r, \sigma\right) - \frac{X}{L} P_{di}\left(S, \frac{L^2}{X}, \frac{L^2}{U}, T, r, \sigma\right)$$

$$+ \frac{U}{L} C_{di}\left(S_t, \frac{L^2 X}{U^2}, \frac{L^3}{U^2}, T, r, \sigma\right) + \frac{L}{U} C_{ui}\left(S, \frac{U^2 X}{L^2}, \frac{U^3}{L^2}, T, r, \sigma\right)$$

$$- \frac{LX}{U^2} P_{ui}\left(S_t, \frac{U^4}{L^2 X}, \frac{U^4}{L^3}, T, r, \sigma\right) - \frac{UX}{L^2} P_{di}\left(S, \frac{L^4}{U^2 X}, \frac{L^4}{U^3}, T, r, \sigma\right)$$

$$+ \frac{U^2}{L^2} C_{di}\left(S, \frac{L^4 X}{U^4}, \frac{L^5}{U^4}, T, r, \sigma\right) + \frac{L^2}{U^2} C_{ui}\left(S, \frac{U^4 X}{L^4}, \frac{U^5}{L^4}, T, r, \sigma\right)$$

and similarly the value of a double barrier in-put can be approximated by

$$P_i(S, X, L, U, T, r, \sigma) \approx P_{ui}(S, X, U, T, r, \sigma) + P_{di}(S, X, L, T, r, \sigma) \tag{5.15}$$

$$- \frac{X}{U} C_{ui}\left(S, \frac{U^2}{X}, \frac{U^2}{L}, T, r, \sigma\right) - \frac{X}{L} C_{di}\left(S, \frac{L^2}{X}, \frac{L^2}{U}, T, r, \sigma\right)$$

$$+ \frac{U}{L} P_{di}\left(S, \frac{L^2 X}{U^2}, \frac{L^3}{U^2}, T, r, \sigma\right) + \frac{L}{U} P_{ui}\left(S, \frac{U^2 X}{L^2}, \frac{U^3}{L^2}, T, r, \sigma\right)$$

$$-\frac{LX}{U^2}C_{ui}\left(S,\frac{U^4}{L^2X},\frac{U^4}{L^3},T,r,\sigma\right)-\frac{UX}{L^2}C_{di}\left(S,\frac{L^4}{U^2X},\frac{L^4}{U^3},T,r,\sigma\right)$$

$$+\frac{U^2}{L^2}P_{di}\left(S,\frac{L^4X}{U^4},\frac{L^5}{U^4},T,r,\sigma\right)+\frac{L^2}{U^2}P_{ui}\left(S,\frac{U^4X}{L^4},\frac{U^5}{L^4},T,r,\sigma\right)$$

The value of double barrier out-options can easily be found using the out-in barrier parity. Static hedging of a double barrier option in this way is naturally not practical. But we still have a closed form formula in a Black-Scholes world, that again will give us the delta, gamma and other risk parameters we need to construct the necessary hedge at least inside the Black-Scholes World.

Table 5.1 shows the difference in value between the Ikeda and Kunitomo (1992)[2] model and our approximation.

TABLE 5.1: THE IKEDA AND KUNITOMO MODEL MINUS OUR INTUITIVE DOUBLE BARRIER MODEL (USING FOUR TERMS IN OUR MODEL AND 20 LEADING TERMS IN THE IKEDA AND KUNITOMO FORMULA),
$$(S_T = 100, X = 100, r = 0.10, b = 0)$$

		T = 0.25			T = 1		
L	U	$\sigma = 10\%$	$\sigma = 20\%$	$\sigma = 30\%$	$\sigma = 10\%$	$\sigma = 20\%$	$\sigma = 30\%$
50	150	0.000000	0.000000	0.000000	0.000000	0.000000	0.000000
60	140	0.000000	0.000000	0.000000	0.000000	0.000000	0.000000
70	130	0.000000	0.000000	0.000000	0.000000	0.000000	0.000000
80	120	0.000000	0.000000	0.000000	0.000000	0.000000	0.000000
95	105	0.000000	0.000000	-0.001244	0.000000	-0.032843	-0.518185

From all the zeros in the table we can see that the two models must give almost identical values for most parameters. First, when the volatility is quite high in combination with long time to maturity, and the difference between the lower and upper barrier is quite small our model gets into trouble. The reason for this is simply because in that case the probability of the asset price hitting the lower and upper barriers many times in succession increases. Using only four terms our model will get into trouble if the asset goes back and forth between the lower and upper barriers more than four times in a row. Then one ends up with two call options instead of one.

In other words, if the probability of many sequential barrier hits is large our missing correction terms will have significant value. In all other cases our formula will work fine. One solution to this is naturally to just add more and more correction terms as the probability of hitting both barriers many times sequentially increases. However, intuitively this must also imply that the probability of at least one barrier hit must be very high. In that case the value of the double barrier option must be very close to that of a plain vanilla option.

Another observation is that our barrier approximation will always overprice double barrier in-options as long as we have even correction terms (2, 4, 6… 14). The reason for this is that even correction terms implies that the last correction term always will be a long position. Again, this means that there exists a probability of ending up with two options instead of one as we should. Combining these observations we can simply increase the accuracy of our model by calculating its value as the minimum of a plain vanilla option and the double barrier approximation with a few even correction terms, (e.g. 2, 4, or 6). Because the value of a double barrier option naturally never can be higher than a plain vanilla option this can do no harm, but only increase the accuracy. Using four correction terms the value of the double barrier in-call option can now be rewritten as:

$$C_t^i(S_t, X, L, U, T, r, \sigma) \approx \tag{5.16}$$

$$\min\Bigg[C_t(S_t, X, T);\ C_t^{ui}(S_t, X, U, T, r, \sigma) + C_{di}(S_t, X, L, T, r, \sigma)$$

$$-\frac{X}{U} P_t^{ui}\left(S_t, \frac{U^2}{X}, \frac{U^2}{L}, T, r, \sigma \right) - \frac{X}{L} P_t^{di}\left(S_t, \frac{L^2}{X}, \frac{L^2}{U}, T, r, \sigma \right)$$

$$+\frac{U}{L} C_t^{di}\left(S_t, \frac{L^2 X}{U^2}, \frac{L^3}{U^2}, T, r, \sigma \right) + \frac{L}{U} C_t^{ui}\left(S_t, \frac{U^2 X}{L^2}, \frac{U^3}{L^2}, T, r, \sigma \right)$$

$$-\frac{LX}{U^2} P_t^{ui}\left(S_t, \frac{U^4}{L^2 X}, \frac{U^4}{L^3}, T, r, \sigma \right) - \frac{UX}{L^2} P_t^{di}\left(S_t, \frac{L^4}{U^2 X}, \frac{L^4}{U^3}, T, r, \sigma \right)$$

$$+\frac{U^2}{L^2} C_t^{di}\left(S_t, \frac{L^4 X}{U^4}, \frac{L^5}{U^4}, T, r, \sigma \right) + \frac{L^2}{U^2} C_t^{ui}\left(S_t, \frac{U^4 X}{L^4}, \frac{U^5}{L^4}, T, r, \sigma \right) \Bigg]$$

Using this modified version of our formula the largest mispricing in Table 5.1 goes from -0.518185 to only -0.000024 and all the other mispricings get even smaller. Extensive numerical investigation shows that this method is extremely accurate and robust for all types of input parameters. Even dropping the last two correction terms, numerical investigation indicates that our formula should be more than accurate enough for any practical purpose. For instance, if we now increase the volatility further in combination with longer time to maturity, and decrease the difference between the two barriers this will only increase the accuracy of our formula.

While the method we are using makes no difference if the strike price is inside or outside the barrier range, the Ikeda and Kunitomo (1992) quickly runs into trouble when the strike price is outside the lower and upper barrier. This is shown in Table 5.2, where we look at double knock-out call options. We are using a very high strike price far above the upper barrier and intuition tells us that the value must be close to zero, while the Ikeda and Kunitomo model returns negative values. Using the Black (1976) formula to value plain vanilla options with the same parameters we will see that the value is zero to four decimal places, as we can see using our method of barrier symmetry we get the correct value even for such extreme input values.

In practice one can often observe a strike price outside the barrier range, in particular for double knock-in options. For double knock-out options it does not make too much sense to have a strike outside the barrier range. Double knock-in options can, however, be created from going long a plain option and short a double knock-out option, either physically in the market or simply by using this as valuation method. That the valuation method holds also when the strike is outside the barrier range is of great importance.

TABLE 5.2: EXAMPLES OF CALL-UP-AND-OUT-DOWN-AND-OUT VALUES

$(S = 100, X = 300, r = 0.10, b = 0)$

			$T = 0.25$			$T = 0.50$	
L	U	$\sigma = 0.15$	$\sigma = 0.25$	$\sigma = 0.35$	$\sigma = 0.15$	$\sigma = 0.25$	$\sigma = 0.35$
			Barrier Symmetry Method Values				
50	150	0.0000	0.0000	0.0000	0.0000	0.0000	0.0000
60	140	0.0000	0.0000	0.0000	0.0000	0.0000	0.0000
70	130	0.0000	0.0000	0.0000	0.0000	0.0000	0.0000
			Ikeda Kunitomo Method Values				
50	150	−48.7657	−48.7017	−46.9406	−44.7299	−36.1031	−24.4045
60	140	−72.4506	−71.5175	−65.3518	−64.1936	−46.0981	−28.3429
70	130	−98.0578	−91.6767	−75.3108	−78.1407	−44.8479	−20.2687

3.1 Dual Double Barrier Options

The technique developed above is extremely flexible and we can easily create new types of complex barrier options. In a standard double knock-in call option you get a call no matter if the upper or lower barrier is hit. However, a customer (trader or hedger) would wish he had a put if the asset hits the lower barrier and a call if the asset price hits the upper barrier. This would be a knock-in double barrier put-down-call-up. Using the technique described above we can now easily value such an option. Here we are also limiting ourselves to the case when the cost-of-carry is zero, that is barrier options on futures or forwards. A very good approximation should be:

$$C_t^{ipc}(S_t, X, L, U, T, r, \sigma) \approx \min\Big[\max[C_t(S_t, X, T, r, \sigma); \tag{5.17}$$

$$P_t(S_t, X, T, r, \sigma)]; C_t^{ui}(S_t, X, U, T, r, \sigma) + P_t^{di}(S_t, X, L, T, r, \sigma)$$

$$-\frac{X}{U} P_t^{ui}\left(S_t, \frac{U^2}{X}, \frac{U^2}{L}, T, r, \sigma\right) - \frac{X}{L} C_t^{di}\left(S_t, \frac{L^2}{X}, \frac{L^2}{U}, T, r, \sigma\right)$$

$$+\frac{U}{L} C_t^{di}\left(S_t, \frac{L^2 X}{U^2}, \frac{L^3}{U^2}, T, r, \sigma\right) + \frac{L}{U} P_t^{ui}\left(S_t, \frac{U^2 X}{L^2}, \frac{U^3}{L^2}, T, r, \sigma\right)$$

$$-\frac{LX}{U^2} P_t^{ui}\left(S_t, \frac{U^4}{L^2 X}, \frac{U^4}{L^3}, T, r, \sigma\right) - \frac{UX}{L^2} C_t^{di}\left(S_t, \frac{L^4}{U^2 X}, \frac{L^4}{U^3}, T, r, \sigma\right)$$

$$+\frac{U^2}{L^2} c_t^{di}\left(S_t, \frac{L^4 X}{U^4}, \frac{L^5}{U^4}, T, r, \sigma\right) + \frac{L^2}{U^2} P_t^{ui}\left(S_t, \frac{U^4 X}{L^4}, \frac{U^5}{L^4}, T, r, \sigma\right)\Big]$$

Similarly, the formula for a knock-in double barrier call-down-put-up is:

$$C_t^{icd}(S_t, X, L, U, T, r, \sigma) \approx \min\Big[\max[C_t(S_t, X, T, r, \sigma); \tag{5.18}$$

$$P_t(S_t, X, T, r, \sigma)]; P_t^{ui}(S_t, X, U, T, r, \sigma) + C_t^{di}(S_t, X, L, T, r, \sigma)$$

$$-\frac{X}{U}C_t^{ui}\left(S_t,\frac{U^2}{X},\frac{U^2}{L},T,r,\sigma\right)-\frac{X}{L}P_t^{di}\left(S_t,\frac{L^2}{X},\frac{L^2}{U},T,r,\sigma\right)$$

$$+\frac{U}{L}P_t^{di}\left(S_t,\frac{L^2X}{U^2},\frac{L^3}{U^2},T,r,\sigma\right)+\frac{L}{U}C_t^{ui}\left(S_t,\frac{U^2X}{L^2},\frac{U^3}{L^2},T,r,\sigma\right)$$

$$-\frac{LX}{U^2}C_t^{ui}\left(S_t,\frac{U^4}{L^2X},\frac{U^4}{L^3},T,r,\sigma\right)-\frac{UX}{L^2}P_t^{di}\left(S_t,\frac{L^4}{U^2X},\frac{L^4}{U^3},T,r,\sigma\right)$$

$$+\frac{U^2}{L^2}P_t^{di}\left(S_t,\frac{L^4X}{U^4},\frac{L^5}{U^4},T,r,\sigma\right)+\frac{L^2}{U^2}C_t^{ui}\left(S_t,\frac{U^4X}{L^4},\frac{U^5}{L^4},T,r,\sigma\right)\Bigg]$$

A call-down-put-up knock-in option naturally has a considerably lower value than a call-up-put-down knock in option. The latter can be seen as a poor man's double barrier option.

Table 5.3 shows the value of dual double barrier options.

TABLE 5.3: DUAL DOUBLE BARRIER OPTIONS
($S = 100$, $X = 100$, $T = 0.25$, $r = 0.08$, $b = 0$)

		call-up-put-down knock-in			put-up-call-down knock-in		
L	U	$\sigma = 0.10$	$\sigma = 0.20$	$\sigma = 0.30$	$\sigma = 0.10$	$\sigma = 0.20$	$\sigma = 0.30$
70	130	0.0000	0.2368	2.6778	0.0000	0.0000	0.0009
75	125	0.0002	0.6753	4.5569	0.0000	0.0000	0.0063
80	120	0.0049	1.7827	5.8601	0.0000	0.0003	0.0400
85	115	0.0895	3.8906	5.8601	0.0000	0.0089	0.1791
90	110	0.8917	3.9088	5.8601	0.0001	0.1161	0.3405
95	105	1.9550	3.9088	5.8601	0.0570	0.2814	1.0719

Such a double barrier option is not just theory, as such options have actually begun to be traded in the OTC FX market.

4 Static Hedging in the Real World

It is worth commenting on static hedging; as simple barrier options with barriers very far out-of the money are not necessarily very liquid one can argue that many of the static hedges described above are not practical. However, even if we use the idea of static hedging to come up with the valuation formula for the more complex barrier options this does not mean that we actually need to use static hedging for our valuation formula to hold. As the static hedging gives us a closed form formula (approximation) we can from that formula find the traditional delta hedge. The traditional continuous delta hedging argument behind the Black-Scholes-Merton model is also valid here, even if we used a very different approach to come up with the valuation formulae for the complex options. The reason we still can use the dynamic delta approach is that the Black-Scholes-Merton argument is simply embedded in our model as our static hedge is built up from a series of simpler options that, to begin with, was based on geometric Brownian motion and continuous delta hedging. A good indication of this is that we get the same value and delta

as an analytical solution built from the ground up based on the Black-Scholes-Merton argument. However, our static hedging model has one advantage, in the case where there actually should be a liquid traded standard barrier options then if we actually can construct a static hedge our valuation method will also be consistent with a symmetric volatility smile (in $\ln(S)$), in other words the method is more robust with respect to stochastic asset price process than geometric Brownian motion. In the foreign exchange interbank market there is a very active market for standard barrier options, and static hedging there seems to be a realistic alternative.

5   Conclusion

Using a mathematical symmetry between standard put and call barrier options we have shown that a double barrier option can be valued in a simple and intuitive way as the minimum of a series of a few single barrier options and a plain vanilla option. Further, we have shown how the same principle can be used to value new and complex barrier options like dual double barrier options. The method is both more intuitive and in many ways more robust than traditional valuation methods.

FOOTNOTES & REFERENCES

1. For an option on a non-dividend paying stock $b = r$, for an option on a stock index paying a continuous dividend yield q, $b = r - q$, for a option on a futures/forwards $b = 0$, and for an option of foreign exchange $b = r - r_f$ where r_f is the foreign risk-free interest rate.
2. Assuming flat barriers. The Ikeda and Kunitomo (1992) formula can also be used for valuation of double barrier options with curved barriers.

■ Bates, D. S. (1991) "The Crash of '87: Was It Expected? The Evidence from Options Markets" *Journal of Finance*, **46**(3), 1009–1044.
■ Bjerksund, P, and G. Stensland (1993) "American Exchange Options and a Put-Call Tranformation: A Note" *Journal of Business Finance and Accounting*, **20**(5), 761–764.
■ Black, F. (1976) "The Pricing of Commodity Contracts" *Journal of Financial Economics*, **3**, 167–179.
■ Black, F. and M. Scholes (1973) "The Pricing of Options and Corporate Liabilities," *Journal of Political Economy*, **81**, 637–654.
■ Carr, P. and J. Bowie (1994) "Static Simplicity," *Risk Magazine*, **7**(8), 40–50.
■ Carr, P. and M. Chesney (1998) "American Put Call Symmetry" *Journal of Financial Engineering*.
■ Carr, P., K. Ellis and V. Gupta (1998) "Static Hedging of Exotic Options," *Journal of Finance*, **53**, 1165–1190.
■ Gao, B., J. Huang and M. Subrahmanyam (2000) "The Valuation of American Barrier Options Using the Decomposition Technique" *Journal of Economics Dynamics & Control*, **24**, 1783–1827.
■ Geman, H. and M. Yor (1996) "Pricing and Hedging Double-Barrier Options: A Probabilistic Approach," *Mathematical Finance*, **6**(4), 365–378.
■ Haug, E. G. (1998) "Put-Call Barrier Transformations" Working Paper Tempus Financial Engineering.
■ Haug, E. G. (2001a) "Closed form Valuation of American Barrier Options," *International Journal of Theoretical and Applied Finance*, **XIX**, 175–192.
■ Haug, E. G. (2001b) "First-then-knockout options," *Wilmott*, August.

- Heynen, R. C. and H. M. Kat (1994) "Partial Barrier Options," *Journal of Financial Engineering*, **3**, 253–274.
- Hui, C. H. (1997) "Time-Dependent Barrier Option Values" *Journal of Futures Markets*, **17**, 667–688.
- Ikeda, M., and N. Kuintomo (1992) "Pricing Options with Curved Boundaries" *Mathematical Finance*, **2**, 275–298.
- Merton, R. C. (1973) "Theory of Rational Option Pricing" *Bell Journal of Economics and Management Science*, **4**, 141–183.
- Reiner, E. and M. Rubinstein (1991) "Breaking Down the Barriers," *Risk Magazine*, **4**(8), 28–35.
- Rich, D. R. (1994) "The Mathematical Foundation of Barrier Option-Pricing Theory" *Advances in Futures and Options Research*, **7**, 267–311.

Clive Granger

Granger on Cointegration

Clive W. J. Granger is a Professor in Economics at the University of California, San Diego. He has published extensively in statistics, econometrics and finance. In 2003 he received the Nobel Prize in Economics for his work on methods of analyzing economic time series with common trends (cointegration). Professor Granger has published several hundred papers and a series of books.

Haug : Where did you grow up?

Granger : Cambridge and Nottingham, England.

Haug : When did you first become interested in science and mathematics?

Granger : High School, Nottingham.

Haug : What is your educational background?

Granger : Undergrad and Ph.D. at the University of Nottingham.

Haug : In simple words what is cointegration?

Granger : Discusses implications that on occasions a pair of "smooth series" can add to an "unsmooth" series. Implies generation by an error-correction model.

Haug : Is the main purpose of cointegration to find stationary relationships between variables?

Granger : Both this and equilibrium relationships.

Haug : When it comes to correlation between financial assets one typically looks at the returns, can cointegration also be used on the prices itself?

Granger : It has to be used on prices, not directly on returns. Potentially leads to extra forecasts on prices.

Haug : It is said that cointegration can be used to find trends, what type of trends are we talking about here? Can cointegration, for example, distinguish between mean-reversion, seasonality in data?

Granger : Yes, but not deterministic trends. They are "stochastic trends" like a random walk.

Haug : **Is cointegration also effective for finding short-run and long-run relationships in a system?**

Granger : No. Cointegration is mostly concerned with long-run but the associated error-correction model does both long-run and short-run.

Haug : **Linear correlation is very sensitive in that one has simultaneous measurements, is the same true for cointegration?**

Granger : No. You can add a white noise error to both variables and not change cointegration.

Haug : **Is the theory of cointegration also fully developed for continuous time processes?**

Granger : Probably, but I do not care as there is no continuous time data.

Haug : **From options and other derivatives instruments trading in the market we can back out implied volatilities as well as correlation and even distributions. Has there been any work on implied cointegration, or is cointegration as a tool limited to the study of historical time series?**

Granger : It is traditionally limited to historical data, "implied" data may be incorrect.

Haug : **Is cointegration dependent on any distributional assumptions about the underlying variables?**

Granger : No. The theory is not, but some of the tests may be.

Haug : **In practice we always have a limited amount of data points. Based on certain distribution assumptions we can calculate the confidence interval around our correlation or volatility estimate, which typically is wider the fewer data points we have. Can we do the same for cointegration?**

Granger : We have the same problem with cointegration.

Haug : **If there is a sudden regime switch causing historical relationships to go wild does this cause problems for cointegration? In such cases will the cointegration from the past be meaningful for the future?**

Granger : Cointegration measures "deeper" relationships, and so may survive the break.

Haug : **Tail events that happen extremely infrequently could easily be missing from the data we are estimating, how can we take this into account, and how sensitive is cointegration to a few outliers in the tail of the distribution?**

Granger : Cointegration should not be sensitive to the inclusion (or not) of outliers.

Haug : **Is there a limit to the number of variables that can be studied practically using cointegration?**

Granger : In theory, no.

Haug : **Do you have any hobbies outside econometrics and finance?**

Granger : Travel, reading and walking.

Haug : In your view where are we in the evolution of econometrics and in particular modeling and understanding of co-movements in data?

Granger : We have concentrated too much on mean and variance; in the future we will do more about predictive distributions and quantiles.

Some of Professor Granger's papers are listed below, for a long list of his many publications see http://econ.ucsd.edu/~cgranger/pubs.html.

REFERENCES

■ Engle, R. F. and C. W. J. Granger (1987) "Cointegration and Error Correction Representation, Estimation and Testing" *Econometrica*, **55**, 251–276.
■ Granger, C. W. J. (1981) "Some Properties of Time Series Data and Their Use in Econometric Model Specification" *Journal of Econometrics*, **16**, 121–130.
■ ——— (1992): "Forecasting Stock Market Prices" *Journal of Forecasting*, **8**, 3–13.

The Haug brothers; Dr Haug and Dr Haug. When I have a math problem I can't solve I simply call my baby brother. In our childhood we used to compete in making the best computer games, this was in the days when they printed the computer code in the computer magazines. My brother got his first computer game published when he was only 13 years old, I got my first computer game published when I was 16. What can I say, my brother got the brains and I got the looks;-)

6

Knock-in/out Margrabe*

with Jørgen Haug

In this chapter we push the Black-Scholes-Merton (BSM) formula to the limit by using it to value exchange-one-asset-for-another options with knock-in or knock-out provisions that depend on the ratio of the two asset prices. These option contracts are relevant to investors and traders concerned with the relative performance of securities, and they crop up in M&As.

1   Margrabe Options

Exchange-one-asset-for-another options give the owner the right to exchange asset S_2 for asset S_1 at expiration and were originally analyzed by Margrabe (1978).[1] The payoff from such a call option is

$$c^e(S_1, S_2; 0) = (S_1 - S_2)^+,$$

where $(\cdot)^+$ is the positive part. Margrabe considered the special case when the two asset prices follow geometric Brownian motion:

$$dS_1(u) = \mu_1 S_1(u)du + \sigma_1 S_1(u)dz_1(u), \qquad S_1(t) = S_1,$$

$$dS_2(u) = \mu_2 S_2(u)du + \sigma_1 S_2(u)dz_2(u), \qquad S_2(t) = S_2,$$

where μ_i and σ_i are the instantaneous return and volatility of asset $i = 1, 2$, and dz_1 and dz_2 are correlated Wiener processes with correlation coefficient ρ. The price of a call option with τ years left to maturity, derived in the appendix as a prelude to extensions with barriers, is then

$$c^e(S_1, S_2; \tau) = S_1 e^{(b_1-r)\tau} N(d_1) - S_2 e^{(b_2-r)\tau} N(d_2), \tag{6.1}$$

where

$$d_1 = \frac{\ln(S_1/S_2) + (b_1 - b_2 + \sigma^2/2)\tau}{\sigma\sqrt{\tau}},$$

$$d_2 = d_1 - \sigma\sqrt{\tau},$$

$$\sigma = \sqrt{\sigma_1^2 + \sigma_2^2 - 2\rho\sigma_1\sigma_2},$$

and b_i is the cost of carry of asset $i = 1, 2$.

---

*We would like to thank Erik Stettler for useful comments.

Margrabe makes the useful observation that we do not need to find a separate formula for a put option. The payoff from a put can be rewritten as

$$p^e(S_1(T), S_2(T); 0) = (S_2(T) - S_1(T))^+ = (1 - S(T))^+ S_2(T),$$

where $S \equiv S_1/S_2$. There is no special reason to factor out S_2, however. If we instead factor out S_1, then the payoff is equivalent to the call option, where S_1 and S_2 interchange roles.

2 Knock-in/out Margrabe Options

Consider first a *down-and-in* exchange-one-asset-for-another option (down-and-in Margrabe) which is knocked in if the ratio of the two asset prices $S = S_1/S_2$ hits the barrier H before maturity. By the reflection principle the price of a call down-and-in Margrabe option is[2]

$$c_{di}^e(S_1, S_2, H; \tau, r, b_1, b_2, \sigma_1, \sigma_2, \rho) = S_2 e^{(b_2-r)\tau} \left(\frac{S}{H}\right)^{1-\frac{2b}{\sigma^2}} c\left(\frac{H^2}{S}, 1, \tau, 0, b, \sigma\right),$$

where $c(S, X, \tau, r, b, \sigma)$ is the BSM call option (Black and Scholes, 1973; Merton, 1973) with current price of underlying S, strike X, time to maturity τ, riskless rate r, cost of carry b, and volatility σ. In the down-and-in Margrabe $b = b_1 - b_2$. Similarly, the value of an up-and-in Margrabe put option is given by

$$p_{ui}^e(S_1, S_2, H; \tau, r, b_1, b_2, \sigma_1, \sigma_2, \rho) = S_2 e^{(b_2-r)\tau} \left(\frac{S}{H}\right)^{1-\frac{2b}{\sigma^2}} p\left(\frac{H^2}{S}, 1, \tau, 0, b, \sigma\right),$$

where p is the BSM put option. It is possible to do with only one of the formulae here too, by observing a simple equivalence. Let $\hat{S} = S_2/S_1 = S^{-1}$, $\hat{H} = H^{-1}$, 1_A equal 1 when A is true and 0 otherwise, $\underline{S} = \min_{u \in [t,T]} S(u)$, and $\overline{S} = \max_{u \in [t,T]} S(u)$. The payoff to the up-and-in put is

$$(S_2(T) - S_1(T))^+ 1_{\{\overline{S}>H\}} = S_1(\hat{S}(T) - 1)^+ 1_{\{\hat{S}<\hat{H}\}},$$

which is equivalent to the payoff to the down-and-in call where the two asset prices interchange roles, and the barrier is H^{-1} rather than H.

Table 6.1 shows down-and-in Margrabe values. The first row shows plain vanilla Margrabe prices. It is evident that the barrier option values converge to the Margrabe option values when the barrier converges to the current price ratio $\frac{125}{100} = 1.25$, because the probability of a barrier hit converges to unity.

The value of *down-and-out* Margrabe options follows from the in-out parity. A down-and-out Margrabe option is equal simply to a long plain Margrabe option plus a short down-and-in Margrabe option. In the special case when $H = 1$ and $b_1 = b_2$ the formula for a down-and-out Margrabe can be simplified to $c_{do}^e = e^{(b_1-r)T}(S_1 - S_2)$. For such parameters this option is "surprisingly" unaffected by volatility and correlation. If $b_1 = b_2 = r$ we naturally get an even simpler formula; $c_{do}^e = S_1 - S_2$, this is the world's simplest two-asset option formula, see Lindset and Persson (2006).

TABLE 6.1: DOWN-AND-IN MARGRABE VALUES
For comparison, the first line shows plain margrabe values without barriers,
$(S_1 = 125, S_2 = 100, \tau = 1, r = 0.07,$
$b_1 = 0.03, b_2 = 0.05, \sigma_1 = 0.45, \sigma_2 = 0.47.)$

H	$\rho = -0.5$	$\rho = 0.0$	$\rho = 0.5$
	45.8421	40.1508	32.7530
1.2499	45.8318	40.1401	32.7418
1.2000	40.7303	34.9214	27.2639
1.1500	35.7986	29.9309	22.1338
1.1000	31.0790	25.2257	17.4500
1.0500	26.6049	20.8523	13.2922
1.0000	22.4108	16.8553	9.7238

Lastly, consider an *up-and-out* Margrabe option. Its price is given by

$$c_{uo}^e(S_1, S_2, H; \tau) = S_1 e^{(b_1-r)\tau} \left[\hat{N}(k_1) - \hat{N}(k_3) - \left(\frac{H}{S}\right)^{1+\frac{2b}{\sigma^2}} \{\hat{N}(k_2) - \hat{N}(k_4)\} \right]$$

$$- S_2 e^{(b_2-r)\tau} \left[N(k_1) - N(k_3) - \left(\frac{S}{H}\right)^{1-\frac{2b}{\sigma^2}} \{N(k_2) - N(k_4)\} \right],$$

where $\hat{N}(x) = N(x - \sigma\sqrt{\tau})$,

$$k_1 = \frac{\ln(H/S) - \left(b - \frac{1}{2}\sigma^2\right)\tau}{\sigma\sqrt{\tau}}, \qquad k_2 = \frac{\ln(S/H) - \left(b - \frac{1}{2}\sigma^2\right)\tau}{\sigma\sqrt{\tau}},$$

$$k_3 = \frac{-\ln(S) - \left(b - \frac{1}{2}\sigma^2\right)\tau}{\sigma\sqrt{\tau}}, \qquad k_4 = \frac{\ln(S/H^2) - \left(b - \frac{1}{2}\sigma^2\right)\tau}{\sigma\sqrt{\tau}},$$

and as before $b = b_1 - b_2$. The equivalence above still holds in this case, so we leave out the expression for the down-and-out put. Table 6.2 confirms that its price converges to zero as the barrier converges to the current price ratio. Moreover, the price converges to the price of a plain vanilla Margrabe as the barrier increases. This is also as expected, since the probability of knocking out the option contract diminishes as the barrier increases.

3 Applications

While it's neat to be able to price a two-asset barrier option by simply using reflection and the BSM formula, the proof of the pudding is still in the eating! In other words, are the option contracts of any use?

The options that we consider are relevant to investors and traders that are concerned with the relative performance of stocks, or for instance a stock versus a stock index. Moreover, Margrabe (1978) indicated that exchange-one-asset-for-another options are often embedded in financial

TABLE 6.2:   UP-AND-OUT MARGRABE VALUES

For comparison, the first line shows plain margrabe values without barriers, ($S_1 = 125, S_2 = 100, \tau = 1, r = 0.07,$ $b_1 = 0.03, b_2 = 0.05, \sigma_1 = 0.45, \sigma_2 = 0.47.$)

H	$\rho = -0.5$	$\rho = 0.0$	$\rho = 0.5$
	45.8421	40.1508	32.7530
1.2599	0.0025	0.0048	0.0136
1.5000	0.3011	0.5503	1.4583
2.0000	3.1487	5.2288	10.7486
2.5000	8.3667	12.5473	20.3393
3.0000	14.2419	19.5300	26.3218
3.5000	19.7277	25.1056	29.5072
5.0000	31.5188	34.3892	32.3216
25.0000	45.7671	40.1490	32.7530
50.0000	45.8399	40.1508	32.7530

contracts, and thereby also relevant to corporate finance. An important case is when a firm bids for another firm by offering its own shares in exchange for shares in the target. The owners of the target in effect receive an option to exchange their shares for shares in the acquiring firm. This is only part of the story, however. The latest M&As frenzy is full of examples of acquiring firms walking away from the deal. Many bidding firms use walk-away covenants that render the offer void if the share price of the target company drops significantly in relation to that of the acquiring firm. Other common walk-away covenants rely on other measures of performance of the target. As long as the stock market is functioning well, any relevant performance measure should be highly correlated with the stock price. Hence, even these cases can be viewed as a Margrabe option that is knocked out when the stock price ratio hits a barrier. In real-world covenants, the level of the barrier is typically not specified well or is even unknown. An obvious extension to our model would be to allow the barrier level to be stochastic.

Appendix

Margrabe: Probabilistic methods allow an easy explanation as to why the price of the plain vanilla Margrabe option is given by (6.1.) Let P be the original probability measure, Q the risk-adjusted measure when the bank account serves as numeraire, and Q_S the probability measure determined by $\frac{dQ_S}{dQ} = \frac{S_2(T)}{E\{S_2(T)\}}$. If we represent investors' information at time t by $\mathcal{F}t$ and let $S(t) \equiv S_1(t)/S_2(t)$ then

$$c^e(S_1, S_2; \tau) = e^{-r\tau} E^Q\{(S(T) - 1)^+ S_2(T)|\mathcal{F}_t\}$$
$$= e^{-r\tau} E^Q\{S_2(T)\}\mathcal{F}_t E^{Q_S}\{(S(T) - 1)^+ |\mathcal{F}_t\}$$
$$= S_2(t)e^{(b_2-r)\tau} E^{Q_S}\{(S(T) - 1)^+ |\mathcal{F}_t\}.$$

This is the BSM formula without discounting, multiplied by $S_2(t)$, strike price 1, current asset price $S = S_1/S_2$, and volatility as stated above.

Down-and-in Margrabe: Adding a barrier is simple, since we have just derived the basic Margrabe formula by using probabilistic methods. Let $\underline{S} = \min_{u \in [0,T]} S(u)$, the lowest level of the price ratio attained during the life of the option contract. Let D be the event that the option is in-the-money at maturity, $\{S(T) \geq 1\} \cap \{\underline{S} \leq H\}$. The payoff of the call is

$$[S_1(T) - S_2(T)]1_D = S_2(T)[S(T) - 1]1_D.$$

The value of the call is therefore

$$
\begin{aligned}
c^e_{di}(t) &= e^{-r\tau} E^Q\{S_2(T)[S(T) - 1]1_D | \mathcal{F}_t\} \\
&= S_2(t)e^{(b_2-r)\tau} E^{Q_S}\{[S(T) - 1]1_D | \mathcal{F}_t\} \\
&= S_2(t)e^{(b_2-r)\tau} \left[E^{Q_S}\{S(T)1_D | \mathcal{F}_t\} - E^{Q_S}\{1_D | \mathcal{F}_t\} \right].
\end{aligned}
$$

Define a new probability measure by $dQ_{SS}/dQ_S = S(T)/E\{S(T)\}$, and recall that for any probability measure $\hat{Q}$, $E^{\hat{Q}}\{1_A | \mathcal{F}\} = \hat{Q}(A | \mathcal{F})$, the conditional probability of the event A. The value of the call can now be rewritten as

$$c^e_{di}(t) = S_2(t)e^{(b_2-r)\tau} \left[S(t)e^{b\tau} Q_{SS}(D | \mathcal{F}t) + Q_S(D | \mathcal{F}t) \right].$$

The role of the reflection principle is to help characterize $Q_{SS}(\cdot)$ and $Q_S(\cdot)$ (Conze and Viswanathan, 1991).

Up-and-out Margrabe: Continuing with the above notation and letting G be the event that $\{S(T) \geq 1\} \cap \{\bar{S} < H\}$,

$$
\begin{aligned}
c^e_{uo}(t) &= e^{-r\tau} E^Q\{S_2(T)(S(T) - 1)1_G | \mathcal{F}_t\} \\
&= S_2(t)e^{(b_2-r)\tau} E^{Q_S}\{(S(T) - 1)1_G | \mathcal{F}_t\} \\
&= S_2(t)e^{(b_2-r)\tau} \left[S(t)e^{b\tau} E^{Q_{SS}}\{1_G | \mathcal{F}_t\} - E^{Q_S}\{1_G | \mathcal{F}_t\} \right] \\
&= S_2(t)e^{(b_2-r)\tau} \left[S(t)e^{b\tau} Q_{SS}(G | \mathcal{F}_t) - Q_S(G | \mathcal{F}_t) \right],
\end{aligned}
$$

where again the two conditional probabilities are computed by the reflection principle.

FOOTNOTES & REFERENCES

1. Rubinstein (1991) and Haug (1997) are other treatments of this class of options.
2. Conze and Viswanathan (1991) apply the reflection principle to lookback options, of which barrier options are special cases. Haug (2001) applies the same principle to value standard American barrier options. A simple discussion of the principle can be found in most text books on probability theory, for instance Durett (1996).

■ Black, F. and M. Scholes (1973) "The Pricing of Options and Corporate Liabilities" *Journal of Political Economy*, **81**, 637–654.
■ Conze, A. and Viswanathan (1991) "Path Dependent Options: The Case of Lookback Options" *Journal of Finance*, **46**, 1893–1907.
■ Durett, R. (1996) *Probability*. 2nd edn, Belmont, CA: Duxbury Press.
■ Haug, E. G. (1997) *The Complete Guide To Option Pricing Formulas*. New York: McGraw-Hill.
■ —— (2001): "The Options Genius" *Wilmott Magazine*, **1**(1), 70–73.
■ Lindset, S. and S.-A. Persson (2006) "A Note On a Barrier Exchange Option: The World's Simplest Option Formula?," *Financial Research Letters*, **3**.
■ Margrabe, W. (1978) "The Value of an Option to Exchange One Asset for Another" *Journal of Finance*, **33**(1), 177–186.
■ Merton, R. C. (1973) "Theory of Rational Option Pricing" *Bell Journal of Economics and Management Science*, **4**, 141–183.
■ Rubinstein, M. (1991) "One for Another" *Risk Magazine*, **4**(7).

Stephen Ross

Stephen Ross on APT

Stephen A. Ross is best known as the inventor of the Arbitrage Pricing Theory, as well as the co-discoverer of the binomial model for pricing derivatives. His book, "Corporate Finance", is in its seventh edition. Stephen Ross is Professor in Financial Economics at MIT Sloan School of Management.

Haug :   Where did you grow up?

Ross : Brookline, Massachusetts, USA.

Haug : What is your educational background?

Ross : BA in physics from CalTech and Ph.D. in economics from Harvard.

Haug :   How and when did the idea of risk-neutral valuation first come into being, and what was your contribution to it?

Ross : I first discovered the equivalence between no arbitrage and the existence of a positive linear pricing. Independently John Cox and I discovered risk neutral pricing in the context of option pricing theory. We subsequently realized that it was a representation of the fundamental equivalence I had discovered earlier.

Haug : In your own words, what is Arbitrage Pricing Theory (APT)?

Ross : It is a simple theory that builds on the most successful idea in modern finance if not in all of economics, namely that there can be no arbitrage possibilities simply available. In the case of the APT it has two components. First, the assumption is made that returns are generated by a linear factor model, i.e., there are a limited number of factors that affect all asset returns and their affects add to the total systematic impact for each asset. Second, the idiosyncratic effects on individual stocks can be diversified away and will play no role in pricing large portfolios. Third, since each such portfolio is linearly related to common factors, to prevent arbitrage the pricing, i.e., the expected return of each asset must be similarly linearly related to its exposure to the factors.

Haug : Is the APT model a replacement, generalization or supplement to the CAPM?

Ross : It is a different theory and each stands alone. The CAPM is an equilibrium model that places rests on the rationality of market participants. The APT relies only on no arbitrage. As a consequence the APT is stronger in the sense that its assumptions are weaker but the price of that is that its conclusions are weaker. In particular, it has little to offer for determining risk premia.

Haug : What are the main similarities and differences between APT and CAPM?

Ross : At a practical level its simple, the APT allows for multiple factors to impact expected returns independent of their influence on the market portfolio. For the CAPM knowing only the market portfolio and the relation of assets to it is sufficient for pricing assets.

Haug : How well does the arbitrage theory fit empirical observations?

Ross : Not as well as I would like. Like all asset pricing theories, to quote Gene Fama: "The data has yet to meet a theory that it likes".

Haug : If one can define a violation of the APT model in an appropriate way, does this imply an arbitrage opportunity?

Ross : Yes.

Haug : With thousands of hedge funds and traders claiming (or at least hoping) that they can beat the market does this mean that practitioners do not believe in APT, or is this the reason APT actually works in practice, that hedge funds and arbitrage traders will quickly bring asset prices back into line?

Ross : The latter is the proper way to think about it. The friction in the market keeps the APT from being perfect and the actions of traders drives the market towards the no arbitrage ideal.

Haug : How do we identify the factors "driving" the APT?

Ross : There are two main methods. First we can take a purely statistical approach and define the factors by decomposing the covariance structure of asset returns to identify portfolios of securities that mimic factors. Second we can specify the factors exogenously by identifying economic forces, e.g., interest rates that we can give names to and that we a priori believe will impact cash flows and discount rates.

Haug : Was the APT intended to be a practical model or is it more an academic model helping us to understand some deeper fundamental principles of investments, or both?

Ross : Both; all good academic models enable us to see the world more simply and clearly and that clearly has pragmatic benefit.

Haug : Is the APT in any way dependent upon the distribution assumptions of the under-lying assets?

Ross : As I said before, one uses a linear factor model. Beyond that assets can have fat-tails or any marginal distributions.

Haug : What about factors that are normally not observable, but can then suddenly have a big impact on the markets, like for example a massive terrorist attack (September 11), or a sudden stock market crash? How does this affect the assumptions and use of the APT?

Ross : It just makes empirical work more difficult. More simply, for example, inflation is obviously a factor and it is obviously for quite long periods of time.

Haug : How has the APT evolved over time, what are the differences between the original and more modern versions of the APT?

Ross : More modern versions have empirical structures, for example the Fama French factor portfolios and they have developed as dynamic models such as the intertemporal CAPM which argues that the state variables are what determine the future evolution of the market opportunities. I always viewed the factors as innovations in such state variables and making this dynamics explicit has been central to our understanding of asset pricing.

Haug : How are dynamic delta hedging of options and its risk neutrality connected to APT?

Ross : They are really the same thing. Locally as in a snapshot option pricing and delta hedging is simply the formation of an arbitrage portfolio in a one factor exact APT with no idiosyncratic risk.

Haug : In the Black-Scholes-Merton and also in the binomial model that you developed together with Cox and Rubinstein, the risk of the option can basically be removed by dynamic delta hedging. In other words we can value the options or derivative security using risk-neutral valuation. However, I understand this argument is based on continuous price moves, while we in practice often observe jumps. Does this imply that we in practice have only a weak form of risk-neutrality?

Ross : No. In the binomial model you can delta hedge but clearly there are jumps and time and prices move discretely. The key is that there be enough assets to span the jumps – two is sufficient in a binomial model – not that time or prices be continuous.

Haug : You also did some work on option valuation under constant elasticity of variance. What was the idea behind this work?

Ross : John Cox did more of this than did I but the basic implication is just to alter the dependence of option pricing on volatility.

Haug : You are also involved in a firm known as Compensation Valuation. What is the idea behind this firm?

Ross : CVI uses modern option pricing technology to value employee stock options for companies that issue them. More generally, CVI solves complicated valuation problems for companies.

Haug : Do you have any hobbies outside financial economics?

Ross : Basketball – I am a fan. Tennis – I am a bad player. Sailing/Boating.

Haug : In your view where are we in the evolution of quantitative finance?

Ross : At a wonderful beginning. Or to paraphrase Winston Churchill, the middle of the beginning.

REFERENCES

■ Cox, J. (1975) "Notes on Option Pricing I: Constant Elasticity of Variance Diffusions" Working paper, Stanford University.
■ Cox, J. C. and S. A. Ross (1976) "The Valuation of Options for Alternative Stochastic Processes" *Journal of Financial Economics*, **3**, 145–166.
■ Cox, J. C., S. A. Ross and M. Rubinstein (1979) "Option Pricing: A Simplified Approach" *Journal of Financial Economics*, **7**, 229–263.
■ Roll, R. and S. A. Ross (1980) "An Empirical Investigation of the Arbitrage Pricing Theory" *Journal of Finance*, **35**(5), 1073–1103.
■ Ross, S. A. (1976) "The Arbitrage Theory of Capital Asset Pricing." *Journal of Economic Theory*, **13**, 341–360.
■ Ross, S. A., R. W. Westerfield and J. Jaffe (2004) *Corporate Finance, 7th ed.* New York: McGraw-Hill.

7

Resetting Strikes, Barriers and Time*

with Jørgen Haug

We suggest a simple technique to price a large class of European reset options. Options where the strike is reset during their lifetime are traded actively in the OTC equity market. They are considered difficult to value because of the inherent path dependency. Our solution shows you how to price these options in a surprisingly simple and intuitive way, by extending the binomial tree of Cox, Ross and Rubinstein (1979) and Rendleman and Bartter (1979). Not only can our method be used to price standard reset strike options, but also to price reset barrier options, and even to reset time itself.

1   Introduction

In a plain vanilla reset call (put) option the strike is reset to the asset price at a predetermined future time, if the asset price is below (above) the initial strike price. More generally the strike can be reset to any function of the asset price at future dates. This makes the strike path-dependent. Gray and Whaley (1999) have derived a closed form solution for the price of European reset strike options.[1] They assume that the asset price follows a geometric Brownian motion $dS_t = \mu S_t dt + \sigma S_t dz_t$, $S_0 = S$. The price of the call option is then given by

$$c_r(S, X) = Se^{(b-r)T} M(a_1, y_1; \rho) - Xe^{-rT} M(a_2, y_2; \rho)$$
$$- Se^{(b-r)\tau} N(-a_1) N(z_2) e^{-r(T-\tau)} + Se^{(b-r)T} N(-a_1) N(z_1),$$

while the price of the put option is given by

$$p_r(S, X) = Se^{(b-r)\tau} N(a_1) N(-z_2) e^{-r(T-\tau)} - Se^{(b-r)T} N(a_1) N(-z_1)$$
$$+ Xe^{-rT} M(-a_2, -y_2; \rho) - Se^{(b-r)T} M(-a_1, -y_1; \rho).$$

---

*We are grateful for helpful comments from Svein Stokke, Citibank New York. Any remaining errors are the responsibility of our secretary.

b is the cost of carry of the underlying asset, σ is the volatility of the relative price changes in the asset, and r is the risk free interest rate. X is the strike price of the option, τ the time to reset (in years), and T is its time to expiration. $N(x)$ and $M(a, b; \rho)$ are respectively the univariate and bivariate cumulative normal distribution functions. The remaining parameters are $\rho = \sqrt{\tau/T}$ and

$$a_1 = \frac{\ln(S/X) + (b + \sigma^2/2)\tau}{\sigma\sqrt{\tau}}, \qquad a_2 = a_1 - \sigma\sqrt{\tau},$$

$$z_1 = \frac{(b + \sigma^2/2)(T - \tau)}{\sigma\sqrt{T - \tau}}, \qquad z_2 = z_1 - \sigma\sqrt{T - \tau},$$

$$y_1 = \frac{\ln(S/X) + (b + \sigma^2/2)T}{\sigma\sqrt{T}}, \qquad y_2 = y_1 - \sigma\sqrt{T}.$$

It takes some complex calculus to come up with such solutions. More importantly, the main weakness of closed form solutions is their lack of flexibility. If there is the slightest change in the option's payoff, one has to come up with a new solution – if one exists. A better solution must allow for greater flexibility, while retaining reasonable levels of accuracy and speed.

To this end, consider a standard European binomial tree. In the setting of Rendleman and Bartter (1979) the probability of going up or down in a node is set equal to $\frac{1}{2}$ (we could also have used the approach of Cox, Ross and Rubinstein, 1979). If p is the probability that the asset price will move up, and $(1 - p)$ is the probability of a move down, then $p = \frac{1}{2} = (1 - p)$. The corresponding sizes of the moves up or down at each time step, Δt apart, are

$$u = e^{(b - \sigma^2/2)\Delta t + \sigma\sqrt{\Delta t}}, \qquad d = e^{(b - \sigma^2/2)\Delta t - \sigma\sqrt{\Delta t}}.$$

Let n denote the number of time steps and i the state. The probability that the asset price ends at node (i, n), starting at S, is $P\{(i, n)\} = \frac{n!}{i!(n-i)!} p^i (1 - p)^{n-i} = \frac{n!}{i!(n-i)!} \left(\frac{1}{2}\right)^n$. The expected value from a single path is simply the path probability multiplied by the corresponding payoff at maturity, discounted at the risk free interest rate,

$$e^{-rT} \frac{n!}{i!(n - i)!} \left(\frac{1}{2}\right)^n \max[Su^i d^{n-i} - X, 0].$$

The value of a European option is simply the sum of all path probabilities multiplied by the payoff from each path. The value of a plain vanilla option is thus given by

$$c(S, X) = e^{-rT} \sum_{i=0}^{n} \frac{n!}{i!(n - i)!} \left(\frac{1}{2}\right)^n \max[Su^i d^{n-i} - X, 0],$$

$$p(S, X) = e^{-rT} \sum_{i=0}^{n} \frac{n!}{i!(n - i)!} \left(\frac{1}{2}\right)^n \max[X - Su^i d^{n-i}, 0].$$

Let n denote the number of time steps to maturity, m the number of time steps to the reset time ($m < n$), i the state at maturity, and j the state at time step m. To value a reset strike option we need the probability $P\{(i, n) \cap (j, m)\}$ that S_t passes through (j, m) and ends at (i, n). We can find this probability by using the relationship $P\{(i, n) \cap (j, m)\} = P\{(i, n)|(j, m)\}P\{(j, m)\}$, where $P\{A|B\}$ is the probability of event A conditional on event B. First the probability of going to (j, m) beginning at S is simply

$$P\{(j, m)\} = \frac{m!}{j!(m - j)!} p^j (1 - p)^{m-j} = \frac{m!}{j!(m - j)!} \left(\frac{1}{2}\right)^m.$$

Second, the probability of ending at (i, n) when starting at (j, m), is

$$P\{(i, n)|(j, m)\} = \frac{(n - m)!}{(i - j)!(n - m - i + j)!} \left(\frac{1}{2}\right)^{n-m}.$$

Starting at S, the probability of going through (j, m) and ending at (i, n) thereby equals

$$P\{(i, n)|(j, m)\}P\{(j, m)\} = \frac{m!(n - m)!}{j!(m - j)!(i - j)!(n - m - i + j)!} \left(\frac{1}{2}\right)^n.$$

The value of a reset call option is simply equal to the sum of the payoffs multiplied by the corresponding probabilities, discounted at the risk free interest rate,

$$c_r(S, X) = e^{-rT} \sum_{j=0}^{m} \sum_{i=j}^{n-m+j} \frac{m!(n - m)!}{j!(m - j)!(i - j)!(n - m - i + j)!} \left(\frac{1}{2}\right)^n g(Su^i d^{n-i}, X_c),$$

where $g(S, X) = \max[S - X, 0]$, and $X_c = \min[\alpha Su^j d^{m-j}, X]$. The constant α determines how much in- or out-of-the-money the reset strike is.

The method can be made more efficient by considering only paths that are in-the-money at maturity. This is achieved by replacing $\sum_{i=j}^{n-m+j}$ with $\sum_{i=a_c(j)}^{n-m+j}$, where $a_c(j) = j + \max[0, a_j + 1]$,

$$a_j = \text{Int} \left\{ \frac{\ln(X_c) - \ln(Su^j d^{n-j})}{\ln(u) - \ln(d)} \right\},$$

and $\text{Int}(x)$ is the integer part of any real number x.[2]

A put reset option p_r is valued by the same expression as for c_r, but with $g(S, X) = \max[X - S, 0]$ and $X_p = \max[\alpha Su^j d^{m-j}, X]$. Similar to the call, the formula for the put can be made more efficient by only taking into account paths that are in-the-money at maturity: replace $\sum_{i=j}^{n-m+j}$ with $\sum_{i=j}^{a_p(j)}$, where $a_p(j) = \min[n - m + j, j + \max[0, a_j]]$.

The main advantage of the suggested approach is its flexibility. Consider for instance a reset power option, with payoff at maturity equal to $g(S, X) = \max[S^2 - X^2, 0]$. This contract is easily valued by replacing the payoff function. What about more complex reset options, like barrier reset options? As simple as one, two, three! Before we deal with these, however, it is of interest to evaluate how accurate the binomial reset method is. In table 7.1 we compare the closed form solution of Gray and Whaley with our binomial method, using 150 time steps. We also report the value of plain vanilla options in the first column, using the formula of Black and Scholes (1973). It is clear that our method yields values that are very close to those of the closed form solution.

**TABLE 7.1: COMPARISON OF CLOSED FORM SOLUTION AND THE
BINOMIAL RESET STRIKE METHOD**
The parameters used are $S = 100$, $X = 100$, $T = 1$, $r = 0.10$, $b = 0.10$, and $n = 150$. BS
denotes the formula of Black and Scholes, for plain vanilla options; GW denotes the reset
formula of Gray and Whaley; HH denotes the binomial reset method.

Volatility	BS	$\tau = 0.25$		$\tau = 0.5$		$\tau = 0.75$	
		GW	HH	GW	HH	GW	HH
Call options							
10%	10.3081	10.9337	10.9293	10.8329	10.8384	10.6559	10.6626
20%	13.2697	14.5827	14.5935	14.5658	14.5846	14.2735	14.2936
30%	16.7341	18.5853	18.6258	18.6627	18.6637	18.3078	18.3288
Put options							
10%	0.7919	1.1690	1.1649	1.3729	1.3794	1.4969	1.5063
20%	3.7534	4.9384	4.9539	5.3269	5.3511	5.3790	5.4064
30%	7.2179	9.2388	9.2876	9.7922	9.8030	9.7543	9.7854

2 Reset Strike Barrier Options

Formulas for valuing standard barrier options are well known from the literature (see, e.g. Merton, 1973; Haug, 1997). We now consider barrier options with strikes that are reset. These are standard reset options where the strike can be reset at a predefined future date, and additionally the options have one or several predefined barriers that can knock them in or out.

To value these options it is necessary to compute the probability of hitting a barrier H. The probability of hitting the barrier along each path can be found analytically (see Brockhaus, Ferraris, Gallus, Long, Martin & Overhaus, 1999). Consider first an *up-and-out* call option where the barrier covers the entire life of the option. If the asset price hits the barrier before maturity the option expires worthless. Its value is given by

$$c_{rb}(S, X) = e^{-rT} \sum_{j=0}^{m} \sum_{i=j}^{n-m+j} \frac{m!(n-m)!}{j!(m-j)!(i-j)!(n-m-i+j)!}$$
$$\times \left(\frac{1}{2}\right)^n g(Su^i d^{n-i}, X_c)[1 - p^H(j, m; i, n-m)],$$

where $g(S, X) = \max[S - X, 0]$, $X_c = \min[\alpha Su^j d^{m-j}, X]$, $p^H(j, m; i, n-m) = p^H(j, m) + p^H(i, n-m) - p^H(j, m)p^H(i, n-m)$ is the probability of hitting the barrier when going through (j, m) and ending up in (i, n),[3] and

$$p^H(i, n) = \begin{cases} \exp\left\{\frac{-2}{\sigma^2 n \Delta t}\left|\ln\left(\frac{S}{H}\right)\ln\left(\frac{Su^i d^{n-i}}{H}\right)\right|\right\} & \text{when } Su^i d^{n-i} < H \\ 1 & \text{when } Su^i d^{n-i} \geq H. \end{cases}$$

The probability of hitting a barrier that covers only the period *after* the reset is given by $p^H(i, n-m)$. Similarly, the probability for hitting a barrier that covers only the time period *before* the reset time is given by $p^H(j, m)$.

Knock-out options are difficult to model, in practice stochastic volatility and jumps can be of great importance!

ASIAN PYRAMID POWER

THE COLLECTOR IN: UNEXPECTED WEATHER

WRITTEN BY: ESPEN HAUG
ILLUSTRATED BY: SEBASTIAN CONLEY

HMM. I COULD USE A NICE SUNNY VACATION!

SUNNY FLORIDA!

SOON...

WHAT! THIS IS FLORIDA?!!

YES. ONE MONTH AGO THE WEATHER SUDDENLY GOT VERY BAD.

THE COLD SEEMS TO BE EMANATING FROM THAT SMALL ISLAND!

TIME TO INVESTIGATE...

LATER THAT DAY ON THE MYSTERIOUS ISLAND...

WHOOOSH!

HUH? WHO ARE YOU?

I'M THE COLLECTOR! YOUR COLD WEATHER MACHINE HAS GONE FAR ENOUGH!

BUT I'VE INVESTED MILLIONS IN FLORIDA COLD WEATHER DERIVATIVES! JOIN ME AND WE'LL BE RICH!

ACTUALLY I THINK IT'S TIME TO PUT YOUR OPERATION ON ICE!

SSSSS!

SOON...

MORE SUNTAN LOTION, COLLECTOR?

FINALLY THINGS ARE HEATING UP!

Blub Blub

end

FROM RUSSIA WITH VOL

IT HAD BEEN A GOOD MONTH. MY OPTION STRATEGY HAD MADE A LOT OF MONEY. I WAS BUYING CHEAP OPTIONS FOR VERY *LOW VOLATILITY*.

TIRED FROM A LONG WEEK, I RETIRED TO BED. WITH A LONG OPTION POSITION WITH LIMITED RISK, I SLEPT LIKE A BABY.

ZZZZZ...

I WENT TO MY LIBRARY AND SEARCHED FRANTICALLY FOR A REFERENCE TO NEGATIVE VOLATILITY.

NOTHING. NOT EVEN IN THE DERIVATIVES BIBLE, "PAUL WILMOTT ON QUANTITATIVE FINANCE."

ALBERT SHIRYAEV? THE RUSSIAN MATHEMATICAL GENIUS? HAD HE FOUND A WAY TO MAKE NEGATIVE VOLATILITY POSSIBLE?

NEXT STOP, MOSCOW, SIR.

THANKS, SARA.

I LEFT FOR HOME WITH PEACE OF MIND. WITH LONG OPTIONS, I COULD AT MOST LOSE THE PREMIUM PAID.

VRUM

THAT NIGHT I HAD A NIGHTMARE. I DREAMT THAT VOLATILITY HAD GONE *NEGATIVE!* MY HEDGE FUND COLLAPSED!

$V = -1$

NEGATIVE

MY HEART WAS BEATING FAST. I DID AN INTERNET SEARCH FOR NEGATIVE VOLATILITY...

WHAT?!

BEEP

WAS THIS A *RUSSIAN SECRET* DEVELOPED DURING THE COLD WAR? I HAD TO GET TO MOSCOW TO FIND OUT.

SARA, READY MY AIRCRAFT.

YES, SIR.

NOW BREAKING THE SOUND BARRIER, SIR.

KERBOOM!

I ENJOYED AN EXCELLENT MEAL AND LOOKED FORWARD TO A QUIET WEEKEND.

TONIGHT'S MENU INCLUDES RUSSIAN CAVIAR, AVOCADO, AND A BOTTLE OF 1947 CHATEAU PETRUS.

THANK YOU, JAMES.

WELL NATURALLY I KNEW NEGATIVE VOLATILITY WAS IMPOSSIBLE. BUT THE DREAM FELT ALL TOO REAL FOR ME TO RELAX.

NOOO!

BOOM

... A SINGLE LINK CAME UP!

YAHOO!

NEGATIVE VOLATILITY [Search]

search results:

NEGATIVE VOLATILITY:
ALBERT SHIRYAEV
STEKLOV MATHEMATICAL
INSTITUTE, MOSCOW, RUSSIA.

no other matches

ON THE WAY TO MY PRIVATE AIRFIELD, MY THOUGHTS RACED. WHILE REAGAN WASTED MILLIONS ON A SPACE ANTI-MISSLE PROGRAM, HAD THE SOVIETS BEEN DEVELOPING A WAY TO CREATE *NEGATIVE VOLATILITY?*

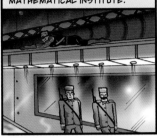

THE COLLECTOR

IN: **NEGATIVE PROBABILITY**

WRITTEN BY: ESPEN HAUG
ILLUSTRATED BY:
SEBASTIAN CONLEY

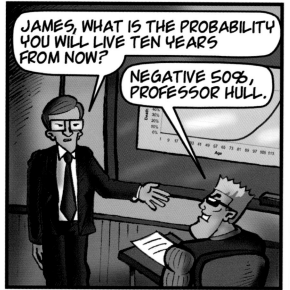

Pompeii (Oil painting on canvas)

The city of Pompeii was lying in the tail of a sleeping volcano. The volcano suddenly woke up with a series of eruptions that destroyed the city completely. In the Gaussian hill we have the Sharpe ratio, basic Value at Risk and much of the modern Gaussian finance theory. In the fat-tail and the high peak volcano we have empirical financial discoveries going back to at least 1915, with Wesley Mitchell, and later Oliver (1926) and Mills (1927). We also have Benoit Mandelbrot, who for much of his life has fought a battle against Gaussians. Many of the theories still taught at business schools today are rooted in Gaussian.

HIDDEN CONDITIONS

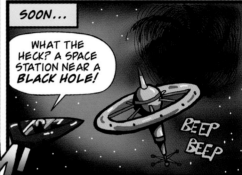

FROZEN TIME ARBITRAGE

The Life of a trader involves probability theory, gambling, a quick mind and meeting a lot of interesting people!

Some of the biggest blow-ups in finance are due to people ignoring that financial models are based on other models, like probability models. You also need to understand the limitation of the model behind the model.

The Alchemy of Derivatives (Oil painting on canvas)

Option trading relies on robust hedging principles, such as the put-call parity. According to modern finance theory, the risk in derivatives can be more or less fully hedged away by dynamic delta hedging. According to the true alchemy of derivatives, most unwanted risk in options can only be hedged away using options against options. In this way, supply and demand for options will affect the option value. In other words, the option is biting its own tail. The alchemy of derivatives is based on the powers of quantitative finance combined with a deeper philosophical understanding of what traders actually do in practice.

Down-and-out barriers can be incorporated in the same way, by using the appropriate probabilities of barrier hits. Simply define

$$
p_H(i, n) = \begin{cases} \exp\left\{ \frac{-2}{\sigma^2 n \Delta t} \left| \ln\left(\frac{S}{H}\right) \ln\left(\frac{Su^i d^{n-i}}{H}\right) \right| \right\} & \text{when } Su^i d^{n-i} > H \\ 1 & \text{when } Su^i d^{n-i} \le H, \end{cases}
$$

and $p_H(j, m; i, n - m)$ as above. Now simply substitute the latter in place of $p^H(j, m; i, n - m)$. For a barrier that covers only the period *after* the reset, the probability of hitting the barrier is given by $p_H(i, n - m)$. A barrier that covers only the period *before* the reset induces a hit probability equal to $p_H(j, m)$.

If the contract specifies different barriers H_S and H_E for the periods before and after reset respectively, the probability of not hitting any of the barriers is $1 - p_{H_S}(j, m) - p_{H_E}(i, n - m) + p_{H_S}(j, m) p_{H_E}(i, n - m)$ (this works for *up*-and-out options too, of course). For barrier put options it is only necessary to change the payoff function $g(S, X)$ from $\max[S - X, 0]$ to $\max[X - S, 0]$, in the usual way.

To value in-options one can use the in/out barrier parity:

In-barrier option = Long out-barrier option − Short plain vanilla option.

Consider next a cash rebate K, which is paid out at maturity to the holder of the option if the barrier is hit during its lifetime. We take this into account by multiplying the rebate by the probability of hitting the barrier, and then discount the product at the risk free rate: $e^{-rT} K p^H(i, n)$ (use $p_H(\cdot)$ for a *down*-and-out option). Use the probability of the complementary event to price a rebate which is paid if the barrier is *not* hit during the option's lifetime.

In practice the barrier is monitored at discrete points in time. Discrete monitoring will naturally decrease the probability of barrier hits, relative to continuous monitoring. Broadie, Glasserman and Kou (1997) have developed an approximate correction for pricing formulae for discrete barrier options. It can also be used for our reset binomial method. The correction shifts the barrier(s) away from the price of the underlying asset. To price a discrete barrier option it is only necessary to replace the continuously monitored barrier H with a discrete barrier level. The latter is given by $H^D(\Delta t) = H e^{\beta \sigma \sqrt{\Delta t}}$ if the barrier is above the price of the underlying asset, and $H_D(\Delta t) = H e^{-\beta \sigma \sqrt{\Delta t}}$ if the barrier is below. Δt is the time between monitoring instants, and $\beta \approx 0.5826$. Broadie, Glasserman and Kou (1997) show both theoretically and experimentally that discrete barrier options can be priced with remarkable accuracy using this simple correction.

3   Reset Barrier Options

Rather than resetting the strike we can just as easily reset the barrier. Consider the case of an up-and-out reset barrier option, where the barrier is reset the first time it is hit. If the initial barrier covers the entire lifetime of the option, the option price is given by

$$
e^{-rT} \sum_{j=0}^{m} \sum_{i=j}^{n-m+j} \frac{m!(n-m)!}{j!(m-j)!(i-j)!(n-m-i+j)!} \left(\frac{1}{2}\right)^n
$$
$$
\times g(Su^i d^{n-i}, X)[1 - p^{H(j)}(j, m; i, n - m)],
$$

where $H(j) = \min(\alpha S u^j d^{m-j}, H)$, H is the original barrier, and α is a positive constant that determines how the barrier is reset as a function of S_t (this can easily be generalized). Other types of reset barrier options can be valued in a similar way. The necessary adjustments are similar to those in the previous discussion.

4   Resetting Time

Trading options is much like dating: timing is everything. Someone who is long a call or put when the market moves in the unfavorable direction could use more time. Using our new flexible reset binomial method we can easily value options where the time to maturity is reset. Consider a call option, and assume the time to maturity is reset at a future date $\tau = m\Delta t$ if the asset price is a predetermined percentage out-of-the-money (alternatively, in-the-money). Its price is given by

$$c_r^\tau(S, X) = \sum_{j=0}^{m} \sum_{i=j}^{n-m+j} D_c(i, j) \frac{m!(n-m)!}{j!(m-j)!(i-j)!(n-m-i+j)!}$$

$$\times \left(\frac{1}{2}\right)^n \max[S_c(i, j) - X, 0],$$

where

$$S_c(i, j) = \begin{cases} S u^i d^{n-i} & \text{when } \alpha S u^j d^{m-j} < X \\ S u^j d^{m-j} & \text{when } \alpha S u^j d^{m-j} \geq X \end{cases}$$

and

$$D_c(i, j) = \begin{cases} e^{-rn\Delta t} & \text{when } \alpha S u^j d^{m-j} < X \\ e^{-rm\Delta t} & \text{when } \alpha S u^j d^{m-j} \geq X. \end{cases}$$

For a put option, the price is given by

$$p_r^\tau(S, X) = \sum_{j=0}^{m} \sum_{i=j}^{n-m+j} D_p(i, j) \frac{m!(n-m)!}{j!(m-j)!(i-j)!(n-m-i+j)!}$$

$$\times \left(\frac{1}{2}\right)^n \max[X - S_p(i, j), 0]$$

where

$$S_p(i, j) = \begin{cases} S u^i d^{n-i} & \text{when } \alpha S u^j d^{m-j} > X \\ S u^j d^{m-j} & \text{when } \alpha S u^j d^{m-j} \leq X \end{cases}$$

and

$$D_p(i, j) = \begin{cases} e^{-rn\Delta t} & \text{when } \alpha S u^j d^{m-j} > X \\ e^{-rm\Delta t} & \text{when } \alpha S u^j d^{m-j} \leq X. \end{cases}$$

Longstaff (1990) has derived a closed form solution for these reset time options. As before, the binomial reset method offers more flexibility, and can be used to value a larger class of reset time options. Using the latter method, reset time options can be combined with reset strike and barriers.

One can for instance extend the method to a call where the time, strike and barrier are reset as a function of the asset price at a predetermined future date. To get some idea of how accurate our approach is take a look at table 7.2. It compares our method to Longstaff's closed form solution.

TABLE 7.2: COMPARISON OF CLOSED FORM SOLUTION AND THE BINOMIAL RESET TIME METHOD

The parameters used are $S = 100$, $X = 100$, $T = 1$, $r = 0.10$, $b = 0.10$, and $n = 200$. Longstaff denotes the formula of Longstaff (1990). HH denotes the binomial reset time method.

Volatility	$\tau = 0.25$		$\tau = 0.5$		$\tau = 0.75$	
	Longstaff	HH	Longstaff	HH	Longstaff	HH
Call options						
10%	5.2526	5.4007	6.6644	6.6167	8.3941	8.3271
20%	8.1299	8.3793	9.7562	9.7096	11.4691	11.3562
30%	10.9954	10.7393	12.9565	13.0889	14.8446	15.0490
Put options						
10%	1.2216	1.2112	1.1417	1.1532	0.9844	1.0015
20%	3.8839	3.8111	4.0780	4.1074	3.9962	4.0557
30%	6.7096	6.8574	7.2482	7.1952	7.3589	7.2203

For a given number of time steps the reset time method is somewhat less accurate than the reset strike method. In other words, it is slower to converge. This is especially pronounced when the time to reset is short relative to the time to maturity. In this case the grid is too coarse at the time of reset. This can be ameliorated either by increasing the total number of time steps in the tree or by locally making the grid finer (Figlewski & Gao, 1999). The latter technique offers better computational efficiency, but is also more complex to implement.

5   Conclusion

We have developed a simple and flexible method to value reset options. It can be adapted to value almost any type of European reset option: reset strike, barriers, strike with barriers, and time, as well as power options and more. Some of our simplifying assumptions are trivial to extend, for instance how to reset the strike as a function of the underlying asset price.

FOOTNOTES & REFERENCES

1. Gray and Whaley (1997) study a slightly different type of reset option.

2. To derive $a_c(j)$ consider the security price at state (j, m), $S_\tau = Su^j d^{m-j}$, and solve for those i that ensure that $S_T > X_c$: At the sub-tree starting at (j, m) we initially sum over $j \leq i \leq n - m + j$. Substituting $k = i - j$, $S_T = S_\tau u^k d^{(n-m)-k}$ where $0 \leq k \leq n - m$. The truncation a_j obtains by solving the inequality $S_T > X_c$ for k, ensuring it is an integer.

3. Recall from probability theory that for two generic events A and B, $P(A \cup B) = P(A) + P(B) - P(A \cap B)$. If A and B are independent events $P(A \cap B) = P(A)P(B)$. We want to compute the probability of the barrier being hit along all paths between $(0, 0)-(j, m)$ or $(j, m)-(i, n-m)$. In our case $P(A) = p^H(j, m)$ and $P(B) = p^H(i, n-m)$. Since the asset price follows a Markov process, these events are independent, and the expression for $p^H(j, m; i, n-m)$ follows (A Markov process is like a bad hangover: the only factor that determines the meal plan of the day is your current state – not how you felt during the party).

■ Black, F. and M. Scholes (1973) "The Pricing of Options and Corporate Liabilities," *Journal of Political Economy* **81**, 637–654.

■ Broadie, M., P. Glasserman and S. Kou (1997) "A Continuity Correction for Discrete Barrier Options" *Mathematical Finance*, 325–349.

■ Brockhaus, O., A. Ferraris, C. Gallus, D. Long, R. Martin and M. Overhaus (1999) *Modelling and Hedging Equity Derivatives*. Risk.

■ Cox, J. C., S. A. Ross and M. Rubinstein (1979) "Option Pricing: A Simplified Approach" *Journal of Financial Economics*, **7**, 229–263.

■ Figlewski, S. and B. Gao (1999) "The Adaptive Mesh Model: A New Approach to Efficient Option Pricing" *Journal of Financial Economics*, 313–351.

■ Gray, S. F. and R. E. Whaley (1997) "Valuing Bear Market Reset Warrants with a Periodic Reset" *Journal of Derivatives*, 5, 229–263.

■ ——— (1999) "Reset Put Options: Valuation, Risk Characteristics, and Application" *Australian Journal of Management*, **24**, 1–20.

■ Haug, E. G. (1997) *The Complete Guide To Option Pricing Formulas*. New York: McGraw-Hill.

■ Longstaff, F. A. (1990) "Pricing Options with Extendible Maturities: Analysis and Applications" *Journal of Finance*, **45**(3), 935–957.

■ Merton, R. C. (1973) "Theory of Rational Option Pricing" *Bell Journal of Economics and Management Science*, **4**, 141–183.

■ Rendleman, R. J. and B. J. Bartter (1979) "Two-State Option Pricing" *Journal of Finance*, **34**, 1093–1110.

Bruno Dupire studying stochastic behavior on Times Square (Photo: Amber Gray)

Bruno Dupire the Stochastic Wall Street Quant

Bruno Dupire has headed various Derivatives Research teams at Société Generale, Paribas Capital Markets and Nikko Financial Products. He pioneered the use of neural networks in finance and is probably best known for his work on local volatility models. He has also worked extensively on stochastic volatility modeling. He is currently a member of the Bloomberg quantitative finance research team in New York. He was included in Risk magazine's "Hall of Fame" of the 50 most influential people in the history of derivatives. In 2006 he received the Wilmott award for cutting edge research.

Bruno Dupire tends to publish his many interesting ideas in short and precise form, with a background in formal mathematics, typical for French quants, some might say. If I had never met Bruno Dupire I would probably have thought of him as a boring formal math quant-geek. But how wrong can one be? Last time I met Bruno at a quantitative finance evening we were competing in car racing. Well, for quants in the middle of Manhattan crowded with traffic and people the solution was stationary racing cars packed with technology and sensors connected to a large wall sized screen. I quickly took the lead, and led for lap after lap. Laughing, Bruno shouted to me that he had to let the customers win. With only one round left I was very confident that I would win. Then suddenly my car went into a spin, I had no idea what happened except that I saw Bruno's racing car jumping ahead of me. With my competitive trading instincts I desperately tried to overtake him but it was too late; Bruno Dupire was the winner.

Afterwards I figured out that as a formal mathematician Dr Dupire had most likely used the early laps to calibrate his model and make me overconfident, then when the time was right he pushed his car to the limit. After the race we switched topic to the discussion of the valuation of a sequential portfolio of options with very short time frame, research I had just begun looking into. Bruno immediately had some insightful comments to make. After meeting Bruno Dupire a few times I could tell that he was someone who did not take himself too seriously, a very important attribute for a quant who wants to apply his ideas in practice, because models are only models. Bruno knows when to have fun and when and how to present his quant ideas in the way of a mathematician.

Haug : Where were you born?

Dupire : In Paris; I spent my youth in Saint-Sulpice, 6th arrondissement, close to Saint-Germain-des-pres, former home of the existentialists, jazz clubs and penniless intellectuals, before it turned into Armani-land. Still, Saint-Sulpice remains a charming village within a city.

Haug : When did you first become interested in mathematics and science?

Dupire : My family background is conspicuously unscientific, but it seems I have always had a fascination for numbers. My parents told me that at the age of four, I used to ask for two four digit numbers to add mentally to get to sleep. A few years later, I was seduced by the aesthetics of mathematical reasoning, the possibility of creating the objects and tools you need, and the purity of the quest of eternal truths that do not rely on our perceptual envelope. Mathematics attempts to transcend our sensorial experience, in contrast with physics which aims at explaining observable phenomena.

Haug : What is your educational background?

Dupire : Mostly mathematics, with many shades. In Paris, I studied at Ecole Normale Superieure, got a Master's degree in Artificial Intelligence, spent some time at an economics school, before taking the brave and unlikely step of emigrating to Brazil for a PhD in fluid dynamics and eventually being involved in biology modeling and even experimental psychology. I think it is essential for a scientist to be exposed to many influences. Part of research is the ability to apply to a field a common place of another field, and beyond that, to cross fertilize different strands of knowledge. For me theoretical finance has been the perfect receptacle to merge these influences and to try to contribute to expand this field.

Haug : Emanuel Derman[1] in his book "My Life as a Quant" categorized you as "As a Frenchman, he had a taste for formal mathematics, and his very brief report proposed an elegant formula for local volatilities". Do you think that in general French quants have a more formal mathematical approach to presenting their quantitative models than most others, or is this a myth?

Dupire : It is a truth but not a monopoly.

Haug : In some of your first jobs in quantitative finance I understand that you were involved in neural networks, were they used for predictions and how did they work out?

Dupire : I got involved in neural networks before entering finance. In 1986, I was working with Francisco Varela, a great theoretician of self-organized systems and we touched upon a wide variety of topics: immune system modeling, understanding pigeon and human color vision and experimenting with neural networks. At the time, it was a brand new branch of cognitive sciences, at the crossroads of neurology, psychology and artificial intelligence. It was attempting to mimic the ability of the human brain to perform high level tasks through the cooperation of a large number of distributed units, in sharp contrast with the then dominating paradigm of formal languages and the procedural approach in Artificial Intelligence (AI). It was plagued with anthropocentered lingo like ability to "learn automatically", "generalize", "selectively forget" and so on. As a mathematician, I was merely seeing it as a tool that associates inputs to outputs and improves its performance by minimizing an error function (it is very much like calibrating the parameters of a model to fit market prices). I realized that neural networks could be used to predict time series, by training them to associate correctly the future to the past on a set of examples. You then pray that it will perform correctly on out of sample examples. I sold the idea to CDC in 1987 and did the study the following year. It seems it was the first attempt ever to apply neural networks to forecasting and it became very popular in finance in the 1990's.

Was it working well? It was quite unstable and was suffering from a rigid representation of data, tied up to a fixed time scale. It is better to reformat the data according to the business time than to the calendar time.

Another application I was developing at the time and which leaves me with some regret at not having pursued it was the concept of "creative networks", which look for the input that maximizes the output and submits the best candidates to the human observer, who in turn categorizes them in order to hone the learning process. We learn best by 1) trying and being corrected, and 2) by distinguishing between limit examples.

Haug : How is your work on local volatility models related to the work of Rubinstein, and Derman and Kani who published their ideas on local volatility models at about the same time as you?

Dupire : In 1991 at the Société Generale in Paris I had incorporated time dependent parameters, typically instantaneous volatility that was a function of time calibrated to fit the term structure of volatility (and the year after a stochastic version of it that fits the term structure of variance swaps, which did not exist at the time but that I needed to define). This was not fitting the market smiles, a problem I addressed in 1992 and solved by calibrating a trinomial tree to the vanillas. Still, it was clear that a continuous time theory was needed to overcome the shortcomings and limitations of the tree and I developed it in early 1993, wrote a paper in March and presented it in June (AFFI conference, La Baule, June 1993). Later that year, Derman and Kani developed a similar approach, albeit merely discrete through a non uniform binary tree, like Rubinstein, although he was simply calibrating to one maturity as opposed to the whole spectrum. Our three approaches were published by Risk magazine in the beginning of 1994. I had mixed feelings at the time: I considered that I had done the most: before them, a better tree, continuous time treatment (which is the crucial feature), risk management (superbucket analysis to decompose the volatility risk across strikes and maturities) and that it was unfair not to receive the proper appreciation for that. At the same time, I was at the time a virtually unknown researcher and it was an honor to be associated with such well respected names, so I happily settled for it.

Haug : What are the differences and similarities between stochastic volatility models and local volatility models?

Dupire : Strictly speaking, the volatility in the local volatility model (LVM) is stochastic, as it depends on the price which is itself stochastic; however, as there is no additional source of risk, it makes more sense to describe it as deterministic, as it is a deterministic function of spot and time. LVM assumes the instantaneous volatility at a future time will be known if we know the spot price at that time. It is a strong limitation, although it is more flexible than Black-Scholes.

As LVM has only one source of uncertainty, it is a complete model and continuous delta hedging with the underlying ensures perfect replication, in contrast with stochastic volatility model which has an inherent volatility risk that cannot be hedged by the underlying alone.

Another difference is that LVM is a non-parametric model that achieves a perfect fit to the implied volatility surface through a formula for the local volatility, as opposed to the usual parametric stochastic volatility models that merely perform a best fit as a result of an iterative calibration procedure.

A similarity that is often overlooked or misunderstood is the fact that if LVM and a stochastic volatility model (SVM) are both calibrated to the same surface, then SVM is a noisy version of LVM. More precisely, the expectation of the instantaneous variance at a future time conditioned on the spot value at that time is equal to the local variance for this spot and time. In short, SVM is LVM plus some centered noise.

The main merit of LVM is to have extracted the notion of instantaneous forward variance conditional to a price level, as my paper "Arbitrage Pricing with Stochastic Volatility" extracted the notion of unconditional instantaneous forward variance. It may be a poor predictor of future volatility but it is the uniquely enforceable one from vanilla options and any calibrated stochastic volatility model has to respect it in expectation.

Haug : Have you tried to extend the local volatility model to incorporate stochastic behavior of the volatility surface and even jumps in the volatility surface?

Dupire : Definitely. Even before LVM I had developed a SVM that was fitting the term structure of variance swaps (although they did not exist at the time, I had to define them!) but not the precise skew for each maturity. On the other hand, LVM is a deterministic volatility model that fits the whole surface perfectly, so it was natural to try to unify these two approaches to get a SVM fitting the whole surface. I did it in 1995–1996 with UTV (Unified Theory of Volatility, see my January 1996 paper, presented for the first time at FORC, Warwick, May 1995). The resulting model is intricate, in general non Markov and is an implementation nightmare. However, it contains the important notion of conditional instantaneous variance (whose expectation is the local variance) and how to lock it. Frankly, I don't think the market was ready to absorb this piece of work at the time. I also have versions with jumps.

Haug : Do the principles of risk-neutral valuation break down if the volatility is stochastic? The argument of dynamic delta hedging cannot remove my risk towards volatility of volatility?

Dupire : Delta hedging with the underlying can remove the volatility risk that is correlated with the underlying, which is why LVM is complete and SVM is not. To hedge the component of volatility that is decorrelated with the underlying, hedging with options is required. My 1992 work, Arbitrage Pricing with Stochastic Volatility (APSV) is along these lines. It was the first work showing that it was possible to find the risk neutral process for volatility from the knowledge of the current surface.

Haug : At a Global Derivatives conference in Madrid in 2004 I remember that you talked about volatility arbitrage and conditional and unconditional forward volatilities. Can you refresh my memory about this?

Dupire : Unconditional instantaneous forward variance is the instantaneous variance at a future date that you can lock today by combining two log profiles of similar maturities, as I showed in APSV (1992).

Conditional instantaneous forward variance is the instantaneous variance at a future date conditional to the spot being at a certain level that you can lock today by combining essentially calendar spreads and butterflies. You have to use forward corridor variance swaps and take some care when going to the limit (maturity first, strike second). This is in my paper UTV (1996).

Haug : I know you also have done some studies on sticky strike and sticky delta modeling, can you update us briefly on the "latest thinking" on this topic?

Dupire : Sticky strike and sticky delta are trader phrases to describe the behavior of volatility when the price moves. Sticky strike means the volatility of a given strike is unaffected by the price move. Sticky delta means the volatility merely depends on the moneyness. In particular, the ATM volatility remains constant, which is typical of models with independent increments. In the absence of jumps, sticky delta and sticky strike regimes are arbitrageable as soon as you do not have flat implied volatility. Even in the presence of jumps, generating a sticky delta regime requires huge jumps, out of proportion with the historical behavior of prices.

Haug : When calibrating derivatives models to historic data isn't there always a danger that we have too little data. We could easily miss out on extreme jumps in the asset or volatility or other tail events that happen extremely infrequently, how can we adjust or compensate for this?

Dupire : It seems you are referring to estimating statistically parameters from historical data, not calibrating model parameters to current market prices. For statistical estimation, scarcity of data is a main issue. By definition rare events rarely occur and almost never occur on short history. This is actually the driving strategy of many hedge funds that take hidden undue risks and look very good until their sudden death. Scarce data in the presence of latent risk calls for a change of paradigm from observation to causality. When the data do not reveal much you have to go beyond them and seek the causal links that may cause a disaster, such as economic turbulence. If my light bulb has not blown out in the past 100 hours, I don't infer it will last forever; I will look for the statistics of this model, the precise operating conditions. Otherwise, if you want to stick to data analysis, extreme value theory can be a guideline to extrapolate the tail events.

Haug : If the at-the-money volatility stays the same, but the skew suddenly makes a twist (Black-Scholes implied volatilities), in terms of a stochastic volatility model does this indicate that the expected correlation between the asset and the local volatility has changed suddenly ?

Dupire : A change in correlation between the asset and the instantaneous volatility would certainly produce this effect. In a jump model, the change of balance between the up jumps and the down jumps would have the same effect.

Haug : In a presentation on volatility skew modeling I know you were also discussing leverage. What type of leverage were you were talking about and how does this affect the volatility skew?

Dupire : Leverage is a term from the equity world which describes the fact that for low firm values the debt/equity ratio increases. It implies that a stock price decline tends to be accompanied by an increase of its instantaneous volatility. In general, it describes the link between price and volatility.

Haug : When it comes to the correlation between volatility and the asset I would think the correlation often changes dramatically in disaster/crisis situations. Do current stochastic volatility models capture this? Should both the correlation and the volatility be allowed to jump?

Dupire : Correlation describes the joint behavior of well mannered processes in time of peace. In times of war, it breaks down and jumps or Markov switching models are better adapted. This being said, models with jumping volatility enjoy some academic popularity.

Haug : As an option trader I often like to distinguish between stochastic realized volatility and stochastic implied volatility. If I am planning to hold the option for a short term compared to the option life time the change in implied volatility is most important for me. While if I want to hold it for a long period relative to the option life time then delta hedging and the behavior of the underlying asset; in terms of its volatility, volatility of volatility, etc seems the most important, do current stochastic volatility models take this into account?

Dupire : Yes, in the sense that in a stochastic volatility model, the implied volatility itself is stochastic and a position held over a short time interval will be marked to market with this implied volatility which reflects the best prediction of the future. So stochastic volatility models exhibit randomness both in instantaneous volatility and in implied volatility and they account for the fact you mention.

Haug : Chicago Board Option Exchange has introduced futures on the volatility index VIX. I know Bloomberg has implemented a model for this. Peter Carr in this book gives you and Arun Verma great credit for the research behind this model. Can you tell us briefly about the VIX futures and potential ways to hedge and model it?

Dupire : I have observed since the late 80's a liking amongst traders for talking about "buying/selling volatility". A more modern term for it is "treating volatility as an asset class". In both cases, it is probably due to the illusion that dealing with abstraction is the stamp of a higher spirit. Anyhow, modern tools like VIX and variance swaps are pure volatility vehicles whilst the volatility deals of the past were mostly vanilla trades that mix in a complex and undesired way volatility exposure and spot exposure, as most of the action takes place close to the strike.

The VIX reflects the global level of implied volatility, across all strikes and not only at the money, of the S&P 500. It is related to the variance swap replication, which entails a portfolio of options of all strikes approximating a log profile. As VIX is homogenous to volatility, the square root of the variance, it induces a concavity bias that depends on the volatility of the volatility. The interesting fact is that this volatility of volatility can itself be estimated from the historical volatility of the VIX itself, so in a somewhat vertiginous circularity, we can estimate the VIX fair value from its own time series!

Haug : **The underlying instruments for hedging volatility products are often options, options that are themselves priced according to a model. Can I classify volatility derivatives models as models on models?**

Dupire : Put more simply, volatility derivative models mostly model the volatility of volatility. The usual take on this is the common sense approach that an option on realized variance, for instance, merely requires the modeling of its underlying, the realized variance. The realized variance is the payoff of a variance swap so market practice is to 1) price with the volatility of the variance swap and 2) hedge with a dynamic position on the variance swap. As a variance swap corresponds to a position in the log profile, bundle of vanillas of all strikes, the classic approach involves treating all strikes similarly (up to a $1/K^2$ factor). I actually showed that, amazingly, a proper inspection of the Skorohod embedding problem (arcane curiosity of stochastic calculus) was giving a tight lower bound for those products and was involving trading selectively across the vanilla strikes. It is a striking example of a long journey in theory that leads to a very practical prescription that the trader can understand but would probably not have thought of beforehand.

Haug : **I have seen variance, volatility and correlation swaps trading in the market as well as options on realized volatility and also forward agreements on implied volatility. I have even seen banks offering contracts on skewness. Where is the limit of product development, will we soon see swaps on kurtosis and higher order moments as well, do such products have any benefits for the economy or are these simply products for traders wanting to put on a new fancy bet, or investment banks and financial institutions searching for new products with higher margins?**

Dupire : There is a sad tendency to deviate from the original economic motive of derivative products, which was to tightly fit the client's risk. Banks were supposed to have the structuring ability to design the proper product and to transfer the risk efficiently to a large globally hedged portfolio. In contrast, there is now a plethora of retail products with digital payoffs that make no sense for the final investor. No sense because they correspond neither to a need nor a view of the investor and because the investor often does not understand them. These products with their digital payoffs or complex correlation exposures create risk both for the bank and the investor, at the antipode of their supposed economic use. This being said, skew exposure is a real risk and it is legitimate to wish to hedge it through skew swaps. However, skew arises as a mix of leverage and return asymmetry and current skew swaps only address the latter.

Haug : **Where is the trade off between having a model that captures the most important aspects of the underlying asset price behavior and a model that has too many parameters to estimate?**

Dupire : The dividing line is the cognitive equipment of the trader who eventually operates this machine. A common view is that it is better to have a simple well understood model than an ideal but opaque and unmanageable one, and I basically share this view. Control must rule over sophistication. However, I am surprised at the reluctance traders have to accept concepts like stochastic volatility which have been around for 20 years and which are so material in many situations.

Haug : What are the fundamental reasons for stochastic volatility and jumps?

Dupire : A common answer is that reality is more complicated than simple constant volatility assumptions and that stochastic volatility and jumps provide a more proper description of the irregularity of the flow of information. If I answer at the level of the modeling choice, I would say that the maturing cycle of a concept (such as volatility) starts from being ignored, then being modeled as 0, then as a constant, then as a time dependent function, then as a random process, then as deploying in several dimensions so it is natural that volatility, measure of randomness, becomes itself random and we can proceed to stochastic volatility of volatility and so on, but I don't think it is fruitful to go further down this line. Jumps enrich the modeling vocabulary in a more radical way and lead to deeper incompleteness, which is anyway an inherent feature of markets.

Haug : When do you come up with most of your great ideas, when staring at your computer screen at work, when drinking some good wine or in the middle of a car race, in other words what is in your opinion the best environment for coming up with great research ideas?

Dupire : Good ideas often come up in front of the computer, great ones rarely. Great ones, if any, come in the middle of the night, in the middle of a heated discussion, or at random times. I remember that it was by the swimming pool of a Miami hotel that in 1994 I realized that local variance was a ratio of two assets, hence a martingale under some probability measure, hence was equal to a conditional expectation of future variance, which is a fundamental fact of the field of volatility. Great ideas can be fed either by obsession or relaxation.

Haug : Do you ever get fed up with quantitative finance?

Dupire : Yes, I took a five year break. I was fed up at the end of 1998 and I stopped on my 40th birthday to enjoy my wife and kids and the French Riviera. I was saturated at the time and came back in January 2004 at full speed with a fresh view on many topics, and it seems to go quite well now. [A fortnight before the interview, Bruno received the Wilmott "Cutting edge research" award for 2006 and was voted the top practitioner contributor for the past five years in the ICBI Global Derivatives industry survey].

Haug : Do you have any hobbies outside quantitative finance?

Dupire : I have a long lasting interest in understanding how aesthetics is conditioned by physiology and how it transcends it. Also, as a researcher, I indeed value ideas over matter. A field that captures my interest is music theory; another one is the study of subtropical insects and of damaged Moldavian stamps (joking).

Haug : Do you also apply option theory to any real life decisions/options?

Dupire : Behavioral finance claims that people often behave irrationally. I think it is true and I sometimes indulge in the pleasures of despising optimized behavior.

Haug : Have there been any jumps in the stochastic process of Bruno Dupire's life so far that you can share with us, or has it been a smooth continuous process of wining and dining?

Dupire : Life is a sequence of catastrophes, in the mathematical sense. A slow maturing process can have dramatic consequences at times and they build the story of our life. For details, hey, it is just a book about finance, not psychotherapy!

Haug : In your view where are we in the evolution of quantitative finance?

Dupire : Quantitative finance has attracted an inordinate number of mathematicians and physicists, because it is a vibrant field and because of obvious financial incentives. Whichever your love of aesthetics or your pursuit of scientific truth, you do not want to be left aside or pitied. This sheer number of (and possibly excess of) researchers, means that many topics are over covered. What strikes me is their inclination to apply their narrow field of expertise to finance, with a tendency to bend financial problems to their methods, when I definitely believe that methods should adapt to problems and not the reverse. To be more specific, it is tempting for a scientist to dive into issues such as finding a characteristic function or developing asymptotic expansions, but it is harder to understand real financial issues such as hedging, transaction costs, statistical arbitrage, liquidity, reserve policies and so on. Another fact that should not be ignored is that quants are increasing in sophistication but traders (although many of them are ex quants) do not participate in this evolution: still few traders use stochastic volatility models and virtually none use jump models. This gap is worrying, but to bridge it, quants have to do their share and come up with a more digestible language.

FOOTNOTE & REFERENCES

1. See Interview with him elsewhere in this book.

■ Derman, E. and I. Kani (1994) "Riding on a Smile" *Risk Magazine,* **7**(2).
■ Dupire, B. (1992) "Arbitrage Pricing with Stochastic Volatility" *Risk Magazine,* **7**(1).
■ ———— (1994): "Pricing with a Smile" *Risk Magazine,* **7**(1), 18–20.
■ ———— (1995) "Exotic Option Pricing by Calibration on Volatility Smiles," in Advanced Mathematics for Derivatives: Risk Magazine Conference.
■ ———— (1996): "A Unified Theory of Volatility," Paribas working paper. Republished in the book *Derivatives Pricing: The Classic Collection,* Risk Books (2004), edited by Peter Carr.
■ Rubinstein, M. (1994) "Implied Binomial Trees," *Journal of Finance,* **49**, 771–818.

Asian options are far from trivial to value

8

Asian Pyramid Power

with Jørgen Haug and William Margrabe

Asian options are among the more popular forms of exotic options. Even though they can be priced by Monte Carlo simulation it is not a popular approach among practitioners. A swarm of researchers from academia and the industry have therefore churned out a number of closed form approximations for arithmetic average options,[1] and there seems to be no end to the interest in improving the approximations in search of the last penny. We choose to focus not on the last penny but rather at the intuition behind the choice of volatility in Asian option pricing. We also demonstrate that it is important to take the term structure of plain vanilla option volatility into consideration. The implications of a term structure of volatility for Asian option valuation have received scant attention in the literature, and most off-the-shelf systems available to Wall Street delivers only Asian option models that ignore the term structure. Could it be that the hunt for the last penny has made academics and practitioners blind to the big bucks? Before we discuss the effect of calibrating Asian options to the term structure of volatility, let us kick off with the intuition behind the relationship between Asian option volatility and the well known rule of thumb that Asian option volatility equals the spot volatility divided by the square root of three.

In 1997 Bill Margrabe (a.k.a. Dr Risk) asked a question on his web page www.margrabe.com regarding Asian options. The Collector (Espen) answered the question in 1999. As you will see, however, Bill Margrabe's own explanation was more intuitive and elegant. The quiz and its solution are reprinted below (feel free to try to figure out the answer before you read on to its solution). After going through the quiz, we discuss when and why it can make a big difference whether you calibrate Asian options to the term structure of volatility or not. As a bonus, we also look into variable time between fixings. But first the quiz and its solution.

1 Celia in Derivativesland

1.1 Quiz (7/9/97)

Carroll Lewis, a don at Christ Church College, Oxford, runs a hedge fund on the side. He specializes in buying and selling short-dated average price currency options, for which the underlying price is the average of the daily closing exchange rates over the life of the option. For example, recently, one Friday he bought a one week, Average Price Call Option that expires on the following Friday, and that pays off the greater of zero and the average of the five daily closing prices.

   Also, Lewis has an interest in child photography. Namely, he has a studio where he takes pictures of little girls. From time to time he employs one of those little girls, Celia, age 10, as a derivatives quant. Unfortunately, Celia is mathematically challenged and is still counting blocks and building (sometimes elaborate) figures with them. Fortunately, Celia is highly reliable when asked to perform tasks within her range.

   Lewis has devised a childishly simple, non-algebraic algorithm for computing a key component of the correct volatility to plug into a Black-Scholes-Merton (BSM) option calculator, so he can price his Average Price Options (Black and Scholes, 1973; Merton, 1973). Celia carries out this algorithm flawlessly. Lewis takes her output, performs a single arithmetic operation on it, then takes the square root of that operation's result, and multiplies it by the volatility for the currency.

   What is Carroll Lewis's algorithm for Celia? (Assume for simplicity the usual BSM framework, and that only business days matter, ignoring weekends and holidays.)

1.2   Solution (2/14/99)

Espen Haug supplies a correct solution that requires nothing more from Celia than the four basic arithmetic operations, plus squaring.

> I am not sure if my algorithm is simple enough, but since Celia no longer is ten (Margrabe posted the problem circa 7/9/97), but at least eleven or probably twelve years old, I believe she can handle it. I am also wondering whether she is Asian or American? If she is Asian I am sure she can handle it. If she is American, she could have big problems understanding it. (Warning: Although your statement may be factually correct, it is not politically correct. While it does not disturb me, it may limit your dinner invitations in some parts of Liberal America – Margrabe.) Well, all she needs to do is taking the number of days in the period and add that number together twice as many times as the number of days in the period, then add the number of days in the period three times more, then add one to that number. Then Mr Carroll Lewis has to divide it all by $6 \times \text{days}^2$, then take the square root of it and multiply it by the spot volatility. More precisely:

$$\sigma_G = \sigma \sqrt{\frac{2n^2 + 3n + 1}{6n^2}},$$

> where σ_G is the average volatility, σ is the spot volatility and n is the number of days/fixings. The formula is based on the assumption that the next fixing is one day (fixing period) away (no weekends, including weekends would make the algorithm a bit more complex). The formula works excellently for discrete geometric averages, and should also be good enough for Government work on discrete arithmetic average options. (Perhaps the BIS allows this calculation for computing capital requirements – Margrabe.) For a very large n the formula converges to the volatility of a continuous time geometric average rate volatility: $\frac{\sigma}{\sqrt{3}}$.

While Dr Risk can't really ditch this algorithm, it might be asking a bit much, even for most young Asian girls. Dr Risk's algorithm, though, is simple enough for even seven year old American girls:

First, the background, which is not so simple:

$$A = (S_1 + S_2 + \cdots + S_5)/5$$
$$= \frac{(S_0 + \Delta S_1) + (S_0 + \Delta S_1 + \Delta S_2) + \cdots + (S_0 + \Delta S_1 + \cdots + \Delta S_5)}{5}$$
$$= \frac{5S_0 + 5\Delta S_1 + 4\Delta S_2 + 3\Delta S_3 + 2\Delta S_4 + 1\Delta S_5}{5}$$

With $T = 5\Delta t$, and Var $\Delta S_i = S^2\sigma^2 T$ we can construct a lognormal process to be input into the BSM-formula, with volatility consistent with that of the average process,

$$\text{Var } A = A^2\sigma_G^2 T = A^2\sigma_G^2 5\Delta t$$
$$= \frac{25 \text{ Var } \Delta S_1 + 16 \text{ Var } \Delta S_2 + 9 \text{ Var } \Delta S_3 + 4 \text{ Var } \Delta S_4 + 1 \text{ Var } \Delta S_5}{25}$$
$$\approx \frac{(25 + 16 + 9 + 4 + 1)S^2\sigma^2\Delta t}{25}$$

Hence,

$$5A^2\sigma_G^2\Delta t \approx \frac{(25 + 16 + 9 + 4 + 1)S^2\sigma^2\Delta t}{25},$$

or

$$\sigma_G^2 \approx \frac{55\sigma^2}{125} = \frac{11}{25}\sigma^2.$$

Here's where Celia gets involved. Carroll asks Celia to construct two figures from blocks and count the blocks involved:

1. Construct a big cube that has five little cubes along an edge. It contains 125 little cubes.
2. Construct a big pyramid that has a base of 5×5 little cubes, a layer of 4×4 cubes on top of that, etc, with one small cube at the peak. That has $25 + 16 + \cdots + 1 = 55$ little cubes in it.

Even a ten year old American girl ought to be able to handle that. My second-grade daughter (age seven) was able to perform it this morning between finishing breakfast and leaving for school. Okay, I helped a bit.

Then, Carroll multiplies the underlying variance by the ratio of the pyramid's volume to the large cube's volume. In the limit, as $n \to \infty$ this ratio goes to $\frac{1}{3}$, as we can see from Espen Haug's expression and we know from high school geometry. The volatility is the square root of the variance.

What we have looked at so far is actually geometric average volatility when we assume the spot price follows a geometric Brownian motion with constant volatility:

$$dS_t = \mu S_t \, dt + \sigma S_t \, dZ_t,$$

where Z is a Wiener process.

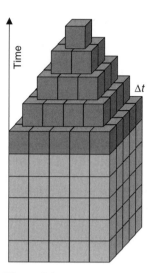

Figure 8.1

In the general case of n fixings we have

$$\sigma_G^2 = \frac{\sigma^2}{n^3} \sum_{i=0}^{n-1} (n-i)^2. \tag{8.1}$$

As in the the case of five fixings, the average variance equals the variance of the spot multiplied by the volume of a pyramid divided by the volume of a cube.

2 Calibrating to the Term Structure of Volatility

It is straightforward to make the model above consistent with the term structure of plain vanilla implied volatilities. We now assume a spot rate process with time dependent deterministic volatility:

$$dS_t = \mu S_t \, dt + v_t S_t \, dZ_t.$$

We can now incorporate the volatility structure by using a different local volatility, $v_i \equiv v_{t_i}$, for each layer in the pyramid, where $t_0, \ldots, t_{n-1}$ corresponds to the pyramid's layers. The formula for the geometric average volatility is then

$$\sigma_G^2 = \frac{1}{n^3} \sum_{i=0}^{n-1} (n-i)^2 v_i^2. \tag{8.2}$$

The geometric variance (squared volatility) is a weighted sum of the local variances (v_i^2) for the various time steps. One algorithm for computing geometric variance is to multiply the ith local variance by the volume of the ith layer of 1×1 cubes in a pyramid with base $n \times n$, sum all layers, and then divide by the volume of the cube with side n (i.e., divide by n^3). For each layer we need the local volatility. The local implied forward volatilities can be computed from global implied BSM volatilities by the formula

$$v_i = \sqrt{\frac{\sigma_i^2 t_i - \sigma_{i-1}^2 t_{i-1}}{t_i - t_{i-1}}},$$

where σ_i is the implied global volatility for an option expiring at time t_i, and σ_{i-1} is the implied volatility for an option expiring at time $t_{i-1} < t_i$. For a plain vanilla option the relationship between local and global volatilities is

$$\sigma^2 = \frac{1}{T} \int_0^T v_t^2 \, dt,$$

or in discrete time

$$\sigma^2 = \frac{1}{T} \sum_{i=0}^{n-1} v_{i+1}^2 \Delta t_{i+1},$$

where σ is the global spot volatility over the period T, or alternatively the implied volatility of a plain vanilla option expiring at time T, and $\Delta t_i = t_i - t_{i-1}$ is the time covered by the discrete local volatility v_i.

Equation (8.2) similarly shows the relationship between local spot volatilities and global Asian volatilities. The pyramid formula (8.2) shows intuitively that the volatilities for the first fixings receive higher weights than the later ones. The volatility of the first fixing receives a weight equal to the base of the pyramid, n^2, while the last fixing receives the weight of one cube. As the number of fixings goes to infinity the last fixing will receive a weight which is negligible relative to the first fixing. The height of the pyramid can be seen as the time to maturity of the average period. Moreover, the height of each layer represents the time between each fixing.

So far we have assumed equal time between fixings. For this reason the height of each layer is equal to Δt. In real applications the time between fixings can vary. Consider the case of daily fixings. Most markets are closed on weekends which results in longer time periods over weekends. The pyramid formula for Asian options with varying time between fixings is

$$\sigma_G^2 = \frac{1}{n^2 T} \sum_{i=0}^{n-1} (n-i)^2 \Delta t_{i+1} v_{i+1}^2 \tag{8.3}$$

We have simply assigned a variable time to each fixing, Δt_i, which corresponds to the height of each layer in the pyramid. The height of the pyramid and the cube is still equal to $\sum_{i=0}^{n-1} \Delta t_{i+1} = T$.

Let us consider the example of a one week Asian option. It is Thursday and the contract expires next Thursday. The option has five fixings, but the time of the second fixing period is three times as long as the other fixing periods. This is illustrated in Figure 8.2.

To find the Asian volatility, simply multiply the volume of each layer by the variance in the corresponding period, sum up, and divide by the volume of a box with height equal to the

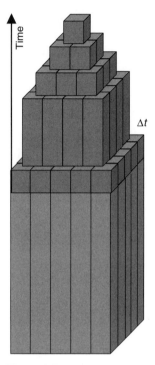

Figure 8.2

pyramid. It does not matter what time scale we use for the height of the pyramid – it could be days or weeks or years – since the ratio of the volume of the pyramid to that of the cube is independent of units. If we only have one fixing in the Asian option, then we naturally end up dividing the volume of a cube by an identical cube (a plain vanilla option).

The value of geometric average options that are calibrated to the term structure can now be computed with the BSM formula:

$$c = Se^{(b_G - r)T} N(d_1) - Xe^{-rT} N(d_2),$$

where X is the strike price, $N(x)$ is the cumulative normal distribution,

$$d_1 = \frac{\ln(S/X) + (b_G + \sigma_G^2/2)T}{\sigma_G \sqrt{T}},$$

and

$$d_2 = d_1 - \sigma_G \sqrt{T}.$$

This is the BSM formula where we have replaced the volatility with σ_G, and the cost of carry with

$$b_G = \frac{\sigma_G^2}{2} + \frac{1}{nT} \sum_{i=1}^{n} (b - \sigma_i^2/2)t_i.$$

Here t_i is the time to each fixing, T is the time to maturity,[2] and σ_i is the global BSM volatility for an option with expiration t_i.

2.1 Global Plain Vanilla to Global Asian

We have so far built pyramids from bricks of local volatilities (a.k.a. 'implied forward volatilities'). Each layer in the pyramid represents the weight we assign to the local volatility at each time step. Alternatively we can build pyramids directly from global plain vanilla volatilities.

To see the relationship between local and global spot volatilities in relation to Asian volatility we can rearrange the pyramid into a special, terrace shaped "ziggurat-pyramid" as in Figure 8.3.

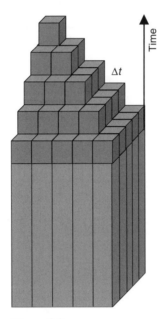

Figure 8.3

The volume of the pyramid and cube is still the same as earlier, however the ziggurat-pyramid helps us visualize the calculation of Asian volatility directly from vanilla global spot volatility.[3] The relationship between local and global volatilities for Asian options is that each pillar in the ziggurat-pyramid represents a global plain vanilla volatility. Each pillar is thus built from local volatilities. For instance a discrete Asian option with five fixings will have a total of 25 pillars $(n \times n)$ in the ziggurat-pyramid. One pillar reaches all the way until expiry (the corner) – that is, the height is T. Three pillars have maturity on the fixing before maturity, at the next step there are four by four pillars, that is 16, but nine are already used so we are left with seven. There are totally $5^2 = 25$ cubes in the first layer of an Asian pyramid, but 16 of the cubes are going into the next layer, so only nine are left with height equal to the time to the first fixing. In the general case of n fixings we can find the Asian geometric volatility directly from the global volatilities (adding the number of pillars in the ziggurat-pyramid, each weighted by its height in time) (Levy, 1997):

$$\sigma_G^2 = \frac{1}{n^2 T} \left[\sum_{i=1}^{n} \sigma_i^2 t_i + 2 \sum_{i=1}^{n-1} (n-i) \sigma_i^2 t_i \right], \tag{8.4}$$

where σ_i now is the implied BSM global volatility from an option that expires at t_i, and t_i is the time to fixing i. This formula yields the same result as equation (8.3).

3   From Geometric to Arithmetic

Most of the traded options are arithmetic average options. Based on the approximation by Levy (1997) the volatility of an arithmetic discrete average, calibrated to the term structure of implied volatilities, can be found as

$$\sigma_A = \sqrt{\frac{\ln(E[A_T^2]) - 2\ln(E[A_T])}{T}}, \tag{8.5}$$

where

$$E[A_T] = \frac{1}{n} \sum_{i=1}^{n} F_i,$$

where F_i is the forward price at fixing i. Moreover,

$$E[A_T^2] = \frac{1}{n^2} \sum_{i=1}^{n} F_i^2 e^{\sigma_i^2 t_i} + 2 \sum_{i=1}^{n-1} F_i e^{\sigma_i^2 t_i} \sum_{j=i+1}^{n} F_j.$$

As before σ_i is the plain vanilla BSM volatility for an option with expiration t_i, where t_i is the time to fixing i. Defining $F_A = E[A_T]$ we can now approximate the value of the arithmetic call option as[4]

$$c \approx e^{-rT}[F_A N(d_1) - X N(d_2)]$$

and a put option as

$$p \approx e^{-rT}[X N(-d_2) - F_A N(-d_1)]$$

where $N(x)$ is the cumulative normal distribution function,

$$d_1 = \frac{\ln(F_A/X) + T\sigma_A^2/2}{\sigma_A \sqrt{T}},$$

and

$$d_2 = d_1 - \sigma_A \sqrt{T}.$$

It is well known that this model works best for reasonably low volatilities, for instance spot volatility less than 30%. We will demonstrate, however, that it is far better to use a relatively simple approximation that takes into account the term structure of volatility than using a more accurate model not calibrated to the term structure of volatilities.

4   The Dollars

Now to the dollars: How important is it to calibrate the Asian volatility to the term structure of plain vanilla implied volatilities? Consider an option with six months to maturity, weekly fixings, and one week to the first fixing. In total there are 26 fixings. Assume we have plain vanilla options expiring every week. In practice one will typically need to do some form of interpolation between plain vanilla implied volatilities. In table 8.1 we assume the six month plain vanilla European option trades for 20% global volatility, and has zero cost of carry. The first four columns in the left hand side of the table shows Asian options[5] calculated with a flat term structure of volatility of 20%. All values take into account discrete fixings. GA represents geometric average options, and MC represents arithmetic Asian option valued using Monte Carlo simulations with 30,000 simulations in combination with antithetic variance reduction. The Monte Carlo can be regarded as benchmark values. Levy is the discrete method of Levy (1992), while CUR is the geometric conditioning approach described by Curran (1992). Curran's method is known to be a bit more accurate than Levy's method. The next three columns report on Asian options with an upward sloping term structure of implied volatilities. We use Curran's method only for a flat term structure.[6] We assume the implied volatilities are increasing by 0.5% per week, while the six-month global spot volatility is 20%.

The last three columns are similar Asian option values with a downward sloping term structure, falling 0.25% per week.

The table shows that the effect of taking into account the term structure of volatility is significant. Table 8.2 is similar to table 8.1, but now with 50% global spot volatility.

Table 8.2 illustrates that Levy's method is no longer as accurate as in the case with lower volatility, compared to the benchmark. It is well known that the Levy approximation is less accurate with higher volatility, relative to both Curran's method and the benchmark. To use a

TABLE 8.1: COMPARISON OF ASIAN OPTION VALUES WITH 20% GLOBAL SPOT VOLATILITY

$(S = 100, n = 26, t_1 = 1/52, T = 26/52 = 0.5, r = 5\%, b = 0\%, \sigma = 20\%)$

Strike	With flat term structure				Upward sloping			Downward sloping		
	GA	MC	Levy	CUR	TGA	TMC	TLevy	TGA	TMC	TLevy
80	19.3722	19.5145	19.5152	19.5135	19.3563	19.5064	19.5063	19.4067	19.5392	19.5387
90	10.0133	10.1287	10.1437	10.1288	9.6861	9.8137	9.8313	10.2815	10.3762	10.3987
100	3.1938	3.2765	3.2700	3.2667	2.2034	2.2785	2.2819	3.7262	3.7984	3.7977
110	0.5306	0.5724	0.5515	0.5647	0.1227	0.1458	0.1314	0.8450	0.8785	0.8701
120	0.0453	0.0555	0.0479	0.0531	0.0015	0.0023	0.0016	0.1204	0.1417	0.1254

TABLE 8.2: COMPARISON OF ASIAN OPTION VALUES WITH 50 % GLOBAL SPOT VOLATILITY

$(S = 100, n = 26, t_1 = 1/52, T = 26/52 = 0.5, r = 5\%, b = 0\%, \sigma = 50\%)$

Strike	With flat term structure				Upward sloping			Downward sloping		
	GA	MC	Levy	CUR	TGA	TMC	TLevy	TGA	TMC	TLevy
80	20.0737	20.7927	20.8747	20.7638	19.5448	20.3095	20.3924	20.3773	21.0187	21.1506
90	12.9318	13.5173	13.6090	13.5006	12.0559	12.6821	12.7695	13.3929	13.8929	14.0490
100	7.6799	8.1837	8.1962	8.1444	6.6509	7.1262	7.1759	8.2094	8.6562	8.7176
110	4.2331	4.6499	4.5884	4.6038	3.2998	3.6521	3.6361	4.7249	5.0932	5.0853
120	2.1867	2.4690	2.4100	2.4678	1.4902	1.7126	1.6800	2.5758	2.8907	2.8122

closed form geometric average option as approximation for arithmetic is as we can see even more inaccurate. It is typically better, however, to use an inaccurate approximation that takes the term structure of volatility into account, than to use a more accurate model that ignores the term structure. The best approach is naturally to use an accurate Asian model that takes the term structure of volatility into account.

Appendix: Inside the Average Period

When we are inside the average period, and m out of n fixings are fixed we can find the value of an Asian option by

$$
\begin{aligned}
\text{Payoff} &= A - X \\
&= \frac{S_1 + \cdots + S_n}{n} - X \\
&= \frac{S_1 + \cdots + S_m + S_{m+1} + \cdots + S_n}{n} - X \\
&= \frac{\frac{m(S_1+\cdots+S_m)}{m} + \frac{(n-m)(S_{m+1}+\cdots+S_n)}{n-m}}{n} - nX \\
&= \frac{mA_m + (n-m)A_{n-m}^* - nX}{n} \\
&= \frac{(n-m)A_{n-m}^* - (nX - mA_m)}{n} \\
&= \frac{(n-m)\left[A_{n-m}^* - \frac{nX-mA_m}{n-m}\right]}{n} \\
&= \frac{n-m}{n} \times \left(A_{n-m}^* - \frac{(nX - mA_m)}{n-m}\right)
\end{aligned}
$$

The value of the Asian option is now equal to $\frac{n-m}{n}$ options, with underlying A_{n-m}^* and strike price $\frac{nX-mA_m}{n-m}$. When only one fixing is left the value of an Asian option can be simplified to the value of plain vanilla option multiplied by $\frac{1}{n}$, with strike equal to: $nX - (n-1)A_m$.

FOOTNOTES & REFERENCES

1. Among others: Kemna and Vorst (1990), Turnbull and Wakeman (1991), Levy (1992), Levy and Turnbull (1992), Curran (1992), Bouaziz, Briys and Grouhy (1994), Geman and Eydeland (1995), Dewynne and Wilmott (1995), Clewlow (1996), and Milevsky and Posner (1998).

2. For a continuous geometric average without term structure we have $b_G = \frac{1}{2}\left(b - \frac{\sigma^2}{6}\right)$.

3. For the case of Asian volatility from local volatility we could just as well have used a ziggurat-pyramid.

4. The Levy formula is unnecessarily complex, and we have modified it to a much simpler expression.

5. We have limited the present analysis to European Asian options. Several papers deal with American Asian options, for instance Hull and White (1993), Hansen and Jørgensen (1997), Chalasani, Jha, Egriboyun and Varikooty (1999), and Dai and Lyuu (2002). For American Asians the importance of taking into account the term structure of implied volatilities should be even higher.

6. It should not be too complicated, however, to modify it to hold also for non-trivial term structures.

■ Black, F. and M. Scholes (1973) "The Pricing of Options and Corporate Liabilities" *Journal of Political Economy*, **81**, 637–654.

■ Bouaziz, L., E. Briys and M. Grouhy (1994) "The Pricing of Forward Starting Asian Options" *Journal of Banking and Finance*, **18**, 823–839.

■ Chalasani, P., S.Jha, F. Egriboyun and A. Varikooty (1999) "A Refined Binomial Lattice for Pricing American Asian Options," *Review of Derivatives Research*, **3**(1), 85–105.

■ Clewlow, L. (1996) "A Model for London Metal Exchange Average Price Options Contracts" *London Metal Exchange*, August.

■ Curran, M. (1992) "Beyond Average Intelligence" *Risk Magazine*, **5**(10).

■ Dai, T. and Y. Lyuu (2002) "Efficient, Exact Algorithms for Asian Options with Multiresolution Lattices" *Review of Derivatives Research*, **5**, 181–203.

■ Dewynne, J. N. and P. Wilmott (1995) "A Note On Average Rate Options With Discrete Sampling" *SIAM J. Appl. Math.*, **55**(1), 267–276.

■ Geman, H. and A. Eydeland (1995) "Domino Effect," *Risk Magazine*, **8**(4).

■ Hansen, A. T. and P. L. Jørgensen (1997) "Analytical Valuation of American-style Asian Options" Working Paper, University of Aarhus, Denmark.

■ Hull, J. and A. White (1993) "Efficient Procedures for Valuing European and American Path-Dependent Options" *Journal of Derivatives*, **1**, 21–31.

■ Kemna, A. and A. Vorst (1990) "A Pricing Method for Options Based on Average Asset Values" *Journal of Banking and Finance*, **14**, 113–129.

■ Levy, E. (1992) "Pricing European Average Rate Currency Options" *Journal of International Money and Finance*, **11**, 474–491.

■ ———— (1997) "Asian Options" in *Exotic Options, The State of The Art*, Clewlow, L. and Strickland, C. (Eds) International Thomson Business Press.

■ Levy, E. and S. Turnbull (1992) "Average Intelligence" *Risk Magazine*, **5**(2).

■ Merton, R. C. (1973) "Theory of Rational Option Pricing" *Bell Journal of Economics and Management Science*, **4**, 141–183.

■ Milevsky, Moshe, A. and S. E. Posner (1998) "Asian Options, the Sum of Lognormals, and the Reciprocal Gamma Distribution" *Journal of Financial and Quantitative Analysis*, **11**, 409–422.

■ Turnbull, S. M. and L. M. Wakeman (1991) "A Quick Algorithm for Pricing European Average Options" *Journal of Financial and Quantitative Analysis*, **26**, 377–389.

Eduardo Schwartz

Eduardo Schwartz: the Yoga Master of Mathematical Finance

Eduardo Schwartz is Professor in Finance at UCLA Anderson School of Management. He has published more than 90 articles in finance and economic journals. He was one of the first to apply finite difference to option valuation, and was also a pioneer in real option valuation as well as in developing models for commodity derivatives. More recently he has done some interesting work on asset allocation and portfolio optimizing under fat-tails.

Haug : Where did you grow up?

Schwartz : I was born and grew up in Santiago, Chile.

Haug : How and when did you first become interested in finance, economics and mathematics?

Schwartz : I became interested in mathematics and economics while I was studying Engineering in Chile. I became interested in finance when I went to Vancouver to get a Masters degree.

Haug : What is your educational background?

Schwartz : I have an Engineering degree from the University of Chile (a six year course) and Masters and PhD in Finance from the University of British Columbia in Vancouver.

Haug : How and when did you first become interested in applying finite difference methods to valuation of derivatives instruments?

Schwartz : Michael Brennan and I realized that there were many interesting options problems that did not have closed formed solution, so I wrote part of my PhD dissertation developing these numerical methods to value derivative instruments.

Haug : Was it clear early on for you that binomial and trinomial trees were special cases of finite difference methods?

Schwartz : We published a paper on this subject in 1977 in which we described these relationships.

Haug : Was there much focus on fat-tails in the distribution at that time? Was this the reason that you looked into finite difference methods applied to jump processes?

Schwartz : I did not work on fat-tails until very recently.

Haug : You have also written multiple papers on valuation of commodity derivatives. What is the main difference in building models for commodity derivatives as opposed to financial derivatives like equity or currency?

Schwartz : The fact that most commodities have (stochastic) convenience yield makes them quite different from other financial derivatives. I started working more intensely on this subject around 1995 when I prepared my presidential address to the AFA.

Haug : If there is suddenly a shortage of a commodity (a short squeeze) can this be seen as a jump in the convenience yield?

Schwartz : It is always hard to distinguish empirically a jump from a diffusion with very high volatility.

Haug : When it comes to electricity derivatives I know that you have looked into modeling seasonality in the spot price, can you describe this model briefly?

Schwartz : In addition to all the other problems, some commodities (like electricity) prices have seasonal variations and you have to take this into account in the pricing of derivatives on those commodities.

Haug : Even if seasonality is important for modeling electricity spot price behavior I would think that seasonality should already be reflected in the forward or futures prices, if not there would be some good relative value trading opportunities?

Schwartz : Sure they are reflected, so that is why you have to take it into account if you want to have a good pricing model.

Haug : You have also done a great deal of work on real options, what are the main differences between valuing real options and financial options, the hedging argument?

Schwartz : In the last few years I have been very interested in this topic. Since the hedging arguments do not go through in real options you have to deal with the problem of estimating market prices of the risk factors which is sometimes a very hard problem.

Haug : Can you also describe how patents and R&D projects are related to option valuation?

Schwartz : In R&D projects there is great uncertainty in costs and in the potential revenues in the future, and there is a lot of flexibility such as the abandonment option at any time if things are not going well. So the real options approach is clearly appropriate to deal with this type of project.

Haug : In 2001 together with Longstaff you published some interesting work on valuing American options by simulation, can you tell us briefly about this method?

Schwartz : Simulation is a very powerful method but until recently it could only be used for solving European type problems since these are forward looking. But in the case of American options you need to start from the end (maturity time) and work backward optimizing at every point in time. At every point in time the holder of the option has to compare the value of immediate exercise with the expected value of continuation. We computed this expected value of continuation using simple linear regression from the simulated values. This was a simple but very powerful idea that now I am using in most of the work I am doing in real options.

Haug : Value at risk (VaR) is often criticized for being based on assumptions of normal distribution while we in practice clearly have fat-tailed distributions (leptokurtotic). Have you looked into how to improve VaR taking into account fat-tails?

Schwartz : It is more exact but it is harder to implement. I am working on this subject with Pedro Santa Clara. Hopefully we will eventually get to a better solution.

Haug : What about asset allocation, will changing the assumption from normal distributed returns to some type of fat-tailed distribution play an important role here?

Schwartz : In some work that I did with S. Rachev and others we showed that they can play an important role.

Haug : Do you have any hobbies outside economics and finance?

Schwartz : I like jogging, biking and yoga. I also enjoy reading and traveling.

Haug : Can your life be best described as a Brownian motion or jump-diffusion?

Schwartz : I think more like a Brownian motion!

Haug : In your view where are we in the evolution of quantitative finance?

Schwartz : I think we have made tremendous progress but there is always more to do.

A list of some of Schwartz's papers can be found below, a more extended list can be found at http://www.anderson.ucla.edu/x4150.xml.

REFERENCES

■ Brennan, M. J. and E. S. Schwartz (1977) "The Valuation of American Put Options," *Journal of Finance*, **32**(2), 449–462.
■ ——— (1978) "Finite Difference Methods and Jump Processes Arising in the Pricing of Contingent Claims: A Synthesis" *Journal of Financial and Quantitative Analysis*, **XIII**(3), 461–474.
■ Cortazar, G. and E. S. Schwartz (1994) "The Valuation of Commodity-Contingent Claims" *Journal of Derivatives*, **1**, 27–39.
■ Gibson, R. and E. S. Schwartz (1990) "Stochastic Convenience Yield and the Pricing of Oil Contingent Claims" *Journal of Finance*, **45**, 959–976.

■ Longstaff, F. A. and E. S. Schwartz (2001) "Valuing American Options by Simulation: A Simple Least-Square Approach" *Review of Financial Studies*, **14**(1), 113–147.

■ Lucia, J. and E. Schwartz (2002) "Electricity Prices and Power Derivatives: Evidence from the Nordic Power Exchange" *Review of Derivatives Research*.

■ Miltersen, K. and E. S. Schwartz (1998) "Pricing of Options on Commodity Futures with Stochastic Term Structures of Convenience Yields and Interest Rates" *Journal of Financial and Quantitative Analysis*, **33**(1), 33–59.

■ Mittnik, S., R. S. and E. S. Schwartz (2002) "Value-At-Risk and Asset Allocation with Stable Return Distributions" *Allgemeines Statistisches Archiv*, **86**(1), 53–68.

■ Rachev, S., E. S. Schwartz and Y. Tokat (2003) "The Stable non-Gaussian Asset Allocation: A Comparison with the Classical Approach" *Journal of Economic Dynamics and Control*, **27**(6).

■ Schwartz, E. S. (1997) "The Stochastic Behavior of Commodity Prices: Implications for Valuation and Hedging" *Journal of Finance*, **52**(3), 923–973.

■ Schwartz, E. S. and Y. Tokat (2002): "The Impact of Fat-Tailed Returns on Asset Allocation" *Mathematical Methods of Operations Research, Special Issue on Mathematical Models in Market and Credit Risk*, S. Rachev (Ed.), **55**(2), 165–185.

■ Schwartz, E. S. and L. Trigerogis (2001): *Real Options and Investment Under Uncertainty: Classical Readings and Contributions*, (Eds). MIT Press.

When standing in Central Park you can feel the power of New York City. New York city is also highly dependent on power; I remember the blackout of August 2003 when I had to sleep on the trading floor.

9

Practical Valuation of Power Derivatives*

In this chapter I look at the practical valuation of power derivatives from a trader's perspective. Most people that have written about valuation of power derivatives are academics or quants working in the research departments of large organizations far away from the trading desk. Most of them have never traded a single power option. In general there is nothing wrong with that as some of the greatest practical research in quantitative finance has come out of academia and research departments. Anyway, when it comes to electricity derivatives most academics have made simple things too complex and at the same time have forgotten simple things that have great importance. Still, as we will see the Black-Scholes-Merton model, or rather the formula will not necessarily suffice without some modifications when applied to the electricity market. This chapter was written during a research sabbatical from trading, to be honest most of this chapter was written in a bar in the town of Trondheim, one of the greatest university towns on this planet. To write or read about formulae and abstract mathematics is in my experience best done in a relaxing atmosphere. A frozen margarita can certainly help you absorb this chapter once you have finished reading it, or better still before.

1 Introduction

The Nordic electricity market with its exchange Nord Pool is today one of the most active exchanges in the word for physical electricity and electricity derivatives. Deregulation of the Norwegian electricity market began in 1991[1] before which it was an inter-utility market. In 1994 an OTC market for trading in electricity forwards and options developed, at about the same time that the Nord Pool exchange was established. New electricity legislation in Finland and Sweden opened up the deregulation of their markets in 1996 and 1998, and followed in 1999 by Denmark. The early deregulation and establishment of an exchange is probably one of the reasons the Nordic market became so successful. Although I will concentrate on the Nordic power market, most of this will also be relevant for other developing power markets, particularly because there are several exchanges trying to build on the Nordic model.

*This chapter was written while taking a sabbatical from trading and spending some time at the Norwegian University of Science and Technology. I would like to thank Stein Erik Fleten and Dan Tudball for some very useful comments. Needless to say, I remain solely responsible for any errors that still remain. This chapter was presented at the ICBI Global Derivatives conference in Paris, May 2006 and in November 2005 at the Norwegian University of Science and Technology.

After the establishment of Nord Pool it was not long before large US energy companies like Enron and TXU became members of the exchange. In Nord Pool's last peak period Enron was one of the largest, if not the largest player at Nord Pool with an active market making and position taking operation in Oslo. Today many international players are members of the exchange, from the member list (http://www.nordpool.no/) we can see that well known banks like Morgan Stanley, Merrill Lynch, Barclays, J. Aron (the commodity arm of Goldman Sachs) and also well known hedge funds like Tudor and D.E. Shaw are exchange members. At the time of writing more than 300 firms are exchange members of Nord Pool. Most of the large US energy companies that used to be members of the exchange left after the collapse of Enron. That most of the trading in the Nordic market at that time was on a well functioning exchange and not OTC meant that Enron (and everybody else) had to pay margin deposits on their contracts. This resulted in no credit losses in the Nordic market for anyone that had traded indirectly with Enron through Nord Pool. However, there were some considerable losses for players that had done OTC transactions with Enron. In the US there were basically no well-functioning exchanges for power derivatives and many players there had large credit exposures to Enron. The result was a chain reaction of losses. As a result power trading in the US market dried up almost completely. At Nord Pool there was derivatives trading as usual although the volumes fell quite dramatically as even Nordic companies became alarmed by losses in the OTC market, and also because some of the biggest market makers and position takers like Enron were simply gone.

Back to the beginning: in 1996 I resigned from my job as a market maker in fixed income options at Chemical Bank (today J.P. Morgan Chase Bank[2]) to set up my own company doing research, software and consulting for the fixed income and particularly the electricity market. I wanted to be part of the New New Thing: the fast growing electricity market. Many traders in the newly developed electricity market had good quant skills, many with backgrounds in engineering, while others had moved over from fixed income trading, FX trading or the stock market, but very few had the combination of a solid option trading background with good quant skills. There were a lot of different opinions on how to value electricity forwards and options at that time, one player explained to me how they used some type of regression analysis to value options. I was wondering if they had ever heard about arbitrage-free pricing models? Or maybe arbitrage principles had no value here, because one could not store electricity? A few very quantitatively oriented players were looking into Monte Carlo models trying to take into account seasonality, mean reversion, temperature, precipitation and a lot of other factors in one massive super simulation. The few people with option trading experience from other markets that recently had switched to the electricity market seemed simply to apply the Black-76 formula. I was skeptical about all of these approaches, but as a trader I always had great respect for other experienced traders. I got hold of some spot price data and looked at the historical distributions. The spot price had extremely fat-tails, further it had several statistical measures indicating mean reversion and seasonality. Also, how could one even use modern finance theory on electricity that was not easy to store? Many academics must have thought the same; over the next few years papers on mean reversion and seasonality were being published in relation to electricity derivatives. When I think back to that time, not even the contract descriptions from the OTC and exchange market were specific on all the details that might be important from a valuation perspective. I spent days and months contacting brokers and other people actively involved in the market to find out what really was the standard. That several people active in the market gave completely different answers did not make things simpler, exactly when was the delivery, and did you get delivery of the forward or was it all completely cash settled, or cash settled plus delivery of the forward, and was the forward delivered at the strike price or the settlement price? In the early days of a completely new market there are also limits to how much data you can back-test your ideas on. It had all the characteristics of a new fast growing market including some confusion about some details, details that can provide opportunities for arbitrageurs. The big differences in opinion about how to value the derivatives contracts in the market told me that I should get involved as a trader rather than as a consultant, and soon enough I was trading the New New Thing.

The physical market was limited to the physical players, namely the power producers, large retailers and energy intensive industry. The Nordic market is dominated by hydro-electric power, later when Sweden became a member it also entailed some nuclear power and to some degree oil, gas and coal generators. To value the forward price is partly arbitrage pricing, because hydro-electric producers can at least in theory store their electricity by letting their water reservoirs fill up, but as storage is limited by several factors, the pricing of forward contracts also involves expectations (knowledge and gambling) about temperature, precipitation, ice melting, you name it. As I worked mainly with the financial players, first with my own consultant software firm and later as a proprietary trader. Because of this I decided early on that I would not compete with the physical players with regard to their knowledge about supply and demand in the physical market. I could not store electricity without buying a hydro-electric power plant, some financial players became involved in this, but most financial players only became involved in the derivative market that all were financially settled against the spot price. In such a situation my view was that one could possibly gain an advantage over the physical players by understanding exactly how one could value derivatives against other derivatives contracts, and this is what this chapter is all about.

The most actively traded contracts soon became the seasonal and annual forward contracts, today Nord Pool have switched from three seasonal forwards to four quarterly forwards contracts per year, but this make little or no difference for the formulae we will soon look at. In the delivery period these exchange traded forwards have daily financial settlement against the spot price. The spot is a physical auction market with a daily fixing price. For example a fourth quarter 2006 forward will have delivery period starting October 1 ending December 31. For every day in the delivery period the contract is financially settled against the daily fixing price of the physical spot market. Each "day" is 24 hours, so the fourth quarter 2006 quarterly contract will have 2,208 MWH (megawatthours), or actually 2,209, because through returning from summer time in October we get one additional hour. The prices at Nord Pool are quoted today in EUR (it used to be in NOK). What the market called and still calls forwards are in reality swaps. In the beginning of the market many players were not really aware of this, or did not care? One player I consulted took advantage of this and arbitraged seasonal swaps against annual swaps, locking in risk-free arbitrage. The mistake was that many players assumed that the forward price was the same as the forward value, by not recognizing it as a swap they simply did not do the correct discounting when comparing forwards against forwards. Now let's move on to some formulas.

2 Energy Swaps/Forwards

Given the presence of traded contracts with quoted market prices, we can come up with a way to value the swap relative to other swaps. For example a strip of quarterly power swaps covering the whole year should have the same value as an annual swap. Otherwise there will be an arbitrage opportunity. All the forward contracts have financial settlement against the daily spot fixing that is set by the physical market. That there is no physical delivery makes it easier for financial players, nobody can for example corner the forward market.

As already mentioned the electricity swaps traded in the Nordic power market are known as forwards, but are (from a valuation perspective) power swaps, a strip of one day electricity forwards. To compare the value of different swaps we simply need to discount the cash flows. The swap/forward market price is not the value of the swap contract, but only the contract price. To compare different power swaps with each other we need to find the value:

$$F_{ValueToday} = \frac{e^{-r_b T_b}}{n} \sum_{i=1}^{n} \frac{F}{(1 + r_{j,i}/j)^i},$$

(9.1)

where $F_{ValueToday}$ is the swap value today and

F is the forward/swap price in the market. In this case 'price' should not be confused with 'value'!

j is the number of compoundings per year (number of settlements in a one year forward contract). We assume here they are evenly spread out. In practice there are no payments during weekends, so every fifth payment does not have the same time interval as the rest of the payments. However the effect of taking this into account is not of economic significance, at least for monthly or longer contracts.

n is the number of settlements in the delivery period for the particular forward contract. Nord Pool uses daily settlement, so this will typically be the number of calendar or trading days in the forward period.

$r_{j,i}$ is a risk-free interest swap rate starting at the beginning of the delivery period and ending at the i the period. Further, it has j compoundings per year.

T_b is the time to the beginning of the forward delivery period.

r_b is a risk-free continuously compounded zero coupon rate with T_b years to maturity.

Equation (9.1) is what a couple of market participants figured out early in the game and was in some cases able to arbitrage a strip of seasonal contracts against annual contracts. We can simplify equation (9.1) to

$$F_{ValueToday} = F e^{-r_b T_b} \frac{\left(1 - \frac{1}{(1+r_j/j)^n}\right)}{r_j} \frac{j}{n},$$

(9.2)

where r_j now is the forward start-interest swap rate, starting at the beginning of the delivery period and ending at the end of the delivery period, with j compoundings per year set equal to the number of settlements per year.

Example Consider a quarterly electricity forward(swap) that trades at a price of 35 EUR/MWH (EUR per mega watt hour), the delivery period is 2,160 hours or 90 days. It is six months to the start of the delivery period. Assume the forward start interest swap rate, starting six months from now and ending six months plus 90 days from now is 5 % converted to the basis of daily compounding. The six months continuous zero coupon rate is 4 %. What is the present value of the power contract when using 365 days per year? $F = 35$, $r_j = 0.05$, $j = 365$, $n = 90$, $r_b = 0.04$, $T_b = 0.5$

$$F_{ValueToday} = 35e^{-0.04 \times 0.5} \times \frac{\left(1 - \frac{1}{(1+0.05/365)^{90}}\right)}{0.05} \times \frac{365}{90} = 34.0940.$$

The present value of the power forward/swap is thus 34.0940 EUR per MWH. The total value of one contract is found by multiplying the number of hours in the contract period by the value per MWH $2160 \times 34.0940 = 73,643.08$ EUR.

Approximation Formula (9.2) can be approximated by:

$$F_{ValueToday} \approx F e^{-r_b T_b} e^{-r_d (T_m - T_b)},$$

where r_d is the forward starting continuously compounded zero coupon rate for the delivery period, multiplied by the time from the start of the delivery period T_b to the middle of the delivery period T_m. This can be simplified further by

$$F_{ValueToday} \approx F e^{-r_e T_m}, \tag{9.3}$$

where r_e is a continuously compounded zero coupon rate from now to the end of the delivery period. This approximation is reasonably accurate as long as we use consistent rates.

Example Consider the same input as in last example. To make the examples equivalent we have to find a rate r_e that is consistent with $r_b = 0.04$ and $r_j = 0.05$. To find r_e from the example above we first need to convert r_j to a continuously compounded rate $r_{cj} = 365 \ln(1 + 0.05/365) = 0.04999658$. Based on no arbitrage opportunities we must have

$$e^{-r_e T_m} = e^{-r_b T_b} e^{-r_{cj}(T_m - T_b)},$$

$$r_e = \frac{r_b T_b + r_{cj}(T_m - T_b)}{T_b + (T_m - T_b)},$$

$$r_e = \frac{0.04 \times 0.5 + 0.049997 \times 90/365/2}{0.5 + 90/365/2} = 0.04198,$$

and we can now approximate the value of the forward price

$$F_{ValueToday} \approx 35e^{-0.04198 \times (0.5 + 90/365/2)} = 34.0961,$$

The approximate value is thus not very different from 34.0940 calculated by the more accurate formula.

3   Power Options

As I have already indicated in the introduction, the spot price in the Nordic electricity market definitely has some seasonality, further statistical tests indicate that it follows some type of mean reversion. The returns also have very fat-tails. In the Nordic market almost all options are not directly on the spot price, but rather on quarterly and annual power swaps. If the spot price is seasonal and mean reverting this should already be reflected in the forward price in a efficient market. For example in the winter months where there is peak demand for electricity in the Nordic countries (heating) if the low demand in the summer months (there is not much air conditioning in the Nordic markets) is not already reflected in the summer months forward then market participants can do very good relative value trades by selling forward contracts for the summer months and, for example, buying the next winter forwards against it. Then there is a high probability that the spot price would come down in the summer and give profit on the short summer contracts.

I don't doubt that one needs a seasonal model, possibly in combination with a mean reverting model and many other factors to value the fair forward price from the spot price, but in an efficient market we must assume that this already is more or less reflected in the forward prices, see also Lucia and Schwartz (2002). If you don't think so you should forget the option market and concentrate on doing relative value trades in spot against forwards and in particular forward against forwards. When valuing options based on arbitrage theory and dynamic hedging the only thing that is important is the option value relative to the underlying, that is the stochastic process and the distribution of the returns of the underlying asset (in a risk neutral world). Many academics have concluded that a geometric Brownian motion and Black-Scholes-Merton type model are useless for electricity derivatives, because they observe seasonality and mean reversion in the spot price.

If we look at the distribution and some statistical properties of the spot price returns they are basically right in their assumptions. We can get a good idea of this simply by looking at Figure 9.1 which plots the histogram for the Nord Pool electricity spot using data from 5 November 2001 to 3 November 2004. From the figure we can see the extremely fat-tails and the large peak, which also is confirmed with a Pearson kurtosis of 11.12 (leptokurtic distribution), remember the normal distribution only has kurtosis of 3. As already mentioned the options trading at Nord Pool are European options on the quarterly and annual forward contract and not directly on the spot. Figure 9.2 shows the return distribution on a annual forward. This is hardly comparable to the spot data, it is much closer to a normal distribution. It still has some fat-tails as is also evident from a Pearson kurtosis of 4.9, but this is not very different from what we observe in a lot of stocks where the Black-Scholes-Merton formula or its binomial equivalent is actively used by many (most?) practitioners. Not convinced? Just look at Figure 9.3 which is the return distribution of Amazon.com, the distribution has much fatter tails (Pearson kurtosis of 13.29) than the annual electricity forward, and I know for sure that many option traders used Black-Scholes-Merton type formula to value options on such stocks. As we know, option traders naturally do not use the Black-Scholes-Merton formula in it's naive way when valuing options on stocks, they fudge the model to work in such a market by pumping up the volatility for out-of-the money options versus at-the money options, we will get back to this later. My point is simply that based on statistical analysis[3] one can conclude that the distribution on quarterly and annual electricity forwards returns is not very different from that on many stocks, except they are maybe closer to the normal distribution than some dot com stocks. In other words at least theoretically we can start to approximate by assuming the forward price (swap) follows a geometric Brownian motion

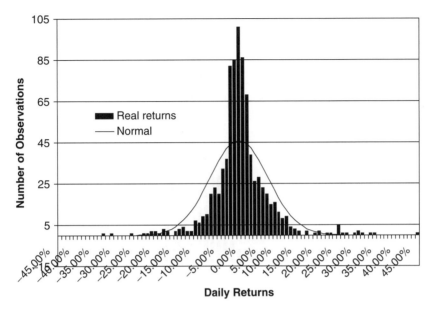

Figure 9.1:   Electricity Spot Daily Returns

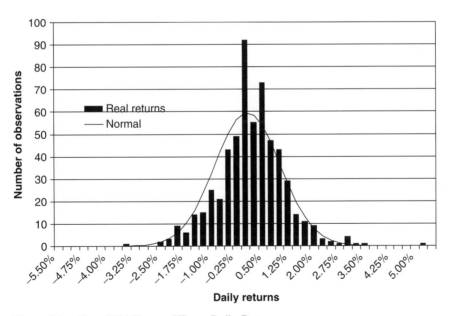

Figure 9.2:   Year 2004 Forward/Swap Daily Returns

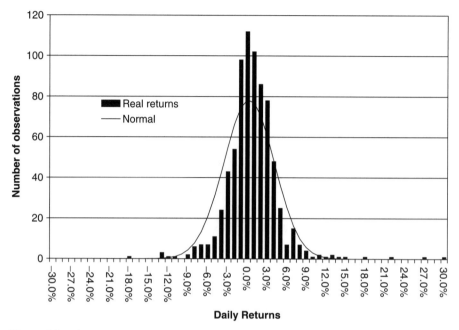

Figure 9.3:   Amazon Daily Returns

$$dF = \sigma F dz$$

where σ is the volatility of the returns of the forward/swap price F and dz is a Winer process. Using Ito's lemma we get the following PDE

$$\left[\frac{\partial f}{\partial t} + \frac{1}{2}\frac{\partial^2 f}{\partial F^2}\sigma^2 F^2\right] dt = rf.$$

Where f is the value of the derivative security. Solving this for a European option with the boundary condition $\max[F - X, 0]$ where X is the strike price we get the well known Black-76 formula

$$c = e^{-rT}[FN(d_1) - XN(d_2)], \tag{9.4}$$

$$p = e^{-rT}[XN(-d_2) - FN(-d_1)], \tag{9.5}$$

where

$$d_1 = \frac{\ln(F/X) + (\sigma^2/2)T}{\sigma\sqrt{T}},$$

$$d_2 = \frac{\ln(F/X) - (\sigma^2/2)T}{\sigma\sqrt{T}} = d_1 - \sigma\sqrt{T},$$

and r is the risk free rate, T is the years to maturity and $N(\cdot)$ is the cumulative normal distribution function.

The experienced option traders that moved into the electricity market early on using the Black-76 formula were probably not far off at all, as we will see they were just on target, except for their delta hedge. The Black-76 formula early on became more or less the standard in the Nord Pool option market. But what about the boundary condition, didn't I just tell you that the power forwards in reality were not forwards but swaps, so that the boundary condition and formula must be modified accordingly? By what I believe was a coincidence, the way Nord Pool had formulated their option contracts actually turned the valuation problem magically into an option on a future/forward (expiring at the same time as the option) and not an option on a swap. The option contracts at Nord Pool were specified in such a way that at expiration they had cash settlement equal to the difference between the forward price and the strike price, and in addition you got delivery of a forward at the settlement price. The forward you got at maturity had no impact on the valuation or hedging problem as you always had the opportunity to close this out immediately at no cost, except the bid offer spread. However, if you had delta hedged the option during its lifetime you were now suddenly left with cash flows from your hedging that did not start to materialize before the swap went into the delivery period. This option may seem difficult to value at first. Things that seem confusing at first typically have a very simple solution. The key was to figure out that the cash flows from just holding the option were exactly the same as a standard European option on a futures or forward[4] contract, so the option value had to be equal to the Black (1976) formula. As mentioned earlier this soon also became the market standard. Still, what you were actually hedging with was not a future or forward but a power swap. To take this into account one simply needed to adjust the delta accordingly. Many market participants got this wrong for years. If the option value is given by Black-76 then we could hedge the option using the Black-76 delta and a forward expiring at option maturity. Now if the forward price move then the Black-76 delta multiplied by the forward price will exactly offset the change in the option value (at least according to traditional theory). However we are not hedging with a forward contract but with a swap, so we need an adjusted delta Δ_H that multiplied by the swap value is exactly equal to the Black-76 delta multiplied by the forward price. Letting $\Delta_{B76} = e^{-rT}N(d_1)$ be the Black-76 delta, the delta for hedging with electricity forwards/swaps must be given by:

$$\Delta_{B76}F = \Delta_H F_{VaT}$$

$$\Delta_{B76}F = \Delta_H F e^{-r_p(T_b-T)} \frac{\left(1 - \frac{1}{(1+r_j/j)^n}\right)}{r_j} \frac{j}{n}$$

$$\Delta_H = \Delta_{B76} e^{r_p(T_b-T)} \frac{nr_j}{j\left(1 - \frac{1}{(1+r_j/j)^n}\right)}$$

$$\Delta_H = N(d_1) e^{-rT} e^{r_p(T_b-T)} \frac{nr_j}{j\left(1 - \frac{1}{(1+r_j/j)^n}\right)},$$

$$\Delta_H \approx N(d_1) e^{-rT} e^{r(T_b-T)} \frac{nr_j}{j\left(1 - \frac{1}{(1+r_j/j)^n}\right)},$$

where F is the swap/forward market price, and F_{VaT} is the swap value at option expiration T, r_p is the risk-free rate from the option's expiration to the beginning of the delivery period. T_b

is the time from now to the beginning of the delivery period, r is the risk free rate until option expiration.

$$d_1 = \frac{\ln(F/X) + T\sigma^2/2}{\sigma\sqrt{T}},$$

and for a put

$$\Delta_{put} = N(-d_1)e^{-rT}e^{r_p(T_b-T)}\frac{nr_j}{j\left(1 - \frac{1}{(1+r_j/j)^n}\right)}. \tag{9.6}$$

3.1 Energy Swaptions

April 2005 Nord Pool changed the contract description of their options on forwards/swaps in order to have delivery of the underlying swap at the strike price and not at the fixing price. For this reason Nord Pool options are today European options on energy swaps (a.k.a. energy swaptions). If a call swaption is in-the-money at maturity the option has delivery of a swap (named forward by the market) delivered to the strike price. The pay-out from the option is thus no longer received immediately at expiration, but rather during the delivery period of the underlying swap (forward). The energy call swaption formula is

$$c = \frac{\left(1 - \frac{1}{(1+r_j/j)^n}\right)}{r_j}\frac{j}{n}e^{-r_p(T_b-T)} \times \text{Black-76}$$

$$= \frac{\left(1 - \frac{1}{(1+r_j/j)^n}\right)}{r_j}\frac{j}{n}e^{-r_p(T_b-T)}e^{-rT}[FN(d_1) - XN(d_2)]$$

$$= \frac{\left(1 - \frac{1}{(1+r_j/j)^n}\right)}{r_j}\frac{j}{n}e^{-r_b T_b}[FN(d_1) - XN(d_2)], \tag{9.7}$$

where r_p is the risk-free rate from the option's expiration to the beginning of the delivery period. T_b is the time from now to the beginning of the delivery period. Moreover,

$$d_1 = \frac{\ln(S/X) + \sigma^2 T/2}{\sigma\sqrt{T}}, \qquad d_2 = d_1 - \sigma\sqrt{T}.$$

For a put we have similarly

$$p = \frac{\left(1 - \frac{1}{(1+r_j/j)^n}\right)}{r_j}\frac{j}{n}e^{-r_b T_b}[XN(-d_2) - FN(-d_1)]. \tag{9.8}$$

Good approximations for calculating the call and put swaption values are

$$c \approx e^{-r_e T_m}[FN(d_1) - XN(d_2)]. \tag{9.9}$$

$$p \approx e^{-r_e T_m}[XN(-d_2) - FN(-d_1)]. \tag{9.10}$$

where r_e is the risk-free rate from now to the end of the delivery period and T_m is the time in years from now to the middle of the delivery period, and

$$d_1 = \frac{\ln(S/X) + \sigma^2 T/2}{\sigma\sqrt{T}}, \qquad d_2 = d_1 - \sigma\sqrt{T}.$$

Example Consider a call on a quarterly electricity swap, with six months to maturity. The start of the delivery period is 17 days after the option expires and the delivery period is 2,208 hours or 92 days. The swap/forward trades at 33 EUR/MWH, the strike is 35 EUR/MWH. The number of fixings in the delivery period is 92. The risk-free rate from now until the beginning of delivery period is 5%. The daily compounding swap rate starting at the beginning of the delivery period and ending at the end of the delivery period is 5%. The volatility of the swap is 18%. What is the option value? $T = 0.5$, $T_b = 0.5 + 17/365 = 0.5466$, $r_b = 0.05$, $r_j = 0.05$, $j = 365$, $n = 92$, and $\sigma = 0.18$ yields

$$d_1 = \frac{\ln(33/35) + 0.5 \times 0.18^2/2}{0.18\sqrt{0.5}} = -0.3987,$$

$$d_2 = -0.3987 - 0.18\sqrt{0.5} = -0.5259,$$

$$N(d_1) = N(-0.3987) = 0.3451, \qquad N(d_2) = N(-0.5259) = 0.2995,$$

$$c = \frac{\left(1 - \frac{1}{(1+0.05/365)^{92}}\right)}{0.05}\frac{365}{92}e^{-0.05 \times 0.5466}[33N(d_1) - 35N(d_2)] = 0.8761.$$

To find the value of an option on one swap/forward contract we need to multiply by the number of delivery hours. This yields a price of $2208 \times 0.8761 = 1,934.37$ EUR. Alternatively we could have found the option value using the approximation (9.9), using time from now to the middle of delivery period $T_m = 0.5 + 17/365 + 92/2/365 = 0.6726$ and assuming the rate from now to the end of the delivery period is $r_e \approx 0.05$:

$$c \approx e^{-0.05 \times 0.6260}[33N(d_1) - 35N(d_2)] = 0.8761.$$

At four decimals accuracy the approximation evidently gives the same result as the more accurate formula.

Put-call parity For a standard put (a.k.a. receiver swaption) or call option (a.k.a. payer swaption) the put-call parity is:

$$p = c + (X - F)\frac{\left(1 - \frac{1}{(1+r_j/j)^n}\right)}{r_j}\frac{j}{n}e^{-r_b T_b}, \tag{9.11}$$

and of course

$$c = p + (F - X)\frac{\left(1 - \frac{1}{(1+r_j/j)^n}\right)}{r_j}\frac{j}{n}e^{-r_b T_b}. \tag{9.12}$$

The put-call parity can be used to construct synthetic put or calls as well as synthetic swaps/ forwards from traded puts and calls. The synthetic/implied forward price from a put and a call is given by

$$F = \frac{c - p}{\frac{\left(1 - \frac{1}{(1+r_j/j)^n}\right)}{r_j} \frac{j}{n} e^{-r_b T_b}} + X.$$

Energy Swaption Greeks

Delta:

$$\Delta_{call} = \frac{\left(1 - \frac{1}{(1+r_j/j)^n}\right)}{r_j} \frac{j}{n} e^{-r_b T_b} N(d_1),$$ (9.13)

$$\Delta_{put} = -\frac{\left(1 - \frac{1}{(1+r_j/j)^n}\right)}{r_j} \frac{j}{n} e^{-r_b T_b} N(-d_1).$$ (9.14)

Vega: The vega is the swaptions sensitivity with respect to change in volatility.

$$\text{Vega}_{call,put} = \frac{\left(1 - \frac{1}{(1+r_j/j)^n}\right)}{r_j} \frac{j}{n} e^{-r_b T_b} F n(d_1)\sqrt{T}.$$ (9.15)

It is necessary to divide by 100 to express vega as the change in the option value for a 1% point change in volatility.

Gamma: Gamma for swaptions:

$$\Gamma_{call,put} = \frac{\frac{\left(1 - \frac{1}{(1+r_j/j)^n}\right)}{r_j} \frac{j}{n} e^{-r_b T_b} n(d_1)}{F \sigma \sqrt{T}}.$$ (9.16)

Rho:

$$\rho_{call} = \left(\frac{(1+r_j/j)^{-n-1}}{r_j} - \frac{\left(1 - \frac{1}{(1+r_j/j)^n}\right)}{r_j^2} \frac{j}{n} - T \frac{\left(1 - \frac{1}{(1+r_j/j)^n}\right)}{r_j} \frac{j}{n}\right)$$
$$\times e^{-r_b T_b}[FN(d_1) - XN(d_2)],$$ (9.17)

$$\rho_{put} = \left(\frac{(1+r_j/j)^{-n-1}}{r_j} - \frac{\left(1 - \frac{1}{(1+r_j/j)^n}\right)}{r_j^2} \frac{j}{n} - T \frac{\left(1 - \frac{1}{(1+r_j/j)^n}\right)}{r_j} \frac{j}{n}\right)$$
$$\times e^{-r_b T_b}[XN(-d_2) - FN(-d_1)].$$ (9.18)

4 Still, What About Fat-Tails?

Even when using a modified Black-Scholes-Merton model that takes into account that the underlying is a power swap one still has the same problem as in any other market, the observation of fat-tails in the returns. Most traders prefer to get around this by fudging the model, inputting some type of volatility smile. In the early development of the Nordic market one could often see a flat volatility smile, providing an opportunity for good relative value trades. As in other markets, in the electricity market we observe jumps from time to time, jump diffusion or more likely jump-diffusion in combination with stochastic volatility models are possibly a way to go if you can just come up with a robust model. Personally I always prefer to have a whole set of models in front of me on a huge spreadsheet. From this I can at least find out quickly how sensitive a given strike and maturity are to different input parameters for volatility of volatility or jumps using models with different assumptions. This will also help me fudge my basic model. In other words I am using a Black-Scholes-Merton type formula without actually using the Black-Scholes-Merton model behind it. See Chapter 2 for more on this.

When it comes to options directly on the spot one typically has to return to modelling the spot directly, here seasonality, mean reversion and very fat-tails can all be of great importance. However, this is only a small fraction of the derivatives market at least in the Nordic market and I have concentrated on the main contracts trading actively.

FOOTNOTES & REFERENCES

1. See Westerberg (1999) for more information on the history of the Nordic electricity market, you had better understand Norwegian in order to be able to read it, or you can hire me as a consultant and I can read it for you.

2. Chemical Bank took over Chase Manhattan Bank and changed its name to Chase, then Chase took over J.P. Morgan and changed its name to J.P. Morgan Chase, then J.P. Morgan Chase took over Bank One but still kept the name J.P. Morgan Chase.

3. Naturally more than what is presented here.

4. With a forward expiring at the same time as the option.

■ Black, F. (1976) "The Pricing of Commodity Contracts" *Journal of Financial Economics*, **3**, 167–179.

■ Black, F. and M. Scholes (1973) "The Pricing of Options and Corporate Liabilities" *Journal of Political Economy*, **81**, 637–654.

■ Hagan, P. S., D. Kumar, A. S. Lesniewski and D. E. Woodward (2002) "Managing Smile Risk" *Wilmott Magazine, September*, **1**(1), 84–108.

■ Lucia, J. and E. Schwartz (2002) "Electricity Prices and Power Derivatives: Evidence from the Nordic Power Exchange" *Review of Derivatives Research*.

■ Merton, R. C. (1973) "Theory of Rational Option Pricing" *Bell Journal of Economics and Management Science*, **4**, 141–183.

■ Westerberg, G. (1999) "Utviklingien i Det Nordiske Kraftmarkedet" *Derivatet*, **11**, 3–7.

Aaron Brown holding a Wall Street poker face
(Photo: Amber Gray)

Aaron Brown on Gambling, Poker and Trading

Aaron Brown is an executive director at the investment bank Morgan Stanley. He has spent many years on Wall Street in trading and risk management, and also in academia as a Professor of Finance. Besides trading and risk management Aaron Brown has devoted a large part of his life to poker. He has recently published a very interesting book on the topic: "The Poker Face of Wall Street". Aaron Brown is a columnist for Wilmott Magazine, in 2005 he received the Wilmott Award as the "Educator of the Year".

I had been invited to Aaron Brown's home for dinner but he never told me that he played poker until one day he sent me an early manuscript of his book. Was it that he did not want to take my money? Or could it simply be that he found it easier to win money from Nobel prize winners than option traders?

Haug : Where did you grow up?

Brown: I was born and raised in Seattle, Washington. In those days, no one came to Seattle on purpose. It was a place people ended up because they got stuck on the way to somewhere else. There was a heavily Scandinavian element, from the high suicide rate to the intensely liberal social/conservative individual outlook. I was fascinated by the rest of Seattle: the Asian culture, the international sailors and the remnants of the Old West. I hear it's a lot different now.

Haug: When did you first become interested in math and quantitative finance?

Brown: I always loved math, statistics and gambling. I came to finance indirectly. I applied to graduate schools in finance and statistics. The University of Chicago offered me $ 1,500 per year more for finance than Berkeley offered me for statistics. Statistics for me was dilettante work: I loved that experts worked hard to gather data, then would explain their field to me, and I got to play with the numbers and tell them what things meant. I loved the philosophy of it, and the practice; expert testimony, scientific papers and counterintuitive insights. But it didn't seem to lead anywhere, I didn't see myself changing statistical practice. Finance offered more opportunity to build something.

Haug: When did you first become interested in gambling and poker?

Brown: I was always interested in gambling in theory and poker in practice. I have no interest in playing a game I can't win, but I'm interested in some of the intellectual problems they pose. I spent most of my efforts, and this goes back to early childhood, on poker and other games of skill people bet on, also horse racing and sports betting.

All of this was just a hobby, until in college when I first started winning significant amounts of money at poker. It's hard to describe the psychological effect of that. The middle class, especially in the era in which I was growing up, has incredibly strong money taboos. There is no shame greater than not having money; no one ever talks about money, not even how much the father earns or how much the house cost.

The ability to take as much money as you want in poker smashed through all that. The best comparison I can make is to the story of the Invisible Man. You feel like you could walk into a bank and take money out of the till, it's the same feeling of unlimited amounts of money with fear of getting caught (you're invisible, but if someone feels you they can grab you and arrest you).

You get a mania, you want to blow all the money on luxuries and gifts. It's silly to buy moderate priced wine or clothes when you can get any money you want without work. But there's a dark side, only frantic extravagance can give you any satisfaction at all. There is a depressive hangover, the next day nothing seems worth doing, and the money seems worthless (especially if you blew it all).

I still feel a bit of that manic depression when I play poker, but I've learned to channel both parts productively. People who can't manage that become gamblers, always ratcheting up the stakes, always blowing any winnings. That's dangerous, but I'd rather risk that than trade places with someone who never feels the excitement or the hangover. It's not the thrill of the thing, it's the creativity it engenders and the fact that it freed me from money taboos. If you think rationally about money, you have a big advantage in the world.

Haug: What is your educational background?

Brown: I have some degrees from good schools, Harvard and the University of Chicago, but I was never much of a student. I couldn't take notes in class, and I couldn't attend a course that bored me. Like a lot of people, I was bright enough to cruise by without doing much work, but I didn't distinguish myself. Everything important I learned from others came in small seminars and one-on-one discussions. I enjoyed hanging around both schools and meeting some of the smart people there, but I don't feel I really earned my degrees. In both cases, I was happier to leave the places than I was to arrive.

Haug: If someone told you that they are not interested in gambling but only in conservative investments what would you say?

Brown: Unfortunately, fate doesn't seem to care much what you're interested in. Most of life's important gambles get chosen for you: whether your heart will continue to beat, how your kids turn out and whether you get born in a high caste in a rich society or not. The biggest gambles you do choose have nothing to do with investment: the people and things you give your heart to, the places you live, the career you pursue, the person you choose to be.

From a purely financial point of view, it's possible to eliminate a good chunk of your risk, but not by choosing only conservative investments. That just concentrates your risk exposure. You have to think like a gambler even if you don't want to gamble.

Haug: Why has the word gambling such a bad reputation?

Brown: Historically, the main criticism of gambling was that it is a waste of time and money. Like drinking, sex and art; it's an important part of being human, but it can also use up a lot of time and energy.

For a host of complicated social reason, over the last three hundred years or so, gambling has acquired some harsher criticisms, particularly from middle-class Europeans. People have accused it of defying religion, eroding character, undermining society and being a mental disease. It has been criminalized, slandered and taxed unfairly.

Haug: What is the origin of the word gambling?

Brown: No one really knows. It appeared in English in the 1700's, with no obvious ancestors or cognates. "Gambler" and "gambling" were pejorative slang terms, the verb "to gamble" came fifty years later as a back formation, and it was much later still that a neutral connotation was possible (even today, the word is more popular among critics of gambling than the "gaming" industry). It probably shares an Old English root with "game" but no one knows where the "b" came from. One conjecture is from the French-derived "gambol" (originally "to leap," then to "frolic"), but there's no evidence for that.

It seems unlikely to be an accident that a new pejorative word for wagering money appeared just at the time and place that serious criticism of the practice became widespread. A modern parallel might be the word "hacker," which appeared in the mid-1970s when the possibility of anti-social, or at least asocial, computer programming entered the mainstream. Like "gambler," "hacker" appeared as a noun with the verb following as a back formation, it was pejorative from the beginning although sometimes defiantly embraced by practitioners and it has no obvious linguistic link to anything.

Haug: Is gambling the same as speculation?

Brown: George Bernard Shaw described some English irregular verbs like "I am firm, you are stubborn and he is a pig-headed fool". In this vein, "I am a bold master of calculated risk, you are a speculator and he is a gambler". These words are too weighted down by connotation and dispute to have clear meanings.

Nevertheless, I would distinguish them as follows. A gambler hopes to take advantage of risk, to harness it the way an engineer harnesses energy. He needs risk, and will create it if it doesn't occur naturally. A speculator accepts risk as a means to an end. A speculator buys a risky stock, then hopes it goes up. A gambler hopes it goes down, then buys more shares. The speculator puts up with the risk to get the return, the gambler requires the risk in order to get the return.

Haug: When I moved from Europe to the USA in 1999 I noticed immediately that many of the traders were involved in poker and other sorts of gambling (beside trading) in their free time. Is there a gambling culture in the USA?

Brown: There is a gambling culture everywhere. There are different cultural manifestations but, of course, not all individuals conform to the common stereotype of their background. American gambling is very much about wealth transfer, it is important to win and acceptable to complain about losing. Gambling back and forth with little net wealth transfer is considered silly.

European gambling is about individual honor and play. Gambling is not supposed to result in significant wealth transfer, and it is important to be a good winner and a good loser. Asian, African, middle Eastern and other cultures have their own traditions.

Haug: Is gambling always a zero sum game, what one loses others gain?

Brown: Only in the narrowest of senses, in which case all financial transactions are zero sum. If I trade you bread for firewood, we can both gain. But if we swap money back and forth, whether in a bank or a poker game, one of us can only gain what the other loses.

But in a larger sense, exchange stimulates economic activity, so everyone can gain. A bank pays back depositors with interest paid by borrowers, which sounds zero sum, until you consider that the borrowers do something useful with the money; things that would not have been done without the loan. This "money is sterile" argument was used against banks and other financial institutions for centuries, but we consider it silly today. Gambling, theft, gifts, taxes and other forms of exchange are not zero sum as long as they stimulate real economic activity. Gambling games have often done this more effectively than banks.

Haug: What makes poker different from, for example, chess?

Brown: If you don't know, let's deal a few hands.

Here are a couple of quick observations. Chess has complete information and no randomness; poker has incomplete information and randomness. While chess can be played for money, it does not have to be, and the stake does not change the game. Poker only makes sense played for money, and the stake is the game. The main mental skill required for chess, as determined by psychometric research, is memory; for poker it is attention. Chess is played against a board, not a person. Your opponent's personality, wealth and mannerisms make no difference. Poker is player with a table of people, the cards are incidental. Poker players make good traders, agents and partners, but bad leaders, followers and team players. Pure chess skill is not good for much, you can be a crazy chess player but not a crazy poker player. However, many chess players are very successful when they combine chess analytic and strategic ability with other talents. Chess players are more likely to be leaders, followers or team players than good traders, agents or partners.

Haug: Does risk management play an important role at the poker table?

Brown: No, but it is essential before and afterwards. Risk management transmutes chaotic profits of traders into predictable revenue streams valued by the equity markets or investors; and it can allow you to integrate the chaotic outcomes at the poker table into a sensible financial life.

Haug: What is the best way to become a good poker player, should one read a lot of poker books or simply learn the hard way by first losing some money at the poker table?

Brown: This is a hard question. In the first place, I think you need some innate talent, or at least interest. You need a lot of practice, and it would be too expensive to acquire this at the table. When I was a kid, I dealt a lot of hands, and later did computer simulations. Today, I'd get a good computer game and just play a lot of hands. You need to recognize patterns and probabilities as second nature, you can't be thinking about them at the table. Today you can get what used to pass for a lifetime's worth of poker experience in a few months.

Of course, this just covers the card play, which is really quite simple (too simple to be any fun if there weren't money involved). You can become an expert in this in the amount of time it takes to learn the rules and basic play of bridge or chess.

Reading books is useful in conjunction with this, but the books alone are not much help. However, anyone with the temperament to sit alone for months reading and playing computer games, probably isn't made for the game of poker.

Good games players have a deep desire to back their own judgment. They'd rather try things themselves and lose, than follow traditional advice or consensus and win. If you have this kink, it shows up young (which is good, because if it showed up late you'd kill yourself learning how to back your own judgment at adult stakes). In that case, you already have the most important skill for poker. If you aren't that kind of person, I don't think you can ever become better than a competent poker player.

At some point, you have to take the step of actually playing. If you are destined to be a good poker player, you probably take this too soon. But either way, you can't learn to play poker without risking money, and if you play before you learn, you will probably lose. The solution is to start with bad players, where you learn slowly but can make money; then increase your level slowly. Still, you can't be a good credit officer until you've made some bad loans, you can't be a good trader until you've made some bad trades, and you can't be a good poker player until you've lost a lot of money.

Haug: How important is a good understanding of probability theory when it comes to poker, gambling and trading?

Brown: You need a feel for practical probabilities. Theory is only useful if it helps you maintain focus and discipline. It's a good way of explaining what you do, and a good way of planning, but not a good way to figure things out on the spot. And bad theory is very dangerous.

Haug: Is it easier to make money from trading or poker?

Brown: It depends how much you want to make. Anyone with half a brain can make the price of a few meals playing poker, but there are a lot more millionaire traders than poker players (and most of the rich poker players got their money from being celebrities and writers than net winnings at the table).

Haug: How do you know you have a positive edge in poker or trading?

Brown: There is too much randomness in both activities to tell directly. You need a network. In poker, you can tell if you are a consistent winner in a game; and you can tell if people from your game are consistent winners other places. Thus you can place yourself within the network, even though you could never measure yourself accurately versus another individual based only on your common results. Similarly in trading, you can tell if you are a valuable member of a profitable desk or fund, and if so, how your desk or fund stacks up against competitors.

Haug: It's one thing is to win and another is to get your money, do you see any relationship between credit risk in poker and trading?

Brown: There is a saying in casino management, "you have to win the money twice". That means once at the tables, then you have to collect it. With casinos, trading and poker; it only makes sense to deal with people you trust, who accept the basic rules of the game. You watch the credit risk, of course, but if it's the main concern, you're in a different business.

A loan that will likely be repaid is useful to both parties, it's an honorable transaction. A lot of suspicion attaches to people who make loans they do not expect to be repaid. Either the lender is stupid, or is taking advantage of the borrower. If you don't expect the losers to pay you voluntarily after a trade or a poker game, find a new game.

Haug: Did you ever beat a Nobel prize winner playing poker?

Brown: I don't try to beat people, that's not the point. You play with people, not against them. In a good poker game, everyone is a winner.

This Nobel-prize stuff has gotten out of hand. When I was pitching my book, one of the salesmen at the publisher asked if I'd played any famous people. I gave a list of some professionals and Wall Streeters, people serious poker players or financial professionals would know, but none had the celebrity status to go on a book jacket. "Well", he said, "we get proposals all the time from people who played with celebrities and at final tables in major championships. What can you offer to compete with that?"

I thought for a bit and said, "I bet I've played more Nobel prize winners than those guys". The salesguy loved it and it appeared in some of the marketing material for the book. I feel kind of silly claiming it for an accomplishment, anyone who wanted to play Nobel prize winners just has to go to places they hang out and get in the games. I can testify that many of them play. You don't have to be good at poker, in fact they're happier to play you if you're not (see, you have to be smart to get the prize). Since I play poker and spent a lot of time at places with lots of Nobel prize winners, it's not surprising that I've played a few.

Then everyone wants me to name them. When I wrote the book, I asked over a dozen people I played with if I could use their names. Except for the professional poker players, every single one said "no". Even well-known tournament players, whose poker playing is a matter of public record, wouldn't consent to be named. Therefore, I didn't name, and won't name, anyone who I didn't contact either, I assume they would also say "no". There's a tradition at poker that what happens at the table is private, you never discuss who won or lost, and you don't share other details in public. I hope if the book is successful, some of them will come out of the closet, but I won't out them.

Given that, I would have preferred not to say anything at all. I don't approve of making a public claim like this, then refusing to give details. But that's just the bed I made and now have to lie in.

Haug: I also heard that you worked with Fischer Black at some point, when was this?

Brown: "Worked with" is too strong. I discussed some ideas with him over several years, some of mine, some of his. We were never collaborators or friends, just professional colleagues.

Haug: Did you ever play poker with Fischer Black?

Brown: No, and to my knowledge he never played. I did mention it once to him, but he didn't say anything. I had the impression he never gambled at all, but a trader friend told me he saw him betting on horses at Saratoga with Ed Thorp.

Haug: Can option theory help you in poker?

Brown: I think there's a breakthrough in poker theory waiting to happen. Each bet is an option, and a good valuation formula would simplify the game a lot. But until someone tackles that problem, I don't think it's useful at the table. Like risk management, however, it can help you before and after you sit down.

Haug: Do you feel that a course in gambling and poker should become part of the many Masters in financial engineering programmes offered?

Brown: I don't know why someone who didn't like games would go into finance in the first place. Those people will do the coursework on their own, making it a class would just kill the fun. The people who don't like games would be discouraged by the need to study them in courses. That might be a good thing for them and for the industry.

Haug: How important is it to keep a poker face at the poker table?

Brown: In poker and life, you should know when to shut up. Your best move is often to say nothing, and give nothing away. So you must learn how to do this. However, it's not something you do very often, especially if you play for fun.

Haug: Can anyone learn to become a good poker player or trader or do you think that genetics plays an important role?

Brown: I have no opinion about nature versus nurture, but I think there is an essential skill that shows up young. Every good poker player or trader became aware of risk young, and was intrigued by the discovery. They reacted in many different ways, but experience taught them all the same lessons. I don't think you can force that on someone who doesn't feel it, nor can you learn as an adult. That's just my observation, I haven't done a systematic study.

Haug: Where does one draw the line between bluffing and cheating at the poker table?

Brown: That's not a line. Bluffing is an essential strategy in poker, perhaps the defining strategy. There's nothing dishonorable about it, and certainly no rule against it. Someone who insisted on playing poker straightforwardly wouldn't be playing the game, he'd just be donating money to the other players.

Haug: On Wall Street I see many traders simply selling risk premium. The result is that they will with a high probability make money for some time before they blow up, in

other words they are underestimating tail events. Have you seen many poker players making same mistake?

Brown: Sure. The classic example in poker is when a limit player tries no limit poker. In limit poker, there is a maximum bet anyone can make, therefore a limited tail risk. It's like buying options. When you go to no limit, anyone can bet up to the amount of chips they have on the table, and you either have to match that bet (or put in all your chips if you have less than the bettor) or fold, giving up all the money you put in previously. That's like writing options.

A player who doesn't understand no limit will often apply strategies that win a small amount almost all the time. In limit that's great, because the one or two times per night you lose only amount to a fraction of the profit you made the other times. In no limit, one hand can easily wipe out all your profit for the night, plus all your other money.

But you see the reverse as well, in traders and poker players, people who don't bet enough when they have the advantage, so they have no reserve for bad times. The classic poker example of this comes in tournament play. Many people just try to survive. They avoid large bets and risky situations, even if they have the edge. They survive as the first half or so of the players are eliminated. But this strategy rarely gets them in the money. The players who make a profit from tournament play are aggressive from the beginning. They may be eliminated early but, if not, they eliminate a lot of other players and get to the late stages with big stacks.

Haug: What is the most extreme tail event that has surprised you at the poker table or in your trading?

Brown: The stock market crash of 1987. Not the crash itself (although that did surprise me) but the realignment of the options market.

I've played enough poker that even the rarest hands wouldn't be tail events. I've never been dealt a five card royal flush, but I have seen one dealt; and I've had straight flushes and fours of a kind. Most of the poker games I play have only a few concealed cards, and I've seen every possible combination of those many times.

I guess the most extreme tail event I've seen at a card table is a bridge player die of a heart attack while berating his partner.

Haug: The sub-title of this book is "Models on Models", what are the biggest mistakes people make at the poker table when it comes to not understanding the deeper assumptions behind their model?

Brown: They don't see how the poker game is embedded in a larger structure. They try to beat opponents in hands, when that does not advance their goal of having a lifetime of winning poker. There's more cooperation than competition at the poker table, and among traders. If you don't see that, you can make good trades and play good hands, but you won't make a living.

Haug: Do you often go to Las Vegas to gamble?

Brown: No. I don't like Las Vegas. More precisely, I like the town a lot, but not the casinos. I have been there, but there are better places for poker, and I don't play casino games. Plus it's far away from everything, I'd rather go to Atlantic City or Europe.

Haug: Is it possible to have positive expected returns in Las Vegas or are all games tilted in the favor of the casinos?

Brown: That's a false dichotomy. Yes, the casinos make money (on the table play that is, they often lose it on overhead, comps, advertising and other expenses). But poker players can have positive expected returns.

In fact, if you sit in a low stakes poker game at a casino, particularly at a busy time, you'll be amazed at the people who come to play. A lot of people come and buy $ 20 or $ 50 or $ 100 worth of chips, lose it in half an hour, then wander off to do the same thing at blackjack or roulette. They expect to lose, they don't see the difference between poker and slot machines.

You realize that you are the casino. The house has brought these people to your table, and you take their money as efficiently as a blackjack dealer or roulette wheel. You make a salary like a croupier, and the house gets its rake. You're just part of the entertainment.

There are "advantage" players in casino games, people who spot down cards, track shuffles and count cards in blackjack, play positive expected return video poker or predict roulette wheels. Everyone I know who has tried this has ended up breaking even on play, but making money on comps. However good they are, the inevitable errors and problems wipe out the profits. Some people claim to make a living that way, I can't say one way or the other from my own experience. Making money from comps, say by getting four different casinos to reimburse your airfare, is more like embezzlement than gambling to me. Anyway, that's much harder than it used to be.

Haug: A great trader told me that his best advice in trading simply was to stay away from trading when one did not see opportunities, even if this sometimes meant that one would not touch a trade for months. Instead one could sit on the sideline working on improving as well as coming up with new trading strategies. Does this "golden rule" hold also for poker and other forms of gambling?

Brown: In principle yes. There's an old story about a poker player who was told he was being cheated, that the game was crooked. "I know", he replied, "but it's the only game in town". This is not smart.

However, I have never witnessed a place where you couldn't find a profitable poker game. It's a lot easier than finding a profitable trade.

Haug: Do you ever play poker with your wife, if so did you take her money?

Brown: I taught her to play, along with my children, but we don't play for money in the family.

Haug: Do you ever buy tickets in the lottery?

Brown: Once in my life. I was standing in the subway when I noticed a very strange looking man edging his way toward me. I got a little nervous, but he kept coming. Then I saw a dollar bill near my foot, he was trying to get it without alerting me that it was there. Without thinking, I picked it up and tried to hand it to him.

He wouldn't take it. He said with absolute conviction that he only wanted the dollar to buy a lottery ticket, and that it was no longer his lucky dollar, it was mine. If he took it, it would lose, but it was sure to win for me. Fate has picked me to win, and he begged me to buy the ticket.

When I got out of the subway, I noticed it was one of those big jackpot days when everyone is lined up to buy tickets. I succumbed to superstition, and bought the ticket. I did pretty well, I matched three numbers when four would have won me $ 15.

Haug: In your view where are we in the evolution of quantitative finance?

Brown: We're at a very exciting time, the next five years will see great discoveries. These will mean tremendous changes in financial services over the subsequent decade, and change the way we think about money.

Haug: What about the evolution of poker, it seems to get more and more popular?

Brown: No, it's already more popular than it should be. It is not a sport, and good players are not celebrities. Once people figure that out, it will be replaced by a new fad and the real game will go on.

Haug: Did you keep the best poker and gambling secrets for yourself or have you given them all away in your new book?

Brown: I'm a teacher first, my book is completely honest.

REFERENCES

■ Brown, A. (2004) "Time Enough for Counting" *Wilmott Magazine*, November, 20–24.

■ ——— (2005) "Table Stakes," *Wilmott Magazine* September, 16–20.

■ ——— (2006) *The Poker Face of Wall Street*. New York: John Wiley & Sons, Inc.

10
A Look in the Antimatter Mirror*

T
ake a look at yourself in the mirror. You will hopefully see a reasonably symmetric image of the real you, though your left and right sides have been reversed. In this chapter I will explore an amazing antimatter-mirror that I stumbled across recently in the files of quantitative finance.

1   Garbage in, Garbage Out?

One day when the market was very quiet, I became bored. As an option trader (and formula collector) what else could I do but play around with my Black-Scholes-Merton calculator (a computer implementation of the Black and Scholes (1973)/Merton (1973) formula[1])? Just for fun, I wondered what would happen if I dared to input negative volatility in the formula. My state-of-the-art self-made options system returned a negative number; at least I didn't get a "catastrophic error: restart immediately" message. Options cannot take negative values, so I guess garbage in, garbage out.

But wait, could there be something to it? By playing around with it a bit more I found, quite interestingly, that inputting negative volatility for a call option, then multiplying the result by negative one actually gave me the value of a put, and vice versa. Some time ago I had listened to Nobel prize winner Richard Feynman lecture on "Einstein's Relativity, Symmetry, and Space-Time", see Feynman (1997). The talk on symmetry, matter and antimatter had been particularly fascinating. Had I just looked at a financial parallel to matter and antimatter? Before we move on, allow me to introduce you briefly to the history behind the discovery of antimatter.

1.1   Does Antimatter Matter?

In 1889, the physicist Arthur Schuster wrote a letter to the journal "Nature", stating the question "If there is negative electricity, then why not negative gold as yellow as our own?". For thirty years, Schuster's letter gathered dust. In 1929 the English physicist Paul[2] Dirac wrote down a equation predicting the existence of antiparticles, underlining the duality idea of Arthur Schuster. Soon scientists set out on an adventure in search of antiparticles. In 1932 Carl Anderson discovered the antielectron (known as a positron). By 1956 the existence of antiparticles was well established.

---

*Thanks to Alexander (Sasha) Adamchuk, Peter Carr, Gordon Fraser and Erik Stettler for their many useful comments. The antimatter Haug is naturally responsible for any remaining errors.

Today physicists speak of protons and antiprotons, neutrino and antineutrino, quarks and antiquarks ... you name it, it has its opposite. As predicted by Dirac, it seems that every particle has an antiparticle with exactly the same mass but an opposite charge. The world of antimatter can best be described as a mirror image of our own world, see Fraser (2000). If a particle and its antiparticle meet, they annihilate each other and liberate their entire mass in the form of energy. Annihilation is the only phenomenon that is fully efficient in converting mass to energy in accordance with Einstein's law, $E = mc^2$. When a nuclear bomb explodes, for instance, only a fraction of 1 % of the atomic mass is converted into energy. When matter and antimatter collide, 100 % of the mass disappears (turns into energy), see for example Lederman (1993).

Leading physicists claim that antimatter can be very useful in the future, for such endeavors as generating super clean, super efficient energy.

Let's fantasize for a while about how such an antimatter world might appear in mathematical finance. If Schuster could suggest negative gold, then why not negative stock prices and strike prices? In such an antimatter world, the volatility would probably also be negative. And then to have a complete theory, there would have to be a connection between options in our world and in the antimatter mirror world.

1.2 Back to the Trading Floor

While playing with negative volatility in my Black-Scholes implementation I became very excited ... was this a new rule of the universe?[3] I contacted the Wizard of option symmetries and magic tricks, Dr Peter Carr,[4] currently at NYU. Almost immediately he replied, saying that this finding was very interesting, and closely related to a recent working paper by Peskir and Shiryaev (2001). Using sophisticated mathematics Peskir and Shiryaev (2001) demonstrated what they named put-call duality:

$$c(S, X, T, r, b, \sigma) = p(-S, -X, T, r, b, -\sigma)$$

where c is the Black-Scholes-Merton call option formula, p is a put, S is the asset price, X is the strike price, T is time to maturity, r is the risk-free rate, b is the cost of carry for the underlying security, and σ is the volatility of the asset. It was actually the genius Alexander (Sasha) Adamchuk from the University of Chicago who first introduced Shiryaev and some other people to the symmetry just mentioned, which he had coined supersymmetry (at the conference on Quantitative Risk Management in Finance, July 31–August 5, 2000, Carnegie Mellon University, Pittsburgh[5]). Without even thinking about it, I had just used my option calculator to combine the Adamchuk/Peskir-Shiryaev antimatter-duality/supersymmetry with a simple state-space transformation:

$$k \times c(S, X, T, r, b, \sigma) = c(k \times S, k \times X, T, r, b, \sigma)$$

where k is a constant. This leads to the interesting antimatter-option-mirror that I had just been looking into (this is what Sasha had coined supersymmetry)

$$c(S, X, T, r, b, \sigma) = -p(S, X, T, r, b, -\sigma)$$

and naturally

$$p(S, X, T, r, b, \sigma) = -c(S, X, T, r, b, -\sigma)$$

But why is it not perfectly symmetrical? A call does not equal an antimatter-call, and a put does not equal an antimatter-put. Interestingly this is also what we see in the matter and antimatter world, in Feynman's own words:[6]

> If we made a left-hand clock, but made it out of the other kind of matter, antimatter instead of matter, it would run in the same way (as a right hand matter clock). So what has happened is instead of having two independent rules in our list of symmetries, two of these rules go together and make a new rule, which says that to the right is symmetrical with antimatter to the left.

In the option world we get the similar rule

> A matter-call (right-handed derivative instrument) is symmetrical with an antimatter-put (left-handed derivative instrument), and vice versa.

The product stems from the fact that the results for both puts and calls can be obtained if one introduces a polarity variable, for example either $+1$ or -1. The polarity variables enter through the boundary conditions and are thus present in the solution. At least this is part of the story.

Not only does this result hold for the option value, but naturally also for all the option Greeks: delta, theta, rho, etc. For example the delta of a call will equal the antimatter-delta of a put.

The matter/antimatter-option rule is not only stimulating for the imaginary brain cells, but the result is actually very robust and simplifies coding and implementation of many derivatives models. You need only the formula and code for a call or for a put, as one can easily be translated into the other using an antimatter-mirror. As Dr Carr the symmetry Wizard pointed out to me, the result only holds when the pricing formulas involve σ times $\sqrt{T}$, rather than $\sqrt{\sigma^2 T}$. The result can easily be extended to several exotic options, like barriers and Asian options.

In the financial markets, empirical research suggests that most assets and commodities have leptokurtic distributions (fat-tails and peaked top). We can use option models to describe the distribution by using higher order moments like skewness and kurtosis.[7] In our matter world the third moment, skewness, can be estimated as

$$\text{Skewness} = \frac{\sum_{i=1}^{n}(x_i - \overline{x})^3 / n}{\sigma^3} \qquad (10.1)$$

where x_i is the asset returns, $\overline{x}$ is the mean of the asset return, n is the number of observations, and σ is the second moment of the distribution (the volatility). Since volatility is negative in the antimatter world, skewness will change sign.

The fourth moment of a distribution known as Kurtosis (Pearson) is defined as

$$\text{Kurtosis} = \frac{\sum_{i=1}^{n}(x_i - \overline{x})^4 / n}{\sigma^4} \qquad (10.2)$$

From this we can see that the antimatter kurtosis would still be positive in both the matter and antimatter world.

Figure 10.1 shows two distributions generated by a very flexible option valuation model that can also take into account a wide spectrum of distributions, more precisely, the Rubinstein (1998) extension of the Cox, Ross and Rubinstein (1979)/Rendleman and Bartter (1979) binomial

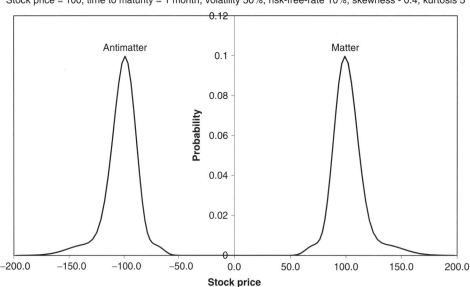

Figure 10.1

model. This is essentially a discrete implementation of the Black-Scholes-Merton model extended for distributions different from log-normal using an Edgeworth expansion (basically a discrete implementation of the Jarrow and Rudd (1982) formula).

The distribution to the right is generated by using normal input parameters (the matter world), and the probability distribution to the left was generated on the basis of antimatter input, that is negative stock price, negative volatility and opposite sign skewness. The stock price process in the antimatter-binomial tree is negative, and the distribution is the antimatter-mirror image of the distribution generated by the normal input parameters. Remember that one of the rules in particle physics is that particles and antiparticles have the exact same mass, but opposite charges. Similarly the two distributions have exactly the same probability mass, but different charges. But just as in a mirror (and as in the matter and antimatter world) a matter-call equals an antimatter-put and vice versa. More formally, when including skewness or kurtosis in our valuation we get the following matter antimatter relationship

$$c(S, X, T, r, b, \sigma, \kappa, \xi) = -p(S, X, T, r, b, -\sigma, -\kappa, \xi)$$

and naturally also

$$p(S, X, T, r, b, \sigma, \kappa, \xi) = -c(S, X, T, r, b, -\sigma, -\kappa, \xi)$$

where κ is the skewness and ξ is the kurtosis of the matter distribution. This result holds for Edgeworth and Gram-Charlier[8] expansions of the Black-Scholes-Merton formula, as well as for multiple discrete implementations. As we have demonstrated, this is a very general result.

1.3 Option-antimatter Philosophy

Yes I know you are already asking: has Haug gone nuts? My imagination has certainly gone wild, and I am nearing a field where my knowledge is approaching zero (if not negative). But before you judge me let me offer a quote from the Master of the Universe

> I am enough of an artist to draw freely upon my imagination. Imagination is more important than knowledge. Knowledge is limited. Imagination encircles the world.
> Albert Einstein

Imagination is certainly important not only in astrophysics. Long Term Capital Management also believed themselves to be the Masters of the Universe, with multiple Nobel prize winners and knowledge that others could only dream about, but still their complete lack of market imagination made LTCM blow up in a Big Bang, leaving behind only a black hole.

Please hang on because now it gets even more interesting. I now ask whether we in an antimatter world could possibly also replace positive probabilities with negative ones.[9] Negative probabilities would twist the probability mass around the x axis and give negative option values (not to be confused with shorting an option). At first this would seem crazy, but on the other hand, this would make our matter and antimatter options "equivalent" to the particle world. We are in a left-right matter antimatter world, in other words we have a lack of perfect symmetry.

Matter and antimatter are not perfectly symmetric as was first assumed (a left-handed neutrino does not equal a left-hand antineutrino but rather a right-hand antineutrino.[10] It was not long before physicists all asked themselves (and are still asking) if there is something more basic underneath it all? Is there a God particle[11] that really is perfectly symmetrical? In the search for perfect symmetry one physicist proposed the super string theory. Could it be that the "shapes" of the particles one observes – quarks, antiquarks, etc are not different particles, but rather super strings (God particles) that vibrate with the speed of light in different modes? Could different vibrations generate different particles just as different vibrations in a guitar string generate an almost infinite number of melodies?

But wait a minute. Don't we have a close parallel in finance: the God particle of Brownian motion? Brownian motion leads to the bell shaped normal distribution which is perfectly symmetrical. Thus a call equals an antimatter-call and a put equals an antimatter-put.[12] From Brownian motion we can generate an almost infinite number of stochastic processes and distributions. Now going from mathematical finance back to physics, could it be that the God particles are simply super strings vibrating/spinning around with Brownian motion? Then by combining such God particles could one generate almost any particle-distribution-shape that again might explain the different particles we observe?

2 Conclusion

Back to reality. When it comes to option pricing, garbage-in (negative stock price, strike and volatility) does not necessary lead to garbage-out, but rather a very interesting relationship regarding matter and antimatter. These results are not only extremely fascinating but also potentially useful practical applications. For many option models there is essentially no need for developing and implementing separate models for call and put options; all one needs is a formula for a call or a put, and then by inputting the antimatter equivalent stock price, strike price, volatility and higher order moments we will get the value for a put and vice versa.

More importantly, if a matter and an antimatter-option met they would annihilate each other. Instead of releasing a huge amount of energy as in the particle world, this would possibly release a lot of money. But who would get all that money . . . God himself? Or would it all simply disappear, as this could probably only happen when a matter and antimatter universe collides (through a black hole?), thus annihilating each other in a Big Bang?

FOOTNOTES & REFERENCES

1. See Haug (1997) for implementation of this formula and many others.
2. Not to be confused with Paul Wilmott who was not yet born at the time.
3. A rule not even described in the two volume Bible of quantitative finance: "Dr Paul on Quantitative Finance", see Wilmott (2000).
4. Dr Carr was one of the first to demonstrate the use of what is known as put-call symmetry (Carr & Bowie, 1994). He later published a whole series of papers demonstrating the use of different symmetry principles in finance Carr and Chou (1997), Carr and Chou (1998), Carr, Ellis and Gupta (1998). See also Haug (1998); Haug (2001a); Haug (2001b) for several implications of reflection and barrier symmetries.
5. Adamchuk's most recent talk on this topic was at the Kolmogorov Memorial Readings: "From Supernova to Discovery of Supersymmetry in Finance. New Vistas in Mathematical Foundations of Finance", The University of Chicago, April 2001: http://finmath.com/Chicago/NAFTCORP/Kolmogorov_Memorial_Readings_2001.html. By the way, Adamchuk would not accept that I had called him a genius. So, that he is a genius is possibly not true? But how can one deny the reality, "You must be able to distinguish between what is true and what is real", Albert Einstein. If you are still not convinced, take a look at http://finmath.com/Chicago/NAFTCORP/Sasha.html, a picture is worth more than a thousand words.
6. Listen to Feynman (1997) audio cd.
7. One of the first papers describing this idea was Jarrow and Rudd (1982).
8. See Corrado and Su (1996) and Brown and Robinson (2002).
9. I am not the first scientist to introduce negative probabilities, see Feynman (1987). However I am probably the first mad quasi scientist introducing it in the field of finance.
10. In physics we are not referring to symmetry in geometrical figures but rather to the symmetries of actions. For a good reference work on symmetries in particle physics and such deep concepts as the CPT Theorem see Lee (1988).
11. Read Lederman (1993) for the story of the search for the God particle.
12. The first to suggest using a normal distribution for option valuation was probably Bachelier (1900).

■ Adamchuk, A. (1998) "From Supernova to Discovery of Supersymmetry in Finance" *New Vistas in Mathematical Foundations of Finance*. unpublished, University of Chicago.
■ Bachelier, L. (1900) "Theory of speculation" in: P. Cootner, Ed., 1964, *The random character of stock market prices*, MIT Press, Cambridge, Mass.

■ Black, F. and M. Scholes (1973) "The Pricing of Options and Corporate Liabilities," *Journal of Political Economy*, **81**, 637–654.

■ Brown, C. and D. Robinson (2002) "Skewness and Kurtosis Implied by Option Prices: A Correction" *Journal of Financial Research*, **XXV**(2).

■ Carr, P. and J. Bowie (1994) "Static Simplicity," *Risk Magazine*, **7**(8).

■ Carr, P. and A. Chou (1997) "Breaking Barriers," *Risk Magazine*, pp. 139–145.

■ ────── (1998) "Static Hedging of Complex Barrier Options" *Bank of America Securities Working paper*.

■ Carr, P., K. Ellis and V. Gupta (1998) "Static Hedging of Exotic Options," *Journal of Finance*, **53**.

■ Corrado, C. J. and T. Su (1996) "Skewness and Kurtosis in S&P 500 Index Returns Implied by Option Prices" *Journal of Financial Research*, **XIX**, 175–192.

■ Cox, J. C., S. A. Ross and M. Rubinstein (1979) "Option Pricing: A Simplified Approach" *Journal of Financial Economics*, **7**, 229–263.

■ Feynman, R. P. (1987) "Negative Probability," First published in the book *Quantum Implications: Essays in Honour of David Bohm*, by F. David Peat (Editor), Basil Hiley (Editor) Routledge & Kegan Paul Ltd, London & New York, pp. 235–248, http://kh.bu.edu/qcl/pdf/feynmanr19850a6e6862.pdf.

■ ────── (1997) *Six Not-So-Easy Pieces, Lecture 2: Symmetry in Physical Laws*, May 20, 1963. Addison Wesley.

■ Fraser, G. (2000) *Antimatter, the Ultimate Mirror*. Cambridge: Cambridge University Press.

■ Haug, E. G. (1997) *The Complete Guide To Option Pricing Formulas*. McGraw-Hill, New York.

■ ────── (1998) "Put-Call Barrier Transformations" *Working paper Tempus Financial Engineering*.

■ ────── (2001a) "Closed form Valuation of American Barrier Options" *International Journal of Theoretical and Applied Finance*, **XIX**, 175–192.

■ ────── (2001b) "First-then-knockout options" *Wilmott*, August.

■ Jarrow, R. and A. Rudd (1982) "Approximate Option Valuation for Arbitrary Stochastic Processes," *Journal of Financial Economics* **10**, 347–369.

■ Lederman, L. (1993) *The God Particle*. Dell Publishing.

■ Lee, T. D. (1988) *Symmetries, Asymmetries, and the World of Particles (Jesse and John Danz Lecture Series)*. University of Washington Press Seattle & London.

■ Merton, R. C. (1973) "Theory of Rational Option Pricing" *Bell Journal of Economics and Management Science*, **4**, 141–183.

■ Peskir, G. and A. N. Shiryaev (2001) "A note on the Put-Call Parity and a Put-Call Duality" *Theory of Probability and its Applications*, **46**, 181–183.

■ Rendleman, R. J. and B. J. Bartter (1979) "Two-State Option Pricing" *Journal of Finance*, **34**, 1093–1110.

■ Rubinstein, M. (1998) "Edgeworth Binomial Trees" *Journal of Derivatives*, **XIX**, 20–27.

■ Wilmott, P. (2000) *Paul Wilmott on Quantitative Finance*. New York: John Wiley & Sons, Inc.

Knut Aase

Knut Aase on Catastrophes and Financial Economics

Knut K. Aase is a Professor in the Department of Finance and Management Science at the Norwegian School of Economics and Business Administration. He has done a great deal of research in Insurance Economics, Financial Economics, Probability Theory, Statistics and even Mathematical Biology. Over the last few years he has focused more on derivatives, but with a quite original approach. Recently Professor Aase has, for example, used option pricing theory with jumps to make inferences about equity premiums.

Haug : Where did you grow up?

Aase : In the little village of Litlebergen on Holsnøy. Holsnøy is an island located about 20–30 km north of Bergen, Norway.

Haug : What is your educational background?

Aase : University of California, Berkeley. PhD (1979: statistics).
University of Bergen, MSc (1975: probability and statistics).
University of Bergen, Bachelor's degree (1973).
Visiting scholar at various universities, primarily in the US. Among others, one year at each of the following institutions: MIT, Sloan School 1985–86; Stanford University, Graduate School of Business 1996–97 and UCLA, Anderson School of Management 2004–05.

Haug : You have done a great deal of research in both insurance and financial economics. What are the similarities and main differences between these areas of research?

Aase : As I see it, both are part of the economics of uncertainty, and thus subject to the same basic principles, or laws. In insurance an agent, or company, could in principle obtain a perfect hedge using the reinsurance market, although the aggregate risk is borne by the members of society at large. In financial economics a perfect hedge can only be obtained in a complete market, and although we have interesting models of such markets, like the Black and Scholes model, few if any real financial markets have this property. Also, in finance the aggregate risk is ultimately borne by everyone.

Haug : I assume that insurance companies to a large degree hedge their risk by diversifying their bets, but what about large-scale disaster/catastrophe scenarios when everything goes down at the same time, for example a massive earthquake, how do you hedge for such risks and how do you model it?

Aase : Large scale risk is normally dealt with using the reinsurance market. But as explained above, the aggregate risk cannot be "hedged away".

One class of models could be random point processes, or marked point processes if you prefer this term, which seem well suited to model such events. Recently, a fair amount of stochastic calculus has been developed for jump models, and statistical inference for these models has been around for quite some time now. In the latter field my advisor from Berkeley, Professor David R. Brillinger, has been a major contributor.

Haug : What are the similarities and differences between disaster scenarios in the insurance business and stock market crashes?

Aase : In neither case have catastrophes so far destroyed the respective industries. In the insurance sector government programs are sometimes triggered in such cases. Also, some insurance contracts become invalid during wars. When natural disasters strike poor and underdeveloped areas, the effect on the insurance industry is often limited since the individuals have little or no insurance coverage, like for example, the tsunami in South-East Asia in December of 2004. In cases like this, multinational efforts are initiated to bring in immediate help. This situation is rather different from a stock market crash.

During stock market crashes it seems that portfolio insurance may be of limited value, for various reasons. In contrast, at least so far, insurance has worked as planned in disaster scenarios, due primarily to the world reinsurance markets. In both cases it may take some time for the market to recover. For an insurance catastrophe event, like the Piper Alpha accident in the North Sea, Hurricane Andrew, or the Northridge earthquake in Southern California, it also takes many years to actually settle the claims. This is due primarily to the complex and not very transparent set of contracts used in the world's reinsurance industry.

Abstracting from institutions for the moment and considering only a market for "risk exchange" (in a consumption numeraire), individuals in society will optimally hold functions of the aggregate risk, a fact which follows from Karl Borch's pioneering research in the field. These functions may be smooth if the preferences are, and if we restrict attention to a one period framework with expected utility and consumption only at the final time point, the Pareto optimal sharing rules are, e.g. affine if and only if the risk tolerances are affine with identical cautiousness. The question is then if markets and institutions can be formed which allow the individuals to obtain this ideal risk sharing arrangement.

Haug : Are insurance companies in general paid too much or too little for selling tail event risk? And do we have time series of data that are long enough to say much at all?

Aase : The insurance industry claims typically "too little", but here, as elsewhere, the market decides, relatively independent of the actuaries' complaints, although the actuaries' probability beliefs should to a certain degree be reflected in the premiums. Actuaries have, of course, a good feel for tail events based on statistical data. There is also an extensive literature on the statistics of extreme events, dating back to the book by Leadbetter, Lindgren and Rootzen

(1983) via Embrechts, Klüppelberg and Mikosch (1997) to the extant literature in the field. Whether or not the time series are long enough, could of course always be debated – for some events they may be, for others the uncertainty may still be larger than desirable.

Haug : In 1990 you published a paper on Unemployment Insurance. What was this about?

Aase : Inspired by a paper on the subject written by E. Malinvaud, I wanted to extend the analysis to include moral hazard, due to the problem of "hidden action", i.e. the unemployed's *efforts* in finding a new job are not directly observable. Dealing with human beings, who, among other things grow older, I could have chosen a non-homogeneous Markov model, but decided on a semi-Markov framework, and managed to obtain some fairly explicit results.

Haug : Several leading investment banks have recently offered economic derivatives on, for example, Nonfarm Payrolls. Can this be seen as a supplement or competition for insurance companies?

Aase : During the last decades the insurance and banking industries have tended to merge. Financial institutions offer today a variety of financial services. But still there exist some notable differences: banks tend to hedge "everything" whereas insurance companies "reserve" instead. The various financial institutions compete with each other, of course, but otherwise I would call this derivative a supplement.

Haug : What about exchange traded catastrophe derivatives, are these supplements or competitors for the insurance industry?

Aase : Both. The direct reason for creating PSC[1] options or catastrophe (CAT) products seems to stem from a belief that the capitalization of the international financial markets may better absorb natural catastrophe risk than the reinsurance markets. For example, the daily fluctuation in the US financial markets – about 70 basis points or \$133 billion on average – exceeds the maximum possible insurance loss that might arise from an earthquake catastrophe, according to simulation experiments.

The more fundamental reason, as I see it, is that catastrophe derivatives and other financial instruments are created in order to improve welfare at large, i.e. in order to get closer to the ideal situation with "Arrow-Debreu" securities, in which a competitive equilibrium is Pareto efficient.

However, adding new instruments will, of course, not entirely achieve this ideal goal, and we know (from, e.g. O. Hart's work on this subject) that merely adding new securities that do not complete the market, may actually lower welfare.

The emergence of markets like these can be thought of as *economic efficiency*; if agents think that such instruments will improve economic efficiency, they will somehow be created.

Haug : Catastrophes, disaster scenarios as well as stock market crashes typically cause all securities to jump in the same direction, in other words such risks are not directly hedgeable simply by holding a well diversified portfolio of the underlying assets (not idiosyncratic). Dynamic delta hedging will typically also fail in such situations. How can we still value derivatives in such a situation, when risk-neutral valuation seems to break down, are we back to some type of equilibrium model?

Aase : As mentioned above, aggregate risk is ultimately borne by the society as a whole, and cannot be hedged away in some black box outside the real world, from which funds could be extracted when needed. In general, the theory of derivatives can usually be made consistent with equilibrium models. In a paper published in 2002, I demonstrate, for example, how the Black and Scholes model can be made consistent with the continuous time version of the rational expectations model of Lucas (1978). In this framework, the price will reflect how the payments of a security covary with aggregate consumption.

As an illustration, consider the case where the dividends from a security are correlated positively with the state price deflator. Such a security would simply possess the fortunate property of tending to pay out more dividends, in units of consumption, in states where the aggregate consumption tends to be low – in other words, in states where these dividends will be relatively valuable – and this characteristic of a security must of course be reflected in its market price. Terms providing this property enter into equilibrium pricing formulae, but may not be part of the financial engineering set up, which is of course a weakness of the latter.

Haug : You have also done some research on Levy processes in relation to stochastic volatility, can you tell us briefly about this?

Aase : In the model you refer to, the volatility became stochastic by construction, so the results could, at least in principle, be compared to those emerging from stochastic volatility models, although these two approaches are indeed very different.

My main motivation for writing this paper was an attempt to incorporate the Normal Inverse Gaussian (NIG) distribution into financial modelling in a non-trivial way, by considering a partial equilibrium model, but my model also contained some ad hoc elements which are hard to defend. The NIG-distribution seems to fit financial data reasonably well, according to empirical research.

Haug : How are the capital asset pricing model (CAPM) and the Equity Premium Puzzle affected by jumps in prices, I know that you did some research on this back in 1993?

Aase : Back then I derived a version of the consumption based capital asset pricing model (CCAPM), where the jumps in the aggregate consumption and in dividends of securities were taken to be exogenous. This assumption causes also equilibrium price processes to contain unpredictable jumps at random time points. The goal was to obtain a richer class of models that deviate from the "locally mean-variance" type that results when only Ito-diffusions are considered. While this approach could be used to explain some of the large equity premiums of the last century for a reasonable level of relative risk aversion (of the representative investor), it does not seem quite as promising in explaining the risk free rate puzzle, as it still provides negative subjective rates.

This analysis also opens up for looking at tail distributions that are very different from the normal one, an approach that may be promising.

Haug : In the early 1980's you published some work related to jumps in asset prices. Can you explain what this was about?

Aase : One motivation for introducing jumps, is to get out of the mean-variance setting of economic modeling under uncertainty. A diffusion model is driven by the Brownian motion, a stochastic process that is Gaussian, and can thus be characterized by its first two moments. This usually results in expressions for economic quantities that only depend upon the two first moments of the relevant probability distributions, even if these are not normal. The cause of the classical mean-variance dependence, usually in a one period setting, has a different origin. Here preferences were assumed to depend only on the two first moments. Although the means and the variances have a different origin in these two settings, the results can sometimes have a striking similarity.

Haug : In the late 1960's the mean-variance framework was criticized by your former college, Karl Borch. Were you inspired by this?

Aase : Originally my main motivation was to obtain more realistic models. Later this debate was inspiring. Recalling the discussion between Borch, Feldstein and Tobin in 1969, Borch, for example, simply pointed out that the probability distribution of a random variable generally depends on more than only its two first moments. Similar remarks were made by Feldstein, and both authors illustrated possible shortcomings from restricting attention to only the two first moments in the representation of preferences of individual decision makers.

Haug : The work on portfolio optimization from 1984 seems to have been "rediscovered" lately by researchers not aware of your original work. Why is this?

Aase : Researchers in mathematical finance do not seem to have been concerned about jumps until relatively recently. Then, some of them at least, set out to solve interesting problems without checking far enough back in time. I have discussed this with one such author, and he said that his (joint) paper would not have been written if he knew about my early results. Still, these results are not discussed in the introduction to this particular paper, a mere reference to my paper is given in the list at the end.

Haug : With the large number of journals publishing quantitative finance papers today, can we expect researchers to know what is already published?

Aase : We cannot expect them to know beforehand, but we can expect them to check when they start their research. This is relatively simple today, using e.g., the internet.

Haug : How important is marketing of a good idea versus just having published a good idea, and how important is it to publish in the "right" journal?

Aase : Previously these matters did not seem all that relevant. The idea was the important issue, not the journal where it was published. Eventually, the interesting results would become known. Today these things have changed, at least at business schools, some with "incentive mechanisms" rewarding publications in the "right" journals. Thus this may become important for the individual researcher's welfare, but perhaps not for his or her reputation as a scientist in the long run, I believe.

Haug : In 2004 you published a paper on "Quantity Contracts". As I understand it, this is a type of option where the underlying quantity is stochastic, can you give us a brief description of this topic?

Aase : In the agricultural sector, the quantity produced is random (as seen from the time of sowing), due to varying meteorological conditions. Something similar happens in the production of hydroelectric power. Since farmers and other agents are normally concerned about revenue, i.e. price times quantity abstracting from costs, quantity or yield contracts become of interest. Such contracts are market based solutions to managing yield risk, and allow for futures contracts and options contracts also on quantity. The presumption is that these contracts may be combined with ordinary futures contracts on price, to provide a hedge, or lock in a certain revenue.

The authorities, at least in the US, encourage market based solutions of say, crop insurance, to state based insurance programs, due partly to the asymmetric information between farmers and the authorities.

Crop Yield Insurance (CYI) futures and options contracts could be a partial solution to this problem, although many practical difficulties arise at the institutional level when the necessary "unbiased" quantity indices are to be constructed. It should also be noted that an element of moral hazard will typically exist in the very construction of these indices. These indices cannot be traded directly, being the basis of the financial instruments, and this will bring about some of the same difficulties that are known from the real options theory, when it comes to pricing and hedging.

Haug : You are known for running up the steepest Norwegian mountains. Is this when you get some of your ideas in quantitative finance and insurance economics, or is it when rolling down?

Aase : In order to get some blood to my brain during an average day at the office, of physical inactivity, some exercise seems to help me. Such activity also provides some additional health benefits, of course. Since I enjoy downhill skiing, perhaps an idea or two may strike on the way down as well.

Haug : You have spent time both at top universities in the US and in Norway (we only have a couple I guess). What are the pros and cons of working at a university in a small country like Norway as opposed to a top university in the US?

Aase : The pressure in Norway, and in parts of Europe, is considerably lower than in a top US institution, although it has also increased somewhat here in recent years. This lower pressure may of course be considered a benefit for one's leisure time, and hence for overall welfare, but perhaps not for the professional output and quality of one's work.

Haug : Do you have any hobbies besides running up steep mountains?

Aase : I do like outdoor life, a hobby I share with my wife Torill, like walking and skiing in the mountains, trips/expeditions that can typically last for several days, and also sea kayaking in our fjords (and lakes). I use swimming as regular exercise, and previously I did some scuba diving; here my wife is still active.

I own the farm where I grew up, located by the sea, where I spend some time with my family, which includes an active girl of 10 years of age, Silje Marie, and my wife's family owns a couple of mountain cabins, all requiring a fair amount of maintenance. We do most of this work ourselves.

Haug : Where do you think we are in the evolution of quantitative finance?

Aase : The field has reached an impressive state of sophistication, partly by applying an ever increasingly advanced set of mathematical and statistical tools to a variety of interesting problems. However, parsimony and transparency may not always be offered the required attention.

If we compare the situation in finance with that of physics, the situation is that some researchers call for a better understanding of the basic physical laws and principles, and a more correct application of the mathematical tools, than the field has seen during the last 30–35 years, when the emphasis has been more or less on "computations without understanding". In string theory, for example, there is a very large number of different, competing models, all having a large number of "free parameters", and as a result a model can often be picked that seem able to explain any experiment, simply by a proper choice of these parameters. The result is that one learns essentially nothing new about the basic unsolved problems of physics, like the "theory of everything". On the other hand, physics contributes very constructively to applied research, as witnessed through the impressive technological advancements of our time.

In finance there may be something of the same dilemma for the time being, since an increasing number of partial analyses are carried out, some undeniably contributing to our understanding of markets, institutions and human economic behaviour, but leaving more fundamental questions untouched.

There is also a danger that in the smoke from all the mathematical sophistication, the researcher loses sight of some of the more fundamental economic principles. As an example, some recent analyses of the selection problem behind insider trading have ignored the fundamental principle that prices must reflect, at least to some extent, the information possessed by the various agents involved. When there is asymmetric information, some sort of game theory can not be dispensed with.

Other examples can be taken from insurance, where, e.g. actuaries have worked with so-called "premium principles" for more than 100 years now, principles that still do not reflect basic economic principles of pricing risk.

Another favorite is optimal risk allocation using "ruin theory". Completely ignoring the large body of economic contract theory that exists, and which is in fact tailor made to analyze insurance contracts, "optimal" insurance contracts are obtained entailing full insurance up to some level, but if the damage is beyond this level, the compensation is zero. At least I have never come across contracts of this sort in real life. Imagine the kind of behavior this gives rise to at loss levels near this specific level. Notice that this topic has surfaced in finance under the heading "value at risk".

Finally, let me mention the popular subject of "optimal dividend policies" analyzed in a world where the conditions of the Miller and Modigliani Theorem are satisfied. Then we know that dividends are irrelevant for the value of the insurance company, but despite this very complicated, mathematical analyses are carried out.

So, I think researchers in the field could sometimes take a few steps back, catch their breath, and try to get in better touch with some of the the underlying principles. This may enhance understanding and bring the field in the right direction also on the more fundamental issues.

Some references related to this interview below, and further references to Knut Aase's many publications can be found at his homepage: http://www.nhh.no/for/cv/aase-knut.htm.

FOOTNOTES & REFERENCES

1. The underlying of such options are not an asset, but a catastrophe losses index provided by the Property Claim Services (PCS), such options trade at Chicago Board of Trade.

■ Aase, K. K. (1990) "Unemployment Insurance and Incentives" *The Geneva Papers on Risk and Insurance Theory*, **15**(2), 141–157.
■ ——— (1993) "A Jump/Diffusion Consumption-based Capital Asset Pricing Model and the Equity Premium Puzzle" *Mathematical Finance*, **3**(2), 65–84.
■ ——— (2000) "An Equilibrium Asset Pricing Model Based on Levy Processes: Relations to Stochastic Volatility, and the Survival Hypothesis" *Insurance: Mathematics and Economics*, **27**(3), 345–363.
■ ——— (2002a) "Equilibrium Pricing In The Presence Of Cumulative Dividends Following A Diffusion" *Mathematical Finance*, **12**(3), 173–198.
■ ——— (2002b) "Representative Agent Pricing of Financial Assets based on Levy Processes with Normal Inverse Gaussian Marginals" *Annals of Operations Research*, **114**, 15–31.
■ ——— (2004) "A Pricing Model for Quantity Contracts" *Journal of Risk and Insurance*, **71**(4), 617–642.
■ Arrow, K. and G. Debreu (1954) "Existence of an Equilibrium for a Competitive Economy" *Econometrica*, **22**, 265–290.
■ Black, F. and M. Scholes (1973) "The Pricing of Options and Corporate Liabilities" *Journal of Political Economy*, **81**, 637–654.
■ Borch, K. (1962) "Equilibrium in a Reinsurance Market" *Econometrica*, **30**, 424–444.
■ Borch, K. H. (1969) "A Note on Uncertainty and Indifference Curves" *The Review of Economic Studies*, **36**, 1–4.
■ Brillinger, D. R. (1975) "Statistical Inference for Stationary Point Processes" In M. L. Puri (Ed.): *Stochastic Processes and Related Topics* (pp. 55–99). New York: Academic Press.
■ Embrechts, P., C. Klüppelberg and T. Mikosch (1997) *Modelling Extreme Events*. Springer Verlag.
■ Feldstein, M. (1969) "Mean-Variance Analysis in the theory of Liquidity Preferences and Portfolio Selection" *The Review of Economic Studies*, **36**, 5–12.
■ Hart, O. D. (1975) "On the Optimality of Equilibrium When the Market Structure is Incomplete" *Journal of Economic Theory*, **11**, 418–430.
■ Leadbetter, M., G. Lindgren and H. Rootzen (1983) *Extremes and Related Properties of Random Sequences and Processes*. Springer Verlag.
■ Lucas, R. E. (1978) "Asset Prices in an Exchange Economy" *Econometrica*, **46**(6), 1429–1445.
■ Malinvaud, E. (1985) "Unemployment Insurance" *The Geneva Papers on Risk and Insurance Theory*, **10**, 6–22.
■ Mehera, R. and E. C. Prescott (1985) "The Equity Premium: A Puzzle" *Journal of Monetary Economics*, **15**, 145–161.
■ Tobin, J. (1969) "Comment on Borch and Feldstein" *The Review of Economic Studies*, **36**, 13–14.

11
Negative Volatility and the Survival of the Western Financial Markets

Knut K. Aase

This chapter discusses situations where certain parameters are given values that are outside their natural ranges. One case is obtained when plugging in a negative value for the volatility parameter σ in the Black and Scholes formula. This leads to seemingly "new" results.

A different setting is considered related to the developments in time of biological populations. Here deterministic models lead to chaotically fluctuating population sizes, which came as a surprise to workers with population data.

It is argued that the origins for the seemingly new and original results may be related.

1   Introduction

The motivation for this chapter is the entertaining chapter by Haug, "A Look in The Antimatter Mirror", including the comic strip "The Collector" in "From Russia with vol". The Collector had a nightmare, dreaming that the volatility had gone *negative*. An internet search for negative volatility came up with a single link – to Albert Shiryaev at the Steklov Mathematical Institute, Moscow, Russia. After kicking in Shiryaev's door, The Collector reveals his mission – to terminate the Russian secret weapon known as negative volatility. The Collector feared that this weapon might destroy the western capitalist system, and in particular ruin his own option strategy, buying cheap options for very low volatility. But Shiryaev reassures The Collector that negative volatility is "just a mathematical concept". The Collector is at first astonished, then relieved, and finally enthusiastic about the prospects of negative volatility.

2   Negative Volatility – A Direct Approach

Instead of starting, as Haug (2002) does, with the classical Merton, Black and Scholes formula, and plugging in a negative volatility directly in this formula, I suggest we take a look at the dynamic equation for the risky asset. It is

$$\frac{dS(t)}{S(t)} = \mu \, dt + \sigma \, dB(t), \tag{11.1}$$

where $S(t)$ is the spot price of the risky asset at time t, μ is the drift parameter and σ is the volatility parameter. $B(t)$ is the Brownian motion stochastic process at time t under the given probability measure P, and $B(t)$ is thus normally distributed with mean zero and variance t (under P). Informally one can think of the increment $dB(t)$ as normally distributed with mean zero and variance dt. The term $\sigma \, dB(t)$ is thus normally distributed with mean zero and variance $\sigma^2 dt$. A representation for the price process S is as follows:

$$S(t) = S(0)e^{(\mu - \frac{1}{2}\sigma^2)t + \sigma \, B(t)}. \tag{11.2}$$

The only stochastic component in this relation is the term $\sigma B(t)$, which has a normal distribution with mean zero and variance $\sigma^2 t$.

When deriving the formula for a call option written on a stock with price process S, Black and Scholes (1973) made the implicit assumption that the volatility parameter is positive, i.e. $\sigma > 0$. Let us assume the opposite, namely that $\sigma < 0$, i.e., a negative volatility. Going back to equation (11.1), the term $\sigma \, dB(t)$ is still normally distributed with mean zero and variance $\sigma^2 dt$. Positive and negative increments in the Brownian motion are equally likely, and multiplying these increments by a constant, it being negative or positive, yields a random increment with the same distribution, regardless of the sign of σ. Similarly the term $\sigma B(t)$ in equation (11.2) has still a normal distribution with mean zero and variance $\sigma^2 t$, so there are in fact no changes in this regard from the case with positive volatility.

This does not mean that the sample paths are the same; the stretch of data $\{S(t); 0 \leq t \leq T\}$ generated from the equation (11.1) with positive σ is different from the same stretch generated from the same equation but only with σ being negative (and with the same absolute value). However, these two stretches would have the same finite dimensional distributions, and that is all that matters when deriving the Black and Scholes formula. Let us see quickly how this can be done.

3   The Value of a European Call Option for any Value – Positive or Negative – of the Volatility

Under the risk adjusted probability measure Q, the equations (11.1) and (11.2) can be written

$$\frac{dS(t)}{S(t)} = r \, dt + \sigma \, dB^Q(t), \tag{11.3}$$

and

$$S(t) = S(0)e^{(r-\frac{1}{2}\sigma^2)t + \sigma B^Q(t)}, \tag{11.4}$$

respectively, where r is the risk free interest rate, and where $B^Q(t)$ is a Brownian motion process under the probability measure Q. From the similarity with the equations (11.1) and (11.2), we notice that the same story as above can be told under the risk adjusted measure Q, since, by Girsanov's theorem, only the drift term has changed.

Using the above representation (11.4), we now demonstrate how the Black and Scholes formula looks like in the case of a negative volatility parameter σ. The price $c(S, K, T, r, \sigma)$ of a European call option having strike price K and time to maturity T is given as

$$c(S, K, T, r, \sigma) = E^Q\{e^{-rT}(S(T) - K)^+)\}. \tag{11.5}$$

This can be written

$$c(S, K, T, r, \sigma) = e^{-rT} \int_{-\infty}^{\infty} \left(S(0)e^{(r-\frac{1}{2}\sigma^2)T + x} - K\right)^+ \frac{1}{\sqrt{2\pi\sigma^2 T}} e^{-\frac{x^2}{2\sigma^2 T}} dx. \tag{11.6}$$

Notice that we have here integrated with respect to the probability density of the random variable $X =: \sigma B^Q(T)$, which, as observed above, has a normal distribution with mean zero and variance $\sigma^2 T$. The result is, of course, the following formula

$$\begin{aligned} c(S, K, T, r, \sigma) = S(0)\Phi\left(\frac{\ln(S(0)/K) + (r + \sigma^2/2)T}{|\sigma|\sqrt{T}}\right) \\ - e^{-rT} K\Phi\left(\frac{\ln(S(0)/K) + (r - \sigma^2/2)T}{|\sigma|\sqrt{T}}\right), \end{aligned} \tag{11.7}$$

where the function $\Phi(\cdot)$ is the standard normal cumulative probability distribution function. The only difference between this formula and the standard Black and Scholes one is the absolute value sign of the volatility, the term $|\sigma|$ instead of only σ, in the denominator of the distribution function $\Phi(\cdot)$.[1]

When the volatility is positive, the formulae are the same. When the volatility is negative, the price of a call option written on the stock has the same value as a call option written on a stock having positive volatility of the same magnitude (absolute value). In this case, for $\sigma < 0$, we could have written $-\sigma$ instead of $|\sigma|$ in the formula above.

A related point of view is that volatility should *never* be negative, based on the convention $\sqrt{\sigma^2} = |\sigma|$. If we assume $\sigma > 0$ and write the term $\sigma(-B(T))$, applying the minus sign to the Brownian motion directly and not via the term σ, we would obtain the same formula, since $-B(T)$ has the same probability distribution as $B(T)$. In this case we would not even need the absolute value sign $|\cdot|$ in the formula. A statistician would, typically, prefer this interpretation.

The Collector may thus rest in peace. His hectic trip to Moscow was not really warranted, and quite likely, the western capitalist system will survive even this crisis of negative volatility.

4 Negative Volatility – The Haug interpretation

In Chapter 10 by Haug, and with reference to a paper by Peskir and Shiryaev (2001), a negative volatility is plugged directly into the standard Black and Scholes (1973) formula without making the adjustment leading to the formula (11.7). Recall that the original formula is derived under the implicit assumption that the volatility parameter is positive. From the properties of the normal cumulative probability distribution function $\Phi(\cdot)$ it is straightforward to show that this leads to the following relation:

$$c(S, K, T, r, -\sigma) = -c(S, K, T, r, \sigma) + S(0) - e^{rT} K = -p(S, K, T, r, \sigma), \qquad (11.8)$$

where the parameter σ is now positive, and $p(S, K, T, r, \sigma)$ is the price of a European put option. The last equality above follows from the put-call parity. The first equality follows from plugging in $-\sigma$, $\sigma > 0$, in formula (11.7) instead of the term $|\sigma|$, and using the antisymmetry of the function $\Phi(\cdot)$.

So, just by this kind of formula shopping, a seemingly new and interesting relationship is discovered. This is of course not incorrect, but should be considered in the light of the previous section. The left hand side of the formula in equation (11.8) has of course little to do with the price of a European call option any more.

At this stage Haug (2002) enters into the field of particle physics in search of a deeper truth in mathematical finance. On this I would like to point out that related to particle physics is of course the *uncertainty principle*, strongly supported by the Danish physicist and Nobel prize winner Niels Bohr,[2] via "The Copenhagen School". He formulated, among other things, the correspondence principle,[3] which postulates a detailed analogy between the quantum theory and the classical theory appropriate to the mental picture employed. This analogy does not merely serve as a guide to the discovery of formal laws; its special value is that it furnishes the interpretation of the laws that are found in terms of the mental picture used.

Bohr's student, Werner Heisenberg (1930), developed the uncertainty principle.[4] The principle has altered our whole philosophy of science.

Albert Einstein, on the other hand, never really accepted this view of the world, and believed that a system of deterministic differential equations would suffice to describe the world.[5.] There is a rumor that the two professors, Bohr and Einstein, had long walks together in the streets of Copenhagen, sometimes taking the bus, but typically they forgot to get off at the right stop, then took another bus in the opposite direction, and again forgot to get off at the intended destination, and so on. Despite these apparent random oscillations, Einstein was not convinced about the existence of genuine uncertainty. Einstein's God was a God of order and there was no place in his scheme of things for a God who, in his famous phrase, "plays dice with the world".[6]

One may conjecture that if Albert had ever turned to finance, he would either have been in for a big surprise, or become a very popular consultant.[7]

5 Chaotic Behavior from Deterministic Dynamics

The following deterministic model has several applications in population dynamics:

$$x_{t+1} = \theta x_t (1 - x_t), \qquad (11.9)$$

$x_0 \in [0, 1]$, $0 \le \theta \le 4$. The process x evolves in the interval $[0, 1]$ for the given range of θ, and displays a rather complex path behavior as a function of this population parameter (see, for example, Lie and York (1975) or May (1976)). Just to illustrate, for $\theta = 0.8$ the path shows only one fixed point $x^* = 0$, which is locally monotone and stable. For $\theta = 2.0$ two fixed points appear, $x_1^* = 0$ and $x_2^* = 1/2$. The point x_1^* is not stable (repelling), but x_2^* is stable (attracting). Increasing the parameter the paths display ever more complex behavior, where pitchfork curves and bifurcation appears.

One can even move the parameter outside its natural range $[0, 4]$ and obtain really chaotic results from this deterministic model. It is not likely that the resulting behavior has much to do with the evolution of biological populations anymore. Still the mathematical behavior can be explored, and even statistical estimation is possible based on observed sample paths, introducing stochastic shocks in the model (11.9) (see, e.g. Aase (1983)). It was surprising that introducing additive noise in this type of model presented no problems when the goal was to estimate the unknown parameters.

6　Conclusions

The starting point of this chapter was the negative volatility "discovered" by "The Collector". We have pointed out that a statistician would simply not accept the notion of negative volatility. For the geometric Brownian motion process it is, nevertheless, possible to explore this subject a bit further, and we have presented the price of an European call option when the volatility is negative. This we have contrasted with the development in Haug (2002) and Peskir and Shiryaev (2001). While this latter interpretation is "just a mathematical concept", its direct application leads to seemingly new formulae, without any real theoretical underpinning.

Instead of connecting this to the theory of antimatter in Physics as is pursued elegantly by Haug (2002), we indicated a connection to this discipline via the uncertainty principle. This leads us to wonder who would have been the best portfolio manager, Bohr or Einstein? We rounded off the chapter by linking to deterministic chaos.

FOOTNOTES & REFERENCES

1. This type of derivation can be found in, e.g. Aase (2002)
2. He won a *real* Nobel prize, the one in Physics in 1922, unlike "The Sveriges Riksbank (Bank of Sweden) Prize in Economic Sciences in Memory of Alfred Nobel", which is the one granted to economists and people in related fields. As we know, Merton and Scholes shared this prize in 1997. Fisher Black had, unfortunately, passed away some time before this event took place. Likewise, of the three creators of the CAPM only Sharpe received this prize in 1990, Lintner and Mossin were both dead when this prize was awarded (Jan Mossin, e.g. died in 1987 at age 50).
3. See Bohr (1923).
4. Werner Heisenberg was also a Nobel Laureate in Physics in 1932.
5. Einstein received the Nobel prize in Physics in 1921 for his discoveries regarding the photoelectric effect.
6. Clark (1973) p. 327. See e.g. Bartholomew (1984) for a treatise on God and Uncertainty.

7. There is a rumor indicating that Einstein was not terribly interested in money. This rumor claims that he promised his first wife Mileva Maric, who had allegedly assisted him a great deal on parts of his work, the future Nobel prize money as alimony (as long as he received the honor).

■ Aase, K. K. (1983) "Recursive Estimation in Non-linear time Series Models of Autoregressive Type" *The Journal of the Royal Statistical Society*, Series B (Methodological), **45**(2), 228–237.
■ Aase, K. K. (2002) "Equilibrium pricing in the presence of cumulative dividends following a diffusion" *Mathematical Finance* **12**(3), 173–198.
■ Black, F. and M. Scholes (1973) "The Pricing of Options and Corporate Liabilities" *Journal of Political Economy* **81**, 637–654.
■ Bartholomew, D. J. (1984) *God of Chance*. London: SCM Press Ltd.
■ Bohr, N. (1923) *Zeitschrift für Physik*, **13**, 117.
■ Clark, R. W. (1973) *Einstein, the Life and Times*. Hodder & Stoughton.
■ Einstein, A. (1922) *The Meaning of Relativity*. Four lectures delivered at Princeton University, May 1921. London: Methuen & Co. Ltd.
■ Haug, E. G. (2002) "A Look in the Antimatter Mirror" *Wilmott Magazine*, 38–42.
■ Heisenberg, W. (1930) *The Physical Principles of the Quantum Theory*, Dover Publications, Inc.
■ Lie, T. Y. and J. A. Yorke (1975) "Period Three Implies Chaos" *Am Math, Monthly*, **82**(2), 985–992.
■ Lintner, J. (1965) "The Valuation of Risk Assets and the Selection of Risky Investments in Stock Portfolios and Capital Budgets" *Review of Economics and Statistics* **47**, 13–37.
■ May, R. M. (1976) "Simple Mathematical Models With Very Complicated Dynamics" *Nature*, **261**, 459–467.
■ Merton, R. C. (1973) "Theory of Rational Option Pricing" *Bell Journal of Economics and Management Science* **4**, 141–183.
■ Mossin, J. (1966) "Equilibrium in a Capital Asset Market" *Econometrica* **34**, 768–783.
■ Peskir, G. and A. N. Shiryaev (2001) "A Note on the Put-Call Parity and a Put-Call Duality" *Theory of Probability and its Applications* **46**, 181–183.
■ Sharpe, W. F. (1964) "Capital Asset Prices, a Theory of Market Equilibrium under Conditions of Risk" *Journal of Finance* **19**, 425–442.

Elie Ayache is known for the convertible bond pricing engines his company, ITO 33, develops. Are we sure these are the only convertibles he had in mind?

Photograph by Roger Moukarzel

Elie Ayache on Option Trading and Modeling

Elie Ayache has more than eight years' experience in volatility trading before starting up a successful software firm, ITO33 developing state of the art convertible bond models, and more general equity to credit derivative valuation frameworks. Elie Ayache is also a columnist for Wilmott Magazine.

Haug: Where did you grow up?

Ayache: I was born in Lebanon in 1966. I moved to France in 1982, partly to flee the Lebanese civil war, and mainly because my father always had plans for me to come to Paris and prepare for the entry exams of the "big French engineering schools", what we call "Les Grandes Ecoles".

Haug: What is your educational background?

Ayache: I was accepted at the Ecole Polytechnique, from which I graduated in the summer of 1987. At the Ecole Polytechnique (at least, in my day), we used to study all kinds of things in all kinds of fields (with an emphasis on theory and abstraction), such as Quantum Mechanics, Statistical Physics, Fluid Dynamics, Economics, Hilbert and Sobolev Spaces, Numerical Analysis, Probability Theory, Measure Theory, Theory of Distributions, Differential Geometry, Chaos Theory and Bifurcations, and even Biology, etc. I was lucky to listen to the greatest teachers in their corresponding fields. However, given the sheer size and variety of the syllabus, practical guidance was missing in the specific topics. For instance, I had no idea what "finite elements" could be used for in practice. We hardly had any course on programming. Stochastic processes and derivative pricing theory were not taught yet. As a matter of fact, the two years you spent at the Ecole Polytechnique were only a luxury intended to give you the broadest overview of the sciences and the techniques. The brochure said literally: "If you can afford to spend two years of your life enjoying the beauty and the richness of the sciences, without necessarily putting it yet to practice, then apply for the Ecole Polytechnique". After graduation, the student is supposed to enter what we call "application school" (such as Ponts et Chaussées, Ecole des Mines, etc.) and then study engineering proper.

Haug: Can you tell us about your first day in option trading, and how it has shaped your view of the market?

Ayache: I had just been hired by Bank Indosuez as an option trader on the 10 year French government bond futures, and on that day my boss thought I would be more helpful "downstairs" on the floor rather than "upstairs" in the dealing room, because he wanted me to provide him (and the other option traders) with a live commentary on the underlying market.

Underlying future contracts were listed on the French future exchange (MATIF) at that time, but options were still an over-the-counter market and Bank Indosuez was one of the major option market-makers. So to execute your delta hedge as a volatility trader, you really needed to telephone your order to a futures broker. What my boss did not tell me was that the reason he wanted me to hang on the phone from the floor that day, and shout every time I witnessed major action, was that we, as well as the rest of market makers, were massively short out-of-the money puts and needed to rebalance the delta of the book. The idea of having me on the phone was to try to establish, every time the market was hit by a selling wave, whether it had reached a bottom and would bounce back up, or whether it would collapse further. That day was 19 October 1987.

I witnessed three successive "limit downs" that day. I still remember the look on the face of the star trader of the largest Parisian brokerage firm, Jean-Luc. I didn't know it then of course, nor could I understand what it meant for a floor broker to be receiving only selling orders and in such size. As that guy was known to be the best "executioner" on the floor, all the selling orders of the Paris marketplace must have flown instantly into his hands. I could see him "make" the market, or may be he was not making it at all but delivering it as a deadly blow to the head of anyone who dared to show him a bid. His face looked like the face of inevitability.

As an absolute beginner I may have had no idea what was really going on that day. I may have even thought that this was a normal trading day and that the craziness was just the way open outcry worked normally. In retrospect, I find it intriguing today that my first introduction to option trading should have been the absolute breakdown of the option hedging paradigm, even the breakdown of the whole volatility paradigm! What kind of volatility is that when the underlying collapses by 2 % three times in a row during the same morning, and trading is suspended, every time, to allow for the margin calls to take place?

You may think that it was just the Black-Scholes model that was breaking down here (as a matter of fact, option volatility smiles and their subsequent literature were born that day): breakdown of the diffusion assumption, breakdown of continuous hedging or even worse, of the whole capacity to hedge, etc. In retrospect, you can always try and reconstruct a theoretical process to try to explain what happened that day, what I call the "re-processing" of the market: "So what? The market was in fact underlain by a jump-diffusion, not a diffusion, and what we witnessed that day was just the rare event of massive multiple jumps in succession". You can even consider the time series and compute the variance of the logarithm of returns and see what a huge number you get.

Someone like Nassim Taleb would totally dispute that. He would argue that it is not clear a priori whether the data generating process is a diffusion, a jump-diffusion, or any other expressible probability distribution. Because of *essential uncertainty* we do not know the probability distribution that the market is drawing its numbers from, and no amount of past data can help us acquire that knowledge. Speaking of variance of returns is easy when all you have to do is compute averages of square returns on a piece of paper, based on a past time series, however it is completely meaningless a priori, because you are not even sure that the data generating process admits of finite moments.

I personally believe that what I witnessed that day on the floor was something else, something that differed from both stances. My position that day was neither one of fitting a known stochastic process to the market data a posteriori, nor one of sitting puzzled prior to the event and wondering what the probability distribution might be. I was standing right in the middle of the event, right in the middle of that gap between analysis and speculation, between potentiality and empirical observation. Right in that crack inside the very heart of representation that I like to call "actuality".

One thing struck me that day on the floor and never left me afterwards, and that is the belief that a market cannot be re-produced but only produced; that it cannot be re-presented but only presented.

Let me explain. Although I had witnessed literally every trade that day, every price that had been traded and every amount of futures that had changed hands – and I was all the more taken by what I saw, that prices at times no longer traded in ticks but in whole figures; this wasn't "market noise" but more like a single, endless, scream – although I had heard every shout ("Buy them!", "Sold!") and spotted every single action that had caused, or contributed to cause, every single price movement, I had the feeling that something more was going on to make the prices unfold like they did; something not reducible to a chain of causes and effects.

For instance, there are cameras that record the whole trading session, so in theory the whole chain of visible and audible causes and effects is available for examination, and even for restaging. Yet something tells me that if you tried to restage the market action by reproducing in sequence every single cause there was, then you wouldn't get the same result. There was something more going on that day on the floor than the mere succession of reproducible events, something beyond the reach of any dynamic model that you cared to imagine in advance to try to simulate the market, and that something was *actuality*.

The actuality of 19 October 1987 is simply non-reproducible outside 19 October 1987.

And by the way, there is nothing special about 19 October 1987 in my philosophy. It just illustrates my point better because it was a remarkable day and the market movement that day was extreme and more evidently inimitable.

I believe there is something special about the market in general, no matter where or when it takes place or to what extremes it swings, and that is precisely that the market *delivers actuality* and that what it produces is unthinkable outside actuality. Market prices are unthinkable as the output of a data generating process that you would, so to speak, hold in your hand in advance, or at least represent in your thoughts, and that would be ready to generate those prices. What I am blocking here is the whole idea of re-creation and re-production, the very essence of theoretical representation.

This is how I think of the market and this is the vision that struck me on 19 October 1987 and shaped my whole way of thinking ever after. It won't help to object that the market is a dynamic system like any other, only more complex (perhaps the most complex), and that it is only a matter of time before it gets imitated or simulated by some dynamic model (or equivalently, algorithm). For I will then *define* the market as precisely that generator of "actualities that cannot be re-produced or re-presented outside their actuality".

Maybe what is so special and inimitable about the market is that it is the concretization of exchanges taking place *between* two inimitable individuals. The thought here is that, because the market takes place *between* the individuals and not within an individual (or worse, within some algorithm); because it doesn't take place at punctual time, in punctual space, but in that *in-between*, or gap, or interval of time and space, which cannot be reduced to a point within a space series or to an instant within a time series; for this reason the market can only belong to its present and it may even serve as the definition of the present! In other words, it cannot be *re*-presented in a theory or *re*-processed in a model.

Later I will have a lot to say about models and stochastic processes and their use for the pricing of derivatives and their trading. However I wanted to first recount to you this view of the market as irreproducible actuality in order to say how suspicious I will be of any philosophical move or methodology whose working assumption consists in stepping *outside the market in order to model the market*. This is like saying that you cannot think of the market unless you are inside it, unless you are a trader.

Later we will come across many arguments that criticize some particular models and propose alternative ones, such as jump-diffusion models as opposed to diffusion or stochastic volatility models as opposed to constant volatility, etc. We will also come across arguments that deliver a sweeping criticism of the whole quantitative enterprise and insist that the whole framework is not available to begin with, where you could think of a model and compare it to another, because there is opacity of knowledge of higher order than, and irreducible to, the mere lack of foresight which led us to conceive of probability in the first place. We may simply *not know* the probability distribution; we may even not know that *it is* a probability distribution. This is essential uncertainty of course, and it is very severe because you cannot replace the uncertainty of knowledge of the probability distribution with a probability distribution over some known probability distributions. Indeed, this would result in just another probability distribution!

My take on essential uncertainty is that, although it poses a nice epistemological problem to the methodology of risk, it may not be relevant to trading or to the market at all! The market trades prices, not probability distributions. Only in our probabilistic models are prices interpreted as expectations of payoffs over different states of the world. And we invent states of the world and probability distributions in order to so interpret the prices. Both the optimistic econometrician who is trying to fit a probabilistic model to a past time series and the pessimistic skeptic who is questioning the availability of the probability model are backward with respect to the market. The market is not a reflective entity and it does not care to *know* the data generating process. The market does not know anything. It is forward looking and is always ahead of any probability assumption or knowledge thereof.

Am I saying that the market is a fleeting arena of unrelated prices and that anything goes so long as it trades? No, because I am not forgetting the derivatives. Prices of derivatives must be related to the price of their underlying and to each other when they are written on the same underlying. As a matter of fact, the derivative is perfectly replicable by its underlying at its maturity, because its payoff is then perfectly determined. When you think of it, the only reason probability models were reintroduced at this stage (call them derivative pricing models, if you wish) is to prescribe a relation, or a replication strategy, between the price of the derivative and its underlying *one step ahead* of expiration time, when the payoff is not yet determined but will be very soon. From there, it naturally became a matter of prescribing a relation a few steps ahead of maturity, and why not as of today, at issuance of the derivative.

Are we back to the epistemological imperative of knowing the probability distribution in order to price the derivatives? No, because it is the market that prices them and no one else.

Does that mean we should invert the derivative pricing model and claim that the derivatives market "implies" a certain probability distribution, or volatility of the underlying? No, because this is again a backward reaction, and is totally irrelevant to the next market move.

Derivatives are revolutionary and to my mind provide the right entry into the question of the relation between the market and the probability models: however, it is a philosophical mistake to interpret their prices epistemologically. When option traders invert the Black-Scholes formula, they don't care about the *knowledge* of implied volatility; they care about the delta hedge to execute in the market. The Black-Scholes formula, when it is a tool in the trader's hand, is an argument for further trading, not for reflective knowledge, criticism or skepticism. It is for trading the underlying against the option, or trading other options against it. It is the trader's way into the next market movement.

Derivatives markets did not wait for the debate between statistical inference and essential uncertainty to settle before they exploded. Quantitative models are an essential component of derivatives markets' growth, perhaps even its main catalyst, and for this reason cannot be ignored. Notice, however, that my whole outlook is immersed in the market and in trading. Derivative pricing models are tools to re-immerse the trader in trading not to fuel further debate about the sex of angels or the shape of the probability distribution that might be waiting behind the scene, or out there in the fantasy of some econometrician, to generate the market prices. And notice that skepticism à la Taleb is beside the point too, because it is also locked in epistemology.

To my mind, *derivatives markets* are the technological revolution which will bring about a total rethinking of probability and its philosophy. Because they are derivative, we need states of the world and probability distributions to express the relationship between derivative prices and underlying prices and to produce no arbitrage derivatives prices (in other words, we need a pricing kernel). Yet because it is a market and is our *given*, we will never use the probability distribution in order to price the derivatives.

Haug: What did you learn from your years in option and volatility trading?

Ayache: There really were two periods in my trading career: the Paris floor experience on the MATIF (1987–1990) and the London floor experience on the LIFFE (1990–1995). In Paris, there were only five market-makers in the option pit, the bank that employed me and four other major French banks. So most of the time, trading looked like a poker game between five players and, when there occurred some major action from the outside, like a game of the musical chairs.

In Paris I really learned how to manage sizeable option books, what mistakes not to make (such as buying longer dated options in order to hedge the short gamma of shorter dated ones). Perhaps the greatest problem we faced was the conundrum of the overall delta hedge of the option book. Since options were traded and booked at different implied volatility levels, how would we aggregate their deltas? And when the underlying shifted and the whole shape of the volatility surface changed, how would we manage the impact on the aggregate delta? Even today, the problem of the smile and the smile dynamics is the hottest topic in volatility trading.

It was in London that I really immersed myself in real market conditions and learnt that the market was an empirical phenomenon and not something you could rule by a model or by the sheer size of the bank that was employing you. The French philosopher Pierre Duhem points to a contrast between the ways that the French and the English look at models. The English are empiricists and are happy to call "a model" any contraption that manages to replicate the empirical phenomena. They don't really care whether their model is made up of wooden sticks, rubber bands, or springs and the thought will never cross their minds to go and see whether the material the model is made up from corresponds to the stuff the world is made of. The French, by contrast, are rationalists. To understand the phenomenon, they need to fit it in properly axiomatized theory. They need to abstract the model from its observable consequences.

So while we spent our time in Paris trying to guess "real" option value and to speculate about the volatility and the reasons behind market movement, in London I learnt that the option was worth the price that it traded on the pit. And that price might very well be the wild offer that some shrewd local shouts to a hurried broker before anybody else, and gets lifted. Perhaps fifty market-makers, or locals, were standing in my Bund option pit, in London. Most of them were playing their own money and they were individually much smaller players than the French bank who employed me. However, it was by working with them and ending up being one of them that I learnt the most about option trading.

First I learnt what it means to trade volatility in an option market, as opposed to trading it with a model. It is so difficult to accept the idea that options of different strike and different maturity have to be treated, and traded, as separate entities, almost unrelated to each other. For instance, a floor broker steps inside the option pit and all he is interested in are the three month 105 % out-of-the money calls. For two weeks, he keeps buying them following the same ritual: ten thousand contracts every day. As a volatility trader you sell him the calls and buy something else, for instance at-the-money volatility. Yet the guy returns the next day, and pays the same price for the calls, or perhaps even a higher price, regardless of the price of the underlying which may have dropped by now. You keep selling them to him. So what are you now? Are you still a volatility trader? Or have you suddenly turned into an option skew trader? Will you now run a model for the volatility skew? And how will you prescribe its dynamics? Who is going to tell you the point at which the 105 % call definitely becomes too expensive relative to the at-the-money?

So you come to accept the fact that the 105 % call trades in a market of its own and that there is nothing to constrain its value except very loose conditions, such that it may not trade, say, at a higher price than a call of lower strike or longer maturity. Because of what I like to call the "scientific episode" in option pricing – and by that I mean the Black-Scholes model or any other episode of *derivation* of option value – option traders, especially the inexperienced ones, have come to believe that option valuation comes in two stages. First, somebody hands them a number, volatility, second they feed it in a formula and they compute the option value. As a matter of fact, young option traders on the floor really did use to apply this schema. The chief trader would set the implied volatility levels for them and all they had to do was shout the option price, trade it, and hedge it.

One thing I have learnt on the floor is how very tacitly the mood can change. Let's go back to the pit and to our 105 % calls. The loud market-makers are still shouting their offered prices as if they were dying to sell those calls to that monomaniac broker at such a high premium relative to at-the-money volatility, when all of sudden, some other broker enters the pit and offers those calls. They get lifted immediately by the market-makers!

Unbeknownst to the young trader who still thinks the pit is in a selling mood (and who is still holding on the volatility levels set by his boss), the market-makers have in fact tacitly resolved to cover their shorts! Privately, the young trader complains that nobody has told him to raise his volatility levels. The "scientific episode" of option valuation simply blinds him to the fact that the pit is now globally short the 105 % call and they want to buy it back and buy no other. The guys with the experience did not even think: "Well, implied volatility must now be higher on the 105 % strike, because the probability distribution implied by the option market is getting more and more skewed, because that broker is buying more and more of those calls, therefore I should now raise my out-of-the-money volatility level, and start bidding for those calls myself". There is no such dialogue going on between the mature option market-maker and his Black-Scholes formula. He didn't speak to anyone about his urge to cover his shorts, not even to the other market-makers who are exactly in the same situation and who start doing the same thing.

Market memory is one other thing you cannot embed in a model. The market rallies one day and that broker comes back to the pit and "challenges" it (as they say) for a quote on the 105 % calls. Only because you remember the history of trades that went on the floor do you know for sure that this broker will now take his profits and sell back massively the calls he had purchased. It is completely up to you and to your fellow market-makers to show an appropriate bid. I will let you imagine what further "volatility trading" or "skew trading" will ensue.

Another interesting experience in option trading is trading them on expiry day. Options listed on the markets I used to trade would expire quarterly, and usually the "boys" in the pit would go have a drink after the market closed in order to celebrate the expiration. A person about to die is said to re-run the entire train of events of his or her life in quick succession. Likewise expiry day puts your whole history of option trading into perspective, even your whole expertise as option trader. This is the day of reckoning when the option finally acquires its meaning as a derivative instrument. It goes without saying that all option pricing models are useless that day. For instance the underlying price is about the settle in the neighborhood of some option strike and you still have an open position in that option. You almost remember all the trades you have done in that option, during its nine-month trading life span. It may have successively been at-the-money, out-of-the-money, in-the-money and at-the-money again, and you may have traded it at an average premium of, say, 60 ticks. What's fascinating about expiry day is that all the little profits that you may have accumulated throughout your whole history of trading that option (that is to say, your whole history of conscientious user of an option pricing model) can be wiped out if you are still short that option on expiry day and the underlying swings twice through its strike.

I can remember a couple of times when I was caught in such a predicament and my boss at the time, who I still think of to this day as the best visionary trader I've ever met, saved me. He simply told me to leave it entirely to him to manage the delta exposure of the book on that expiry day! I can't describe in a few words the trading prowess he showed that day, buying and selling futures ahead of time, in anticipation of the breach of the strike level. He even ended up making money trading those futures, when in fact we were massively short gamma! The bottom line is that it is indeed very easy to call oneself an option trader and to claim to be part of all the spectacular option trades that had gone on floor when one has the insurance that someone else, as skilled as my boss, would take over the delta of the book on expiry day! There is an alternative to the smooth and continuous Black-Scholes-Merton hedging strategy during the lifetime of the decaying option and that is to "swing" its whole delta in a bang-bang fashion (100 % or nothing) every time the underlying crosses its strike, and to do so until expiry day. This alternative derivation of option value is known as "Brownian local time" and it leads to the same option theoretical value as Black-Scholes. It is as though, within a single day that day, my boss had relived (and expiated) my whole story as an option trader and hedger – and even performed better than me!

Today, Erich Bonnet runs one of the largest European hedge funds, specializing in alternative derivative investment and volatility trading. He was the second boss I had in my trading life as he had succeeded to the boss who had sent me on the floor, on that fateful 19 October 1987. As to that first boss, he proved to be a savior of a different kind. All five Parisian banks involved in option market-making had lost money massively the day the market crashed, and the bank that employed me was no exception. They all decided to stop making the market in the following days, for fear of further losses and in order to close their positions one way or the other, except for my boss. On the contrary, he managed to convince the management of the bank that such a wild market would offer unbelievable trading opportunities. And he was right. Imagine Bank Indosuez being the sole market-maker in the middle of a crowd of market participants half of whom had made incredible profits on their long put positions and wanted to unwind them at any price and half of whom were panicking and wishing to buy options at any cost! In the following week, our profits amounted to tenfold our loss on the first day.

Maroun Eddé now runs one of the largest and most successful software companies specializing in derivatives straight-through processing and risk management. This company was the product of the very simple and robust ideas for option risk management and risk visualization that Maroun had already been applying during his days as option head at Indosuez. Stressing the option book under different volatility scenarios and different market levels, as elementary as it may sound today, was hardly imaginable in those days. Systems simply lacked the notion of "aggregate option book" back then. Not to mention the concept of "gamma-topography", pioneered by Maroun, which enabled him to visualize the overall gamma of the option position as one rich landscape of valleys and hills extending across the whole range of strike prices and maturity dates.

I wouldn't describe Maroun as someone who "made the market" but as someone who "made the rules". His reputation was such, in the period that followed the October crash, that brokers would call him personally or flock around him on the floor when they needed quotes on massive option trades. The period following the crash was peculiar in that options would trade in massive size (because somebody was unwinding a position, or liquidating a whole portfolio, or taking a massive bet), yet for all that the option market was not liquid. Brokers would call Maroun rather than a fickle market-maker because they knew he would quote a price which would be fair both for him, who was taking over the risk from the customer, and for the customer. Like I said, options were not yet listed on the Paris exchange, so when the market authorities decided to list them, later in 1988, it was only natural that they consulted with Maroun in order to establish the rules of the clearing house and the margin calls, even to establish the size and the features of the standardized option contract.

This is what I learnt from my years as option trader. You will notice that the lesson I learnt almost always consisted of cases of failure of quantitative modeling, either routine failure such as we witnessed with "empirical and foresighted Erich" or massive failure, putting in question the very possibility of a market, such as we witnessed with "transcendental Maroun". Yet the two men were as much quantitative traders as can be and were more than familiar with the quantitative tool and the quantitative techniques, because they were familiar with their limit. I am still in close contact, even in business, with the two of them, and there is no doubt that each has modeled a different side of my personality, even of my present business.

Haug: Are you a philosopher, quant, retired trader or a financial software engineer?

Ayache: The answer to this question may have already transpired through my answers above. "Philosopher" or "trader" is not something you are or are not. It is something you enact, something you perform. "To be a philosopher" or "to be a trader" is a performative statement not a descriptive one. You cannot be a "trader at rest", even less so a "retired trader". To be a trader is to be-in-a-market and markets, by the way, have no other way of being (no other way of being thought of, or represented) than of being-been-in-by-the-trader. I am not in the market as I write these lines, so I cannot be a trader.

Likewise, you never *are* a philosopher. When you think, and reflect in writing, about some topic, your thinking "clears its way only by its own questioning advance" (Heidegger). You are both at one with your thought and ahead of it. "The way that is cleared does not remain behind, but is built into the next step, and is projected forward from it". So how can you possibly break this continuous forward motion and step outside your thinking in order to describe yourself, if for one second, as a philosopher? And when you do not think, you altogether do not think and can even less be a philosopher or someone who "has been" philosophizing lately.

I am certainly no quant and as for the products of my company, I do indeed like to call them "financial engines". However, I intend them in the original, revolutionary sense of the term "engineering", not the sense of everyday technological accumulation. As I say in my *OpSession* interview in Wilmott, our engines are the result of "*original thinking*, the kind of thinking that can be both simple and creative; that is capable of reaching back to the origin while producing the latest technology".

Now to answer your question technically, I left the floor in 1995 and returned to Paris. By that time, I had understood that my reflective stance during my eight year immersion in the market was philosophical through and through. This was the turning point in my thought: from trader to writer. I convinced the bank to employ me part time, and for the following three years, I spent half of my time developing option pricing models and learning to be a quant, and the other half learning philosophy at la Sorbonne. In 1998, after earning a Masters degree in philosophy, I felt I would address the problems of quantitative finance more properly, both in their theoretical setting and their numerical application, if I created my own company. This is how ITO 33 was born. Paul Wilmott's first book, *Option Pricing*, was a revelation as concerns PDEs.

Haug: Everybody talks about volatility but what exactly is volatility?

Ayache: By itself, this question sums up the whole philosophy of derivative pricing, even of the market at large. So here is my short answer:

I don't *know* what volatility is.

I shall indeed argue that you *may not know* what volatility is and yet be perfectly able to trade options. Better still; the philosophical upshot of my argument will be that it is in fact *necessary* not to know volatility (in the usual sense of estimating it, or inferring it, or forecasting it) in order to trade and hedge options robustly.

So what is volatility? It is definitely not the statistical estimate that everyone has in mind, i.e. the square root of the average of squared returns. This is simply a formula written on paper. Indeed, nothing stops you from listing the time series of daily closing prices of the underlying on a piece of paper, estimating the average of squared returns and calling it the "volatility". Will that be the volatility of the underlying? What if the underlying process were a jump-diffusion of the kind that is now popular in credit-equity literature, where a Poisson process, whose intensity is also known as the "hazard rate", can suddenly trigger a jump to zero and throw the company into bankruptcy? By definition, default could not have happened in the past otherwise the company wouldn't be alive and we wouldn't have the time series of closing prices of the underlying equity. In other words, "historical volatility" (as this statistical average of squared returns is called) can by definition only capture the diffusion component of the credit-equity process and will show no trace of the potentiality of jumping to zero and dying. By contrast, options, and generally derivatives written on that stock, will have the risk of default priced into their premiums, because they are forward looking. Since everybody knows that the "volatility" of the underlying (whatever that means) and derivatives prices must be related, historical volatility cannot be the volatility we are looking for.

Notice that the above argument against historical volatility was based on the assumption that the underlying process was in fact *known* to be a credit-equity process (or jump-diffusion). So you might want to give the definition of volatility another try and argue that, since the process is known to be what it is, one should not look at history but at the present day or even better, the present instant. "Volatility of the underlying" should really be defined as its instantaneous, or "real" (notice the circularity here), volatility, and by that we mean a measure of the propensity of the underlying to be volatile in the next instant. This includes both its propensity to diffuse and to jump to zero.

The problem is, how could this new definition of volatility not be begging the question? How do we know what the *real* underlying process is? So in a sense, this new definition is even worse than the old. At least historical volatility was based on empirical evidence, the observed time series of prices. "Instantaneous volatility", by contrast, has nothing to rely on but strong metaphysical faith in the existence and persistence of the postulated data generating process.

As a matter of fact, the seemingly empirical definition of volatility as "historical volatility" is also infected by metaphysics. There is no such thing as pure empirical evidence, for empirical evidence as we know it is always theory-laden. For "historical volatility" to be satisfactory as an estimate of "real volatility" the historical sample must contain enough data. (Imagine a massive jump looming at the horizon and the historical sample stopping a few days short of that.) And what is to tell us how much data is enough other than the prior assumption that the probability distribution of the underlying is of a certain sort, for instance a Gaussian, and the corresponding bounds of estimation error? As Nassim Taleb points out, "we need data to discover a probability distribution and a probability distribution to tell us how much data we need. This causes a severe regress argument."[1]

I agree with Taleb that the whole business, even the whole paradigm, of statistical inference needs revising, and like him I shall describe my branch of philosophy as the eradication of metaphysics and the redefinition of statistical inference. Unlike Taleb, however, I will turn to the derivatives markets as my observable reality and avoid talking about (unobservable) probability distributions altogether.

Like I said, Taleb is still locked in epistemology. His topic is still the *knowledge of* the probability distribution, only his point is that such knowledge cannot be had because of essential uncertainty. I propose to be even more radical and to forget about knowledge altogether. This is what I meant when I said "I don't know what volatility is". When the market trades derivatives, does it have to know the probability distribution of the underlying?

Surely enough, people talk of the probability distribution that is *implied* by the derivatives market, or of the volatility that is *implied* by the option prices. They even personify the market and they talk of the "market forecast" of volatility, of the market being right or wrong, etc. We can indeed lend to the market any personality we wish and project on it any human fantasy we please, however, I think the only business the market has in trading derivatives is to *then* go ahead and trade derivatives.

Now of course, the whole theory of derivative pricing is based on the prior knowledge of the states of the world and of the probability distribution. But this is theory. Notice that in practice the trader always trades prices. He trades option prices against underlying prices or other option prices. He never trades probability distributions. We need states of the world and (risk-neutral) probability distributions in order to *interpret* derivative prices as averages of payoff. But who says we have to so interpret them? We need to assume some stochastic process for the underlying (in the real probability) in order to hold the derivative one day before maturity and argue that, since it will be perfectly replicable by the underlying at maturity, i.e. tomorrow, it might also be replicable today, perhaps only probabilistically, or statistically, or optimally in some sense of optimality. And if inter-temporal rebalancing of the hedge is allowed, we will then argue that the derivative is not only replicable one day before maturity but quite a few days before that. But who says we have to replicate the derivatives prior to maturity in order to price them? When Black Scholes and Merton came up with their perfect replication argument and their "exact" option pricing formula, this came as a shock to many an investor who had thought that warrants and options were substantial and independent entities, certainly not redundant with the underlying.

Am I then calling for the complete liberation of derivative prices, a kind of alternative modeling assumption where the price processes of derivative instruments would be postulated independently of each other and of the process of the underlying? Derivatives admit of markets of their own after all, and the dynamics of implied volatility and of implied skew can often be quite independent of the dynamics of the underlying, as in the example of the 105 % calls above.

While certainly a theoretical possibility, this independent postulation of derivative price processes will have to verify certain constraints. For one thing, the derivative price must converge to a known function of the underlying price at maturity, which is none other than its payoff. Also, derivative prices have to be related to each other in such a way as to avoid arbitrage opportunities. A sufficient and necessary condition for this to be the case is the existence of a pricing kernel, in other words, the existence of fixed states of the world and the availability of prices of hypothetical securities paying off $ 1 in the corresponding state of the world and zero otherwise. Derivative prices would be assembled out of these building blocks rather than modeled independently. This is the reason why the next reasonable step for making option prices stochastic independently of the underlying has always been to postulate a stochastic process for the volatility *of the latter* (e.g. Heston, 1993), rather than directly postulating independent stochastic option price processes.

To repeat, the market is a trading arena where all instruments trade at the same level, derivative or no derivative, following the law of supply and demand. The market is handed over a derivative and so it trades this derivative, at a certain price. It doesn't know probability, or volatility, or probability distributions. It is derivative prices that move, not "volatility", or "correlation", or "probability distributions", or any other fancy theoretical entity. However, because derivatives are *structured* and are precisely *derivative*, their price movements cannot be totally unstructured and this minimum structural requirement is what is expressed by this fiction of states of the world and probability distributions overlaying them.

Haug: What you are saying is that there is a gap between the way researchers and theoreticians believe their models are used and the way traders and markets actually price derivatives. In my view derivatives models are often used more as advanced interpolation tools to find the correct price for the next few hours rather than a magic model for finding the fair value.

Ayache: Absolutely. Call this fiction of the states of the world and of the probability distribution overlaying them – in other words, this derivative pricing model – a fancy "interpolation tool" if you will. It is here to guarantee you the required coherence between derivatives prices and the required hierarchy between the derivative and its underlying, also known as replication or hedging.

In philosophy, such a view is called "instrumentalism". It says that theories are mere tools and that there is nothing mysterious or metaphysical in the theoretical entities that they postulate beyond the function they serve in the tool. So if you ask me what volatility is, my ready answer will be at this point: "It is that number you input in your option pricing formula, or that you imply by inverting the formula".

Note, however, that there is potentially a big problem here, even a paradox. You need the theoretical construct of states of the world and probability distributions in order to price derivatives consistently and respect their derivative nature, yet the postulation of fixed states of the world says ultimately that some derivative will be replicable perfectly by the others, therefore will be redundant and will not be able to have its own market. (For instance, all derivatives are redundant in Black-Scholes as they can be replicated perfectly by the underlying; barrier options are redundant in Heston as they can be replicated perfectly by a dynamic strategy involving the underlying and one vanilla option; so on and so forth.) What seems to be the source of trouble is the very idea of a *derivatives market*. Either you have the structure and the hierarchy between derivative and underlying and you don't have the market; or you have the market and you don't have the structure. Another way of putting the paradox is to wonder, with Philippe Henrotte, whether "the prices of all assets and commodities should not be part of the description of a state of the world". "If states are fixed and given", Henrotte argues, "then the introduction of new securities help create powerful hedging strategies which help complete the market". And this we do not want, as a complete market is ultimately no longer a market. However, "if the definition of a state includes the prices of the securities", Henrotte argues further, "new securities mean new prices and a larger state space".[2]

Haug: Should how I hedge my options affect how I look at volatility?

Ayache: And what is volatility, in my instrumentalist view, other than the way that you hedge your option? So my answer will be a tautological "yes of course". Let me postpone for a while reflection on the paradox above and on the way to solve it and let me try to address the hedging question.

What we know for sure for now is that we want to believe in a derivatives market. We don't want to dismiss it. This means prices (of derivatives) get primacy in our philosophy, not states of the world. Prices are our primitive notion not the probability distribution which is in fact itself a secondary and derived concept and has no other purpose but to interpret prices as expectations.

Because we believe in a derivatives market, we can use the Black-Scholes-Merton model (or any complication thereof such as smile models) only in one direction, and that is plugging the option market price in the formula and implying a number called "implied volatility". Because of what we said earlier we will refrain absolutely from reading in that number some magic forecast the option market would be making for the volatility of the underlying, or some probability distribution it would be implying. Why bother with probability distributions and their knowledge when we already *have* a derivatives market? This is what has always had me opposed to Taleb. I say forget about contemplative epistemology. Taleb is certainly right in saying that people who just assume some probability distribution and try to infer its moments from the market do not in fact know anything. They even end up with something worse than lack of the knowledge and that is that they don't know that they don't know. Taleb says: We have this massive phenomenon, called the "market", and our standard categories or theories of knowledge do not apply to it. So we have to look for another answer or despair of ever getting any. I say: Maybe the market itself is the answer! No wonder that the category of probability doesn't apply to the market, for the market – especially with the advent of derivatives – may very well be the technology that is here to replace probability altogether! Historically, probability came after expectation, which was the primitive notion. In fact, probability was introduced in order to find a fair way of splitting the gains in interrupted games of chance (Hacking, 1975). You can see the value of the interrupted game as an "exchange" if you will, as a way of providing liquidity to the players before the end of the game, in a word, as a "market". Back then, games of chance involved fixed, and very often finite, states of the world. So probability worked. But who said probability is adapted to this new and amazing game of chance known as the derivatives market, where states of the world keep expanding?

You might find this questioning quite extreme and you might wonder, now that derivatives markets have been recognized by us as the primitive concept and probability has become the derived and secondary concept (which we're not even sure can be of any help anymore), what higher aim or higher knowledge derivatives markets can serve. It can't be the knowledge of the probability distributions as we have called this move "backward" and said the market was always ahead of it. So if the markets don't serve the knowledge of probabilities what other knowledge can they serve?

The most extreme form of the thought here is this: that we do not *know* anything with the markets – they just don't belong in epistemology – rather, we *do* something with them. Performativity, not representation. And what do we *do* with the market? What higher aim or higher task than knowledge do we accomplish? Time. I think we just do *time*. True the markets are here to "forecast" the future and to make it trade today. However, knowledge is not the right channel here. We don't *know* the future in the markets, we just *do* it (in other words, we trade it).

Haug: The sub-title of this book is "Models on Models", in order to try to illustrate that all quant finance models are based on more fundamental presuppositions such as probability, which is in fact itself a model of higher rank, a model *of knowledge*. I can see now how this criticism relates to your philosophical thinking about quant finance.

Ayache: Yes, absolutely. The hidden assumption behind quantitative finance and derivative pricing models is the availability of states of the world and their fixity. So before we even start wondering what probability to distribute over these states of the world and whether (following Taleb) any could ever be found, derivatives market confront us with a prior and greater challenge and that is that, by themselves, derivatives markets contradict the idea of fixed states of the world. I even think they contradict representational thinking altogether, and that the only way to address them is to be a performer *in* them, not a thinker *about* them. Derivatives are here to be traded, not to help us form knowledge about the probability distributions, and what not. However, derivatives have to be hedged and hedging will definitely require a derivative model. It is through the hedging that I think the necessity of theory can be reconciled with the actuality of the markets and with the performative imperative attached to that actuality. Indeed, although hedging requires a model and an assumption of states of the world and a probability distribution, it does not lock the trader in a contemplative attitude which is all absorbed in knowledge. It sends him back to the market, as it further immerses him in dynamic trading action.

Like I said, the only acceptable use of the Black-Scholes formula in my philosophy is to feed in it the option market, invert it, and compute the number known as "implied volatility". Try to read knowledge of volatility in that number if you wish, however, the real output of the model is the delta hedging ratio that the *volatility trader* will then have to trade in the market. This, to my eyes, is quite revolutionary. In it lies the whole revision of the paradigm of statistical inference that I was talking about. For the first time, a forward looking "statistical estimate", implied volatility, is extracted from the market. However, one must not interpret it as a provider of *forward looking* knowledge (the market forecast of the volatility of the underlying, etc.) but as a reason, even a rationale, for *further* action, namely dynamic hedging.

Thus I may summarize my view: I don't know what volatility is because the only volatility number that is meaningful to my eyes – the only volatility number that is truly forward looking – is implied volatility and implied volatility is not something we should address with knowledge. Its only use is to be fed back in the formula in order to yield the hedge. So to answer your initial question, it is not that the way I hedge should affect the way I look at volatility. Volatility is not here to be looked at, contemplated, or even represented. Rather, I look for implied volatility in order to find a way to hedge. The Black-Scholes-Merton formula or generally derivative pricing models, when calibrated to the market prices of derivative instruments, are not just interpolation tools that help us form the price of other derivative instruments, but algorithms that implicate us in dynamic hedging.

Speaking of dynamics, you can see at once, from the way I have set the problem and prescribed the use of the model, that what dynamics will prevail will certainly not be the dynamics internally assumed by the model but the dynamics of the trader's actual usage of the model: the dynamics of calibrating the model every day to the derivatives markets, of computing the hedges and the prices of other derivatives, and of trading both the derivatives and the underlying. In other words, the real dynamics will be recalibration.

Haug: A great deal of literature is written on calibration of quant finance models, but apart from what you have written on the subject, little is written on recalibration. In your Wilmott Magazine interview on *OpSession* **you propose that recalibration be part of the initial model itself. You say it is an "a priori requirement that must be fulfilled by every system supposed to tackle volatility trading and arbitrage". Whether an option trader uses the Black-Scholes-Merton model, stochastic volatility or implied trees, he will in practice recalibrate his model all the time. How could recalibration be built into the more modern models?**

Ayache: You are aware of course of the insuperable difficulty this question poses. If the dynamics of recalibration are built into the model through a *model* of recalibration, this will yield another model which will bring back the question of recalibration. Say you observe that option traders calibrate their Black-Scholes formula every day to the market and that implied volatility is stochastic as a result. Your next move is to try to model this phenomenon. Because of the necessity of having a pricing kernel and consistent derivative prices, you may not model the Black-Scholes *implied volatility* as stochastic. You have to take a step back and model the volatility of the underlying. So you come up with the Heston model (or some other stochastic volatility model). But then the trader will again recalibrate the Heston model every day; its parameters will become stochastic and we are right back where we started!

So the answer seems to be *not* to try to build recalibration into the model a priori, but to conceive a model which gives us reasons to believe that it will be robust under recalibration a posteriori. And what needs to be robust here is the hedging of course, since derivatives prices are fed from the market anyway.

The difficulty here is that the hedging algorithm (I no longer want to call it a "model" at this stage) *will require* both an assumption for the dynamics of the underlying and the assumption that this assumption will not change. This is the fate of the theory of derivative pricing and hedging and we cannot escape from it!

Our proposed solution is a model which is open to recalibration and to the expansion of the state space, although it respects the requirement of fixed states of the world and of the pricing kernel, in each calibration instance. I have already described it in previous publications (Wilmott, January and May 2006). It is a regime-switching model whose characteristic feature is that the regimes bear the name of no particular stochastic variable. They can be regimes of volatility, or interest rates, or hazard rates, or any other meaningful financial variable. It all depends on the variety of the derivative instruments we are calibrating the model against and on their price manifold.

This model imposed itself on us because it was deduced from a set of three basic rules which I had enunciated, at one time, as the logical summary of my thinking about derivative models: (1) Derivative models are calibrated to the market price of derivative instruments in order to compute the hedge: hedges are the real output of derivative models, not the forecasts; (2) If derivative models are calibrated to the market, this means they will be recalibrated: calibration is recalibration; and (3) As new derivative structures are introduced, whose prices deviate from the prediction of the model, they are calibrated against and they are used as hedges: this is the expansion of the state space.

The key observation regarding the regime-switching model is that it is self-similar under its own stochasticization. It incorporates its own meta-model. Recalibration will make the regime-switching model stochastic like any other model. However, since stochastic variables are expressed in regimes, regimes of regimes are also regimes. So all we have are regimes; we don't have to model recalibration a priori; recalibration and expansion of the state space occur whenever they occur and they put new names on the regimes. Since the regimes have no predefined names, it is not clear that the new, richer stochastic model and its larger state space were not with us all along, only we didn't distinctly perceive them. The model is open to change and upgrading, because at no point do we lock ourselves in the myth of perfect calibration and its correlate, perfect hedging. Rather, we propose optimal hedges and we measure the standard deviation of the P&L. This provides just the right leeway for the model to be robust under successive recalibrations.

Haug: What is your view on the idea of continuous dynamic delta hedging?

Ayache: It is a theoretical fiction of course but then it is very useful. A game theorist friend of mine once told me that the infinite is often the best approximation of the finite. So continuous hedging is the "best" approximation of the more realistic discrete hedging because if we were to model discrete hedging we would have to worry about the choice of the hedging frequency, etc.

I think recalibration is a more serious breach of the integrity of the theoretical model than the fact that hedging is actually discrete rather than continuous. Yet we have to live with recalibration and even try to build it into the model because it is a "necessary accident". This, I have shown, can only be had at the cost of no longer believing in the theoretical fiction which the model sets (fixed state space, known probability distribution) and in trusting that the hedges proposed by the model will *as a matter of fact* prove to be robust. I think the same pragmatism should apply to the issue of discrete vs. continuous hedging.

The myth of a priori modeling and of a priori representation has to be given up in this field that I would still like to call "scientific" (in an upgraded sense of the word). Indeed our science of derivative pricing and hedging is the realm of actuality and any attempt at folding back this actuality into a model, or a generator, or a representation, supposed to hold before the fact, leads to paradox, as we have seen with recalibration, or indeed with the very idea of a derivatives market. This does not mean, however, that chaos should reign. I don't believe in flat empiricism and skepticism is not an option. The only reason why representational thought can lose its supremacy in our science of derivative pricing and yet the science and its scope (I don't want to say the "knowledge") still make progress is that the failure of representation is supplemented by performativity. Only because a regime-switching model such as I have proposed is in the hands of the trader and the trader is immersed in his market can recalibration and the expansion of the state space not be modeled a priori and yet the final result be guaranteed (and that is that hedging will have proven to be robust after all and the trader will have managed to remain afloat in the middle of that big wave which is called the "market").

Quantitative modeling cannot sustain its paradoxes alone. Only because it is a tool in the hands of the trader and because the trader "knows better" than knowledge to deal with the market – i.e. his actions and "knowledge" are performative rather than representational – can quantitative modeling ultimately work and be part of the science. And once it is acknowledged that no model and no theoretical representation can replace the trader's presence and sense of actuality, it won't in the least worry us that hedging should be continuous in the theoretical model and discrete, or even discretional, in actuality.

Haug: There is a great deal written about stochastic volatility and jumps in the underlying asset, but much less about jumps in volatility, can you comment on this?

Ayache: The literature is after closed form formulas, and models of diffusive volatility seem easier to solve than models with jumping volatility. Volatility is unobservable, mind you, so nobody can tell whether it diffuses or jumps and in my philosophy it is no more than a useful fiction.

Notice that volatility is essentially jumping in the regime-switching model I have proposed because it admits of a small number of discrete states, or regimes. We solve the model numerically anyway so closed form solutions are of no concern to us. Why should we worry about an infinite number of states of volatility when a finite number of discrete states can address all the practical issues that are of concern, namely calibration, recalibration and hedging?

Haug: Do you have any views on risk-neutral valuation and the relationship between risk neutral and real probability distributions?

Ayache: Risk neutral probability is just the expression of the fact that derivative prices must be interpreted as expectation of payoff in order to avoid internal arbitrage. It is the same as having a pricing kernel. So if derivative pricing is your sole concern, then naming a pricing kernel, or a risk-neutral probability distribution, is all you need. This risk-neutral probability distribution (call it a derivative pricing operator, if you will) can even be reverse engineered from the known prices of derivatives. This is calibration.

Real probability becomes a concern when we start worrying about replicating the derivative with the underlying process (in incomplete markets, of course). This dynamic replication, or hedging, takes place in the real world where the real process of the underlying is given.

Haug: When it comes to calibration of a model to the past (historical data) and to the present (current market prices), how can you be sure a future tail event will not make the calibration blow up in your face?

Ayache: I only believe in calibration to the present traded prices of derivatives. And calibration is useless if it is not followed by hedging, using the instruments you have calibrated against (or instruments of similar sort). Say you calibrate your model to an option smile. Since smiles are produced by stochastic volatility, this means your model has got to be a stochastic volatility model (not a local volatility model, or an implied tree) because the third rule in my set of three rules above compels you to use the underlying *and at least one option* as dynamic hedges. If you calibrate your model to a credit default swaption, you will use it as hedging instrument and your model has got to be a model of stochastic credit spread.

Now of course a future tail event will make the calibration, even the whole model I had momentarily assumed, blow up in my face. But the hedging is here to defend the calibration, and the next day I will have to recalibrate anyway. Also, do not forget that the models I propose are models for trading (and for immersion in the market), not models for knowledge. The tail event will make any form of knowledge, or even category, you had relied on initially look ridiculous (this is essentially Taleb's point), but are you saying it makes the market and the trader look ridiculous?

Haug: What do you think about Nassim Taleb and his philosophy of randomness and Black Swans?

Ayache: I definitely agree with Taleb that markets are the natural habitat of Black Swans. Black Swans signal the breakdown of representational knowledge because they are events which were not only hidden from knowledge but from its very categories. My thinking about derivatives markets shows that representational knowledge is out of the question anyway because it simply contradicts the idea of derivatives markets. So Black Swans seem to be a constitutive necessity here! Where I diverge from Taleb is then simply that with derivatives markets (and generally markets), we are *way past* the astonishment of seeing a Black Swan for the first time. The market itself, I argued, can be (and must be) seen as a replacement of the whole category of knowledge that was powerless in front of the Black Swan. So the Black Swan shouldn't be a reason to flee the market. On the contrary, the trader's and the market's way should be the way to approach Black Swans. This supposes of course that the trader is immersed in the market and addresses it with performativity rather than representation. This inside view is by definition incompatible with an external view which would judge the trader through the canon of randomness. How can we speak of randomness anymore when we have seen the fate of the states of the world and of probability distributions in the derivatives markets?

Haug: Are you open about the quantitative models in your software or do you keep it secret so it ends up being a black box for the traders using it?

Ayache: I am very open about the philosophy of modeling (as I hope this interview has shown) and the quantitative models in my software are open to change, upgrading, dialogue and recalibration in the full sense of the words.

FOOTNOTES & REFERENCES

1. See Taleb, N. (2007) *The Black Swan*. New York: Random House.
2. See Henrotte, P. (2006) "Buckets in the Hold of the Titanic" *Wilmott Magazine*, March, 24–27.

■ Ayache, E. (2006a) "OpSession" *Wilmott Magazine*, May, 32–42.
■ ———— (2006b) "What is Implied Volatility?" *Wilmott Magazine*, January, 28–35.
■ Black, F. and M. Scholes (1973) "The Pricing of Options and Corporate Liabilities" *Journal of Political Economy*, **81**, 637–654.
■ Duhem, P. (1954) *The Aim and Structure of Physical Theory*. (Philip P. Wiener trans.), Princeton: Princeton University Press.

■ Hacking, I. (1975) *The Emergence of Probability*. Cambridge: Cambridge University Press.

■ Heidegger, M. (1968) *What is Called Thinking?*. (J. Glenn Gray, trans.), New York: Harper and Row.

■ Henrotte, P. (2006) "Buckets in the Hold of the Titanic" *Wilmott Magazine*, March, 24–27.

■ Heston, S. L. (1993) "A Closed-Form Solution for Options with Stochastic Volatility, with Applications to Bond and Currency Options" *Review of Financial Studies*, **6**, 327–343.

■ Merton, R. C. (1973) "Theory of Rational Option Pricing" *Bell Journal of Economics and Management Science*, **4**, 141–183.

■ Taleb, N. (2001) *Fooled by Randomness*. New York: Texere.

■ —— (2006a) "Tales of the Unexpected," *Wilmott Magazine*, March, 30–36.

■ —— (2007) *The Black Swan*. New York: Random House.

■ Wilmott, P., J. Dewynne and S. Howison (1993) *Option Pricing: Mathematical Models and Computation*. Oxford: Oxford Financial Press.

The illusion of time and the illusive models describing financial markets change with time, but time does not change, only its illusion changes. The picture below is based on a genius oil painting done by my artistic hedge fund friend W^2

12
Frozen Time Arbitrage*

Received 29 February 2100
Revised 2 March 1999

> The distinction between past, present, and future is only an illusion, even if a stubborn one.
> Albert Einstein

Time is money. In finance time plays an essential role in everything from calculating how much interest is earned on your bank account to discounting uncertain cash flows, using the most sophisticated option formulas.[1] Unlike physicists, finance plodders always consider the speed of time as given,[2] something they can simply read off the calendar. But time is relative. This and many other aspects of the time have been ignored in finance literature, and with this chapter I intend to focus on time itself.

From Einstein's relativity theory we know that time exists as part of space-time. According to Einstein, the flow of time is affected by gravity and how fast we move with respect to the speed of light in a vacuum. Hundreds of books and papers have been written about the theory of relativity, and the main reason why it is ignored so entirely in finance is probably that with today's technology it has a negligible effect on practical financial calculations. To manipulate time according to Einstein's theory of relativity with any significance for financial calculations, we would need to travel close to the speed of light, or alternatively we would need to be close to a massive gravitation source, for example the Trump Tower or a Black-Hole. More on this later.

But there is another way. Using modern technology we can actually change time and therefore the time value of money, and based on this we can construct a pure time arbitrage. The first time arbitrage has already occurred in laboratories, without the human race even thinking about it ... until now. I am referring here to time travel, and this is not some silly fantasy of mine, but a reality.

Before we move on to time travel arbitrage, we will first concentrate on some "well known" simple forms of time arbitrage. Time arbitrage can be divided into two main groups; the first concerns how to measure time, and the second and much more interesting one involves time travel. Let's start with the boring one.

---

*I would like to thank Erik Stettler and Kent Martino, any remaining errors are due to my past, current and future girlfriends.

1 Time Measure Arbitrage

In today's modern society the length of a second is defined by very accurate atomic clocks, more precisely as 9,192,631,770 oscillations associated with the cesium atom, see for example Langone (2000) or Audoin and Guinot (2001) for more details. Unfortunately, even a clock this accurate is not good enough to keep time in sync. The problem is how to link atomic clocks to the irregular rotation of the Earth. Between 1972 and 1999, 22 leap seconds were added to our clocks to keep in sync with the Earth's rotation. Because the Earth's rotation continues to slow, the gap between the duration of an "Earth second" and that of an "atomic second" continues to widen. If the Earth should speed up, we would need to add negative leap seconds. Still, leap seconds should have a minimal effect on financial calculations, at least in a human's short lifespan, though that is not the case with leap years.

1.1 Leap year arbitrage

A tropical year is 365.2422 days long (the time it takes the Earth to move from one vernal equinox to another one). To make our 365 day calendar work properly we add a leap year every four years. Especially with fixed income derivatives like swaps, this can have significant effect on the valuation. Not all derivatives software systems take leap years properly into account. Several systems that I have seen used by major players try to average it out by using 365.25 days in a year. For a one year swap quoted on a Act/360 basis this will easily lead to a price error of a basis point. Assume the swap rate is 6.00 %. Using 365.25 days per year gives 6.088 %, while 366 days gives 6.10 %, a difference of more than a basis point, which is significant in a market where the bid/offer spread is typically only a few basis points. This difference is probably not enough to lock in a risk-free arbitrage, going long the swap with one counterpart and short with another counterpart, but if you are entering a swap, one basis point on a 100 million dollar notional one year swap adds up to about $10,000. If you don't care about saving $10,000 then please send me a check.

To make things even more complicated, since the tropical year is 365.2422 days long and not 365.25, the calendar is adjusted further by skipping leap years every year evenly divisible by 100 but not by 400. This is why we didn't have a leap year in the year 1900 but had it in 2000. The next time we skip a leap year will be in 2100.

1.2 Time Zone arbitrage

The OTC (over-the-counter) currency market is a global 24 hour market. With respect to option expiration, time zones can play an important role. Let's say you trade USD/JPY options. During New York hours the standard is New York cut, that is the option will expire at 10 a.m. New York time, at the expiration date. Tokyo cut (expiration) is 3 p.m. Tokyo time. New York is normally 12 hours behind Tokyo. For short term options with only a couple of days to expiration, the NY versus Tokyo cut difference is obviously significant. When comparing option prices from different banks, make sure they quote you expirations that are in the same time zone. If not, it will be hard to compare the prices, or even worse, someone might be time zone arbitraging you.

1.3 Summer time/winter time arbitrage

Many countries adjust their clock for summer time in the spring and autumn. I assume the idea is to make the summer evenings have one more hour of daylight, which I see as an idiotic idea enforced by politicians in order to disturb my sleep rhythms and to make life more complex for electricity derivatives quants. In my home country, Norway, we in the very north have 24 hours of daylight in the summer, thus I never got the point of introducing summer time adjustments. We don't need more daylight in the summer, what we need is more daylight in the winter, when there are 24 hours of darkness.

In the electricity market the base load consists of delivering electricity for a 24 hour period. However, in the spring the day before the summer time adjustment is officially only 23 hours long, while the subsequent day is 25 hours. If you made a derivatives contract for the next day and the contract value was specified as 24 hours when the underlying physical commodity is only for 23 hours, you could have a problem. One hour is $\frac{1}{24} = 4.17\%$ of that day's value, which is significant.

1.4 Day Count Arbitrage

For interest rate calculation, the number of days used in a year (day conventions) plays an important role. Let's assume two banks quote you a one year interest swap. Bank A gives you a quote of 5.50 % and bank B gives 5.52 %, both with annual compounding. If you are a payer in the swap, you should naturally go for bank A. Or should you? Make sure to check if they use same day convention first. Assume bank A quoted you on Act/360 basis, and bank B on Act/365 basis. To compare the rates you can convert bank A into an Act/365 quote, assuming a non-leap year this is $5.50\% \times \frac{365}{360} = 5.58\%$. So bank B actually gave you the best quote.

1.5 Stealing time

Stealing money is illegal, but rules about stealing time are more diffuse. In warrant issues, the management and key personnel in the company sometimes get a considerable amount of warrants themselves. As they are typically not allowed to short shares in the company they work for, the only way they can make money is if the warrants end up in-the-money. One way to make this happen is naturally, as we have seen too often; manipulation of accounting numbers to inflate the stock price. An alternative to this, or more likely an addition, is to steal time from the shareholders. When the warrants are getting close to expiration, if they are still not in-the-money then one will from time to time see a sudden and entirely free extension in their expiration. There can be several reasons for this. To issue new warrants costs quite a bit of money, thus it can be optimal for a company to simply extend the current warrants, in the hope that a higher share price in the future will get the warrant holder to exercise, and thus raise more capital. Another reason is because the managers loaded with warrants want to get rich, and stealing time instead of money is one way to do it.

2 Time Travel Arbitrage

Now let's move to time travel arbitrage. First we will consider some "theoretical" ways of doing time arbitrage based on Albert Einstein's theory of relativity. In the end we will look at a very practical way of doing time travel arbitrage.

2.1 Space Travel Arbitrage

Albert Einstein proposed the Special Theory of Relativity in 1905. One of the theory's main contributions is the relationship between space and time. To make it simple; to get to an interview in Manhattan you need four coordinates, street, avenue, floor and time. If you get any of the coordinates wrong you will most likely not get the job, having missed the interview in space or time. Instead of space and time being separate entities they can be considered as space-time, thus giving us a four-dimensional world. According to Einstein's theory, the only thing that is constant in space-time is the speed of light in a vacuum; 299,792,458 meters per second[3] or about 186,300 miles per second. Not impressed? This is actually one of the strangest aspects of the universe. In this world a moving clock will run slower. A person who is traveling quickly through space will experience time dilation relative to a person staying behind on earth. This can be used to travel through time and to do time arbitrage. To calculate time travel arbitrage in Einstein's Universe[4] we can use the Lorentz transformation;[5] time in a moving system will be observed by a stationary observer as running slower by

$$\Delta t_{EarthTime} = \frac{\Delta t_{SpaceCraftTime}}{\sqrt{1 - \left(\frac{v}{c}\right)^2}}$$

where v is the velocity of the time traveler and c is the speed of light. This formula tells us that time moves slower and slower as we approach the speed of light. At the speed of light time stands still.

Let's assume you travel in a space craft for five years at 98 % of the speed of light, $\frac{v}{c} = 98/100$. How many years of earth time will have gone by when you return to mother earth?

$$\Delta t_{EarthTime} = \frac{5}{\sqrt{1 - \left(\frac{98}{100}\right)^2}} \approx 25.13$$

While everybody on earth has grown 25 years older, you have only aged five years, though you have become 25 years richer because during your five years of space travel you have accumulated 25.13 years of earnings on the bank account that you left behind at earth. The value of 100 thousand dollars invested at 7.00 % annual interest rate when you left earth is now worth an amazing

$$100,000 \times (1 + 0.07)^{25.13} = \$547,538.09$$

if you had stayed on earth for five years you would only got

$$100,000 \times (1 + 0.07)^5 = \$140,255.17$$

Time travel in Einstein's Universe is possible in theory[6] but is difficult to do in practice for anything larger than atomic particles due to our primitive technology. Unfortunately, the human race is far from getting close to traveling at any speed significantly relative to the speed of light.[7] Today's best spacecraft only move at a speed of 0.01 % of the speed of light. Even if the Special Relativity Theory and its time dilation are well tested in experiments, accelerating spacecraft requires much more advanced technology than do accelerating particles.

2.2   Gravitational Arbitrage

Gravitation influences space and time (space-time). Not only does time run faster at higher altitudes, it does so at just the rate that Einstein always said it would. The General Relativity Theory actually holds important practical consequences. For example, the clocks on GPS (General Position System) satellites run a little too fast because of the weaker gravity in space, and need to be slowed down relative to Earth-based clocks. If left uncorrected, this would result in the satellite clocks going one second too fast every 70 years. This might not seem like much, but it's an important effect for a precision system like GPS, where timing is everything.

The gravitational effect on time dilation has a minimal effect on Earth for any practical financial calculations. On the other hand, if your financials are strongly dependent on meeting at a specific geographical location such as at sea or in a desert, the gravitational effect on time can naturally have large indirect effects through GPS. Or if you should ever settle down in a black-hole, the gravitation effect on time could suddenly be alfa omega. See Chapter 13 on Space-time Finance for more detail on this subject.

2.3   Frozen Time Arbitrage

The speed of physical processes depends on temperature, and in particular on biological clocks, see Palmer (2002). For hundreds of years people have slowed down biological clocks by lowering the temperature. Your refrigerator slows down the biological and chemical processes so you can store and preserve food for a longer time. The colder the temperature, the slower the food ages and the longer you can store it.

There is an urban legend that Walt Disney arranged to have himself frozen in a chamber full of liquid nitrogen upon his death, and that he now awaits the day when medical technology will make his re-animation possible. At very low temperatures it is possible, right now, to preserve dead people indefinitely with essentially no deterioration. However, this is only half the battle, and so far medical science have not been able to wake up dead-frozen humans. But what about living people? The size of the American population depends on whether you count the frozen part of it or not. Current estimates[8] hold that somewhere between 200,000 and 1,000,000 human embryos are "in storage", frozen in liquid nitrogen, at fertility clinics nationwide. Whether they are awaiting the date of their awakening or of their destruction will be determined by the outcome of the national debate on stem cell research. Freezing human embryos is an interesting topic from a moral and legal perspective. The first court case with parents suing each other over the right to a frozen embryo has already happened in the USA.

Well, let us leave the moral and legal discussion for another time, or for the Wilmott forum, www.wilmott.com, and instead concentrate on how to construct frozen time arbitrage. Let's assume two twin embryos. One is frozen and the other is growing up. The first baby is getting $100k at its birth. The frozen embryo is at the same time given only $50k. The $50k is invested in inflation adjusted treasury bonds, paying 3.5% above inflation, annualized. Sixty five years later the frozen twin embryo is woken up. Assuming 3.5% inflation the $50k has grown to an amazing

$$(\$50,000 \times 1.07^{65}) = \$4,063,643$$

To compare this with the $100k the first twin got 65 years ago we need to adjust for inflation. Still the $50k is worth a whopping

$$\frac{\$4,063,643}{1.035^{65}} = \$434,302$$

By freezing the biological clock, the frozen twin has arbitraged the rest of the world. This is of course independent of the embryo being a twin or not. If everybody was frozen, there would naturally be no people to produce and make returns on the capital, and the interest rates and the arbitrage would quickly go to zero. But as most of the population is not frozen, the few frozen can arbitrage the rest of us. So the first time travel arbitrage has most likely already occurred without the parents even thinking about it. In a not too distant future we can naturally have robots producing and giving return on our capital while we take a break, freezing time and chilling out while waiting for our investments to grow.

You might be wondering about the storage cost of frozen embryos. Is the storage cost so high that it would eat up the arbitrage? If that is the case we could simply start with a higher initial amount, but that means you need to be wealthy in the first place. Still, the answer is No. Each clinic sets its own price. The cost typically falls between $100 and $250 a year but in rare cases may reach $500. Including a cost of $100 per year for freezing time, and this is still a good arbitrage.

What about the risks? As with any investment, even treasury bonds are based on a probability of the government and the human race still existing tomorrow. A high probability of an asteroid hitting the earth (as shown in various bad movies) and terminating the human race as it probably did with the dinosaurs would make frozen time arbitrage less lucrative. The probability of a Deep-Impact in the short run, next year, or next hundred years or so is very low indeed. However, when it comes to Frozen Time Arbitrage, time flies by fast, and when you wake up the government can be bankrupt or even life on earth gone, which would not be the most pleasant of surprises. In contrast to options, high volatility is in general bad for frozen time arbitrage. What you want is stability for a long, long time. When time is frozen you don't care much about the annualized returns as long as they exceed inflation. Just decide how much money you want and calculate the length of time that you need to be frozen. Who knows? In the future when a full grown body can be frozen and then reawakened, if you lose your job in an economic down turn you can simply sell your apartment, put the money in inflation adjusted treasury bonds, give your resumé to a job hunter, jump in the fridge and wait for the next upturn.

2.4 Frozen Light

Freezing an embryo slows down the physical processes and thus the biological clock. In Einstein's theory of relativity time is related to the speed of light. But what about temperatures and light? In our world we are used to matter in three forms; solid, liquid and gas. Since the 1920s it has been known that there is a fourth form of matter generated in the nuclear furnace of the sun – plasma. Bose and Einstein predicted in 1924 that a fifth form of exotic matter called a "Bose-Einstein condensate" would occur at extremely low temperatures. This state of matter was first observed in 1995 by a research team at Cornell University.

Almost 80 years after the theory was developed by Bose and Einstein the Danish scientist Lene Hau and her research team were able to slow the speed of light to 17 metres per second (the speed of a racing bicycle), 20 million times slower than normal. This was done by sending the light through Bose-Einstein matter, which has a temperature close to absolute zero. Absolute zero is the lowest temperature possible, a temperature where atoms and molecules stop their motions, see Shachtman (1999). More recently, Hau and her team have been able to stop light completely and then release it under experimental control.

Does this mean that Einstein's theory was wrong? No, remember that Einstein's theory was based on the speed of light in a vacuum. The slowing of light in a material will not result in any distortions in time. Time dilations depend on moving close to the light's ultimate speed in a vacuum and not to the speed of light in a material, see Glegg (2001). A black hole with a mass a few times larger than that of the sun would have a temperature of only one ten millionth of a degree above absolute zero, see Hawking (1998). So we can ask ourselves: is the reason a black-hole does not allow any light to escape only because of the extreme gravitation, or could it also be that the Bose-Einstein condensate material is playing a role, freezing the light in a similar way as in the Hau experiment?

Even if extreme cold does not cause time dilations, we can still use it to slow biological and physical processes. Time travel through slowing the biological clock is possible, and can be used for frozen time arbitrage.

So far we have only looked at how to travel into the future by slowing down time and how to use it to arbitrage the world. Traveling back in time could possibly be even more profitable. Andreasen and Carr (2002) have recently written an interesting paper where they show how time reversal symmetry between derivatives can be used for hedging, but without explaining how to travel back in time.

3   Conclusion

In financial calculations we cannot assume that time is constant anymore, not even on Mother Earth. The most important of all finance rules; "Time is Money" still holds true, and due to Frozen Time Arbitrage it has a deeper meaning than ever before. I think and hope that you consider me to be crazy, or as the Danish Physicist and Nobel Price winner Neils Bohr would say

> We all agree your theory is crazy; what divides us is whether it is crazy enough to be correct.

So far we have looked at time dilation, but we have avoided the question of what is time. Some researchers actually believe that time is only an illusion. In 1967 the American physicist Bryce DeWitt published an equation that, if his reasoning is sound, can describe the whole universe. John Wheeler, who coined the term "black hole", played a major role in its discovery, thus the equation is called the Wheeler-DeWitt equation. The Wheeler-DeWitt equation describes a possible reality that has no time variable. The equation indicates that the universe is static and that time is frozen for all of us, thus time is only an illusion. For various reasons many physicists do not like it, and it is therefore known as "that Damn Equation". However, recently the theory of timeless reality or of the end of time has received more attention from physicists like Barbour (1999) and Stenger (2000). Illusion or not, who gives a damn, as long as I can freeze my illusion of time in a fridge of liquid nitrogen while the rest of you are passing by in the illusion of time or whatever it is? As a trader, what matters is arbitrage and relative value, and the first Frozen Time Arbitrage has already been done. Who's next!

FOOTNOTES & REFERENCES

1. See Haug (1997).
2. A possible "exception" is Derman (2002), naturally a physicist.
3. As defined officially at the 1983 General Conference on Weights and Measures.
4. See Einstein (1912), Einstein (1961) and Taylor and Wheeler (1992) for more detail on special relativity.
5. This transformation derives its name from Hendrik Antoon Lorentz (1853–1928), a Dutch physicist.

6. See for example Gott (2001), Davies (1995), Davies (2001), Pickover (1998) and Nahin (1998).
7. "In 1971 Joe Hafele and Richard Keating put highly accurate atomic clocks into airplanes, flew them around the world, and compared their readings with identical clocks left on the ground. The results were unmistakable: time ran more slowly in the airplane than in the laboratory, so that when the experiment was over the airborne clocks were 59 nanoseconds slower than the ground clocks – exactly the amount predicted in Einstein's theory". Davies (2001).
8. http://www.cruzada.net/frozen_embryo.htm.

■ Andreasen, J. and P. Carr (2002) "Put Call Reversal" Working Paper, Corant Institute, New York.
■ Audoin, C. and B. Guinot (2001) *The Measurement of Time*. Cambridge: Cambridge University Press, Original in French 1998, English translation.
■ Barbour, J. (1999) *The End of Time*. Oxford: Oxford University Press.
■ Davies, P. (1995) *About Time*. Simon & Schuster.
■ ——— (2001) *How to Build a Time Machine*. Viking Penguin.
■ Derman, E. (2002) "The Perception of Time, Risk and Return During Periods of Speculation" Working Paper, Goldman Sachs.
■ Einstein, A. (1912) *Einstein's 1912 Manuscript on the Special Theory of Relativity*. George Braziller, Publishers in the association with the Jacob E. Safra Philanthropic Foundation and the Israel Museum, Jerusalem, 1996.
■ ——— (1961) *Relativity, The Special and the General Theory*. Random House.
■ Glegg, B. (2001) *Light Years and Time Travel*. New York: John Wiley & Sons, Inc.
■ Gott, R. J. (2001) *Time Travel in Einstein's Universe*. New York: Houghton Mifflin Company.
■ Hau, L. V., S. Harris, Z. Dutton and C. Behroozi (1999) "Light Speed Reduction to 17 Metres per Second in an Ultracold Atomic Gas," *Nature 397*.
■ Haug, E. G. (1997) *The Complete Guide To Option Pricing Formulas*. New York: McGraw-Hill.
■ Hawking, S. (1998) *A Brief History of Time, Tenth Anniversary Edition*. Bantam Books.
■ Langone, J. (2000) *The Mystery of Time*. National Geographic.
■ Nahin, P. J. (1998) *Time Machines, Time Travel in Physics, Metaphysics, and Science Fiction*, 2nd ed. AIP Press.
■ Palmer, J. D. (2002) *The Living Clock, The Orchestrator of Biological Rhythms*. Oxford: Oxford University Press.
■ Pickover, C. (1998) *Time, A Traveler's Guide*. Oxford: Oxford University Press.
■ Shachtman, T. (1999) *Absolute Zero and the Conquest of Cold*. A Mariner Book, Houghton Mifflin Company.
■ Stenger, V. J. (2000) *Timeless Reality*. Prometheus Books.
■ Taylor, E. F. and J. A. Wheeler (1992) *Spacetime Physics, Introduction To Special Relativity*. New York: W. H. Freeman and Company.

Paul Wilmott

Haug on Wilmott
and Wilmott on Wilmott

I first learned the name Paul Wilmott through his book with the green cover entitled "Option Pricing" written together with Jeff Dewynne and Sam Howison. This was the first book on derivatives focusing extensively on the PDE method and finite differences. Paul Wilmott soon came out with his third book "Derivatives". This was a wonderful book packed with useful information. I found a minor typo in his computer code accompanying his book. As I had recently written a book myself ("Option Pricing Formulae") I knew that it was impossible to get a first edition completely free of typos, so I sent the typo to Wilmott in a e-mail suggesting that he could fix it in a potential second edition. This was how I first established contact with Paul who through exceptional talent, hard work and unlimited enthusiasm would soon transform himself into a guru of quantitative finance. The second edition of "Paul Wilmott on Quantitative Finance" consists of three volumes and is nearly 1,400 pages long. This book not only shows how Paul Wilmott's knowledge has grown over the years, but also illustrates how fast the field of quantitative finance has grown, and there seems to be no end to it.

Beside his books Paul has published a large number of papers and is also the founder and editor of a leading quantitative finance magazine known as "Wilmott". This magazine is different in that it is much more open minded in terms of style and ideas than most academic finance journals. If I have understood Paul correctly his idea is that over time the market will decide anyway, a great idea will be acknowledged over time, and bad ideas will sooner or later be seen as bad (hopefully not too many of my own ideas). Established academic journals have a tendency to be extremely conservative in what they publish, they are already well known, and feel probably they have more to lose than gain by publishing ideas outside what is currently in the mainstream. This is often why the most interesting ideas are not accepted in the most prestigious academic journals.

Beside his books and magazine Paul has also started what has become the most popular website where quants meet: www.wilmott.com. If anyone mentions "Derivatives" then "Wilmott" comes immediately to most quants' minds. Paul Wilmott with his books, magazine and website and unlimited enthusiasm for quantitative finance and derivatives is himself in many ways a Derivative of Derivatives, what would Wilmott be without derivatives? Simply a juggler or a Ballroom Dancer?

Haug : Where did you grow up?

Wilmott : I grew up in the north west of England, in a place called Birkenhead, in Mersey-side – the opposite side of the river Mersey from Liverpool.

Haug : What is your educational background?

Wilmott : School, school, more school. Undergraduate in Maths at Oxford, and then a DPhil at Oxford, both at St Catherine's college, and always in Mathematics, and as applied mathematics as possible.

Haug : When did you become involved in ballroom dancing and juggling and did it involve stochastic calculus?

Wilmott : I did indeed once upon a time do ballroom dancing. I did compete for Oxford University. Actually, I'm a triple half blue, because I competed against Cambridge three times. And juggling – for a while in my twenties I was a professional juggler with a troupe of jugglers called the Dab Hands. There was a period in my life when juggling was the only source of income I had. Funny you should mention juggling because the great Claude Shannon of Information Theory built a mechanical juggler as well as being very successful in terms of investing.

Haug : You started out in academia, at Oxford, and then decided to leave in order to become more involved in practice, what made you take this decision?

Wilmott : The decision was a mutual one – Oxford and I didn't get on as well as perhaps we could have done, and after 21 years we decided by mutual consent that a separation was probably the best way forward.

Haug : Having worked both in academia and practice what is the main difference?

Wilmott : The main difference has to be the politics, and in my case the freedom. There's an awful lot more politics in academia. And of course because I'm self-employed there's absolutely no politics in my life right now and I'm sure all my employees would agree with me on that.

Haug : If one resorts to dynamic delta hedging an important question is what volatility to use to calculate the delta. You have recently done some interesting research on this topic, can you tell us briefly about this?

Wilmott : I'm glad you asked that question. This is something which is very little understood. Let me give you a very simple example. You see an option in the market, trading at a 20 % volatility. But you think that volatility's going to be 40 % and let's suppose that you are the world's greatest statistician, so 40 % it will be. So that option is cheap. How can you make money from that option? Well obviously you buy the option. To get at the volatility you need to hedge but do you hedge with the 20 % market volatility or the 40 % that you believe in. This is a very fundamental question, very little addressed in the textbooks at all. And I expect that the reasons it's not addressed in the textbooks is because it assumes that there are arbitrage opportunities, shock horror. And of course, we're all brought up to believe in no arbitrage.

Haug : You also don't like risk-neutral valuation too much, do we have a practical alternative?

Wilmott : I love risk neutral valuation! I would have its children if I could. The only thing about risk neutral valuation is that it gets people thinking too abstractly about what is really a very concrete problem. And really the problem is about hedging. I mean in the real world you can't hedge as well as people say you can in the textbooks, and so once you move outside that nice comfortable risk-neutral world suddenly things are not as straightforward as one is led to believe and real distributions do start to raise their ugly heads, I'm afraid.

Haug : Models are only models, on the one hand we want a model to be as realistic as possible, on the other hand traders often prefer simple models, where is the trade off?

Wilmott : Well, I've seen this first hand because I started life in quantitative finance going back, gosh, twenty years, and in those days working in academia I didn't see people in banks very much. So worked in a very isolated, antiseptic environment where there was no talk about data analysis. I worked on these wonderful models which in practice aren't necessarily that great because of volatility – volatility is not the nice constant for example that you'd read about in early research papers. I started to do most of my research based in this very nice simplistic world, and then as I had more contact with banks and started looking at data I quickly realized that the assumptions in the models were not that great so I started doing more complicated models, in particular, volatility models. And then, when I became the partner in a hedge fund and had to do this for real, all my fancy volatility models may be fantastic, but they were just too darn slow to use in practice, so I've now gone full circle, back to using very simple fast models but understanding about the pitfalls, not dissimilar to your own "Know Your Weapon" articles [that can be found in this book].

Haug : In one of the chapters of your book "Paul Wilmott on Quantitative Finance" you describe interest-rate modeling without resorting to probabilities, how is this possible?

Wilmott : Well this comes from the idea that interest rate models, as a class of models, are notoriously bad, I think it was Emanuel Derman who said, and if it wasn't, whoever it was I apologize, that to appreciate how bad the models are in finance you have to have seen good models. And because I've come from a hard-science background I've seen lots of good models. I know how bad the models are in finance. People who come to finance, from econometrics for example, think the financial models are fantastic. The uncertain interest rate model is in the framework designed to try and do build a model which is scientifically accurate as possible, and it side-steps the whole stochastic framework by talking about uncertainties in interest rates. And instead of having a probabilistic model, with expectations, real or risk neutral, we have an uncertain interest-rate model with no talk about probabilities, instead you talk about worst-case scenarios – what is the worst possible thing that could happen to interest-rates for your portfolio and it's a completely different framework.

Haug : You have done some work on optimal static hedging, how does this work and what types of assets and risk can it hedge?

Wilmott : Optimal static hedging, yes this is about hedging your exotic options with vanilla options to try and reduce as much as possible model risk. And there's a lot of work in the literature about how to do this. The approach I like is that of for example Marco Avellaneda on his uncertain volatility models. Anytime you have a non-linear model, and his uncertain volatility model is an example of this. Whenever you have a non-linear model you have the wonderful situation that you gather a portfolio of options – let's call them option A and option B, then the value of the portfolio made up of A and B is not the same as the value of A plus the value of B. In particular the value of A plus B, the portfolio A plus B is going to be no less than – possibly greater than – the value of A plus the value of B, so because of nonlinearity you can have benefits hedging an exotic with a vanilla. You have some exotic that's worth 10 and you see some vanilla trading at 5, you buy this vanilla, put it into your portfolio and now you've got a portfolio that's worth 17. Not 10 plus 5, but 17. And that's the beauty of nonlinearity.

Haug : How is your risk management invention, CrashMetrics different from risk measures like VaR and stress testing?

Wilmott : It is a form of stress testing – a very extreme form of stress testing – where you assume that the correlation between all assets are one or minus one. And this is relevant when you have crashes or extreme markets. Now when you have an extreme market you find the market all moves south together, you don't have some things going down and some things going up – you have a great deal of perfect correlation – so the mathematics of your portfolio becomes very, very simple when you have perfect correlation. Suppose you've got a thousand different underlyings. If you want to plot a picture of how the value of your portfolio varies with these thousand underlyings, you need to be able to plot something in a thousand and one dimensions. Just think of the vertical axis as being the value of the portfolio and the thousand horizontal axes as being the individual stocks. If you have a crash and everything becomes perfectly correlated then the thousand and one dimensions can be drawn much simpler on a two dimensional picture, the vertical access being portfolio value and the horizontal axis being some measure of the market as a whole because everything is correlated to the market as a whole. So this is the idea of CrashMetrics – very simple to implement, very robust – we like it, investors like it.

Haug : When calibrating any model there must be a risk that we underestimate tail events, even if we include the crash of 87 in our model there is no guarantee that we will not see a bigger crash or disaster in the future, how can we take this into account?

Wilmott : This is very true, but then we also have to make a living and I don't really see this is any different philosophically from how we run our daily life. When we're crossing the street we are used to dealing with cars, buses, the cyclists of course crashing into us, but we are used to avoiding these things, and so we build these into our models of crossing roads. And it's the same with finance, we don't think when we're crossing a road that we are going to be abducted by an alien – well apparently 2 % of Americans do believe that they've been abducted by aliens so maybe this isn't relevant in the States, anyway we don't, at least I don't, worry about being abducted by an alien when I am crossing the street. Similarly when I'm building a portfolio I will try and build in as many things that are realistically possible – maybe think outside the box a little bit – but there's usually a common sense.

Haug : Many investors investing in hedge funds seem to focus on Sharpe Ratios, but how good are Sharpe Ratios for describing risk reward in portfolios that often contain many of derivatives instruments?

Wilmott : Sharpe Ratio is very good when you have the conditions that are right for the central limit theorem, because the central limit theorem tells us that if we have a lot of random things and we add them up we're going to get normal distribution and the normal distribution depends on means and standard deviations of the individual things in our portfolio. So the question really is: under what conditions does the central limit theorem hold. And there are things like independence of events, identical distribution, large numbers of events, finite variance. And these are all wrong to a greater of lesser degree in finance, but I don't think these are so wrong that we should just throw away Sharpe Ratios, I think Sharpe Ratios are still a fantastic starting point for measuring portfolio performance.

Haug : There is a great deal of focus on stochastic volatility, but what about jumps in volatility? How is this affecting valuation of options and other derivatives?

Wilmott : Yes, you can go as far as you want in terms of modeling volatility stochastically and jumps et cetera, and I suspect that when people do this most people are doing this because it's in the recipe book for modeling. If you can imagine a recipe book for Modeling in Finance, and in the first part of this recipe book where you'd normally have starters and soups you'll have deterministic models and deterministic volatility and local volatility certainly. And then for the main courses you would have stochastic volatility, stochastic models for things, and then the dessert part of the cookbook is, in this case, it is a jump in whatever you are modeling, a jump in volatility. So you see people using their recipe book in this fashion without thinking too much outside the box, unfortunately.

Haug : Why do you typically prefer finite difference implementations instead of trees?

Wilmott : Trees are just a simple version of finite difference methods, so I don't have anything against trees; I just think there are so many more sophisticated versions outside the simple tree models that I'd rather work with. Don't forget how long the tree model the Binomial tree has been around. It was published in finance in the 1970s but it was used going back to 1911 by someone called Richardson who used it for solving equations for weather forecasting. So the typical binomial tree which you see in textbooks is nearly a hundred years old now.

Haug : How many assets (or stochastic variables) can be implemented practically in finite difference methods?

Wilmott : I usually stop at three, so I'd have three stochastic variables and one time. That's about where you'd go over to Monte Carlo.

Haug : Did you ever get fed up with quantitative finance?

Wilmott : Er, can we cut that?

[short pause before interview is resumed]

Haug : I know you also like to gamble, what is so fascinating about Blackjack and poker?

Wilmott : Well I don't actually. I don't like to gamble. This goes back to my times at school as a 13 year-old playing Blackjack, or Pontoon as we used to call it, and Three Card Brag – I can't even remember what three card brag is now but it's a simple version of poker – playing these at school. Although I think I was moderately successful I do still bear the scars of a few rather large monetary losses. We are still talking pennies, but I never really recovered, so by nature I am now financially very risk averse, so no I don't like gambling.

Haug : How can you make sure you have an edge in Blackjack and what about trading?

Wilmott : It's much harder to have an edge in Blackjack now than it used to be. To win at Blackjack you need to know about ideas of what is the optimum strategy. Do you take a card, do you stand, do you split pairs, that kind of thing, double down. And that's based on the cards that you have and the card that the dealer is showing. So you need to know what the optimum strategy is first of all, and that's a matter of memorizing various tables. But then even after that, that still doesn't mean you'll win. You need also to have an idea of what's left in the deck, which means you need this idea of counting cards. Keeping track for example of how many high count cards there are versus low count cards, the more high-count cards and aces there are in a deck, the better for you. And then finally you need to be able to manage money, which means, once you've found yourself in a position where the cards are favorable because a lot of low cards have left the deck, you need to know how much should you bet. You roughly speaking size the bet with the edge that you have. So these are three skills you need. You also need a lot patience, you need to be able to drink vast quantities of alcohol without impairing your decision-making, very difficult these days. Very difficult.

Haug : Do you have any hobbies outside quantitative finance?

Wilmott : Certainly not.

Haug : Do you discuss quantitative finance with your beautiful wife?

Wilmott : We discuss all sorts of exciting things – quantitative finance being just one of them.

Haug : Is your wife the silhouette on the cover of "The Best of Wilmott One"?

Wilmott : Is this another one of those scandalous rumors about me? Shocking.

Haug : You include Wilmott in the title of all your books, etc., are you trying to become the Donald Trump of quantitative finance?

Wilmott : I do have a modicum of talent for self-publicity so I've been told, but then I do believe that everyone should attach their names to everything they do.

Haug : What is the biggest tail event you have experienced in life?

Wilmott : Actually, my life is pretty much only tail events. I rarely experience anything within two standard deviations of normal. Mostly they've been good tail events, not always, but one gets used to them, and you get to enjoy them perhaps.

Haug : How important is it to have some programming skills for someone trying to develop new quant finance models?

Wilmott : I think it's very important to have some programming skills. They don't have to be sophisticated, just a little bit of VB or spreadsheets so you can implement your ideas and test them out. This is a fantastic subject for trying out new ideas and I don't think people should be dissuaded too much by received wisdom. You can experiment quite a lot and if you can program then you can experiment even more.

Haug : Most investment banks and hedge funds pay a bonus on an annual basis, I would think this could encourage traders to sell risk premium (tail even risk). This is so that they with a large probability would get high return this year, even if they know they will blow up sooner or later, do you have any views on this?

Wilmott : That is true – I think something like that is really more about personality types than about people making rational decisions, I don't think people will say "Hey look this is how I'm being compensated so the rational thing to do is X", I think people are naturally either risk averse, or risk-taking, and although they will exploit this, I don't think it will be a rational thing – I think it would be more a case that there aren't enough controls on people's activities as perhaps there should be. I do think that the human element within this business of finance is the most important in terms of blow up and extreme events are concerned. I am much more worried about operational risk for example than I am about trading loss.

Haug : Is the underlying asset price behavior independent of the trading in derivatives and the valuation models used, or can it be that the derivatives market affects the asset price behavior itself?

Wilmott : Well you do see this in the convertible bond markets, because almost all convertible bonds are now held by hedge funds and these hedge funds are all delta hedging in the same way and they are all long convertible bonds, so typically they will be selling stock for hedging. So you do find that as the stock goes up they will be selling more stock to hedge and so that causes the stock to go down. So stock goes up, goes down again; stock goes down, goes up again. It's a kind of stabilizing or volatility reducing effect. You see this happening. I have done some work with the great Philipp Schöenbucher, the credit derivatives man, whom I was fortunate to have for a student for a year and we did some work on this feedback effect.

Haug : If derivatives trading and replication of derivatives affects the underlying asset itself then how can it be that all modern finance theory simply concentrates on modeling the underlying asset completely independent of the derivative instrument?

Wilmott : Because most people work in the comfort zone of modeling and this kind of thing is very much outside most people's comfort zone. I think there's a lot more scope outside the comfort zone, the classical no arbitrage, complete markets world, I think there's a lot more scope for more interesting work, and that's the kind of place I like to fool around in.

Haug : That derivatives trading and replication affect the underlying asset and that the underlying asset affects the derivative instrument seems to be dangerous particularly in market crashes?

Wilmott : I am told that one of the explanations for the '87 crash is of course portfolio insurance, a dynamic version of portfolio insurance.

Haug : We live in a time of globalization and particularly when it comes to financial instruments, derivatives and trading, has this reduced or increased the total risk?

Wilmott : Oh definitely increased the total risk. Definitely increased it. The issue really is that there are so many more instruments being traded for pure speculation purposes than there are say for hedging. Only a tiny percent of FX trades are associated with people who have a genuine exposure to exchange rates, the rest are just people just speculating. I think that's a very dangerous situation. But there are so many possible effects of globalization that we should worry about much more than finance.

Haug : What about the OTC market? A large proportion of outstanding derivatives is concentrated on a few massive banks that have exposure to other massive banks, is there a chance one of these banks could default in some type of market crash, and is there a danger for chain reactions, or should we expect these banks with their many PhD's and quants to have mastered the art of risk control?

Wilmott : Yes definitely very serious danger. I don't think having any number of PhDs or quants is necessarily going to help the situation. Not that I've got anything against quants, because I am one, I think in this business people do tend to concentrate on the details, they don't see the bigger picture too much, it's a case of not being able to see the wood for the trees, and also I don't think there's really much incentive for people to look at the bigger picture, unfortunately.

Haug : Why do financial researchers always start with continuous time and then use numerical methods like trees, finite difference or Monte Carlo simulation to approximate the continuous process? I thought that price movement and possibly even time are discrete, so why not the other way around? All price moves that I have seen in practice are discrete, and my clock says tick tick tick, do you have any views on this?

Wilmott : Two things: one is that it's much easier to solve the continuous problems than the discrete problems, whether that's analytically or numerically – it's a much more user-friendly, shall we say, framework. However, the fact that the market moves are not continuous – and in particular if you're talking about derivatives, if you have to hedge discretely that has a really, really big effect on your P&L. Just do a Monte Carlo simulation of an option, doing the delta hedging and just see how far off your P&L is and what it should be. A correctly priced option, delta hedged should give you zero profit – see what happens, and you might be surprised at what the error is.

Haug : In your view where are we in the evolution of quantitative finance?

Wilmott : Well I think – I think, you mentioned about globalization and disasters, I wouldn't be at all surprised if within in a few years we are all living back in caves, thanks to globalization. In particular, lawyers are going to cause the downfall of mankind, way before we start working on our seven factor this, that and the other model, we'll all be back living in caves, but lawyers will be living in bigger caves than anyone else.

Haug : Where can people find out more about your theories?

Wilmott : My theories about caves? In "Paul Wilmott on Quantitative Finance" 2nd edition – available in all good bookshops.

REFERENCES

■ Ahmad, R. and P. Wilmott (2005) "Which Free Lunch Would You Like Today, Sir?: Delta Hedging, Volatility Arbitrage and Optimal Portfolios" *Wilmott Magazine*, Nov/Dec, 64–79.
■ Schönbucher, P. and P. Wilmott (2000) "The Feedback Effect of Hedging in Illiquid Markets" *SIAM Journal of Applied Mathematics*, **61**(1), 232–272.
■ Sharpe, W. (1966) "Mutual Fund Performance" *Journal of Business*, 119–138.
■ Wilmott, P. (2006) *Paul Wilmott on Quantitative Finance*, 2nd edn. New York: John Wiley & Sons, Inc.
■ Wilmott, P., J. Dewynne and S. Howison (1993) *Option Pricing: Mathematical Models and Computation*. Oxford: Oxford Financial Press.
■ Wilmott, P. (Ed.) (2004) *The Best of Wilmott 1 : Incorporating the Quantitative Finance Review*. New York: John Wiley & Sons, Inc.

Espen Haug

13

Space-time Finance The Relativity Theory's Implications for Mathematical Finance*

Little or nothing is written about the relativity theory in relation to mathematical finance. I will here explore the relativity theory's implications for mathematical finance. One of the main results of my reflections on this topic is that the volatility σ is different for every observer. However, what we will call volatility-time $\sigma\sqrt{T}$ is invariant, that is the same for any observer. Further, we will see how the relativity theory will lead possibly to fat tailed distributions and stochastic volatility. Parts of the chapter are admittedly speculative, but not even mathematical finance can escape the fundamental laws of physics.

1   Introduction

The wind was blowing through my hair, I was pushing my Harley to the limit. At 120 miles per hour the 50 mile trip felt like nothing, I slowed down and stopped in front of my girlfriend. She had been waiting on the side walk with a clock that we had synchronized with my wristwatch just before the ride. She gave me her clock. I compared it with my wristwatch. Huh, they showed exactly the same time, not even one hundredth of a second in difference, where was the time dilation? Well, this was some years ago, before I understood that my bike actually hardly moved and that my wristwatch was not accurate enough to measure the slight time dilation that should have been there as predicted by the special theory of relativity.

Einstein's special and general relativity theories are considered to be among the greatest scientific discoveries of our time. Besides having changed our view of the universe, they have practical implications for nuclear physics, particle physics, navigation, metrology, geodesy, and cosmology (see Barone, 1998 for more detail). Strange enough, with the thousands of papers[1]

*I would like to thank Gabriel Barton, Peter Carr, Jørgen Haug, John Ping Shu, Alireza Javaheri, Ronald R. Hatch for useful help and discussions. Any errors or fatal views are naturally my own responsibility.

and books written about relativity and its various implications little or nothing is written about its implications for mathematical finance.[2] In the Wall Street Journal, 21 November 2003, I read about relativity and how physicists were looking at how we might travel through time. Disappointingly not even in the Wall Street Journal is there a single word on how relativity can, will and possibly is already affecting quantitative finance.

In this chapter I take a look at the relativity theory and its implications for mathematical finance. Combining relativity theory with finance, I am naturally running the risk of being considered a crank, but what the heck – I can afford to take that chance: I'm not a Professor who has to publish in conservative academic journals (publish or perish) in order to keep a low paid job.

The present theories of mathematical finance hold only for a society in which we all travel at approximately the same speed and are affected by approximately the same gravitation. It is reasonable to believe that the human race will develop fast moving spacecraft for interstellar travel. There is also a positive probability that we one day will find intelligent life in other places in the universe where the gravitation is much higher than on earth – or maybe aliens will first find us. Going from a world economy to a universe economy will have important implications for financial calculations, just as results for a model of a closed economy might not carry through to an open economy. Almost every formula and theory in mathematical finance has to be modified or generalized. Generalization of the mathematical finance theory that will hold in any part of the universe at any velocity and gravitation is what I will call Space-time Finance.

Most traders I know are typically concerned only with the next minute (spot traders), a day, a week or at maximum a few years in the future. When it comes to the non-financial aspects of life most people appear to be interested in the time frame of a few generations at most. Developing spacecraft traveling at speeds close to the speed of light or making contact with intelligent life could easily take many more generations. For this reason I expect that this chapter in all likelihood will have little or no practical relevance to readers of our time. However, this chapter could hopefully have some entertainment value for the curious mind. Without any direct comparison, recall that Bachelier's (1900) theory on option pricing gathered dust for more than 50 years before attracting wide attention. There are also examples in physics of crazy ideas that later had a real-world impact: in 1895 the President of the Royal Society (in science), Lord Kelvin, claimed that "heavier-than-air flying machines are impossible". His claim was based on our best understanding of physics at that time. Just a few years later in 1903, as we all know, the Wright brothers achieved the "impossible". So travel at speeds significantly close to that of light may not be that far fetched after all.

With billions of galaxies, more solar systems, and probably even more planets there could easily be civilisations on other planets that are far more advanced than ours. Interestingly, some of these civilisations are possibly already using Space-time Finance. Not having developed colonies travelling at speeds close to the speed of light is no excuse for us not to start developing the mathematical finance necessary for participating in a universe economy – especially considering the cost when some of us are nutty enough to consider it a fun spare time activity.

> What is the difference between reality and fiction? In fiction everything has to make sense. I will tell you about the reality.

1.1 The Special Relativity Theory

The relativity theory is far from a one man show, even if Einstein played a major role in the development of the theory as we know it today. When Einstein wrote his 1905 paper on special relativity, the basis for his theory was already laid out by giants like Larmor, Fitzergald, Lorentz, and Poincaré. There is no doubt that Einstein, with his very intuitive mind, came up with many key insights for the foundation of relativity theory. For example, Einstein was the first to understand properly the physical implications of time dilation.[3] Lorentz himself initially did not believe in time dilation, which was a result of his own transformation[4] (Lorentz, 1904), that Einstein based much of his work on. Lorentz himself said:

> But I never thought this had anything to do with real time ... there existed for me only one true time. I considered by time-transformation only a heuristic working hypothesis ...

In his 1909 paper Lorentz took time dilation seriously and formulated a relativity theory closely related to Einstein's special relativity theory. More on this later.

Einstein based his special relativity theory on two postulates (Einstein 1905, Einstein 1912):

1. *Principle of special relativity:* All inertial observers are equivalent.
2. *Constancy of velocity of light:* The velocity of light is the same in all inertial systems.

Einstein accepted that the speed of light had to be constant in any frame (we will discuss this in more detail later), and he figured out that something else had to vary: time. Time dilation will play a central role in space-time finance. Even though time dilation is covered in any basic book on special relativity, we will spend some time on the basics here before we move on to Space-time Finance. Before that a few basic definitions are in order:

Reference frame   In most of our examples we will use two reference frames. First, a stationary inertial frame, which obeys Newton's first law of motion. Any object or body in such a frame will continue in a state of rest or with constant velocity and is not acted on by any forces external to itself. In most examples we will for simplicity assume that the earth and everything on it is a stationary inertial frame. We will later loosen up on this assumption.

Second, as a moving frame we will typically use a spacecraft leaving and returning to Earth. This is actually a non-inertial frame as the spacecraft must accelerate and decelerate. To begin with we will assume this is an inertial frame. We will later look at more realistic calculations where we directly take account of the acceleration.

Observer   With observer we think about anyone in the same frame. This can be a person (possibly hypothetical) or a clock, or even a computer calculating the volatility of a stock.

Asset frame   Where in space-time does an asset trade? One could possibly think that the properties of a financial asset are independent of where the asset trades, since it is not a physical object. This holds only because all humans at the current time are in approximately the same frame. In Space-time Finance the exact space-time location of the trade will have an impact. For a gold futures listed at COMEX (the metal exchange) the exact location will typically be in the trading pit in New York, downtown Manhattan. For a electronic market the trade would typically take place in a computer. The computer will be in a place in space and the trade will be executed at a given time inside the computer. Thus, any trade takes place in an exact point in space-time. After the computer accepts the trade it is too late for anyone to cancel it, even if the trader is far away and possibly not even aware that the trade has been carried out.

Buying or selling a securities in a location very far from you could make it difficult to communicate with each other, due to the maximum speed limit of any signal. For example how could you trade a security on earth if you lived one light year away in a space station? This could easily be solved by having someone close to the location managing your investment.

Proper time and proper volatility   The proper time is the time measured by one and the same clock at the location of the events. That is we can think about a clock "attached" to the object or even the asset we are considering. For example, a wristwatch worn by the same person could measure the proper time for a lifespan of this person, another name for proper time is wristwatch time. "Attaching" a clock to an asset could be done for example by measuring the time with the same computer as where the trade took place. The proper volatility of an asset will be the volatility as measured in the proper time of the asset.

2   Time Dilation

High speed velocity leads to several unexpected effects, like time dilation, length contractions, relativistic mass, and more. All these effects can be predicted using Einstein's special relativity theory. The time elapsed for a stationary observer T and a moving observer $\hat{T}$ is related by the simple, yet powerful formula

$$T = \frac{\hat{T}}{\sqrt{1 - \frac{v^2}{c^2}}}, \tag{13.1}$$

where v is the velocity of the moving observer, and c the speed of light in vacuum. See Appendix A for a short summary of one way to come up with this formula.

2.1   The Twin "Paradox"

Special relativity induces effects that can seem counter intuitive at first. Probably the best known of these is the twin paradox (also known as the clock paradox), see for example Taylor and Wheeler (1992), Sartori (1996), Tipler and Llewellyn (1999), Ellis and Williams (2000). As the twin paradox will play an important role in space-time finance a short introduction to the topic is in order. The twin paradox is basically about two identical twins, let's name them Tore and Kjell. Tore is leaving earth in a spacecraft that travels at a constant velocity of 80 % of the speed of light, $0.8c$, to the star Alpha Centauri approximately 4.2 light years away. When the spaceship reaches Alpha Centauri it instantaneously turns and returns to earth.

The paradox arises because either twin can claim that it is the other twin who is in motion relative to him. But then each twin should expect to find his twin brother younger than himself. The mistake is that we assume the situation is symmetric for the two twins. Einstein had predicted there had to be an asymmetry, and that the twin leaving in the spaceship would end up being younger. In the 1950s and 1960s there was a lively discussion over the twin paradox. Professor of Philosophy Dingle (1956) published a paper in "Nature" where he attacked Einstein's relativity theory. He claimed that the twin paradox could not be resolved and that for this reason the special relativity theory was inconsistent. There then followed a series of papers dissecting the twin paradox (see Sartori (1996) and Marder (1971) for a good reference list). The theoretical discussion came out in Einstein's favor.

A few years later the asymmetric solution to the twin paradox was tested experimentally. Haefele proposed flying atomic clocks around the earth, (Haefele 1970, Haefele 1971), and carried it out in collaboration with Keating, in 1971. After flying highly accurate atomic clocks around the world, they compared their readings with identical clocks left on the ground. The results were unmistakable: time ran more slowly in the airplane than on the ground by the exact amount predicted by Einstein's theory, (Haefele and Keating 1971b, Haefele and Keating 1971a).

Back to the twins. The twin leaving in the spacecraft has to accelerate and decelerate to get back to earth. This makes the situation asymmetric between the two twins. An observer that has to accelerate before reunion with someone that has moved at a uniform velocity (inertial frame) must have traveled faster. However the acceleration itself is not affecting time directly, only indirectly because acceleration affects velocity. This hypothesis, used implicitly by Einstein in 1905, was confirmed by the famous time decay experiment on muons at CERN. The experiment accelerated the muons to 10^{18}g, and showed that all of the time dilation was due to velocity (Bailey et al., 1977). The twin paradox and its time dilation will be the foundations for much of our Space-time Finance. Several other experiments are consistent with the time dilation predicted by the special relativity theory.

2.2 The Current Stage of Space-Time Finance

A relevant question is how fast we need to move for Space-time Finance to have any practical implications. The relativity theory already has practical implications for navigation, metrology, communication and cosmology. It turns out that we already have the technology and people to conduct an experiment with measurable effects for Space-time Finance. The technology in question is the space shuttle. The space shuttle has a typical velocity of about 17,300 miles per hour (27,853 kph). Let us, for simplicity's sake, assume that a dollar billionaire got a free ticket to travel on the space shuttle. Further, assume that he leaves 1 billion dollars in a bank that pays interest equivalent to 10 % compounding annually, but compounding every thousandth of a second to make the calculation more accurate. The speed of the space shuttle is 7,737 meters per second. If the billionaire travels for one year in the space shuttle, or 31,536,000,000 thousandths of seconds, then the time gone by at earth is

$$T = \frac{31,536,000,000}{\sqrt{1 - \frac{7,737^2}{299,800,000^2}}} \approx 31,536,000,011$$

If the billionaire spends one year on Earth then according to his wristwatch he will receive $ 100,000,000.00 in interest income, while he will receive $ 100,000,000.04 in interest rate income if he stays one year in space as measured by his wristwatch. That is a difference of 4 cents. This is a measurable quantity of money, but of course not economically significant, especially not for someone already a billionaire. The barrier to significant profits is that we are at a very early stage of space travel.

3 Advanced Stage of Space-time Finance

3.1 Relativistic Foreign Exchange Rates

When, and if, humans develop large spacecraft transporting populations that travel at speeds close to that of light, why not also have them develop their own currencies? We will now extend the theory of currency exchange to a world with stationary and moving populations. In order to simplify assume that there are only two populations. One is stationary, for example Earth, and one is moving relative to Earth, for example a large space station. Denote the currency on the space station by Moving Currency Dollars (*MCD*) while on Earth we simply assume that everybody is using EURO (*EUR*). The space station has not left Earth yet. Further, assume that the continuously compounded rate is r_m and r in the spacecraft economy and on Earth respectively. The assumption of constant rates can easily be extended to stochastic interest rates. So far this is just like having two different currencies on Earth. Let's say the spot currency exchange rate is quoted as *MCD* per *EUR*, $H = \frac{MCD}{EUR}$. To prevent arbitrage the forward rate F expiring at a future earth time T, must then be

$$F = He^{(r_m - r)T},$$

Assume now that the space station leaves Earth at a uniform speed v to return when the currency forward expires (we are ignoring acceleration for now). It is now necessary to take into account relativistic interest rates. Denote the rate on earth as observed from the moving frame $\hat{r}$, and similarly the rate on the spacecraft as observed in the stationary frame $\hat{r}_m$. To avoid any arbitrage opportunities we must have

$$\hat{r} = \frac{r}{\sqrt{1 - \frac{v^2}{c^2}}},$$

and

$$\hat{r}_m = r_m \sqrt{1 - \frac{v^2}{c^2}}.$$

The currency forward as observed from the spacecraft time must be

$$\hat{F} = He^{(r_m - \hat{r})\hat{T}}.$$

Similarly the forward price at Earth must be

$$F = He^{(\hat{r}_m - r)T},$$

which naturally implies $F = \hat{F}$ to prevent arbitrage opportunities. Similar relationships will hold between any dividend yields or cost of carry on any asset.

A special, but unlikely case is when the proper risk free rates are identical in the two economies $r_f = r$. In this case the stationary Earth currency *EUR* will appreciate against the other currency. The intuition behind this is simply that if we assume the two worlds start with exactly the same resources and technology, the productivity on the moving space station will still be much lower because time and all physiological processes are slowed down. The total rate of return can of course still be higher in the space station if the rate of return is high enough to offset time dilation. The space-time equivalent rate (break-even rate) of return on the space station is simply

$$r_m = \frac{r}{\sqrt{1 - \frac{v^2}{c^2}}}.$$

Consider for instance a rate of return of 5 % on Earth, and that the space station moves at half the speed of light. Then the rate of return on the space station must be 5.77 % per year to give the same return per year as on Earth. Traveling at 98 % of the speed of light the rate of return on the space station must be 25.13 % to offset the time advantage (faster moving time) of the stationary population.

4 Space-time Uncertainty

Geometric Brownian motion assumes constant volatility. This can only be true in an inertial frame where everybody is traveling at the same speed. If we are comparing geometric Brownian motion (or any other stochastic process) in different frames then strange effects appear.

4.1 Relativistic Uncertainty

In the case of one moving frame and one stationary frame we will no longer have one volatility for a given security, but two. If the asset trades on Earth we will have

- the volatility of the asset in the stationary frame, σ, (for example Earth – the proper Earth volatility).
- the volatility of the Earth asset as observed in the moving frame, $\hat{\sigma}$, (spacecraft).

Consider a spacecraft leaving Earth at speed significant to that of light, to return at a later time. Mr X on the spacecraft buys an option on IBM corp. that trades at one of the main exchanges on Earth from Mrs Y who lives on Earth. For simplicity's sake let us assume that the stock price in an inertial frame follows a geometric Brownian in its stationary frame on Earth[5]

$$dS_t = \mu S_t dt + \sigma S_t dz.$$

In the frame of the moving observer (the spacecraft) what volatility must be observed for the stock price to make the option arbitrage free with respect to Earth-inhabitants trading in the same option? The volatility measured by someone on Earth is naturally σ. Let the volatility measured by someone in spacecraft time be $\hat{\sigma}$. As we already know from Einstein's theory the time measured by each observer is different. For a European option the value naturally depends on the uncertainty in form of $\sigma \sqrt{T}$ and not on σ or T independently. This holds also for American options, although it is harder to establish (a mathematical proof is given by Carr, 1991). A contingent claim will in general depend on what we will call the uncertainty-time or volatility-time, $\sigma \sqrt{T}$. To avoid any arbitrage opportunities the relationship between the volatilities as observed in two different frames must be

$$\sigma\sqrt{T} = \hat{\sigma}\sqrt{\hat{T}}$$

$$\hat{\sigma}^2 = \sigma^2 \frac{\hat{T}}{\sqrt{1-\frac{v^2}{c^2}}}$$

$$\hat{\sigma} = \sigma\left(1 - \frac{v^2}{c^2}\right)^{-\frac{1}{4}}.$$

Similarly we can naturally have an asset trading in the moving frame. The proper volatility of that asset in its own frame we name σ_m. The same volatility as observed from the stationary frame we name $\hat{\sigma}_m$. To avoid any arbitrage opportunities we must have

$$\sigma_m\sqrt{\hat{T}} = \hat{\sigma}_m\sqrt{T}$$

$$\hat{\sigma}_m^2 = \sigma_m^2 \frac{T\sqrt{1-\frac{v^2}{c^2}}}{T}$$

$$\hat{\sigma}_m = \sigma_m\left(1 - \frac{v^2}{c^2}\right)^{\frac{1}{4}}.$$

These are relativistic volatilities. The geometric Brownian motion of an asset trading on Earth, as observed by a moving observer, must behave according to what we will call a velocity-moved geometric Brownian motion. The various parameters in the model are shifting their value due to the velocity of the moving frame,

$$dS_{\hat{t}} = \hat{r}S_{\hat{t}}d\hat{t} + \hat{\sigma}S_{\hat{t}}dz$$

Similarly, the velocity-moved geometric Brownian motion of an asset trading in the space station, as observed by a stationary observer, must be

$$dS_t = \hat{r}_m S_t dt + \hat{\sigma}_m S_t dz$$

Invariant Uncertainty-Time Interval From the special relativity theory it is well known that the time interval and distances will look different for different observers, due to time dilation and length contraction. However the space-time interval[6] is invariant, i.e. the same for all observers. A similar relationship must exist when it comes to uncertainty:

> The volatility of an asset, σ and the time, T, will look different for different observers. However the uncertainty-time interval, $\sigma^2 T$, of an asset will be the same for all observers.

Invariant uncertainty-time interval is actually a condition for no arbitrage in Space-time Finance. The "shape" of the uncertainty-time interval can naturally be different for different stochastic

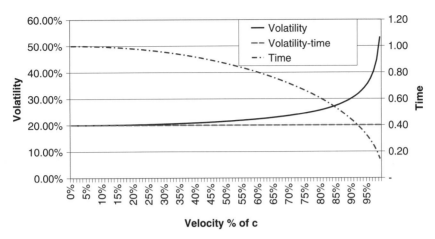

Figure 13.1

processes. Instead of, for instance, $\sigma\sqrt{T}$ we could have a square root $\sqrt{\sigma}\sqrt{T}$, or a $\sigma^{\frac{3}{2}}\sqrt{T}$ volatility process.[7] Time and uncertainty are interrelated and cannot be separated. Even if different observers observe different volatility and time for an asset trading in a given place in space and time (over time), they will all agree on the uncertainty-time. For this reason all agree on the same price for the derivative security, based on the assumption of flat space-time. In addition to velocity we must also take into account curved space-time, as we will soon do. Figure 13.1 illustrates relativistic time T, volatility σ, and volatility-time $\sigma\sqrt{T}$ for a security trading on Earth (stationary frame), as observed from a moving frame at different velocities. The time frame is one year in stationary time. Volatility and volatility-time is measured along the left y-axis, and time against the right y-axis. Time and volatility evidently varies with the velocity, while volatility-time remains constant.

5   Is High Speed Velocity Possible?

We have seen that a trip in today's spacecraft has a measurable effect in terms of Space-time Finance. However, to say that the effect is economically significant would be a gross overstatement. For this to happen we would need a much faster means of travel.

Science fiction books and movies often involve spacecraft traveling at extremely high velocities. It is important to also have in mind that the high velocity travel must be within the laws of physics, and it must also be physiologically possible for humans to survive the trip. For example a spacecraft accelerating at 1000g would get very fast up to high speeds, but the g-force is far beyond what any human can withstand. We will here give a short summary of what can actually be possible in the future when it comes to high velocity travel. Marder (1971) discusses the theoretical and technological limits of space travel, and this section will take as its basis his calculations (see also Barton, 1999 and Nahin, 1998).

Let us assume that we have a spaceship accelerating at 1g. As this is equivalent to the gravitation on Earth such a spaceship would naturally be a very comfortable place for a human population. When we talk about gravitation we must be careful. We will assume the 1g gravitation is in the frame of the space traveler. From Earth the gravitation of the spacecraft will be observationally different. Here the acceleration of the spacecraft will approach zero as the spacecraft approaches the speed of light. Even if the special relativity is valid only for observers moving with a constant velocity (inertial frame) this does not mean that we cannot use it to predict what will happen in an accelerated frame. To do this we will make use of the "clock hypothesis". The clock hypothesis is basically a statement about the instantaneous rate of a (suitable)[8] clock depending only on its instantaneous speed. Let us define v as the speed of the spacecraft as measured from the Earth frame. Further, assume that at any instant there is a second system moving at a fixed speed V (Earth frame) moving parallel to the spacecraft (co-moving frame). The spacecraft's speed in the second system is u. If we divide the journey of the spacecraft into infinitely small time steps, dt, we can assume that the change in velocity, dv, is close to zero in such a brief time interval. In other words we can still calculate the time dilation over a very short time period using the special relativity theory

$$d\hat{t} = \sqrt{1 - \frac{v^2}{c^2}} \, dt. \tag{13.2}$$

The interval, $\hat{T}$, of "proper time" registered by the accelerated clock in its movement between t_1 and t_2 can now simply be calculated by integrating over equation (13.2)

$$\hat{T} = \int d\hat{t} = \int_{t_1}^{t_2} \sqrt{1 - \frac{v^2(t)}{c^2}} \, dt, \tag{13.3}$$

where $t_2 - t_1 > \hat{T}$ is the elapsed time between two events as measured on Earth (stationary frame). Furthermore, we have to be aware that the constant acceleration α, as observed on the spacecraft (the proper acceleration), will look different from Earth. The acceleration in the Earth frame, a is equal to (see Appendix B)

$$a = c\frac{d\beta}{dt} = \alpha(1 - \beta^2)^{3/2}, \tag{13.4}$$

where $\beta = \beta(t) = \frac{v}{c}$ the speed of the spacecraft in percentage of light in the Earth frame. Assuming the speed of the spacecraft is zero, $\beta(0) = 0$ at the start of the journey, $t = 0$, and $\beta(t) = \beta$ we can integrate

$$\int_0^t \frac{\frac{d\beta(u)}{du}}{(1 - \beta(u)^2)^{3/2}} \, du = \int_0^t \frac{\alpha}{c} \, du,$$

this gives us

$$\frac{\beta}{\sqrt{1 - \beta^2}} = \frac{\alpha t}{c}. \tag{13.5}$$

Solving for β we get

$$\beta = \frac{\alpha t/c}{\sqrt{1 + \left(\frac{\alpha t}{c}\right)^2}}. \tag{13.6}$$

Assume that the spacecraft is leaving Earth at Earth time $t_1 = 0$ and spacecraft time $\hat{t}_1 = 0$, that is $t_1 = \hat{t}_1$ at the start of the journey. The spacecraft is constantly accelerating at 1g as measured on the spacecraft for $\hat{T}$ spacecraft years (T Earth years). Next the spacecraft decelerates at the same rate until the spacecraft is at rest with respect to the stationary frame (Earth). This means that the spacecraft travels for $2\hat{T}$ spacecraft years away from Earth. The spacecraft then follows the same procedure back to Earth. The whole trip takes $4\hat{T}$ spacecraft years and $4T$ Earth years. The maximum velocity of the spacecraft is reached at time $\hat{T}$ and is given by replacing t by T in equation (13.6). We thus find that the maximum velocity as observed on Earth is

$$\beta_{\max} = \frac{\alpha T/c}{\sqrt{1 + \left(\frac{\alpha T}{c}\right)^2}}. \tag{13.7}$$

To find the distance as measured from Earth that the spacecraft will reach we need to integrate once more

$$x(t) = \int_{t_1}^{t_2} v(t)dt = \frac{c(\sqrt{\alpha^2 t^2 + c^2} - c)}{\alpha}. \tag{13.8}$$

The maximum distance in light years as measured from Earth that the spacecraft will reach after $2T$ Earth years ($2\hat{T}$ spacecraft years) is $2x(T)$.

We can next find the proper spacecraft time between event $t_1 = 0$ (the spacecraft leaving Earth) and event t_2 (the spacecraft returning to Earth) by integrating

$$\hat{T} = \int_{t_1}^{t_2} \sqrt{1 - \beta^2}dt = \int_{t_1}^{t_2} \frac{dt}{\sqrt{1 + \frac{\alpha^2 t^2}{c^2}}}, \tag{13.9}$$

carrying out the integration we get

$$\hat{T} = \frac{c}{\alpha} \ln\left(\frac{\alpha T}{c} + \sqrt{1 + \frac{\alpha^2 T^2}{c^2}}\right), \tag{13.10}$$

which can be simplified further to

$$\hat{T} = \frac{c}{\alpha} \sinh^{-1}\left(\frac{\alpha}{c}T\right), \tag{13.11}$$

or in terms of the stationary reference frame time

$$T = \frac{c}{\alpha} \sinh\left(\frac{\alpha}{c}\hat{T}\right), \tag{13.12}$$

where $\sinh()$ is the hyperbolic sine function and $\sinh^{-1}()$ is the inverse hyperbolic sine function.

Volatilities in an Accelerated Frame   We now have the tools to look at volatilities in an accelerated frame. The fact is that geometric Brownian motion can only exist at a constant velocity, in an inertial frame. With any form of acceleration the drift and also the volatility of the geometric

Brownian motion will as a minimum be a deterministic function of the velocity, as observed from any other reference frame.

From mathematical finance it is well known that we can calculate the global volatility σ over a time period starting at t_1 ending at t_2 from a local time dependent deterministic volatility $b(t)$ by the following integral

$$\sigma^2 = \frac{1}{t_2 - t_1} \int_{t_1}^{t_2} b^2(t)dt. \tag{13.13}$$

In a similar fashion we can calculate a velocity dependent deterministic volatility in an accelerating frame

$$\hat{\sigma}^2 = \frac{1}{\hat{T}} \int_{\hat{t}_1}^{\hat{t}_2} \hat{b}(\hat{t}; v)^2 d\hat{t} = \frac{1}{t_2 - t_1} \int_{t_1}^{t_2} \frac{\sigma^2 dt}{\sqrt{1 + \frac{\alpha^2 t^2}{c^2}}},$$

which gives the relationship between the volatilities in the two frames

$$\hat{\sigma} = \sigma \sqrt{\frac{c}{T\alpha} \sinh^{-1}\left(\frac{T\alpha}{c}\right)},$$

or in terms of the volatility of an asset traded in a moving frame, as observed from the stationary frame,

$$\hat{\sigma}_m = \sigma_m \sqrt{\frac{c}{\hat{T}\alpha} \sinh\left(\frac{\hat{T}\alpha}{c}\right)}.$$

Numerical Examples Table 13.1 illustrates the consequences of a spacecraft's journey accelerating at 1g. If we, for instance, take a look at a trip that takes ten years as measured by a wristwatch on the spacecraft, the time passed by on earth will be 24.45 years at return. The spacecraft reaches a maximum speed of 98.86 % of the speed of light after 2.5 years. What a velocity! And remember, we are only at 1g! The next column tells us that over 5 years, $\hat{T} = 5$, the spacecraft will be able to travel a distance of 10.92 light years (as measured from Earth). How can the spacecraft travel more than 10 light years in only 5 years? The answer is naturally because the time dilation on the spacecraft. Recall that on Earth 12.71 years have gone by at the same time. The distance as measured from the spacecraft will naturally be different.

Consider next the effects on Space-time Finance. The relativistic volatility shows the global volatility, i.e. the "average" volatility the space crew would have measured over the whole trip for a stock that on Earth had 20 % constant volatility, as measured on Earth.

The last column is the maximum level the instantaneous volatility attains, when the spacecraft reaches its maximum velocity.

TABLE 13.1: SPACECRAFT ACCELERATING CONTINUOUSLY AT 1G (9.81 M/S^2),
($C = 299,800,000$ M/S).

Roundtrip time $4\hat{T}$	Roundtrip time 4T	Maximum Speed %c	Distance light years	Volatility $\hat{\sigma}$	Maximum $\hat{b}(v(t))$
1	1.01	25.24 %	0.065	20.111 %	20.332 %
2	2.09	47.46 %	0.264	20.445 %	21.317 %
3	3.31	64.92 %	0.610	21.003 %	22.932 %
4	4.75	77.47 %	1.127	21.791 %	25.151 %
5	6.51	85.91 %	1.849	22.815 %	27.956 %
10	25.43	98.86 %	10.922	31.891 %	51.517 %
15	92.85	99.91 %	44.527	49.759 %	97.927 %
20	337.40	99.993 %	166.774	82.146 %	186.599 %
30	4,451.94	99.99996 %	2,224.030	243.637 %	677.792 %
50	775,040.09	99.99999 %	387,518.106	2,490.044 %	8,943.021 %

5.1 High Velocity Spacecraft

Today's spacecraft accelerate using mainly propulsion technologies. The energy content we get out of contemporary fuels is low. Uranium fission yields about 6 million times as much energy per kilogram as the burning of hydrogen. Fusion of hydrogen into helium (hydrogen bomb) yields another factor of 10. The most efficient energy for a given mass is achieved by the complete annihilation of matter with antimatter. This turns all mass into energy, and gives about 140 times more energy per kilogram than hydrogen fusion. One day we might be able to have spacecraft where acceleration is achieved by a matter-antimatter annihilation engine (photon engine). This is the most efficient engine we can build, and it is based on the fundamental laws of physics. For more information on this see Marder (1971).

One of the dangers with such trips would be that space is far from a perfect vacuum. Traveling through space involves frequent collisions with stray hydrogen atoms (about one for each cubic centimeter, Nahin, 1998). The result would be a high irradiation of the entire ship, with a lethal dose of gamma rays. Whether we can ever build protective shields against this is another question. Luckily there is possibly an even faster and safer means of high velocity travel, but because of limited space I will have to shy away from a discussion of this.

6 Black-Scholes in Special Relativity

In their model Black-Scholes-Merton (BSM) assumed constant volatility (geometric Brownian motion). However as we know today, the BSM model is also fully consistent with deterministic time-varying volatility. This means that it is also consistent with a deterministic velocity-dependent volatility.

In Space-time Finance we will have several versions of the BSM formula. The standard form of the BSM formula is simply a special case for a inertial frame as observed from the same frame. For an option trading on the spacecraft, on a security trading on Earth, in the Earth currency *EUR* we will have to use the velocity-moved geometric Brownian motion as the basis for the modified

BSM formula

$$dS_{\hat{t}} = \hat{r} S_{\hat{t}} d\hat{t} + \hat{\sigma} S_{\hat{t}} dz.$$

This gives us

$$c = S N(d_1) - X e^{-\hat{r}\hat{T}} N(d_2),$$

where

$$d_1 = \frac{\ln(S/X) + (\hat{r} + \hat{\sigma}^2/2)\hat{T}}{\hat{\sigma}\sqrt{\hat{T}}},$$

and

$$d_2 = \hat{\sigma}\sqrt{\hat{T}}.$$

Similarly for an option trading on Earth on an asset trading on the spacecraft we would have to replace the volatility and the risk-free rate in the Black-Scholes formula with $\hat{\sigma}_m$ and $\hat{r}_m$. Further, we could have an option trading on the spacecraft in the spacecraft currency on an asset trading on earth, or an option trading on Earth in the Earth currency (EUR) on an asset trading on the space-craft. This would complicate it further, but can easily be valued by making appropriate changes for relativistic effects in addition to using the well known techniques to value foreign equity options struck in domestic currency, as described in detail by Reiner (1992), see also Haug (1997).

6.1 Velocity Sensitivities

When trading options it is important to keep track of risks, summarized efficiently by the option sensitivities with respect to the key parameters, delta, gamma, vega, theta, etc. (see Haug, 2003). In the age of Space-time Finance it will naturally also be essential to know the derivative instruments' sensitivities to changes in velocity. The following is the sensitivity of a stationary volatility to a small change in velocity as observed by a moving observer (here we for simplicity ignore any acceleration).

$$\frac{\partial \hat{\sigma}}{\partial v} = \frac{v\sigma}{2c^2 \left(1 - \frac{v^2}{c^2}\right)^{\frac{5}{4}}}.$$

This partial derivative is positive and tells us that the stationary volatility as observed by a moving observer, in the moving frame, will increase the faster she travels.

The sensitivity of volatility in the moving frame to a small change in velocity, as observed by an observer in the stationary frame, is given by

$$\frac{\partial \hat{\sigma}_m}{\partial v} = -\frac{v\sigma_m}{2c^2 \left(1 - \frac{v^2}{c^2}\right)^{\frac{3}{4}}}.$$

As expected this partial derivative is negative. This implies that uncertainty decreases the faster the moving frame moves as observed by a stationary observer.

7 Relativity and Fat-Tailed Distributions

The distribution of many physical phenomena, including stock price returns and commodities, exhibit fat-tails. Empirically the returns are typically non-normally distributed, as opposed to, for instance, geometric Brownian motion. There can be many reasons for this phenomenon. Here we are interested in what physical laws can induce fat-tailed distributions. Assume that we observe the volatility from two moving frames with different velocity, and then look at the "portfolio" volatility. If we, for the sake of simplicity, assume that each particle has a normal distribution, the combined distribution of the two particles will often be fat tailed and leptokurtic, with Pearson kurtosis larger than 3.

7.1 Stochastic Volatility

In the real world the velocity of a single particle or a system of particles will typically change randomly over time. According to quantum mechanics and Heisenberg's uncertainty principle, it is not possible to have perfect knowledge simultaneously of both position and momentum of a particle (Heisenberg, 1927). With uncertain velocity this will lead to stochastic uncertainty-time $\sigma\sqrt{T}$, where both the volatility σ and the time T will appear stochastic. More precisely, with background in relativity theory stochastic velocity v will give us apparently stochastic volatility and time (stochastic clocks). The idea of using a stochastic clock to generate stochastic volatility (uncertainty-time) is not new to finance. It dates back to the 1970 PhD thesis of the now Professor Clark, later published in "Econometrica" (Clark, 1973). Stochastic clocks were later used as the basis for stochastic volatility models (see, for instance, Geman, Madan & Yor, 2000, Carr, Geman, Madan & Yor, 2003, and Carr & Wu, 2004). Instead of Brownian motion they consider stochastic time changed Brownian motion.

This literature makes few or no claims about what drives the stochastic clocks. At a talk at Columbia University (March 2004) Peter Carr indicated that trading volume could drive it, news coming out, etc. In Space-time Finance we need only consider what physical laws that possibly drive stochastic clocks and volatility. We can assume that velocity is stochastic and that the apparently stochastic clock simply is a deterministic function of the stochastic velocity.

Do we need to wait for the age of high velocity spacecraft before stochastic velocity changed processes will have any practical implications on mathematical finance? There is a possibility that stochastic velocity and the relativity theory is today what drives at least part of the stochastic volatility observed in financial markets, as well as any other stochastic uncertainty. The main question is probably whether relativity here on Earth has any economically significant impact on the stochastic part of volatility.

Even if we have so far assumed that the Earth is an inertial frame where we all travel at approximately the same speed with respect to light, this is not true when we are moving down at particle level. All physical macroscopic objects, like people, cars and buildings are in general traveling at the same speed relative to light. At the particle level, however, there are many particles traveling at very high speeds, or even at the speed of light. Particles are all the time emitting and absorbing photons, in the form of visible light or black body radiation. Every single particle, even photons, have in reality their own clock. The clock in a free moving photon is according to the special relativity theory "frozen": traveling at the speed of light we can cross the whole universe without any proper-time going by. A photon emitted from a particle is accelerating from zero speed to c basically instantaneously. This does not mean that we are measuring the time for every single particle here on Earth, we measure the time in the form of the time of macroscopic objects only, using atomic stationary clocks. Thus even if we are all the time affected by particles where the time and velocity are highly different from the average speed of the particles that makes up, for example, your body, we are not adjusting for this directly in our formulae. In the Earth frame we measure the time as if it was moving at one rate using atomic stationary clocks. So instead of observing stochastic clocks in other frames, they all show up as stochastic volatility, and for this reason stochastic uncertainty-time.

The number of particles that affect a stock through corporate activities; etc. at any given time is just astronomical and the number of particles affecting a stock price varies partly randomly partly deterministic over time. It is possible but not necessary that relativity theory for this reason can, to some degree, explain stochastic volatility for a security. To model the volatility of a security at particle level requires modeling the stochastic velocity and possibly other properties of each "particle" affecting the security. This requires super computers far more powerful than we can dream about today (but who knows what's around the "corner"). This would even include the physics of psychology: the human brain and its emotions that naturally lead to trades, at a quantum physics level.

It is most likely that the relativistic effects on stochastic volatility and fat-tailed phenomena are extremely small and probably not even measurable. There are other laws of physics that are much more important for stochastic volatility, jumps and fat-tailed distribution. I will publish a possible solution for this in 2007.

8   General Relativity and Space-time Finance

We have so far limited ourselves to the special theory of relativity. In 1916 Albert Einstein published his general relativity theory. The theory describes how gravity affects space-time. In the case of a spherical symmetric body (like the Earth, Sun or a black hole) Karl Schwarzschild (1873–1916) was able to come up with a beautiful closed form solution (in 1916). Just before his death, from a war-induced illness, Karl Schwarzschild sent his closed form metric solution to Einstein. Einstein wrote to him "I had not expected that the exact solution to the problem could be formulated. Your analytic treatment of the problem appears to me splendid". Karl Schwarzschild derived his closed form metric from Einstein's field equation. Einstein's field equation is given by

$$R_{ik} - \frac{1}{2}Rg_{ik} - \Lambda g_{ik} = \frac{\kappa}{c^2}T_{ik},$$

where Λ is the cosmological constant, often considered to be zero, and T_{ik} is the energy momentum tensor. The κ is Einstein's gravitational constant: $\kappa = \frac{8\pi G}{2c}$ where G is the Newtonian constant of gravitation, and c is the speed of light in vacuum. In many cases Einstein's field equation is very hard to solve and often requires numerical methods. Luckily most objects in the universe are spherical and we can use the closed form Schwarzschild metric for most practical problems. In time-like form the Schwarzschild metric is given by[9]

$$d\tau^2 = \left(1 - \frac{2M}{r}\right)dt^2 - \frac{dr^2}{\left(1 - \frac{2M}{r}\right)} - r^2 d\phi^2 \tag{13.14}$$

where τ is the proper time (wristwatch time), M is the mass of the center of attraction as measured in units of meters, r is the reduced circumference (the circumference divided by 2π), t is the far away time, ϕ is the angle and has the same meaning in Schwarzschild geometry as it does in Euclidian geometry, and $rd\phi$ is the incremental distance measured directly along the tangent to the shell. The Schwarzschild solution gives a complete description of space-time external to a spherically symmetric, non-spinning, uncharged massive body (and everywhere around a black hole but at its central crunch point, the singularity; see Taylor and Wheeler, 2000 and Misner, Thorne and Wheeler, 1973 for excellent introductions to this topic). Actually the vast majority of experimental tests of general relativity have been tests of the Schwarzschild metric. All test results have so far been consistent with Einstein's general relativity theory(?). The general relativity theory has significant implications for the General Position System (GPS). The GPS system consist of multiple satellites containing atomic clocks. The elapsed time for each atomic clock has to be adjusted for both the special and general relativity. This because the effect of Earth's gravity is lower far from Earth and also the speed at which the satellites; travel affects time. The GPS system is actively used by the military for high precision bombs, as well as for civilians like myself, to navigate the car to a new restaurant to meet up with a date.

It is the time dilation caused by gravity that is of greatest interest to space-time finance. The time-like Schwarzschild metric leads us to the formula we need:

$$d\tau = T_{shell} = T\sqrt{1 - \frac{2M}{r}}, \tag{13.15}$$

where T_{shell} is the elapsed time of a clock that is at the radius r on the shell, and T is the time leaps of a far-away time. The far-away time will in practice refer to a clock that is so far away from the gravitation source that the effects of gravitation on time is insignificant compared to the calculation we are doing. From equation (13.15) we can see that the time at the shell (and all physical processes) will go slower than the far-away time.

Next let's take a look at a numerical example (this is also the explanation behind "The Collector" cartoon in this book, as well as the animated cartoon story "Black Hole Hedge Fund"). The mass of the sun is 1,477 meters, assume a black hole with 10 solar masses (14.77 kilometers). The Schwarzschild radius of the black hole is $2M = 2 \times 14{,}770 = 29{,}540$ meters. This is the radius where there is no return (except for Hawking radiation), even light itself will be caught by the Schwarzschild radius. Assume a space station is hovering around the black hole at a radius of 29,552 meters. As the mass of the Earth is insignificant to that of the black hole we can consider the time elapsed at Earth as the far-away time. For one year passed at the space station we will have the following number of years passing by on Earth

$$T_{earth} = \frac{T_{shell}}{\sqrt{1 - \frac{2M}{r}}} = \frac{1}{\sqrt{1 - \frac{29{,}540}{29{,}552}}} \approx 50$$

That is, for every year passing by in the space station 50 years will be passing by on Earth. Assuming next that we place cash at Earth with 10 % annual return. Over 50 years on Earth one million dollars will grow to

$$1{,}000{,}000 \times 1.1^{50} = 117{,}390{,}853$$

But remember only one year has gone by in the space station, so what is its equivalent annual rate of return?

$$1,000,000 \times (1+r) = 117,390,853$$
$$r = \frac{117,390,853}{1,000,000} - 1 = 11,639\,\%$$

That is the annual return on the space station is an incredible 11,639 %. This explains how and why Einstein in the cartoon can promise 10,000 % return from his black hole hedge fund. The additional 1,639 % is simply his management fee!

Can We Survive the Tidal Forces of High Gravity If we should ever settle down in areas with very strong gravitation it can have significant consequences for Space-time Finance. An important question is whether humans will be able to survive the high tidal forces one would experience there.

A pilot will normally die of acceleration stress when reaching about 10g, while a quartz wristwatch will probably still continue to work normally. In 1960, astronaut Alan Shepard experienced 12g during the re-entry of the Mercury spacecraft Freedom 7 (Pickover, 1996, p. 19). There is reason to believe that even moderate g-forces (2–5g) will lead to high stress on our bodies if exposed for a considerable amount of time. We have to conclude that humans are currently not capable of withstanding g-forces necessary to settle down in parts of the universe where the g-force is strong enough to have significant effect on Space-time Finance.

8.1 From Black Holes to Black-Scholes

Many years ago I got hold of the book "From Black-Scholes to Black-Holes". The book was interesting, but the title was misleading because it had nothing to do with the relationship between black holes and the formula of Black-Scholes and Merton. To use the BSM formula anywhere near a black hole we need to modify the original formula by taking into account the gravitational effects on volatility and time. Assume that we are hovering around a black hole, and want to value an option trading on Earth. Because of the relatively much lower gravitation on Earth we can assume that Earth time is far away time. By some simple reflections and calculus we find that the value must be

$$c = SN(d_1) - Xe^{-\hat{r}_f T_{shell}} N(d_2),\tag{13.16}$$

where

$$d_1 = \frac{\ln(S/X) + (\hat{r}_f + \hat{\sigma}_f^2/2)T_{shell}}{\hat{\sigma}_f \sqrt{T_{shell}}},$$

$\hat{\sigma}_f$ is the volatility on the asset as observed from the black hole at radius r, and σ_f is the far away volatility, or basically the volatility of an asset trading on Earth as observed on Earth:

$$\hat{\sigma}_f = \sigma_f \left(1 - \frac{2M}{r}\right)^{-\frac{1}{4}},\tag{13.17}$$

and the relationship between the far-away risk-free rate r_f and $\hat{r}_f$ as observed at the shell

$$\hat{r}_f = \frac{r_f}{\sqrt{1 - \frac{2M}{r}}}. \tag{13.18}$$

Similarly the volatility of an asset trading at the space station hovering around the black hole would be

$$\hat{\sigma}_{shell} = \sigma_{shell} \left(1 - \frac{2M}{r}\right)^{\frac{1}{4}}, \tag{13.19}$$

where σ_{shell} is the proper volatility of an asset trading at a space station hovering around the black hole at radius r, and $\hat{\sigma}_{shell}$ is the volatility of the same asset as observed far away from the gravitational field. The risk-free rate at the spacecraft as observed from a far away observer would be

$$\hat{r}_{shell} = r_{shell}\sqrt{1 - \frac{2M}{r}}. \tag{13.20}$$

When observing a moving frame near a gravitational field we will naturally need to take into account both the special and general relativity theory.

9   Was Einstein Right?

When it comes to the special theory of relativity was Einstein right? Many of the aspects of the relativity theory have been tested experimentally with great precision, but other aspects of his theory are not so well tested. We will here mention briefly a few of the topics where there are still untested aspects of the special and general relativity theory.

9.1   Alternatives to Einstein

Several alternative relativity theories all agree with experimental results at least as well as the special relativity theory. Out of 11 well known independent experiments, said to confirm the validity of Einstein's special relativity theory none are able to distinguish it from, for example, Lorentz's relativity, Flandern (1998) or Taiji relativity, see Hsu (2000). Both Lorentz's and Einstein's (1905) relativity theories are based on the principle of relativity first discussed by Poincaré in 1899. Lorentz assumed a universal time, a preferred frame and a luminiferous ether (a solid medium that electromagnetic waves had to travel through).

In his 1905 paper Einstein denied the existence of the luminiferous stationary ether that Lorentz believed in. Lorentz acknowledge Einstein's insight in relativity theory but never gave up on the ether theory, see Lorentz (1920). Later Einstein modified his negative attitude to the ether and developed his own theory about what he named "the new ether" and also "gravitational ether", see Einstein (1922) and Kostro (1998).

The ether is today one of the most interesting and mysterious topics in physics. However few physicists talk about the ether, today they like to call it empty space, see Genz (1998) for an interesting introduction to nothingness.

9.2 Constancy of the Speed of Light?

In the special relativity theory Einstein's second postulate was that the speed of light is constant in any frame. Einstein assumed that clocks in an inertial frame could be synchronized with a clock at the origin of the frame by using light signals. However to synchronize the clocks in this way we must have an assumption of the speed of light. If Einstein's prescription to synchronize clocks is used, then measured speed must be the speed of light per definition. In other words the synchronization of clocks and the measured speed of light is closely connected (Reichenbach, 1958). The test of the universal speed of light therefore leads to a circular argument. The most advanced laboratory we have for measuring the speed of light, the GPS system, confirms that the measured speed of light does not change over time or the direction of the satellite in orbit. However it cannot tell us what the speed of light is, and in particular the one-way speed of light (Reichenbach, 1958, Flandern, 1998, Hsu and Zhang, 2001). Long before Einstein's time, Maxwell (1831–1879) wrote

> All methods . . . which it is practicable to determine the velocity of light from terrestrial experiments depend on the measurement of the time required for the double journey from one station to the other and back again. . .

Reichenbach (1958), Ruderfer (1960) and others claim that Einsteins' second postulate cannot even be tested. No physical experiment has been able to test whether the one-way speed of light is constant in every direction (i.e. isotropic) as assumed by Einstein. There are several extensions of the special relativity theory that do not assume that the one-way speed of light is constant. They do not necessarily claim that Einstein's special relativity theory is wrong, but that it is simply a special case of a more general relativity theory.

If the one-way speed of light is not constant, but only the two-way speed of light, the time dilation in the twin paradox will still be there, because it is based on two-way time dilation. A possibly nonisotropic one-way speed of light will naturally have an impact on time dilation during a given point on the trip, but the end result will still be the same when the stationary and the moving frame re-unites.

In 1898 Poincaré expressed his view that the constancy of the speed of light was merely a convention. Edwards (1963) replaced Einstein's second postulate with the assumption that only the two-way (round-trip) speed of light is constant. Hsu, Leonard and Schneble (1996) have extended the original formulations of Reichenbach's extended simultaneity and Edwards' universal two way speed of light to be consistent with the 4-dimensional symmetry of the Lorentz and Poincaré group. They have named this extended-relativity.

After Einstein's introduction of the special relativity theory some physicists considered whether they could construct a consistent relativity theory, based only on the first postulate. Ritz (1908), Tolman (1910), Pauli (1921) and others had to conclude that this was impossible. The reason was that they had failed to recognize a 4-dimensional symmetry associated only with the first postulate. Hsu and Leonard (1994) recognized this and were able to come up with a relativity theory based only on the first postulate, and that remarkably still agree with all experiments. They named this generalized relativity theory Taiji relativity. Taiji relativity does not conclude that Einstein's special relativity theory is wrong, it simply says that the second postulate is unnecessary to confirm experimental results. Furthermore, it shows us that our concept of time (e.g. Einstein's relativistic time or Reichenbach time) and also the speed of light in the 4-dimensional symmetry framework are human conventions rather than the inherent nature of the physical world. Special relativity, extended relativity, common relativity and other relativity theories are typically all a special case of the generalized Taiji relativity. However Taiji relativity agrees on the experimental fact that the speed of light is independent of the source velocity (Hsu, 2000; Hsu and Zhang, 2001).

9.3 Faster than the Speed of Light?

In 1992 Professor Günter Nimtz and colleagues at the University of Cologne have done experiments where they claimed to have observed speeds faster than light for microwaves using quantum tunneling. When sending light "particles" (microwaves is just another type of light/electromagnetic waves) against a thick barrier one would think that all the light particles would be stopped. Quantum mechanics tells a different story. According to quantum tunneling there is always a small probability of the particle jumping through the barrier. Another expert at quantum tunneling, Professor Chiao at the University of Berkeley at California, claimed to be able to send photons of visible light at superluminal speeds (faster than light). However he was not very concerned that this would make it possible to send information backwards in time and disrupt causality. His explanation for this is basically that the photons travelling through the barrier were random and could for this reason not be used to send any form of information.

At a physics conference in 1995 Professor Günter Nimtz played Mozart's 40th symphony on a Walkman. The bizarre part was that he claimed that this was the recording from a signal sent at 4.7 times the speed of light. Many leading physicists were, and still are, very skeptical about Professor Nimtz's results (Glegg, 2001).[10]

10 Traveling Back in Time Using Wormholes

So far we have discussed Space-time Finance within the limitations of traveling forward in time (time dilation). Time dilation, as predicted by the relativity theory, is as we already have mentioned confirmed by many physical experiments. Whether it will ever be possible to travel backwards in time is another question. One theoretically possible way to do this is by using wormholes. A wormhole is basically a short-cut through space and time. Wormholes can possibly be created by strong warping (bending) of space-time.

Wormhole physics can be traced back at least to the paper by Flamm (1916). In their 1935 paper Einstein and Rosen discussed a bridge across space-time, today known as an Einstein-Rosen bridge. The term "wormhole" had not yet been coined. After their 1935 paper little work was done on the subject until 20 years later when Wheeler (1955) followed up on the topic. Over the years the physics community has come up with a variety of theoretical wormhole solutions. Most wormhole solutions are practical, however, for neither space travel nor time travel. The gravitational tidal forces will rip humans apart. They can be strong enough even to disrupt the individual nucleus of atoms. The size of some wormholes (Wheeler wormholes) are predicted to be as small as the Planck length, 10^{-35} cm. For humans to travel through such wormholes clearly seems impossible. Still, even if you cannot send a book through a telephone line you can fax its content in the form of electrons or photons. The admittedly speculative movie "Timeline" uses the same idea to "fax" humans through a tiny wormhole, basically by ripping the body apart into its sub-atomic elements (electrons, photons...). In this context is it worth mentioning that in 1988 Morris and Thorne came up with a theoretical wormhole system where humans could possibly pass "safely" through in a reasonable amount of time. By inducing a time-shift and bringing such wormhole mouths together, one would at least in theory create a time machine. However, in contrast to time dilation in the relativity theory there are so far no physical experiments that can confirm the existence of wormholes.[11]

11 Conclusion

Many aspects of the relativity theory are well tested empirically. However, as we have pointed out there are still many open questions. Even if we still do not have all the answers for relativity, and therefore also not for Space-time Finance, I enjoy the idea that Space-time Finance will play some role in the future. Even quantitative finance can not escape the fundamental laws of physics.

Appendix A: Special Relativity and Time Dilation

Because many readers probably have little or no background in relativity theory we will here take a brief look at the math behind time dilation in the special relativity theory. To really exploit the special relativity theory we need the Lorentz transformation, however when it comes to the time dilation factor all we need is actually Pythagoras, theorem (and some reflections that took Einstein many years). Assume that we have a moving train. Inside the moving train we have a light clock. The light clock is constructed from one mirror on each side of the inside of train. The width between the mirrors we call w (the rest length). What is the relationship between the time it takes for the light to go back and forth between the mirrors as measured on the train and on the platform?

The time measured by the moving observer, $\hat{T}$, must be

$$\hat{T} = \frac{2w}{c}.$$

The distance traveled by the light as seen from the platform, p, must be longer than the distance as measured by an observer on the train. Assuming the speed of light is constant, then more time must have passed by for the light to travel the longer path. In other words the platform time between each light clock tick is

$$T = \frac{2p}{c}. \tag{13.21}$$

The length p is unknown, but can easily be found by using Pythagoras' theorem $a^2 = b^2 + c^2$

$$p^2 = w^2 + \left(\frac{1}{2}L\right)^2$$

$$p = \sqrt{w^2 + \left(\frac{1}{2}L\right)^2},$$

where L is the distance traveled by the train between each time the light reflect on the mirror. We know the velocity of the train is $v = L/T$ which gives $L = vT$. Replacing this measurement of p into (13.22) we get

$$T = \frac{2p}{c} = \frac{2\sqrt{w^2 + \left(\frac{vT}{2}\right)^2}}{c}.$$

Further we can eliminate w by replacing it with

$$w = \frac{c\hat{T}}{2}.$$

This gives

$$T^2 = \frac{4\left(\frac{1}{4}c^2\hat{T}^2 + \frac{1}{4}v^2 T^2\right)}{c^2}$$

$$T^2 - \frac{v^2}{c^2}T^2 = \hat{T}^2$$

$$\hat{T} = T\sqrt{1 - \frac{v^2}{c^2}},$$

Figure 13.2 illustrates the classical time dilation example just given. Many apparent "paradoxes" can here be made, for example assume the train will reach the woman in 3 seconds as measured by a clock on the train. The Collector needs 4 seconds to save the woman. The train is traveling at 70 % of the speed of light; will the Collector be able to save the women?

Appendix B: Relationship Between Acceleration in Different Frames

Here we will look at how to obtain the relationship between the acceleration of a point P moving in the x direction in an inertial system $G(x, t)$, and its acceleration in a second, parallel, system $\hat{G}(\hat{x}, \hat{t})$, which is moving with the speed V along the same direction. This section is based on Marder (1971), except that I am using slightly different notation, as well as having fixed what appears to be a typo in his calculations.

Assume v is the velocity of a point in G, and u is the velocity in $\hat{G}$ then by the rules of adding velocities under special relativity we have

$$v = \frac{u + V}{1 + \frac{Vu}{c^2}},$$

and from the Lorentz transformation we have

$$T = \frac{\hat{T} + V\hat{x}/c^2}{\sqrt{1 - V^2/c^2}}.$$

Figure 13.2

Taking differentials we get

$$dv = \frac{du}{1 + \frac{Vu}{c^2}} - \frac{u + V}{\left(1 + \frac{Vu}{c^2}\right)^2}\left(\frac{V}{c^2}\right)du$$

$$= \frac{(1 - V^2/c^2)}{(1 + Vu/c^2)^2}du, \tag{13.22}$$

$$dt = \frac{d\hat{\imath}}{\sqrt{1 - V^2/c^2}}\left(1 + \frac{Vu}{c^2}\right). \tag{13.23}$$

Now to get the acceleration a as observed in the G frame we simply divide (13.22) by (13.23) and get

$$a = \frac{dv}{dt} = \frac{(1 - V^2/c^2)^{3/2}}{(1 + Vu/c^2)^3}\frac{du}{d\hat{\imath}}. \tag{13.24}$$

where $\frac{du}{d\hat{\imath}}$ is the acceleration in the $\hat{G}$ frame. If $\hat{G}$ is the instantaneously co-moving system of the point P, then $u = 0$, $V = v$, and let $\alpha = \frac{du}{d\hat{\imath}}$, then we can simplify (13.24) to

$$a = \frac{dv}{dt} = (1 - V^2/c^2)^{3/2}\alpha, \tag{13.25}$$

which gives us the relationship between the acceleration a as observed in G and the acceleration α as observed in $\hat{G}$.

FOOTNOTES & REFERENCES

1. Already in 1922 there were more than 3,400 papers written about relativity, Maurice LeCat, "Bibliographie de la Relativité", Bruxelles, 1924.

2. Haug (2002) touches upon some of the relativity theory's implications for finance.

3. Larmor (1900) was actually the first to introduce time dilation, but in the context of "ether theory". In his paper there is little or no discussion of the physical implications of time dilation.

4. Larmor (1900) was the first to discover the exact space-time transformation, today known as the Lorentz transformation. Lorentz probably did not know about Larmor's paper. The final rediscovery of this space-time transformation was actually done by Poincaré (1905), based on Lorentz's earlier work. Lorentz himself clearly admitted this:

> My considerations published in 1904 ... have pushed Poincaré to write this article in which he has attached my name to the transformations which I was unable to obtain ...

The Lorentz transformation is given by

$$\hat{x} = \frac{x - vT}{\sqrt{1 - v^2/c^2}}, \qquad \hat{y} = y, \qquad \hat{z} = z, \qquad \hat{T} = \frac{T - vx/c^2}{\sqrt{1 - v^2/c^2}}.$$

Voigt (1887) was the first to derive a type of 4-dimensional space-time transformation, which differs slightly from the Lorentz transformation.

5. We could assume alternatively that we had, for instance, stochastic volatility. We will look at this later.

6. That the wristwatch time, a.k.a. the proper time, is invariant, independent of the reference frame, is one of the well known results of the special relativity theory.

7. The square root volatility model was to my knowledge first introduced by Heston (1993), in the form of a stochastic volatility model. Lewis (2000) is a good reference for an overview of other modeling choices for volatility.

8. For example an Einstein-Levine light clock.

9. In the space-like form the Schwarzschild metric is given by

$$d\eta^2 = -\left(1 - \frac{2M}{r}\right)dt^2 + \frac{dr^2}{\left(1 - \frac{2M}{r}\right)} + r^2 d\phi^2$$

where η is the proper distance.

10. I can recommended the video "Time Travel" with interviews with both Nimtz and Chiao; by NOVA Television, BBC, 1999.

11. For a great introduction to wormholes see Thorne (1994), for a more mathematical introduction see Visser (1996).

■ Bachelier, L. (1900) *Theory of speculation*, in: P. Cootner, Ed., 1964, *The random character of stock market prices*, Cambridge, Mass.; MIT Press.

■ Bailey, J., et al. (1977) "Measuring Time Dilation Via the Lifetime of High-Speed Muons in a Storage Ring" *Nature*, **268**, 301–304.

■ Barone, M. (1998) *Some Almost Unknown Aspects of Special Relativity Theory*, in the book: *Open Questions in Relativistic Physics*, Edited by Franco Selleri. Apericorn.

■ Barton, G. (1999) *Introduction to the Relativity Principle*. John Wiley & Sons.

■ Begley, S. (2003): "Physicists Are Looking at How We Might Take a Trip Through Time," *Wall Street Journal, Marketplace section*, p. B1.

■ Black, F. and M. Scholes (1973): "The Pricing of Options and Corporate Liabilities" *Journal of Political Economy*, **81**, 637–654.

■ Carr, P. (1991) "Deriving Derivatives of Derivative Securities" Working paper, Johnson Graduate School of Management.

■ Carr, P., H. Geman, D. B. Madan and M. Yor (2003) "Stochastic Volatility for Lévy Processes" *Mathematical Finance*, **13**(3), 345–382.

■ Carr, P. and L. Wu (2004): "Time-Changed Lévy Processes and Option Pricing" *Journal of Financial Economics*, **71**, 113–141.

■ Clark, P. K. (1973) "A Subordinated Stochastic Process Model with Finite Variance for Speculative Prices" *Econometrica*, **41**(1), 135–155.

■ Dingle, H. (1956) "Relativity and Space Travel" *Nature*, **177**, 782–784.

■ Edwards, W. F. (1963) "Special Relativity in Ansiotropic Space" *Am. J. Phys.*, **31**, 482–489.

■ Einstein, A. (1905) "Zur Elektrodynamik Bewegter Körper" *Annalen der Physik*, **17**.

■ ──── (1912) *Einstein's 1912 Manuscript on the Special Theory of Relativity*. George Braziller, Publishers in the association with the Jacob E. Safra Philanthopic Foundation and the Israel Museum, Jerusalem, 1996.

■ ──── (1922) *Sidelights on Relativity*. E. P. Dutton and Company.

■ Einstein, A. and N. Rosen (1935) "The Particle Problem in the General Theory of Relativity" *Phys. Rev.*, **48**.

■ Ellis, G. F. R. and R. M. Williams (2000) *Flat and Curved Space-Time*, 2nd edn. Oxford University Press.

■ Field, P. (1992) *From Black-Scholes to Black Holes*. Risk/Finex.

■ Flamm, L. (1916) "Beiträge zur Einsteinschen Gravitationstheorie," *Phys. Z.*, **17**.

■ Flandern, T. V. (1998) *What the Global Positioning System Tells Us about Relativity*, in the book: *Open Questions in Relativistic Physics*, Edited by Franco Selleri. Apericorn.

■ Geman, H., D. B. Madan and M. Yor (2000) "Stochastic Volatility, Jumps and Hidden Time Changes" *Finance Stochast.*, **6**, 63–90.

■ Genz, H. (1998) *Nothingness, the Science of Empty Space*. Cambridge: Perseus Publishing.

■ Glegg, B. (2001) *Light Years and Time Travel*. John Wiley & Sons, Inc.

■ Haefele, J. C. (1970) "Relativistic Behaviour of Moving Terrestrial Clocks" *Nature*, **227**, 270–271.

■ ──── (1971) "Relativistic Time for Terrestrial Circumnavigation" *American Journal of Physics*, **40**, 81–85.

■ Haefele, J. C. and R. Keating (1971a) "Around-the-World Atomic Clocks: Observed Relativistic Time Gains," *Science*, **177**, 168–170.

■ ──── (1971b) "Around-the-World Atomic Clocks: Predicted Relativistic Time Gains" *Science*, **177**, 166–167.

■ Haug, E. G. (1997) *The Complete Guide To Option Pricing Formulas*. New York: McGraw-Hill.

■ ——— (2002) "A Look in the Antimatter Mirror" *Wilmott Magazine*, www.wilmott.com, December.

■ ——— (2003) "Know Your Weapon, Part 1 and 2" *Wimott Magazine*, May and August.

■ Heisenberg, W. (1927) "Über den Anschaulichen Inhalt der Quantentheoretischen Kinematik und Mechanik," *Z. Für Phys.*, **43**, 172–198.

■ Heston, S. L. (1993) "A Closed-Form Solution for Options with Stochastic Volatility, with Applications to Bond and Currency Options" *Review of Financial Studies*, **6**, 327–343.

■ Hsu, J.-P. (2000) *Einstein's Relativity and Beyond, New Symmetry Approaches*. World Scientific.

■ Hsu, J.-P. and H. Leonard (1994) "A Physical Theory Based Solely on the First Postulate of Relativity" *Phys. Letters A*, **196**, 1–6.

■ Hsu, J.-P., H. Leonard and D. A. Schneble (1996): "Four-dimensional Symmetry of Taiji Relativity and Cordinate Transformations Based on a Weaker Postulate of the Speed of Light," *Nuovo Cimento B*, **111**.

■ Hsu, J.-P. and Y.-Z. Zhang (2001): *Lorentz and Poincaré Invariance*. World Scientific.

■ Kostro, L. (1998) *The Physical and Philosophical Reasons for A. Einstein's Denial of the Ether in 1905 and its Reintroduction in 1916*, in the book: *Open Questions in Relativistic Physics*, Edited by Franco Selleri. Apericorn.

■ Larmor, J. J. (1900) "Aether and Matter: A Development of the Dynamical Relations of the Aether to Material Systems" Cambridge: Cambridge University Press.

■ Lewis, A. (2000) *Option Valuation under Stochastic Volatility*. Newport Beach, CA: Finance Press.

■ Lorentz, H. A. (1904) "Electromagnetic Phenomena in a System Moving with any Velocity less than that of Light" *Proc. Acad. Scientific, Amsterdam*, **6**.

■ ——— (1909) "The Theory of Electrons and its Application to the Phenomena of Light and Radiation Heat". New York: Columbia University Press.

■ ——— (1920) *The Einstein Theory of Relativity, 3rd edn.* Brentano's.

■ Marder, L. (1971) *Time and the Space-Traveler*. London: George Allen & Unwin,

■ Merton, R. C. (1973) "Theory of Rational Option Pricing" *Bell Journal of Economics and Management Science*, **4**, 141–183.

■ Misner, C., K. Thorne and J. Wheeler (1973) *Gravitation*. Freeman.

■ Nahin, P. J. (1998) *Time Machines, Time Travel in Physics, Metaphysics, and Science Fiction*, 2nd edn. AIP Press.

■ Pauli, W. (1921) "The Postulate of the Constancy of the Speed of Light," *Collected Scientific Papers by Wolfgang Pauli* (Edited by R. Kronig and V. F. Weisskopf, 1964).

■ Pickover, C. (1996) *Black Holes, A Traveler's Guide*. John Wiley & Sons.

■ Poincaré, H. (1905) "On the Dynamics of the Electron" *Comptes Rendus*.

■ Reichenbach, H. (1958) *The Philosophy of Space and Time*. Translated edition, New York: Dover Publications.

■ Reiner, E. (1992) "Quanto Mechanics" *Risk Magazine*, **5**, 59–63.

■ Ritz, W. (1908) "Recherches Critiques sur L'Électrodynamique Générale" *Annàles de Chimie et de Physique*, **13**(145).

■ Ruderfer, M. (1960) *Proc. IRE*(48).

■ Sartori, L. (1996) *Understanding Relativity*. University of California Press.

■ Taylor, E. F. and J. A. Wheeler (1992) *Spacetime Physics, Introduction To Special Relativity*. W. H. Freeman and Company, New York.

■ ——— (2000) *Exploring Black Holes*. Addison Wesley Longman.

- Thorne, K. S. (1994) *Black Holes & Time Warps*. Norton.
- Tipler, P. A. and R. A. Llewellyn (1999) *Modern Physics, Third Edition*. New York: W. H. Freeman and Company.
- Tolman, R. C. (1910) "The Second Postulate of Relativity,," *Phys. Rev.*, **31**.
- Visser, M. (1996) *Lorentzian Wormholes*. AIP Press, Springer.
- Voigt, W. (1887) "Über das Doppler'sche Princip," *Nachr. Ges. Wiss. Göttingen*, **41**.
- Wheeler, J. A. (1955) *Geons. Phys. Rev.* **97**.

Andrei Khrennikov

Andrei Khrennikov on Negative Probabilities

Over the last few years it has occurred to me that negative probabilities are not necessarily nonsense, and can possibly even be of use in finance. Negative probabilities go back at least to the Nobel prize winner Paul Dirac's introduction of the idea in a paper in 1942. One of today's true probability masters is Andrei Khrennikov, whose first (student) papers on negative and complex probabilities were published in *Dokl. Acad. Sc* by the recommendation of A. N. Kolmogorov – the founder of modern probability theory. However, Khrennikov did not simply accept the axiomatics of modern probability theory. By looking into the very foundation of probability Khrennikov could no longer exclude negative probabilities. While Nobel prize winners like Dirac and Feynman had considered negative probabilities only as formal quantities useful in certain calculations, Khrennikov found the deep roots of negative probabilities. Based on this he has been one of the most important figures behind the development of a profound mathematical theory of probability, where negative probabilities are just as natural as positive ones.

Andrei Khrennikov is currently a Professor of Applied Mathematics, and the Director of International Center in Mathematical Modeling in Physics and Cognitive Sciences, University of Växjö, Sweden. He has written more than two hundred papers on probability theory, applied mathematics and quantum physics. Many of his ideas in probability theory, including negative probabilities are summarized in two of his books "Interpretation of Probability", 1999 and "Non-Archimedean Analysis: Quantum paradoxes, dynamical systems and biological models", 1997

Haug: What do you think about the axiomatics of the modern probability theory – Kolmogorov measure – theoretical axiomatics?

Khrennikov: I was lucky to speak with Andrei Nikolaevich Kolmogorov on a few occasions when he submitted some papers at the same time as myself and my supervisor Professor Smolyanov to *Dokl. Acad. Sc.* In particular, one of these papers was about analogs of the central limit theorem and the law of large numbers for signed and complex measures and distributions. In particular, we obtained the Feynman-Gauss distribution (having a complex quadratic exponent) as the limit distribution. We had long discussions with Kolmogorov on the foundations of probability theory. First of all I was surprised that Kolmogorov did not consider the creation of the axiomatics of modern probability theory as his most important contribution to science. Moreover, it was my impression that he was still not satisfied by his own axiomatics. I think that his theory of algorithmic complexity which can be considered as a return to the von Mises frequency probability theory is also a sign of such dissatisfaction. Personally I think that Kolmogorov's axiomatics were well done from the purely mathematical viewpoint, but the question of its application was not discussed on a sufficiently deep level. The most important question is the relation between frequency and probability. A. N. Kolmogorov paid some attention to this question in his fundamental book "Foundations of Probability Theory" (1933). He motivated all his axioms, besides sigma-additivity of probability, by using the von Mises definition of probability as the limit of relative frequencies. At the same time it was pointed out that the condition of sigma-additivity is a purely mathematical condition that was introduced into the theory only to make use of the Lebesgue integration theory to define the expectation of a random variable. I think that the disappearance of the frequency basis from the Kolmogorov model is one of the main disadvantages of this model. There is the common opinion that this basis can be reconstructed through the law of large numbers. However, as R. von Mises pointed out on many occasions the law of large numbers proved as a theorem in the Kolmogorov measure-theoretical framework cannot be considered as an equivalent of the von Mises frequency construction. In the latter case we start with a collective-random sequence generated by a complex of experimental conditions (physical, social, financial) – and the probabilities appear only at the the second level of this model as limits of relative frequencies for collectives. In the von Mises approach we cannot use the Lebesgue measure and expectation is defined with the aid of the Jordan integral. So the Kolmogorov model is a good mathematical model, but when applying this model we should not forget that this is just a rather special idealized representation of real stochasticity. In particular, a Kolmogorov probability measure is just a mathematical structure representing in a very special way – by using the real analysis and the Lebesgue integral – the real frequency data.

Haug: What is the origin of negative probabilities?

Khrennikov: There are no negative probabilities in the Kolmogorov model, since he used the frequency motivation for his axioms, but the limits of relative frequencies (rational numbers belonging to the segment [0, 1]) are always positive (and belong to the same segment). Thus one of the possibilities to get negative probabilities is to go beyond the ordinary frequency probability theory. The main point is that von Mises collectives represent only a part of random reality. There can exist "generalized collectives" which could produce negative probability distributions. So (from my point of view) the main source of negative probabilities is the extension of random reality beyond standard probabilistic models.

Haug: Why are people afraid to use negative probabilities?

Khrennikov: I would like to start with a counter-question: Why are people not afraid to use positive real probabilities? Such a use of arbitrary real probabilities from [0, 1] is just a consequence of a rather common belief that is, in fact, totally unmotivated. Well you can use such real numbers in your mathematical calculations, but you should be very careful to interpret them as "real probabilities". A. N. Kolmogorov was aware of this problem and he drew the attention of readers of his book to the fact that not all sets belonging to the sigma-field of "events" of his model could be interpreted as actual events. He understood well that by starting with a field F of actual events we obtain a sigma-field which elements do not have a reasonable probabilistic interpretation. Kolmogorov underlined that "the extended field of probability still remain merely a mathematical structure". So "probabilities" which are used in the standard measure-theoretical framework are just symbols which are used for calculations in the framework of real analysis. For some psychological reason people are not afraid to use these ideal symbols. But by starting with a field F of actual events we can obtain extensions of the original (positive probability) P which are not more positive. I studied this question in detail in my book "Interpretations of Probability". By using the Hahn-Banach extension theorem we can obtain signed measures by starting with the positive probabilistic measure. Of course, such extensions differ from the standard Lebesgue extension. But why should one be so concentrated on this special mathematical construction – the Lebesgue measure? In this case one would obtain ideal mathematical structures – "events" which can have "negative probabilities". However, for some psychological reason people are afraid to use such mathematical idealization. Personally I think that the use of "negative probabilities" is no less justified than the use of arbitrary real positive probabilities. Of course, one should be careful with the frequency interpretation of these probabilities, but the same is valid for ordinary positive real probabilities that do not correspond to events belonging to the field of actual events F. Unfortunately, I met A. N. Kolmogorov when I was a student and I did not have such a deep understanding of the problem as I have nowadays. I missed the opportunity to ask him about this problem. In any case he recommended our paper to *Dokl. Acad. Sc.* But it was only after this that we understood how strong was the common prejudice against the use of negative probabilities. The paper recommended by Kolmogorov was sent for additional refereeing (Kolmogorov was a member of Academy of Sciences, all papers recommended by him were usually published automatically). After two years of refereeing the paper was finally published on the basis of the original recommendation of Kolmogorov, since "all referees showed total incompetence in this problem".

Haug: When did you first become interested in negative probabilities?

Khrennikov: In the eighties a group of mathematical physicists from Steklov Mathematical Institute (Moscow), first V. S. Vladimirov and I. V. Volovich and then many others (including me; in the USA, e.g., P. G. O. Freund and E Witten) started to use so-called p–adic numbers (instead of real or complex numbers) to describe some physical models, including superstrings. The basic idea beyond these investigations was that only rational numbers are "physical numbers"; all experimental data is represented by rational numbers (as a consequence of the finite precision of measurements). To create a theoretical model we should extend the system of rational numbers to get a complete metric space. Then there should be taken into account the famous theorem of number theory – Ostrovsky's theorem – that there are only two different types of completions of rational numbers: real numbers and one of systems of p–adic numbers. Here p-is a prime number which determines the corresponding system of p–adic numbers. In models of p–adic quantum physics there arose quantities which should have the meaning of probabilities, but they belong not to the segment $[0, 1]$ of the real line, but to the system of p–adic numbers. I developed a p–adic generalization of frequency theory of probability.

Haug: Is it right to say that negative probabilities have mainly found their use in quantum mechanics?

Khrennikov: At least physicists were not afraid to use these generalized probabilities. Maybe this was a consequence of the terrible problem of renormalization of some quantities in quantum field theory. It is well known that there appear to be many divergent quantities which can get some definite value only through rather counterintuitive procedures of renormalization.

Dirac was the first who observed that one can escape to use such procedures by introducing into consideration negative probabilities. Roughly speaking physicists had only two choices:

(a) to work with infinite quantities and

(b) to work with negative probabilities. Some top-scientists preferred to work with negative probabilities.

Haug: Have negative probabilities ever been detected by any physical experiments?

Khrennikov: No, there were no experiments where we can say that there were directly "detected negative probabilities". But what would it mean to detect directly negative probability? This means that the limit of relative frequencies would be a negative number. This is impossible, simply because by using the standard real metric on the set of rational numbers we would never get a negative limit of positive rational frequencies. To find negative probability in the frequency approach, we should use another metric, e.g., the p–adic one. Such investigations have never been performed. p–adic theory of probability tells us that p–adic limit of relative frequencies typically exists when the ordinary real limit does not. Thus the standard law of large numbers should be violated. I spoke with many experimenters (I am especially thankful to my colleagues from the Institute of Atomphysics of Austrian Universities) on this problem. It seems that the modern methodology of experiments does not give us any opportunity to pay attention to situations where negative frequency probability might be detected. My colleagues told me that if one gets data violating the law of large numbers, then the standard conclusion is that the experiment was not well done or designed. So it may be that we have negative probabilities in experimental data-waste. This was about "experimental detection" of negative frequency probability. But, as I have already remarked, negative probabilities can appear in the measure-theoretical approach when we extend the field of events beyond Lebesgue's theory. Here we can have some indirect experimental evidences. For example, the p–adic probability theory tells us that negative probabilities can be useful to represent infinitely small probabilities. Here we do not neglect events with such probabilities. We can speculate that such negative probabilistic distributions can be useful in the study of anomalous phenomena.[1] In statistical investigations of anomalous phenomena negative probabilities can appear as probabilities of events which are totally impossible from the point of view of ordinary probability theory.

Haug: In short what is p–adic probability theory, and how is this related to negative probabilities?

Khrennikov: The starting point is that relative frequencies are always rational numbers. Therefore we can consider them as being in the system of real numbers as well as in any system of p–adic numbers. Then we can use different metric structures to study the behavior of relative frequencies. If we use the ordinary real metric then we come to the frequency theory of von Mises. But if we consider the behavior of frequencies with respect to one of p–adic metrics then we can develop a p–adic frequency theory of probability. Here we can get negative rational numbers, e.g., -1 (as well as rational numbers larger than 1) as limits of relative frequencies. Thus in the p–adic model negative probabilities appears quite naturally and they have equal rights with other probabilities. As was already remarked, negative probabilities often appear in the situation when a sequence of relative frequencies does not stabilize with respect to the ordinary real metric: in a long run of trails frequencies can fluctuate between 0 and 1. But at the same time these frequencies can stabilize with respect to one of p–adic metrics. So from the point of view of ordinary probability theory we have total chaos: fluctuating frequencies. But from the point of view of the p–adic probability theory we have well defined random behavior described by p–adic probabilities. I and my students performed extended computer simulation of for p–adic probabilistic models.[2] There were presented quite realistic statistical models which produce p–adic and, in particular, negative probabilities. Starting with the p–adic frequency probability theory we can proceed in the same way as in the ordinary probability theory (as A. N. Kolmogorov did): properties of p–adic frequency probabilities (limits of relative frequencies in the p–adic topology) are used for the measure-theoretical axiomatization of theory.

Haug: What is the main difference between p–adic probability theory and Komologrov's probability theory?

Khrennikov: It would be natural to compare the Kolmogorov model with the p–adic measure-theoretical model. The main purely mathematical difference is that the only p–adic valued sigma-additive measures defined on sigma-fields are discrete measures. Thus the condition of sigma-additivity is not so fruitful in the p–adic case. One of the main differences of two models is the theory of limit theorems. In the p–adic case we cannot formulate an analog of the law of large numbers or the central limit theorem as being about the existence of limits for distributions when the number of trials goes to infinity. In the p–adic case by choosing different subsequences of trials we get in principle different limit distributions. In my book[3] there were described all limit points of normalized sums of independent random variables. We remark that such theorems could be obtained even in the 19th century, if one studies the behavior of frequencies not only with respect to the ordinary real metric, but also with respect to p–adic metrics.

Haug: In your very interesting book "Interpretations of Probability" you discuss the Einstein Podolsky and Rosen argument (EPR) as well as the famous Bell's inequality. What does any of this have to do with negative probabilities and probability theory?

Khrennikov: R. Feynman pointed out that quantum physics can be considered as an extension of classical statistical mechanics in which probabilities can take negative values. This point was explored in numerous papers in physics journals. In my book I discussed Feynman's viewpoint in more detail. In particular, it was demonstrated that negative probabilities can naturally appear as the result of regularization of some divergent statistical expressions.

Haug: In quantitative finance negative probabilities often seem to arise from the discretization of a continuous diffusion process, do you see any parallels to this in your work on quantum physics and probability theory?

Khrennikov: I have never tried to study this problem. But spontaneously I can say that there can be some similarity with quantum physics where negative probabilities arise as regularization of some divergent statistical expressions.

Haug: Nobel prize winners like Paul Dirac and Richard Feynman seemed to take negative probabilities seriously, why is it that most people still ignore negative probabilities?

Khrennikov: I think for merely psychological reasons. I had numerous discussions at various seminars on probability theory. People were from the very beginning educated on the basis of one very special probabilistic model – the Kolmogorov one. Therefore for them there is no random reality outside this model; in particular, they reject automatically negative probabilities as totally meaningless ("unreal") symbols. On the other hand, the same people use freely other symbols which they consider as real – these are real numbers from [0,1] which they obtain by extending the probability P from the field of actual events F to various sigma-fields.

Haug: Stochastic processes and probability theory are today used a great deal on Wall Street for valuation and risk management of options and other complex derivative instruments. As a leading expert on probability theory have you ever considered making a move from academia to Wall Street?

Khrennikov: It is an interesting idea. The world of finance is a world of huge complexity; perhaps it is even more complex than the quantum world. Therefore it would be extremely interesting to try to apply new probabilistic methods, in particular, various non-Kolmogorovian models in this domain. However, it would not be easy for a person who became a Professor at the age 32 to make a crucial life change at 45 and move directly to applied financial investigations. If there was created a kind of Institute for Fundamental Financial Investigations, I would be really happy to work there.

FOOTNOTES & REFERENCES

1. See (Khrennikov, 1999a).
2. Khrennikov A.Yu., p–adic valued distributions and their applications to the mathematical physics (1994).
3. Khrennikov A.Yu., Non-Archimedean analysis: quantum paradoxes, dynamical systems and biological models (1997).

■ Khrennikov, A. Y. (1997) *Non-Archimedean Analysis: Quantum Paradoxes, Dynamical Systems and Biological Models*. Kluwer Academic Publishers.
■ ———— (1999a) "Classical and Quantum Mechanics on Information Spaces With Applications to Cognitive, Psychological, Social and Anomalous Phenomena" *Foundations of Physics*, **7**, 1065–1098.
■ ———— (1999b) *Interpretations of Probability*. Coronet Books.

14

Why so Negative about Negative Probabilities?*

What is the probability of the expected being neither expected nor unexpected?

1   The History of Negative Probability

In finance negative probabilities are considered nonsense, or at best an indication of model-breakdown. Searching the finance literature the comments I found on negative probabilities were all negative,[1] see for example Brennan and Schwartz (1978), Hull and White (1990), Derman, Kani and Chriss (1996), Chriss (1997), Rubinstein (1998), Jorgenson and Tarabay (2002) and Hull (2002). Why is the finance society so negative about negative probabilities? The most likely answer is simply that we "all" were taught that probabilities by definition must be between 0 and 1, as assumed in the Kolmogorov measure theoretical axioms. Our negativity about negative probabilities might be as short sighted as if we decided to limit ourselves to consider only positive money. I am not the first one to think that negative probabilities can be useful. Negative probabilities were to my knowledge first introduced by Paul Dirac. Dirac is probably best known for his mathematical prediction of antimatter, a feat for which he was awarded the Nobel prize in 1933. In 1942 Paul Dirac wrote a paper: "The Physical Interpretation of Quantum Mechanics" where he introduced the concept of negative energies and negative probabilities:

> Negative energies and probabilities should not be considered as nonsense. They are well-defined concepts mathematically, like a sum of negative money . . .

The idea of negative probabilities later received increased attention in physics and particularly in quantum mechanics. Another famous physicist, Richard Feynman (1987) (also with a Nobel prize in physics), argued that no one objects to using negative numbers in calculations, although "minus three apples" is no valid concept in real life. Similarly, he argued how negative probabilities as well as probabilities above unity can be very useful in probability calculations:

> Trying to think of negative probabilities gave me a cultural shock at first, but when I finally got easy with the concept I wrote myself a note so I wouldn't forget my thoughts . . . It is usual to suppose that, since probabilities of events must be positive, a theory which gives negative numbers for such quantities must be absurd. (Richard Feyman, 1987)

*Thanks to Jørgen Haug for useful comments. Any errors or views in this chapter are naturally my own responsibility. The ideas from this chapter were presented at the ICBI Global Derivatives Conference, 26 May 2004, Madrid, Spain.

Feynman discusses mainly the Bayes formula for conditional probabilities

$$P(i) = \sum_{\alpha} P(i|\alpha)P(\alpha),$$

where $\sum_{\alpha} P(\alpha) = 1$. The idea is that as long as $P(i)$ is positive then it is not a problem if some of the probabilities $P(i|\alpha)$ or $P(\alpha)$ are negative or larger than unity. This approach works well when one cannot measure all of the conditional probabilities $P(i|\alpha)$ or the unconditional probabilities $P(\alpha)$ in an experiment. That is, the variables α can relate to hidden states. Such an approach has therefore been used in quantum physics to solve problems involving hidden variables.

There has since been a multitude of papers in theoretical physics that focus on the use of negative probabilities. I have included a few examples in the references list, that can also be downloaded from the web: Castro (2000), Cereceda (2000), Curtright and Zachosy (2001) and Peacock (2002). There seems to be a continuing interest in negative probabilities in physics:

> I have done some work recently, on making supergravity renormalizable, by adding higher derivative terms to the action. This apparently introduces ghosts, states with negative probability. However, I have found this is an illusion. One can never prepare a system in a state of negative probability. But the presence of ghosts that one can not predict with arbitrary accuracy. If one can accept that, one can live quite happily with ghosts. (Stephen Hawking)

2 Negative Probabilities in Quantitative Finance

In this section we look at a few examples of where negative probabilities can show up in finance. My examples are not revolutionary in the sense that they solve problems never solved before. I hope, however, that they will illustrate why negative probabilities are not necessarily "bad", and that they might even be useful.

2.1 Negative Probabilities in the CRR binomial tree

The well-known Cox, Ross and Rubinstein (1979) binomial tree (CRR tree) is often used to price a variety of derivatives instruments, including European and American options. The CRR binomial tree can be seen as a discretization of geometric Brownian motion $dS = \mu S dt + \sigma S dZ$, where S is the asset price, μ is the drift and σ is the volatility of the asset. In the CRR tree the asset price in any node of the tree is given by

$$Su^i d^{j-i}, \qquad i = 0, 1, \ldots, j,$$

where the up and down jump size that the asset price can take at each time step Δt apart is given by

$$u = e^{\sigma\sqrt{\Delta t}}, \qquad d = e^{-\sigma\sqrt{\Delta t}},$$

where $\Delta t = T/n$ is the size of each time step, and n is the number of time steps. The layout of the asset price (the geometry of the tree) we will call the sample space (the set of all asset price S_{ij} node values). The probability measure P is the set of the probabilities at the various nodes. The probabilities related to each node in the CRR tree follow from the arbitrage principle

$$Se^{b_i \Delta t} = p_i u S + (1 - p_i) d S, \qquad (14.1)$$

where p_i is risk-neutral probability of the asset price increasing at the next time step, and b_i is the cost-of-carry of the underlying asset.[2] The i subscript indicates that we can have a different probability and also cost-of-carry at each time step. Solving 14.1 for p_i we get

$$p_i = \frac{e^{b_i \Delta t} - d}{u - d}.$$

The probability of going down must be $1 - p_i$ since the probability of going either up or down equals unity. As mentioned by Chriss (1997) a low volatility and relatively high cost of carry in the CRR tree can lead to negative risk-neutral probabilities.[3] More precisely we will have negative probabilities in the CRR tree when[4]

$$\sigma < |b_i \sqrt{\Delta t}|.$$

In this context it is worth mentioning that even if the CRR binomial tree can give negative and higher than unity probabilities the sum of the down and up probability will still sum to one.

What to do with negative probabilities? Assume that we are using a CRR binomial tree to value a derivative instrument, and consider the following numerical example. The asset price is 100, the time to maturity of the derivative instrument is 6 months, the volatility of the underlying asset is 2 %, the cost-of-carry of the underlying asset is 12 % for the first month, and are increasing by 0.5 % for every month thereafter. For simplicity we use only six time steps. That is $S = 100$, $T = 0.5$, $b_1 = 0.12$, $\sigma = 0.02$, $n = 6$. From this we have $\Delta t = 0.5/6 = 0.833$ and

$$u = e^{0.02\sqrt{0.0833}} = 1.006, \qquad d = e^{-0.02\sqrt{0.0833}} = 0.9942,$$

Further we get a risk-neutral up probability of

$$p_1 = \frac{e^{0.12 \times 0.0833} - 0.9942}{1.006 - 0.9942} = 1.3689.$$

and we get a down probability of

$$1 - p_1 = 1 - 1.3689 = -0.3689$$

As expected, we get negative probabilities. In this generalized version of the CRR tree we can have different probabilities for every time steps, so we could have probabilities outside the interval [0, 1] for some time steps and inside for other time steps, in this particular numerical example all the probabilities will be outside zero and one. When we observe negative probabilities in a tree model we have at least three choices:

1. We can consider negative probabilities as unacceptable, and any model yielding negative probabilities as having broken down. The model should be trashed, or alternatively we should only use the model for input parameters that do not results in negative probabilities.

2. Override the negative probabilities. Basically replacing any transition probabilities that are negative or above unity with probabilities consistent with the standard axiomatic framework. For example Derman, Kani and Chriss (1996) suggest this as a possible solution in their implied trinomial tree when running into negative probabilities.

3. Look at negative probabilities as a mathematical tool to add more flexibility to the model.

From these choices I have only seen choice 1 (most common) and 2 being discussed in the finance literature. I am not saying that choice 1 and 2 are wrong, but this should not make us reject choice 3 automatically.

Back to the CRR binomial tree example. In this case what we do about the negative probabilities should depend on the use of the model. Let's consider case 1. In this case we would simply say that for this numerical case the model is useless. In the CRR model case we can actually get around the whole problem of negative probabilities, but let us ignore this for the moment.

In case 2 we could override the few negative probabilities in some "smart" way. This will in general make the model lose information (in particular if calibrated to the market in some way) and is not desirable, as is also indicated by Derman, Kani and Chriss (1996) in the use of their implied trinomial tree.

Consider now case 3. The problem with the CRR tree is in my view actually not the negative probabilities, but the choice of sample space. The negative probabilities simply indicate that the forward price is outside the sample space. The forward price is in a "hidden state", not covered by the sub-optimal location of nodes in the tree. The sub-optimal choice of sample space could certainly be a problem when trying to value some options. Actual realizations of the asset price of relevance to the option price could easily fall outside the sample-space of the model. The strike price X can also be outside the sample space of the tree. This seems to be the main problem with the CRR tree, and not the negative probabilities. We could easily think of an example where the user of the CRR model simply used it to compute forward prices, taking into account a deterministic term structure of interest rates and dividends (b_i). Computing the forward price can naturally be achieved in a simpler and more efficient way, but there is nothing wrong with using a complex model to value a simple product, except possibly wasting computer speed. Even with negative probabilities (and probabilities larger than unity) the CRR tree will still give the correct forward price. Allowing negative probabilities still leaves the model partly intact. The negative probabilities actually seem to add flexibility to the model.

It is also worth reminding ourselves that most probabilities used in quantitative finance are so called risk-neutral probabilities, including the binomial probabilities we have just looked at. As every reader probably already knows, risk-neutral probabilities[5] should not be confused with real probabilities. Risk neutral probabilities, sometimes also called pseudo-probabilities, are simply computational devices constructed for a "fantasy world" (in this case a risk-neutral world) to simplify our calculations. For this reason I can see nothing wrong with at least starting to think about negative probabilities as a mathematical tool of convenience. This expands to outside the world of binomial trees, a binomial model can simply be seen as a special case of a explicit finite difference model, see for example Heston and Zhou (2000) or James (2003). In the same way a trinomial tree can also be shown to be equivalent to the explicit finite difference method (see for example James (2003)) when the probability of the asset price going up p_u and down p_d and stay at the same are set to[6]

$$p_u = \frac{1}{6} + (b - \sigma^2/2)\sqrt{\frac{\Delta t}{12\sigma^2}}$$

$$p_d = \frac{1}{6} - (b - \sigma^2/2)\sqrt{\frac{\Delta t}{12\sigma^2}}$$

$$p_m = \frac{2}{3}$$

This will lead to negative up probability p_u if

$$\sigma > \sqrt{2b + \frac{2}{3\Delta t} + \frac{2\sqrt{1 + 6b\Delta t}}{3\Delta t}}$$

and negative down probability p_d if

$$\sigma < \sqrt{2b + \frac{2}{3\Delta t} - \frac{2\sqrt{1 + 6b\Delta t}}{3\Delta t}}$$

For example with cost-of-carry 20 % and 20 time steps and one year to maturity, we will then get a negative down probability if the volatility is below 7.63 %, this is far from a totally unrealistic case. Similarly, we can also get probabilities higher than unity.[7] In the same way a CRR equivalent trinomial tree can also give negative probabilities, see Appendix.

If you take a close look at The Collector cartoon in negative probability in the mid section of this book you will see that it is surprisingly similar to the binomial and trinomial tree just described. By believing that he is talking to James, the Professor has no idea that the expected death of James is far outside his sample space. The Professor is selecting a sub-optimal sample space, only the future, as basis for his model. The Collector, admittedly having more information, is recognizing that the Professor uses a sub-optimal sample space, but is still able to answer the question with remarkable accuracy, by allowing negative probabilities (pseudo probabilities). This is very much a parallel to considering a node of a tree model outside the geometry of the tree.

3 Getting the Negative Probabilities to Really Work in Your Favor

In the case of the discretization of a geometric Brownian motion through a binomial or trinomial model we can admittedly avoid negative probabilities altogether. In the CRR or trinomial tree just described this can be done simply by respectively setting the number of time steps n equal to or higher than

$$\text{Integer}\left[\frac{T}{(\sigma/b)^2}\right], \quad \text{Integer}\left[3bT\left(-1 + \frac{b}{\sigma^2} + \frac{\sigma^2}{4b}\right)\right] + 1.$$

For very low volatility and high cost-of-carry this will typically require a lot of time steps, and can for this reason be very computer intensive. A better way to avoid negative probabilities is to choose a more optimal sample space, for example in a binomial tree this can be done using a geometry of the tree as suggested by Jarrow and Rudd (1983), setting

$$u = e^{(b-\sigma^2/2)\Delta t + \sigma\sqrt{\Delta t}}, \quad \text{and} \quad d = e^{(b-\sigma^2/2)\Delta t - \sigma\sqrt{\Delta t}},$$

which gives equal up and down probability of

$$p = 0.5, \qquad 1 - p = 0.5.$$

Even if the CRR tree and the Jarrow-Rudd tree use different sample space and probability measure they are both equivalent in the limit, for many time steps. For a binomial tree there are an almost unlimited amount of sample spaces to choose from, each with their own probability measure, but all leading to the same result in the limit.

For more complex models and stochastic processes we will not necessarily be able to avoid negative probabilities. Does this mean that the model has to be trashed? In the introduction to this chapter I told you that all papers I have seen in the finance literature are negative about negative probabilities. This is not entirely true; in a recent and very interesting paper by Forsyth, Vetzal and Zvan (2001): "Negative Coefficients in Two Factor Option Models" the authors illustrate how some finite difference/finite element models with negative probabilities are still stable and consistent. They show how the requirement of positive pseudo-probabilities are not only unnecessary but can also even be detrimental. Forsyth, Vetzal and Zvan seem to try to avoid the term "negative probability", and are consistently using the term "negative coefficients". What they call negative coefficients are closely related to the binomial and trinomial probabilities we have just discussed (as also indicated by the authors). That the authors possibly try to avoid the term negative probability seems to be somewhat of a parallel to how many physicists treat the Wigner distribution. Wigner and Szilard developed a distribution function which for the first time was applied by Wigner to calculate quantum corrections to a gas pressure formula. Wigner originally called this a probability function. The Wigner distribution gives apparently negative probabilities for some quantum states. For this reason many physicists prefer to call it the Wigner function, this even though it has no other physical interpretation than a probability distribution. Khrennikov (1999) gives a detailed mathematical description of why it should be considered a probability distribution, and also explains why the Wigner distribution results in negative probabilities.

Even if Forsyth, Vetzal and Zvan seem to avoid the term negative probabilities, their paper is an excellent illustration of just what I have been looking for, a demonstration that allowing negative probabilities potentially can make a difference in quantitative finance models.

The binomial, trinomial and finite difference models we have touched upon so far were developed originally by assuming probabilities in the interval [0, 1]. So even if negative probabilities seem to add flexibility to some of these models we must be careful with the interpretation of any such negative pseudo-probabilities.

4   Hidden Variables in Finance

Feynman's idea of applying negative probabilities to hidden variables might possibly have some parallels in finance. Expected return, and expected risk (expected volatility, correlation, etc.) are hidden variables that cannot be observed directly. Such hidden variables in finance still play an important role and can affect other observable variables. Derman (1996) describes these as hidden variables in the context of the somewhat related topic of model risk, where he indicates that such variables may simply be individuals' opinions. Much modern financial modeling deals with uncertainty for such hidden variables, however it looks like no one has considered including negative probabilities in such calculations. Inspired by Dirac, Feynman and Hawking could there be that negative probabilities could also be of use to model hidden financial ghosts? Ultimately one would naturally like to see research that proves that using negative probabilities gives a clear advantage.

4.1 Negative Probabilities Hidden in Waste from Model Break Downs?

Personally I don't know of any financial model that at some point in time has not had a breakdown – there's a reason why we call them "models". Just as an example, any derivatives valuation model I am aware of assumes that the current asset price is known. When valuing, for example, a stock option we take the latest traded stock price from our computer screen as input to the model. In reality this price is not known. Every year there are many incorrectly reported prices, due to a human error, or a hardware or software problem. One can naturally reduce the uncertainty surrounding the current price by double-checking several independent providers, etc. However, there is uncertainty concerning any price, even the current one. In some sense almost any asset in financial markets can be affected by "hidden variables". For example in the interbank Foreign Exchange markets, if you physically trade an option at a price over the phone you cannot with 100 % certainty know that you actually traded at that price. It is not uncommon that the counterpart calls you up hours later to cancel or adjust the price of a deal, because they claim they priced it using wrong input parameters, human error or whatever. Few or no models in quantitative finance take such situations into account.

Others examples of model break downs occur when asset prices take values completely outside our expected sample space. I remember some years ago, when the electricity price in a part of Norway actually went negative for a few hours during the night. The electricity was produced by hydropower using large turbines. When there is an over supply of electricity on the grid one can naturally shut down some of the turbines, however this can be a costly process. In this case, instead of shutting down the turbine the power producer was willing to pay someone to use the electricity. The Scandinavian electricity markets are probably the most efficient electricity markets in the world, including futures, forwards and options. We can easily think about a derivative model assuming positive prices breaking down in such a scenario. Finance professors' assumption of "no free lunch" is probably only a reality on the university campuses.

My main point is that there are almost unlimited examples of cases where the real uncertainty is outside the sample space of our quantitative models. A whole new field of finance has grown out of model errors, going under the name "model risk". Can it be that negative probabilities are hidden in the "data waste" from such model breakdowns? There are obviously many ways that we can improve our models and still stay inside the standard assumption of probabilities between 0 and 1, but could it be that building our models from the ground up to allow negative probabilities in the first place could help us make the models more robust, closer to reality?

5   The Future of Negative Probabilities in Quantitative Finance

The main reason that negative probabilities have not yet found much use in quantitative finance is probably that the researchers that have developed these models have been doing this under the belief that any probability must lie between 0 and 1, limiting their view to Kolmogorov probabilities. So far, I have only made a feeble attempt to trace the footsteps of Dirac and Feynman. That is, we have considered negative probabilities as just formal quantities that can be useful in certain calculations. Most people in quantitative finance are interested in finance and not the foundation of probability theory and have probably for this reason ignored the fact that the Komologrov model is not necessarily the complete picture of stochastic reality. To take the next step we need to use a rigid mathematical foundation for a probability theory that also allows for negative probabilities. Andrei Khrennikov has developed such a theory, he has found the root of negative probabilities in the very foundation of probability theory: ensemble and frequency. With the background to his theory described in mathematical detail in his brilliant book: "Interpretations of Probability" (1999), see also Khrennikov (1997), there is reason to believe that negative probabilities applied to finance could be the next step. The Kolmogorov probability theory that is the basis of all mathematical finance today can be seen as the limited case of a more general probability theory developed by a handful of scientists standing on the shoulders of giants like Dirac and Feynman. The probability that the future of quantitative finance will contain negative probabilities is possibly negative, but that does not necessarily exclude negative probabilities.

> If you eliminate the impossible, whatever remains, however improbable, must be the truth. (Sherlock Holmes)

6 Appendix: Negative Probabilities in CRR Equivalent Trinomial Tree

Trinomial trees introduced by Boyle (1986), are similar to binomial trees and are also very popular in the valuation of derivative securities. One possibility is to build a trinomial tree with CRR equivalent parameters, where the asset price at each node can go up, stay at the same level, or go down. In that case, the up-and-down jump sizes are:

$$u = e^{\sigma\sqrt{2\Delta t}}, \qquad d = e^{-\sigma\sqrt{2\Delta t}},$$

and the probability of going up and down respectively are:

$$p_u = \left(\frac{e^{b\Delta t/2} - e^{-\sigma\sqrt{\Delta t/2}}}{e^{\sigma\sqrt{\Delta t/2}} - e^{-\sigma\sqrt{\Delta t/2}}} \right)^2$$

$$p_d = \left(\frac{e^{\sigma\sqrt{\Delta t/2}} - e^{b\Delta t/2}}{e^{\sigma\sqrt{\Delta t/2}} - e^{-\sigma\sqrt{\Delta t/2}}} \right)^2.$$

The probabilities must sum to unity. Thus the probability of staying at the same asset price level is

$$p_m = 1 - p_u - p_d.$$

When the volatility σ is very low and the cost-of-carry is very high p_u and p_d can become larger than one and then naturally p_m will become negative. More precisely we will get a negative

probability $p_m < 0$ when

$$\sigma < \sqrt{\frac{b^2 \Delta t}{2}}.$$

From this we can also find that we need to set the number of time steps to $n \geq \text{Integer}\left[\frac{b^2 T}{2\sigma^2}\right] + 1$ to avoid negative probabilities. Alternatively we could avoid negative probabilities by choosing a more optimal sample space.

Figure 14.1:   The impossible staircase hedge fund

The impossible staircase was more or less invented by the Swedish artist Oscar Reutersvard in the early 1950s. It was independently re-discovered by Lionel and Roger Penrose in 1958, which inspired the famous Dutch graphic artist Maurits Cornelis Escher to make several artistic pieces based on it. In terms of finance, every step on the staircase illustrates the steady stable returns, month-by-month, step-by-step, that many funds and traders promise. The impossible staircase is simply an illusion due to the fact that we try to get a three-dimensional world into a two-dimensional one, ignoring a real dimension. Many funds and traders are simply generating excess returns by ignoring hidden risk dimensions. These risk-dimensions will sooner or later show up, with the result of funds and traders suddenly and unexpectedly blowing up.

FOOTNOTES & REFERENCES

1. At least in the sense that they urge one to avoid negative probabilities.

2. For stocks $(b = r)$, stocks and stock indexes paying a continuous dividend yield q $(b = r - q)$, futures $(b = 0)$, and currency options with foreign interest rate r_f $(b = r - r_f)$.

3. Negative risk-neutral probabilities will also lead to negative local variance in the tree, the variance at any time step in the CRR tree is given by $\sigma_i^2 = \frac{1}{\Delta t}p(1-p)(\ln(u^2))^2$. Negative variance seems absurd, there are several papers discussing negative volatility, see Peskir and Shiryaev (2001), Haug (2002) and Aase (2004).

4. This is also described by Hull (2002), page 407, as well as in the accompanying solution manual, page 118.

5. Risk-neutral probabilities are simply real world probabilities that have been adjusted for risk. It is therefore not necessary to adjust for risk also in the discount factor for cash-flows. This makes it valid to compute market prices as simple expectations of cash flows, with the *risk adjusted probabilities*, discounted at the *riskless interest rate* – hence the common name "risk-neutral" probabilities, which is somewhat of a misnomer.

6. Hull (2002) also shows the relationship between trinomial trees and the explicit finite difference method, but using another set of probability measure, however as he points out with his choice of probability measure one can get negative probabilities for certain input parameters.

7. We will get a up probability p_u higher than unity if

$$\sigma < \sqrt{2b + \frac{50}{3\Delta t} - \frac{10\sqrt{25 + 6b\Delta t}}{3\Delta t}},$$

and down probability of higher than unity if

$$\sigma > \sqrt{2b + \frac{50}{3\Delta t} + \frac{10\sqrt{25 + 6b\Delta t}}{3\Delta t}}.$$

■ Aase, K. K. (2004) "Negative Volatility and the Survival of the Western Financial Markets" *Wilmott Magazine*, Issue 12, July 2004, 64–67.

■ Boyle, P. P. (1986) "Option Valuation Using a Three Jump Process" *International Options Journal*, **3**, 7–12.

■ Brennan, M. J. and E. S. Schwartz (1978) "Finite Difference Methods and Jump Processes Arising in the Pricing of Contingent Claims: A Synthesis" *Journal of Financial and Quantitative Analysis*, **XIII**(3), 461–474.

■ Castro, C. (2000) "Noncommutative Geometry, Negative Probabilities and Cantorian-Fractal Spacetime" Center for Theoretical Studies of Physical Systems Clark Atlanta University, http://arxiv.org/PS_cache/hep-th/pdf/0007/0007224.pdf.

■ Cereceda, J. L. (2000) "Local Hidden-Variable Models and Negative-Probability Measures" *Working paper*, http://arxiv.org/PS_cache/quant-ph/pdf/0010/0010091.pdf.

■ Chriss, N. A. (1997) *Black-Scholes and Beyond*. Chicago: Irwin Professional Publishing.

■ Cox, J. C., S. A. Ross and M. Rubinstein (1979): "Option Pricing: A Simplified Approach," *Journal of Financial Economics*, **7**, 229–263.

■ Curtright, T. and C. Zachosy (2001) "Negative Probability and Uncertainty Relations," *Modern Physics Letters A*, **16**(37), 2381–2385, http://arxiv.org/PS_cache/hep–th/pdf/0105/0105226.pdf.

■ Derman, E. (1996): "Model Risk" Working paper, Goldman Sachs.

■ Derman, E., I. Kani and N. Chriss (1996): "Implied Trinomial Trees of the Volatility Smile" *Journal of Derivatives*, **3**(4), 7–22.

■ Dirac, P. (1942) "The Physical Interpretation of Quantum Mechanics" *Proc. Roy. Soc. London*, (A 180), 1–39.

■ Feynman, R. P. (1987) "Negative Probability" First published in the book Quantum Implications: Essays in Honour of David Bohm, by F. David Peat (Ed.), Basil Hiley (Ed.) London and New York: Routledge & Kegan Paul Ltd, pp. 235–248, http://kh.bu.edu/qcl/pdf/feynmanr19850a6e6862.pdf.

■ Forsyth, P. A., K. R. Vetzal and R. Zvan (2001): "Negative Coefficients in Two Factor Option Pricing Models" *Working paper*, http://citeseer.ist.psu.edu/435337.html.

■ Haug, E. G. (2002): "A Look in the Antimatter Mirror" *Wilmott Magazine*, www.wilmott.com, December.

■ Heston, S. and G. Zhou (2000): "On the Rate of Convergence of Discrete-Time Contingent Claims" *Mathematical Finance*, **10**, 53–75.

■ Hull, J. (2002) *Option, Futures, and Other Derivatives*, 5th edn. Prentice Hall.

■ Hull, J. and A. White (1990) "Valuing Derivative Securities Using the Explicit Finite Difference Method" *Journal of Financial and Quantitative Analysis*, **25**(1), 87–100.

■ James, P. (2003) *Option Theory*. New York: John Wiley & Sons, Inc.

■ Jarrow, R. and A. Rudd (1983): *Option Pricing*. Chicago: Irwin.

■ Jorgenson, J. and N. Tarabay (2002): "Discrete Time Tree Models Associated to General Probability Distributions" *Working paper*, City College of New York.

■ Khrennikov, A. Y. (1997) *Non-Archimedean Analysis: Quantum Paradoxes, Dynamical Systems and Biological Models*. Kluwer Academic Publishers.

■ —— (1999) *Interpretations of Probability*. Coronet Books.

■ Peacock, K. A. (2002) "A Possible Explanation of the Superposition Principle," *Working paper*, Department of Philosophy University of Lethbridge, http://arxiv.org/PS_cache/quant-ph/pdf/0209/0209082.pdf.

■ Peskir, G. and A. N. Shiryaev (2001) "A note on the Put-Call Parity and a Put-Call Duality" *Theory of Probability and its Applications*, **46**, 181–183.

■ Rubinstein, M. (1998) "Edgeworth Binomial Trees" *Journal of Derivatives*, **XIX**, 20–27.

David Bates

David Bates on Crash and Jumps

David Bates is a Professor of Finance at the University of Iowa. Early on he specialized in jumps and stochastic volatility. David Bates was one of the first to demonstrate practically how implied distributions from liquid options could be used to extract useful market expectations.[1] He has shown us that options are not only of interest to traders and hedgers but also to anyone who wants to obtain information about what some of the smartest people in the market (option traders) know and expect.

David Bates does not only develop fancy models he is also an empiricist, spending a great deal of time testing if the models work reasonably well. As an option trader I am particularly interested in tail events, and especially what I call models of models risk. When most people buy an exchange traded put option and the underlying stock falls in value below the strike price they are certain that they will get paid. Most people forget that underlying their derivatives model they have a model of default risk in the clearinghouse. David Bates has looked empirically into such types of risk, something we soon will learn more about.

Haug : When did you first become interested in quantitative finance?

Bates : Largely by accident. As a grad student at Princeton, my primary interests were in international finance. I was trying to come up with an explanation for uncovered interest parity rejections – the fact that putting money in relatively high-interest currencies has been surprisingly profitable. I thought a peso problem might be the answer, and currency options struck me as the right place to look for evidence of peso problems. Once I started, I got more and more interested in options.

Haug : What exactly is a peso problem?

A "peso problem" is a rare event: something major that investors think may occur, but that econometricians have trouble identifying statistically. The term refers to the Mexican peso in the 1970's. Mexican-U.S. interest differentials suggested a future peso devaluation, yet the exchange rate remained fixed for years – until the peso was ultimately devalued in 1976. I was hypothesizing that something similar might be happening with the dollar versus European currencies in the early 1980's: investors might have been deterred from investing in relatively high-interest dollars by fears of a dollar crash. I figured such crash fears should show up in relatively high prices of out-of-the-money call options on Deutsche marks – which I did indeed find in 1984 and early 1985, as the dollar peaked.

Haug : What is your educational background?

Bates : I was an undergraduate math major at MIT. I loved math, but I realized there that it would be hard for me to push the frontiers. So I gradually switched to economics, ultimately ending with a Ph.D in economics from Princeton. Princeton was a great place at the time to do finance; John Campbell, Pete Kyle and Sandy Grossman were there.

Haug : You were to my knowledge one of the very first to extract implied distributions from liquid option prices, in a paper you published in the Journal of Finance in 1991. How did you come up with this idea and what was the paper about?

Bates : It was really a spin-off of the peso problem research in my dissertation. I was looking at foreign currency options for evidence of fears of a dollar crash – this was in the summer of 1987. When the stock market crashed that fall, it was obvious that the same methodology could be used with stock index options. So I got CME data for options on S&P 500 futures, and ran the same diagnostics I had run for Deutsche mark futures options: my skewness premium measure of implicit skewness, and daily implicit parameter estimates of a jump-diffusion model roughly based on Merton (1976). Backing out implicit jump-diffusion parameters was essentially the same idea as computing implicit volatility; but the more general model allowed greater flexibility in implicit distributions and assessing crash risk.

Haug : Based on the implied distributions, you backed out. Did the stock option market anticipate the stock crash of 1987?

Bates : Yes and no. I did find substantial fears of a crash implicit in option prices during the year before the actual crash; in particular, during October 1986 to February 1987 and again in June to August, 1987. Indeed, the negative implicit skewness during those periods was comparable to the pronounced negative skewness we have observed since the crash of '87. However, the implicit crash fears subsided quickly after the market peaked in August 1987, and were negligible in the weeks leading up to the crash.

Haug : What are the differences and similarities between implied risk neutral distributions and expected real distributions, is it only the mean that is different, what about volatility, skewness, kurtosis and even higher order moments?

Bates : The conditional mean always changes. The impact on other moments depends upon what sorts of risks are being priced: stochastic volatility risk, for instance, or jump risk. A stochastic volatility risk premium primarily affects the term structure of expected average variances (actual versus risk-neutral), but has less impact on other moments. At short maturities, the actual and risk-neutral variances should be identical if the only risk is stochastic volatility.

A jump risk premium primarily changes the actual versus risk-neutral jump intensity; there are also effects on the mean jump size. These directly affect variance assessments at all maturities, but also affect skewness and kurtosis. For stock market crash risk, the risk-neutral jump intensity is higher than the actual jump intensity, creating higher variance under the risk-neutral distribution and also more downside risk.

Haug : **You were also the first to describe put-call symmetry, how was this related to extracting implied distributions?**

Bates : I called it the "skewness premium:" the proposition that call options x % out-of-the-money should be worth x % more than comparably OTM put options, for a broad class of quasi-symmetric distributions with small degrees of positive skewness. I had noticed it was a property of the Black-Scholes-Merton call and put formulas. I subsequently realised it was also a property of other popular option pricing models: the Hull and White (1987)/Scott (1987) stochastic volatility option pricing models, the Merton (1976) jump-diffusion model with mean-zero jumps. Furthermore, it held for exchange-traded American futures options, for which I could get data, as well as for European options in general.

The advantage of the skewness premium was that I could say all of these models were wrong, and that we needed models with more skewness, without having to get into model-specific estimation. It was a simple and intuitive nonparametric diagnostic. Now, of course, we routinely build skewness into our option pricing models.

Haug : **How was the jump-diffusion model you introduced in 1991 different from the Merton-76 jump-diffusion model?**

Bates : Primarily in pricing jump risk. Merton's model assumed jump risks were firm-specific and idiosyncratic, so that the actual and risk-neutral jump intensities and jump distributions were identical. Since I was working with stock index options, for which jump risk must be systematic, I had to come up with a method of pricing that risk. I did that in my dissertation, by extending the Cox, Ingersoll and Ross (1985) general equilibrium production economy model to jump-diffusions. My 1991 paper did it more simply, by working more directly with the distribution of what we now call the "pricing kernel".

Haug : **What are the fundamental reasons for jumps in financial markets?**

Bates : Good question, but I don't know the answer. Small jumps can often be attributed to announcement effects, or major pieces of news. However, it's the large jumps that we worry about, and we don't really know what causes those.

Haug : **If you use an option model assuming continuous hedging and you cannot hedge continuously in practice due to transaction costs, etc then I assume this also must have an impact on the implied distribution you are backing out from an option model?**

Bates : Not necessarily. It is possible to derive option pricing models from equilibrium grounds, rather than from no-arbitrage grounds. Indeed, the original Black-Scholes paper primarily derived the formula from the continuous-time CAPM. I think I recall that Fischer Black preferred that justification, precisely because he was skeptical as to whether the no-arbitrage strategy was implementable.

Haug : **Every good option trader I am aware of knows that jumps are extremely important for option valuation and especially out-of-the money options with short time to maturity. Relatively few option traders I know use option models that takes into account jumps, instead they try to fudge a simpler model. Why is this, is it to difficult to estimate the parameters, are the jump models not good enough or is it simply that most traders are not smart enough?**

Bates : The analogy I draw is Newton versus Ptolemy in planetary orbits. Academics are interested in identifying the underlying deeper structure: the fact that orbits are elliptical. Practitioners are interested in what works; their fudge factors are the equivalent of epicycles and epicenters. And such fudge factors did work; I gather the Ptolemaic model could indeed predict planetary orbits as well as the Newtonian model, for the data available in Newton's time.

In option pricing, we don't yet have a simple, perfectly fitting model equivalent to Newton's model. A simple jump model has difficulty matching option prices at all maturities, even when calibrated to one day's data. We're moving to more complicated models that do fit progressively better; but maybe we too are just engaging in the equivalent of adding more epicycles and epicenters. Furthermore, the academic research is focused more on pricing, whereas practitioners are more interested in hedging. So it is perhaps not surprising that practitioners have their own methods, which presumably work for them.

Haug : **Even if I calibrate a jump-diffusion model to many years of historical data I think that I would always underestimate the potential jump size, even if I include the crash of '87 in my data. How do we know that we will not have an even bigger crash at some point ahead?**

Bates : I currently view the '87 crash (down 23 %) as a "normal" 10–15 % crash that was made worse by the DOT system getting overloaded; remember that the market rebounded the following two days. If the order flow system has adequate capacity, then another '87-like crash would appear unlikely. But predicting rare events is inherently difficult, as illustrated by Irving Fisher's famous 1929 comment about stocks having reached a permanently high plateau.

Haug : **In practice is there any way we can hedge options against jump risk without using other options?**

Bates : One can get a partial hedge by delta-hedging with the underlying asset, or with futures, but a more exact hedge does indeed require using other options.

Haug : **What is the latest on jump risk research?**

Bates : I would say there is increasing recognition that not only is there jump risk, but that it varies over time. My 2000 J.Econometrics paper shows that models with stochastic jump intensities fit option prices better, and there has been some time series research by, e.g., Eraker, Johannes and Polson supporting that model. We're making substantial progress in devising methods of estimating models with stochastic volatility and/or jump risk directly from time series data – as opposed to calibrating the models from option prices. Finally, the models with Lévy processes are exploring alternate fat-tailed specifications, and are using random time changes to capture stochastic volatility as well.

Haug : **In some recent research, "Hedging the Smirk" you look at a "model free" method for inferring deltas and gammas from the market. What is the main idea behind this and how are these deltas and gammas different from those of Black-Scholes-Merton?**

Bates : The paper came out of some consulting work I did some time ago: how do you hedge options when the volatility smirk clearly indicates that the Black-Scholes-Merton model is wrong? The paper exploits Euler's theorem: for any homogeneous option pricing function, we can compute deltas (and gammas) from the observable cross-sectional sensitivity of option prices to the strike price. Most of our option pricing models, for stochastic volatility or jump risk, possess this homogeneity property. Translated into implicit volatilities, it creates simple correction terms for deltas and gammas relative to the BSM values for cases when the implicit volatility curve is not perfectly flat.

Haug : The Black-Scholes-Merton delta for deep-out-of-the-money options is extremely sensitive to the volatility used to calculate the delta, does your "model free" method help here as well?

Bates : Unfortunately, no; the procedure only identifies how to hedge against delta or gamma risk. It can be used to hedge against pure jump risk; delta-gamma hedging works pretty well for that. However, asset price jumps are typically accompanied by implicit volatility jumps, especially in stock index options, and a delta-hedged position will still have vega risk. Delta-gamma neutral positions will do better; if you neutralize the gamma, you neutralize much of the vega as well.

Haug : When the market is in a normal period; low or moderate volatility individual stocks tend to jump in different directions. So by having a portfolio of stocks, some short and some long, I will be more or less hedged, some stocks will typically jump up while others jump down. But in a market crash all stocks tend to jump in the same direction, can you comment on this, how can one model and hedge such behavior?

Bates : I gather there is some interest in "dispersion trading" to exploit this: buying portfolios of stock options and writing stock index options. Since individual stock options generally appear to be fairly priced while stock index options are overpriced, it's been a profitable strategy historically. However, it's not a riskless strategy, given that a portfolio of options is not the same as an option on a portfolio. One is betting on the overall level of idiosyncratic stock risk.

Haug : You have also studied crash aversion, in short what is this about?

Bates : That's theoretical work in progress aimed at modeling how the option markets function as a market for trading crash risk. Crash aversion reflects individuals' attitudes towards crash risk; while I express it in utility terms, it is fundamentally equivalent to individuals' subjective beliefs as to the frequency of crashes. For trading to take place, people have to differ in some fashion; and differing crash aversion gives them a motive to trade options. Ultimately, I want to introduce frictions, and model the role of option market makers within this market, but I haven't got there yet.

Haug : You have also done some research on the clearinghouse's default exposure during the 1987 crash, did any of the clearinghouses default at that time and what are the main results of your research on this?

Bates : None did, but some came close. The work, with Roger Craine, was more aimed at providing additional analytical tools for assessing default exposure. The CME's SPAN system is essentially a VaR approach: setting margins such that the probability of a margin-exceeding move is less than 1 %. We were pointing out that clearing houses might also be interested in how much in additional funds would be needed, conditional on margin being exhausted. In the worst-case scenario, the clearing house's responsibility for covering positions means it is essentially short a strangle: a combination of an OTM call and an OTM put. We have methods of evaluating such exposures, from option prices directly or from time series analysis.

Haug : Have we learned from the past, what is the probability that we will get clearing house defaults in the future in the case of a giant market crash?

Bates : I would say yes. Paul Kupiec found that the CME was especially cautious when setting margins on its S&P 500 futures over 1988–92, in the aftermath of the '87 crash. Whether they are still careful, I can't say; it's not something I monitor.

Haug : What about the large number of OTC derivatives that big banks have against other big banks, if one of the big banks defaults could this lead to a chain reaction, to more and more banks going under? Do we have control of the derivatives market?

Bates : That's the issue of systemic risk – something the Fed is rather worried about. There is also considerable concern about the large positions taken by hedge funds. I don't know if much is being done at the regulatory level. We do have a rapidly growing market in credit derivatives, to hedge against individual defaults.

Haug : A currency is in one way similar to a share in the government of that country, can implied distributions from FX options be used to predict defaults of government obligations and financial crises for a country?

Bates : In principle, yes, but it's a bit indirect. Also, FX options are relatively short-maturity. I'd be more inclined to look at fixed-income markets; the country-specific spread over LIBOR on adjustable-rate notes, for instance.

Haug : How good are modern jumps and stochastic volatility models, what is the empirical research telling us?

Bates : We continue to make great progress with stochastic volatility models, and now have a better understanding of volatility dynamics. For instance, we now know that volatility has both short-term and long-term swings. Research into jumps has been evolving more slowly, but using intradaily data is providing some new insights. For instance, whereas the jump-diffusion model appears reasonable for daily data, it's less good for intradaily. The 1987 crash did not occur within 5 seconds, for instance; it took all day to fall. A better model is volatility spikes; realized intradaily volatility jumped from its normal level of about 1 % daily, to 12 % daily on the day of the crash. Aggregated up to daily data (close to close), that looks like a crash; but the intradaily pattern is different.

Haug : With your research background in jumps, stochastic volatility, crash risk and clearinghouse defaults what would you say about VaR and Sharpe ratios as risk management tools for options and other financial instruments?

Bates : It's a starting point, and is better than not having any risk management in place. But one has to be careful, given distributions can be far from normal.

Haug : Who was the first to discover fat-tails – was it Mandelbrot?[2]

Bates : Mandelbrot certainly drew attention to the issue, in the 1960's. Not many use Mandelbrot's stable Paretian specification, however. Infinite-variance processes are rather hard to use in finance, and the prediction that weekly or monthly returns should be as fat-tailed as daily returns appears counterfactual. Merton drew attention to jump-diffusion processes, which are certainly easier to work with. Currently, there's a lot of interest in Lévy processes, which predate Mandelbrot.

Haug : You have spent your career in academia. Have you ever considered working as an option trader, trying to apply your models and ideas to making big bucks and driving sports cars?

Bates : I did work for a couple of years at the First National Bank of Chicago, before returning to Princeton for my doctorate, so my career hasn't been purely academic. But yes, it has been mostly academic. And no, I have not considered working as an option trader. I would assume that requires a wholly different set of skills.

Haug : Have you experienced any jumps in stochastic process life integral so far, and if so were they positive or negative.

Bates : Moving from Wharton to the University of Iowa was certainly a shock, but overall it has worked out well. I grew up in a college town, in Sewanee, Tennessee, and the life style is comfortable. My family certainly enjoys it.

Haug : Do you have any hobbies outside quantitative finance?

Bates : Mostly reading; I'm a great history buff. I used to play tennis, but do less of that, now. I enjoy cycling, and generally try to arrange a cycling trip when I go to Europe.

Haug : In your view where are we in the evolution of quantitative finance?

Bates : At this point, I think we're reaching diminishing returns in terms of modeling univariate stochastic processes. We can argue over precise fat-tailed specifications, jumps versus other Lévy, for instance, but the important issue was just recognizing that there are indeed fat-tails. Similarly, I'm not sure how much further we can push our stochastic volatility models. There's probably room for improvement in modeling multivariate processes; correlation risk, for instance.

I think we need more work on the finance side, as opposed to the math side. Derivatives permit individuals to trade other risks: credit risk, jump risk and volatility risk, for example. How well do the markets for these risks work? Judging from the profit opportunities from selling OTM puts on stock indexes, not very efficiently.

Those with predominantly a math background feel comfortable with stochastic processes and continuous-time finance; but I see a certain amount of hand-waving when it comes to the transformation from objective to risk-neutral distributions. The use of Esscher transforms, for instance; they work, but what's the rationale? The transformation of probability measure is the issue of compensation for risk – a fundamental finance question. If it's too high, as it appears to be, why isn't money pouring in to exploit the opportunities? I think we need more realistic models of market structure – in particular, of the market makers. But that's an academic's perspective; the practitioners can just go on happily making money off of the market inefficiencies.

FOOTNOTES & REFERENCES

1. See also Breeden and Litzenberger (1978).
2. Actually after asking this question I found out that Mandelbrot (1963) referred to Mitchell (1915) as probably the first known to have described fat-tails in price series. However, there is no doubt that Mandelbrot did a great job of drawing attention to this subject.

■ Bates, D. S. (1991) "The Crash of '87: Was It Expected? The Evidence from Options Markets" *Journal of Finance*, **46**(3), 1009–1044.
■ ———— (1996) "Dollar Jump Fears, 1984–1992: Distributional Abnormalities Implicit in Foreign Currency Futures Options" *Journal of International Money and Finance*, **15**(1), 65–93.
■ ———— (2000) "Post-'87 Crash Fears in the S&P 500 Futures Option Market" *Journal of Econometrics*, **94**(1/2), 181–238.
■ ———— (2003) "Empirical Option Pricing: A Retrospection" *Journal of Econometrics*, **116**(1/2), 387–404.
■ ———— (2005) "Hedging the Smirk" *Finance Research Letters*, **2**(4), 195–200.
■ ———— (2006) "The Market for Crash Risk" Working paper, University of Iowa and NBER, March.
■ Bates, D. S. and R. Craine (1999) "Valuing the Futures Market Clearinghouse's Default Exposure During the 1987 Crash" *Journal of Money, Credit, and Banking*, **31**(2), 248–272.
■ Black, F. and M. Scholes (1973) "The Pricing of Options and Corporate Liabilities," *Journal of Political Economy*, **81**, 637–654.
■ Breeden, D. T. and R. H. Litzenberger (1978) "Price of State-Contingent Claims Implicit in Option Prices," *Journal of Business* **51**, 621–651.
■ Cox, J. C., J. E. Ingersoll and S. A. Ross (1985) "An Intertemporal General Equilibrium Model of Asset Prices," *Econometrica*, **53**, 363–384.
■ Eraker, B., M. Johannes and N. Polson (2003) "The Impact of Jumps in Volatility Returns" *Journal of Finance*, **LVIII**(3), 1296–1300.
■ Hull, J. and A. White (1987) "The Pricing of Options on Assets with Stochastic Volatilities" *Journal of Finance*, **42**(2), 281–300.
■ Kupiec, P. (1994) "The Performance of S&P500 Futures Product Margins under the SPAN Margining System" *The Journal of Futures Markets*, **14**(7), 789–812.
■ Mandelbrot, B. (1963) "New Methods in Statistical Economics" *Journal of Political Economy*, **61**(5), 421–440.
■ Merton, R. C. (1976) "Option Pricing When Underlying Stock Returns are Discontinuous" *Journal of Financial Economics*, **3**, 125–144.
■ Mitchell, Wesley, C. (1915) "The Making and Using of Index Numbers" *Introduction to Index Numbers and Wholesale Prices in the United States and Foreign Countries* (published in 1915 as Bulletin No. 173 of the U.S. Bureau of Labor Statistics, reprinted in 1921 as Bulletin No. 284).
■ Scott, L. (1987) "Option Pricing When the Variance Changes Randomly – Theory, Estimation, and an Application" *Journal of Financial and Quantitative Analysis*, **22**, 419–438.

15
Hidden Conditions and Coin Flip Blow Up's*

1 Blowing Up

I will now take a quick look at the danger of ignoring hidden conditions in quantitative finance. How many times have we heard about traders, hedge funds and trading desks being surprised by sudden unexpected massive losses? I am not speaking only about inexperienced traders, for some of the most talented people in this field have lost their shirts. The LTCM blow up with Meriwether and his team, including Nobel prize winners Scholes and Merton, offers only one example. Personally, I was lucky enough to burn a considerable amount of my own wealth at an early age, so let's start with the inexperienced trader blowing up. Fortunately, my net wealth was also very low at that time, so despite the large percentage losses, the dollar amount did not make the press, until now. In 1986 I was studying garden plants at a university in southern Norway, and in-between classes I would go out to the phone booth and call my stock broker. As this was before the internet and cell phones were commonplace, an old-time coin phone booth was my only weapon. By mid 1987 I had made fantastic returns simply by flipping in and out of long stock positions, and I of course felt like the master of the universe. Soon my small savings that I had originally saved up from hard physical work at my grandmother's farm blossomed into a money tree that simply had to be watered daily and would grow predictably, and I planned to cash it in soon and buy a red sports car. On 20 October 1987, the Oslo stock exchange crashed and took my profits with it. I felt the pain, the frustration, and the panic, dumping my stock as fast as possible, and losing almost all my profit, causing my red sports car to ride off and vanish into the sunset.

Now, when trading options on Wall Street, I am very happy that I learned this lesson at an early stage in my career. Losing my red sports car in a stock market crash was far better than losing it in a car crash; at least all my body parts were intact, though I had possibly lost my mojo (which I got back later). Most importantly, this instilled in me a great respect for the markets. What had I done wrong? I had been listening carefully to my broker, who was a professional and had to know what he was doing! Furthermore, the local bank that had given me a loan to invest in stocks had instructed me not to invest in shipping-related ones, deeming them far too risky, and advising instead that I invest in banks and real estate companies. I listened to these self-proclaimed experts, and also thought of myself as one. Why not, I had already built an impressive track record. I ended up investing most of my hard-earned cash in banks and in fast growing real

---

*I would like to thank Erik Stettler for helpful comments.

estate stocks (that would soon go bankrupt). It all worked very well for a while, until the crash of 1987. In more mathematical terms, I had been assigning a very high probability to the notion that these people, including myself, actually knew what they where doing, and had ignored the fact that this was all based on the condition that basically anybody can make money going long stocks in a bull market, at least for a while. But I soon learned the hard way that making money in a bull market should never be confused with one's IQ. I was a green investor with green fingers studying garden plants, with little or no knowledge about investing or trading, blowing up my own money. Still, why is it that even smart and talented people with many years of experience can also blow up? Can it be that the inexperienced and experienced traders have something in common?

2 Coin Flip Blow Up's

A model, whether it is based simply on years of experience and common sense or on state-of-the art quantitative financial mathematics, might work well in most situations, but in some cases it can and will break down. You would then typically blow up, or be lucky enough to get unexpectedly rich. As Dr Nassime Taleb once said, "If you are so rich why are you so dumb?", see Taleb (2001). That is why we call it a model. More precisely, any model is a conditional model. It is based typically on certain explicit assumptions, but often also on some implicit conditions. When it comes to the explicitly stated assumptions, it is easier to determine in what cases the model will break down or have to undergo major adjustments. For example, Black and Scholes stated explicitly in their 1973 paper that the model was based on the assumption of constant volatility. Based on this, it is not hard to see that the model will possibly (but not necessarily) break down under stochastic volatility. It should come as no big surprise that much of the modern option literature has been focusing on this assumption and on how stochastic volatility and jump-diffusion processes affect option values.

The main danger in applying any quantitative model is not when there is a breakdown in explicitly stated assumptions, for these can be stress-tested relatively easily, or alternatively, we can replace the model with another one closer to reality. Most of the finance literature tends to focus on breakdowns in explicitly stated assumptions. For example, there are hundreds of papers looking into how stochastic volatility will affect the option value relative to the Black-Scholes world. This is naturally fine, but it is easy to forget that almost any model is also dependent on many implicit conditions. Many of these conditions are often hidden in such a way that it takes some serious thought to identify them. One good method is to ask what other models (or common sense) this particular model is based on. For example, almost any option or derivatives model is based on probability theory, typically the Kolmogorov's probability theory that is the corner stone of modern probability. As described by Ballentine (2001) in Kolmogorov's probability theory, the conditional probability is relegated to secondary status,[1] while the mathematical fiction of "absolute probability" is made primary. According to Ballentine (2001) there are several objections to taking Kolmogorov's axioms as the foundation of Probability Theory; it should be seen rather as a model of a more fundamental Probability Theory. Among other things, the secondary status of conditions in Kolmogorov's model can easily make us forget that in reality any probability actually has to be a conditional probability. As an illustration, let's look at the flip of a coin.

Not too long ago, I asked a group of people, some traders, some academics and some quant nerds, for the probability of getting heads-up on a coin toss. Most of them looked at me as if I was wasting their time with common sense. One trader thought I was trying to trick him and told me that if it was a fair coin then the probability of heads up would be close to 50 %, or actually slightly smaller if one included the very slight probability of the coin ending on its edge. As an options trader, he at least considered some extreme tail events in his model. Even with a fair coin, our answer of a roughly 50 % probability of heads-up is still based on many implicit conditions. The reason we would typically not mention or even think about them is that we base our answer on common sense, historical experience and what we learned at school. But common sense is dangerous, or as Einstein once said, "Common sense is the collection of prejudices acquired by age eighteen". The answer of 50 % probability is based implicitly on a fair coin as well as on the exact time, place and all the particulars that make the event (in this case a coin flip) unique and unrepeatable, see Rocchi (2001) for more detail on this. For example, a 50 % probability of heads-up on a coin flip is based on gravity. What is the probability of ending heads-up or even on the edge in a zero gravity environment? Most of the universe is comprised of "empty space" with close to zero gravity, so a 50 % probability of the coin landing heads-up can actually be seen as a tail event. Actually what we consider an extreme tail event, edge up, using our collection of prejudices, could very well be a quite common event in most of the universe(?). Who knows, next time you walk into a party and someone challenges you to a coin flip bet, it could be an astronaut planning to perform the coin flip in outer space. Of course, to meet a astronaut in a bar is in itself probably a 4 sigma event, so the probability for that condition is no doubt too low to be taken seriously. Or wait a minute, this is also conditional on what type of party you are invited to. If it is a farewell party for astronauts, then the probability of such an event suddenly becomes significant.

By thinking about probabilities as being always conditional, we have uncovered several hidden conditions behind a coin flip bet. Then after we have uncovered the hidden conditions we can consider the probability of the various conditions and thus better judge if it is a good trade or not. But let's get back to reality – what does a coin flip in space have to do with quantitative finance and trading? We are still not in the age of space-time finance.[2] But too often, risk managers, traders, portfolio managers and corporations ignore possibly hidden implicit conditions behind their models and their trades. I can see no other reason why so many smart people have blown up hundreds if not billions of dollars. But didn't I just ignore a possibly hidden condition, in that I just assumed that these people were smart in the first place? Well, I'd better stop before I turn myself into an arrogant besser weiser,[3] my point is simply that by thinking about every probability as a conditional probability, we will have a greater chance at uncovering what conditions the model is actually based on, and thus in avoiding blow-ups and instead make big bucks. In other words, "Don't assume. It makes an ass out of you and me".

Models are often based on simplified unrealistic assumptions. Before using a model always ask yourself how robust is this model, and what explicit and implicit assumptions is it built on.

FOOTNOTES & REFERENCES

1. Kolmogorov's axioms are basically (1) $P(\Omega) = 1$. (2) $P(f) \geq 0$ for any f in Ω. (3) If $f_1, \ldots f_n$ are disjoint then $P(f) = \sum_i f_i$, where f is the union of $f_1, \ldots f_n$. (4) if $f_i \rightarrow \emptyset$ (the empty set then) $P(f_i) \rightarrow 0$.
2. See Chapter 13.
3. If you don't understand this, just look up in a German dictionary.

■ Ballentine, L. E. (2001) "Interpretations of Probability and Quantum Theory" in *Foundations of Probability and Physics*, A. Khrennikov (Ed.). Singapore: World Scientific.
■ Black, F. and M. Scholes (1973) "The Pricing of Options and Corporate Liabilities" *Journal of Political Economy*, **81**, 637–654.
■ Rocchi, P. (2001) "Is Random Event the Core Question? Some Remarks and A Proposal" in *Foundations of Probability and Physics*, A. Khrennikov (Ed.). Singapore: World Scientific.
■ Taleb, N. (2001) *Fooled by Randomness*. New York: Texere.

Peter Jäckel, the specialist on Monte Carlo simulation and random numbers, seems to believe that rubbing the soles of Billiken will guarantee a positive outcome. The Monte Carlo master has certainly switched into low-discrepancy numbers. (Billiken is "the God of things as they ought to be")

Peter Jäckel on Monte Carlo Simulation

Peter Jäckel is Global Head of Credit, Hybrid, Inflation and Commodity Derivative Analytics at ABN AMRO, he has also worked in quantitative research for Nikko Securities, Royal Bank of Scotland and Commerzbank Securities. Doctor Jäckel has published a great book entitled "Monte Carlo Methods in Finance" (2002), I hope we will see a second edition before too long.

Haug : Where did you grow up?

Jaeckel : Darmstadt, Germany.

Haug : When did you first become interested in mathematics and quantitative finance?

Jäckel : As for mathematics, probably as soon as I could grasp the concept of numbers. Quantitative Finance was more of a chance event – I was thinking about leaving academic research in theoretical physics and spoke to some recruitment agencies who suggested to me to go for some interviews in the City of London.

Haug : What is your educational background?

Jäckel : Physics, specifically Nonlinear Dynamics and Bifurcation Theory in applied Theoretical Physics. First degree from Darmstadt, D. Phil. from Oxford.

Haug : What is the origin of the name Monte Carlo simulation, did it come from the casinos of Monte Carlo?

Jäckel : Nicholas Metropolis is said to have come up with the term, in allusion to his colleague Stanislaw Ulam's liking of Poker and other card games. Both worked with John von Neumann on the Manhattan project. The method itself is said to have been conceived by Stanislaw Ulam who, in 1946, likened the calculation of a solitaire game's statistics by simply iterating the game to the calculation of neutron diffusion statistics. Yes, it was a reference to the fact that the method back then relied on random numbers generated by a roulette wheel or any other truly random number source.

Haug : Did you ever go gambling in Monte Carlo?

Jäckel : After writing the book, I had to, didn't I?

Haug : **Is it true that Monte Carlo simulation also played an important role in developing the atomic bomb?**

Jäckel : That is not so clear. It only became publicly known as a numerical tool in theoretical physics just after the end of WWII. All references point to it first being used in 1946, i.e. one year after the first nuclear bombs had been deployed. It definitely was used from then on as part of the Manhattan project.

Haug : **Was it Phelim Boyle who first applied Monte Carlo simulation to finance?**

Jäckel : He certainly has the first publication in that area. In a way, it was a natural step given the close relationship of the original application of the Monte Carlo method (stochastic diffusion processes in physics) and the models used in quantitative finance. It took a great leap of faith, though, to consider the technique for financial calculations as early as the 1970's when a standard computer was still a large piece of machinery. Respect to the man!

Haug : **What is the definition of a good random number generator?**

Jäckel : Asymptotic uniformity and serial decorrelation.

Haug : **When should one use pseudo-random number generators and when should one use quasi-random numbers?**

Jäckel : I have not used random or pseudo-random numbers for anything other than teaching purposes in years. I have yet to see an application of Monte Carlo methods in finance that I wouldn't prefer doing with low-discrepancy numbers. I would also not use the term *quasi*-random numbers since low-discrepancy numbers have no concept of randomness, quasi- or otherwise. In a nutshell: random numbers – never; low-discrepancy numbers – always. Provided that you adhere to the rules that come with the use of low-discrepancy numbers, that is: always draw vectors of the full dimensionality required, never construct paths incrementally, and sort dimensions by relative importance.

Haug : **Is it also possible to combine low-discrepancy and pseudo random numbers or is this of no use?**

Jäckel : It is possible to do that and may be useful at times. A lot of the early publications on low-discrepancy numbers were on this subject, mainly because of the myth that low-discrepancy numbers cannot be used for more than, say, 10 dimensions. Since it has become more widely known that properly initialized Sobol's numbers work extremely well much further than that, the publications on mixing approaches have diminished.

Haug : **There are so many types of low-discrepancy numbers; Halton, Faure, Neiderreiter and Sobol. What are the differences between these?**

Jäckel : For me, the differences are that none of them are usable in high dimensions apart from properly initialized Sobol numbers. In more mathematical terms, the decisive difference is the dependence of the dimensionality-dependent convergence coefficient $c(d)$. For most low-discrepancy methods, this coefficient grows very rapidly with d. It has been shown by number theoreticians that generation methods can be conceived that do not show this detrimental growth in $c(d)$. Properly initialized Sobol's numbers, Niederreiter (1988) numbers, and Niederreiter-Xing numbers belong to that family. For very low dimensionalities, say around 5, Niederreiter-Xing numbers outperform all others, even Sobol's numbers but only ever so slightly. The construction of Niederreiter-Xing numbers is so complicated, and readily available only up to moderate dimensionalities, that, overall, Sobol's numbers rule, hands down. Provided you initialize them properly, that is, but Sobol himself knew this and published how to do it already in the early 1970's, i.e. even before Phelim Boyle suggested the use of conventional Monte Carlo methods in finance! It is mysterious to me how it could ever have happened that the myth arose that low-discrepancy numbers only work for very low dimensionalities (but I have my own conspiracy theory on this subject). To combat this myth was the main motivation for my writing the book on Monte Carlo methods in finance. I am very glad that these days it appears to be reasonably widely accepted that Sobol's numbers are useful even for high-dimensional problems.

Haug : When it comes to low-discrepancy Monte Carlo simulation is there a limit to the number of assets we can simulate at the same time?

Jäckel : No, though, the relative performance benefit decreases the more equally important dimensions there are. Luckily, in financial applications it almost never happens that we have a high number of equally important dimensions.

Haug : What are the limitations of Monte Carlo simulations in quantitative finance?

Jäckel : What limitations?

Haug : Is there any simple way to calculate, for example, the Vega for an option without running the simulation twice?

Jäckel : Yes, and no. A risk management department will almost always insist on a complete revaluation. For other purposes, a variety of tricks and techniques exist, e.g. likelihood ratio methods to pathwise differentiation, etc. In general, though, the most important thing about a Monte Carlo implementation is to make it fast, *really fast!*

Haug : In short what is a Brownian bridge, and in what context is it most useful?

Jäckel : A Brownian bridge is the mathematical concept of constructing a Wiener process path satisfying all the required statistical features of such a process in a recursive refinement procedure. It is very similar to the construction of a Cantor set. Norbert Wiener's construction of a standard Brownian process by the aid of the Brownian bridge was, allegedly, the breakthrough required to prove that the concept of a continuous but non-differentiable process that we now know as a Wiener process really is mathematically consistent. The construction algorithm of the Brownian bridge has since been formalized as the process $W(t) - t \cdot W(1)$ created from a standard Wiener process $W(t)$.

Haug : When using Brownian bridges might I just as well start at the maturity of the derivatives and go backwards, or does Monte Carlo simulation always start now and then run forward?

Jäckel : Reverse constructions are possible. In fact, some Monte Carlo algorithms are based on reverse evolution of Wiener processes, similar to the use of the forward Kolmogorov equation in the calculation of Arrow-Debreu prices.

Haug : What if I need to simulate a stochastic bridge between start and end points, but including jumps and stochastic volatility? Is this easy to implement?

Jäckel : It may not be easy, but it can certainly be done. The easiest way to use Brownian bridges is always to construct a set of driving standard Wiener processes using Brownian bridges, and to construct all other paths as deterministic functions of the given $W_i(t)$ paths.

Haug : Do you have any views on patenting in finance? I know Columbia University has some patents on the use of quasi-random Monte Carlo simulation in finance applications, do you have any views on this?

Jäckel : Their patents will expire not that far in the future. The impact those patents had on Columbia's reputation will be remembered for much longer.

Haug : What is the best way to measure and model co-dependence between assets?

Jäckel : Some form of rank correlation. Better even, retain the full multi-dimensional probability function. Always keep the original data, if it was sampled data.

Haug : Correlation between assets tends to increase or break down during market crises. How can we take this into account in our models?

Jäckel : Practically? Reserve against it. Ideally? Lemming-effect modeling, i.e. make codependence a function of movement speed.

Haug : In your book "Monte Carlo Methods in Finance" you state, "If you can't hedge it, you better guess right", can you tell us more about your experience with this?

Jäckel : Too often, I am asked how to calibrate models to certain data. Too often, it turns out that the data the model is supposed to be calibrated to are only interpolated, or worse even, extrapolated market quotes, i.e. they are *not* tradeable at all, neither as a bid nor as an offer, let alone two-way. This means that calibrating a model to those data would express an explicit guess as to the distribution of the relevant financial quantities. Since these guesses can not be hedged out (since the given points are not tradeable), we are essentially plugging in our own views as to the real world probabilities, not risk-neutral ones. Since we can't hedge, we are fully exposed to those views coming true. Well, as we saw with the disastrous popularity of endowment mortgages in the UK in the 1980s and 1990s, gambling on real world views can be very painful indeed. You better guess it right or at least make sure you can stomach the potential loss. A lot of exotic structures are outright exposures to barely hedgeable correlation assumptions. We got rid of the raw asset risk, but we are stuck with realized correlation risk. The quote you give is meant to be a reminder that with all we do in the mathematics of financial derivatives, in the end of the day, we are still dealing with the concept of buying and selling. That's all we do. If you can't buy and sell the raw ingredients to your product, it is no good to rely on the price being a certainty based on what you think the fair price of the raw ingredients *should* be.

Haug : Monte Carlo simulation is often used in Risk Management, how do you make sure you take into account fat-tails when looking at your risk?

Jäckel : The most common approach for this is to use historical data.

Haug : When modeling a great number of assets using Monte Carlo we need to feed the model with a correlation matrix. This as I understand it is not always as simple as it seems, can you tell us briefly about this?

Jäckel : Correlation numbers, if estimated from historical time series, are themselves just an estimate associated with a distribution of uncertainty. The uncertainty is surprisingly wide! If you only have 100 data points or so, and your correlation estimate is near zero, the uncertainty (estimated as a standard deviation) is about 20 % or so, and that is in absolute terms [see Numerical Recipes chapter on the Fischer transformation on this subject]! Time series often are not properly synchronized either, and this alone often gives rise to sampled correlation matrices not being positive semi-definite.

Haug : What about operational risk, is Monte Carlo simulation also of use here?

Jäckel : Given its flexibility, and today's computer speeds, it probably is.

Haug : How important is it to know programming when it comes to Monte Carlo simulation, and what is the preferred programming language?

Jäckel : Quantitative finance without programming is like quantitative finance without knowing what a natural logarithm is. The programming language depends on your environment. If you build numerical derivatives models, it can only be C, C++, or possibly assembler if you are of that kind of inclination. Raw speed is paramount, and the closer the language is to assembler, the better.

Haug : More and more computers come with dual processors and computers with multiple processors are just around the corner. At the moment we are typically generating one random number at a time in sequence, what if we had thousands of multi processors generating thousands of random numbers parallel in time? I would think that this would be closer to the reality and could lead to a breakthrough in how we calculate risk and value derivatives. Do you have any views on this?

Jäckel : I am confused. I haven't done any single threaded simulations in years. Are you telling me that some people out there still don't do every single simulation with one thread per CPU? Just kidding. Yes, multi-threading is a major advantage and it is actually surprisingly simple to do. If you imagine that it takes years of studying, and up to several months to implement an industrially usable implementation of importance sampling methods, it looks comparatively cheap to spend three or four days to modify your code to run multithreaded. The simpler the paradigm, the better. I always use the simple but robust concept of a draw increment. I set the *draw increment* to the number of threads that I use. Each thread has a number generator object, started off with an offset in the sequence equal to its own thread number. In each iteration, each number generator advances not by one in the sequence but by the draw increment. That way, I can use pseudo-random number generators as well as low-discrepancy number generators, and I retain equality in the convergence diagram by adding up equal chunks of the convergence diagrams of each of the thread's individual results. As for proper distributed parallel computing, this is also common practice throughout most investment banks for their overnight risk report generations.

Haug : What does a typical work day look like for Dr Jäckel?

Jäckel : Some meetings with business heads, some administrative work, a lot of interactive sessions and reflections with team members, some writing of documentation, and some programming. Also, quite a lot of work and project management relating to ongoing developments, both on the quantitative side and regarding implementation. Sometimes even some thinking about new ideas, but there is very little time left for that.

Haug : What is in your opinion the main difference between doing quantitative finance for a bank and academia?

Jäckel : In the business, you have to be able to switch context and keep in mind the business relevant criteria which means that thinking about blue sky ideas is reserved for rare occasions or weekends. It feels a lot more rewarding, though, in more than one way. One of the things I love about working in the business is that I can simply prove theories by experiment, and that, equally, I can disprove theories by demonstrating counterevidence obtained from numerical experiments. I love the space for the inventor's mind, the entrepreneurial spirit, as they call it. Having a short attention span myself, the business environment's fostering of fast returns is right up my street.

Haug : What do you think good quants have in common?

Jäckel : Solid background maths, structured thinking, lateral thought, flexibility, perseverance, good communication skills, serious numerical analysis, good programming knowledge, and good work ethics. One definitely does *not* have to be a genius, though.

Haug : Did you ever get fed up with quantitative finance?

Jäckel : Never for long enough not to start thinking about new ideas within days.

Haug : Do you have any hobbies outside quantitative finance?

Jäckel : There is not that much time left for it, and I enjoy tinkering with new ideas too much.

Haug : Can life itself be described as a Brownian bridge, we know the start point; birth, and the end result; death, but in between it can be a very stochastic ride?

Jäckel : Nice one. Perhaps more as a Variance Gamma bridge: we know where we arrive, but not exactly when or how much happens in between.

Haug : Do you apply Monte Carlo simulation to any of your daily life challenges?

Jäckel : Admittedly, when I need to cover a large area of possible solutions quickly, I tend to employ some form of stratified sampling, i.e. group all possible ways in sets of resemblance, and try a representative sample for each set. Then, refine in the most promising area. Also, having used Monte Carlo simulations for long enough helped me to overcome inhibitions to solve some problems by brute rote application of procedure, aided by simple tools. Sometimes, doing something manually, no matter how simple-minded, is the fastest way out of a pickle. It is never the preferred approach, of course, but excluding the brute force method right from the start seriously limits your flexibility. And if you can employ a machine to do it for you, even better.

Haug : **What do you think about my idea of arranging a Monte Carlo simulation conference in Monte Carlo, would you sign up as a speaker?**

Jäckel : Definitely.

Haug : **In your view where are we in the evolution of Monte Carlo simulation as well as quantitative finance in general?**

Jäckel : Quantitative finance is both advanced as well as in its infancy. It is advanced in that it managed to employ many techniques well established in other areas of science and mathematics, and in its developments in numerical analysis. It is in its infancy in that we are still thinking about financial processes only in terms of stochastic processes. I like stochastic processes because of their elegance, appeal, and usefulness as a model for financial processes. I do not believe in them, though. I believe some people will come up with models introducing more of a structural inter-dependency between financial agents. We may be a long way from such models being numerically tractable, but I am confident that it will happen.

REFERENCES

■ Boyle, P. P. (1977) "Options: A Monte Carlo Approach" *Journal of Financial Economics*, **4**, 323–338.
■ Halton, J. H. (1960) "On the Efficiency of Certain Quasi-Random Sequences of Points in Evaluating Multi-Dimensional Integrals" *Numerische Mathematik*, **2**, 84–94.
■ Jäckel, P. (2002) *Monte Carlo Methods in Finance*. New York: John Wiley & Sons, Inc.
■ Niederreiter, H. (1988) "Low-discrepancy Sequences and Low-dispersion Sequences" *Journal of Number Theory*, **30**, 51–70.
■ Niederreiter, H., and C. Xing (1995) "A Construction of Low-discrepancy Sequences Using Global Function Fields" *Acta Arithmetica*, **73**(1), 87–102.
■ —— (1996) "Low-discrepancy Sequences and Global Function Fields with Many Rational Places" *Finite Fields and Their Applications*, **2**, 241–273.
■ Sobol, I. M. (1967) "On the Distribution of Points in a Cube and the Approximate Evaluation of Integrals" *USSR Journal of Computational Mathematics and Mathematical Physics (English Translation)*, **7**, 86–112.

This photo was taken during a tapas evening in Madrid during the Global Derivatives Conference of 2004. From left; Paul Wilmott, Jesper Andreasen, Bruno Dupire, Emanuel Derman, Nero?, Dr. Haug, two unknown?, at the table but outside the picture were also Alan Lewis, Alireza Javaheri (as shown in photo 2). Not often so much derivatives brain power can be found in a cluster of Madrid. If you walked every day around Madrid and asked people about quantitative finance the knowledge would unsurprisingly not be too high, then suddenly walking into this quant dinner would be a tail event in space and time. Why do the rich tend to get richer and why do quants tend to cluster, is it the same law of nature driving it? Why did the conference take place in Madrid, why did exactly these quants cluster at that time and that place, what is randomness and what is deterministic, everything seems so clear and deterministic afterwards, but who would have predicted this tail event to happen in 1999?

Haug, Taleb and Wilmott meeting in New York City for a lively discussion. Did I have too much wine?

Index

361

corridor variance swaps,
  concepts 124, 171
cost of carry 129–30, 136, 145–6,
  182–3, 325, 327–8
Courant Institute 121
covariance 126, 154
Cox, J.C. 44, 104, 116–18, 153, 155,
  157–8, 225, 337
Cox-Ross-Rubinstein (CRR) binomial
  framework 104, 116–18, 155,
  157–8, 225, 324–7, 332
Craine, Roger 339
crashes
  1929 22–3
  1987 6–8, 218, 248–9, 254, 280,
    283, 336–40, 343–4
  APT 154–5
  aversion studies 339
  blow-ups 343–6
  catastrophe scenarios 232
  causes 283–4, 335–6, 338–40
  globalization effects 283–4
  jump risk 54
  peso problems 335–6
CrashMetrics 280
crazy ideas 110–11, 273, 288
credit default swaps 108
credit derivatives 108, 283, 341
credit risk 4, 108, 216, 341
Crépey, Stéphanie 105
Crop Yield Insurance (CYI) 236
CRR (Cox-Ross-Rubinstein binomial
  framework) 104, 116–18, 155,
  157–8, 225, 324–7, 332
cultural issues, gambling 213–14
cum-dividend process 81–6, 89–90,
  94–5
cumulative normal
  distributions 182–3, 184–5
Curran, M. 185–6
currencies 52, 106, 137, 192, 284,
  292–3, 335–6, 340
  peso problems 335–6
  space-time finance 292–3
  speculation 284, 335–6
currency options 52, 106, 137, 192,
  335–6, 340

day count arbitrage 269
DdeltaDvol 49
de la Vega, Joseph 35
death, attitudes 13
debt/equity ratios, leverage 171–2
delta hedging 4–6, 10–11, 27,
  33–61, 69, 170, 205, 248,
  251–4, 260–1, 278–9, 284
  see also dynamic...; static...
  alternatives 33–61
  concepts 4–6, 10–11, 27, 33–61,
    69, 170, 205–6, 248, 251,
    260–1, 278–9, 284

critique 60, 69, 170, 260–1,
  278–9
  geometric Brownian
    motion 39–40, 44–50
  greatest breakthrough 43–4
  historical background 33–61
  implied volatilities 260–1
  jump diffusion 50–4, 62
  knowing your weapon 33–64,
    279
  left over risk 37
  real-world situation 33, 50–61,
    137–8
  risk 33–4, 60–1, 170
deltas 4–6, 33–61, 134, 171, 205–8,
  278–9, 300, 338–9
  calculation considerations 278–9
  DdeltaDvol 49
  energy swaptions 205–8
  sticky delta concepts 171
demand/supply effects, options 54,
  58, 61
Demeterfi, Kresimir 108
Denmark 197–8, 242
derivatives
  see also futures...; options...;
    swaps
  market concepts 258–60
  revolutionary aspects 250–1
Derivatives (Wilmott) 277
Derman, Emanuel 4, 5, 44, 49,
  55–60, 100–14, 115, 126,
  168–9, 279, 323, 326, 328–9,
  356–7
Derman-Taleb approach, options
  pricing 55–60
deterministic dynamics, chaotic
  behaviour 242–3
Deutsch, Henry 38
DeWitt, Bryce 273
Dewynne, Jeff 277
Dictionary of Financial Risk
  Management (Gastineau and
  Kritzman) 109–10
Dingle, H. 290–1
Dirac, Paul 84, 223–4, 317, 321–3,
  329
Dirac's delta function 84
discounted expected pay offs,
  options 55–6
discrete dividends 67, 79–98
  see also dividends
  concepts 79–98
  liquidation/survival options 83–4,
    87–95
  multiple dividends 86–7,
    94–5
  new approach 67, 79–98
discrete time, continuous time 14,
  44, 48–9, 55, 58–9, 112,
  262–3, 284, 321, 324–7,
  337
dishonesty 7–9

Disney, Walt 271
dispersion trading 339
distributions 2–5, 6–7, 9, 11, 23,
  248–9, 256–9, 263–4
  see also fat tails
  classes 2–3
  critique 2–5, 6–7, 9, 10–14
diversification, risk 5, 14, 51–3,
  232–4
dividends
  see also discrete dividends
  arbitrage 81–2
  concepts 67, 79–98, 234, 237
  critique 81–2, 237
  cum-dividend process 81–6,
    89–90, 94–5
  escrowed dividend model 79–81,
    90, 92, 96
  ex-dividend process 80–1, 83, 85,
    87
  liquidation/survival options 83–4,
    87–95
  model comparisons 87–9
  multiple dividends 86–7, 94–5
  policy selections 83–5, 237
  weaknesses 81–2
DOT system 338
double barrier options 129–38
  see also complex barrier options
double black diamonds 1, 12–13
down-and-in options 116–18,
  131–5, 146–50
down-and-out options 146–50,
  161–4
draw increments, threads 353
Drexel 28
dual double barrier options 136–8
Duanmu, Zhenyu 109
Dupire, Bruno 104–5, 121, 125,
  166–75, 356–7
dynamic delta hedging 4–6, 10–15,
  27, 33–61, 69, 103, 122,
  137–8, 155, 170, 233–4,
  262–3
  see also delta hedging
  concepts 4–6, 10–11, 42–61,
    122, 137–8, 155, 170,
    233–4, 262–3
  critique 60, 122, 170
  Derman and Kamal
    approximation 48–9
  geometric Brownian
    motion 44–50
  greatest breakthrough 43–4
  jump diffusion 50–4, 61
  Monte Carlo simulations 45–6,
    48–9, 50–1
  replication hedging errors 46–54
  risk 60–1, 170
  robustness 44, 58–9, 122,
    129–30, 137–8
Dynamic Hedging (Taleb) 1